# WILD WEST SHOWS

Paul Reddin

University of Illinois Press
Urbana and Chicago

© 1999 by the Board of Trustees of the University of Illinois
Manufactured in the United States of America
1 2 3 4 5 C P 5 4 3 2 1

∞ This book is printed on acid-free paper.

Library of Congress Cataloging-in-Publication Data
Reddin, Paul.
Wild West shows / Paul Reddin.
p. cm.
Includes bibliographical references and index.
ISBN 0-252-02464-8 (cloth : alk. paper)
1. Wild west shows—United States—History. I. Title.
GV1833.R43   1999
791.8'4'0973—DDC21
98–58008
CIP

To Gordon and Lelia
Annie, Sue Ann, and Jed

# CONTENTS

# ACKNOWLEDGMENTS

A goodly number of people made working on this book enjoyable. It began years ago in a reading seminar at the University of Missouri offered by the late Professor Lewis Atherton. He directed my dissertation on Wild West shows and encouraged me with many letters to get it in print. Although it has been nearly thirty years since I completed it as a dissertation, this gentleman's admonitions remained as I worked on the manuscript. Could I stay "intellectually buttoned," avoid pretense, and remember that good history appeals to both scholars and the general public? The person who pushed the project along in later years was my assistant, Janet Mease, a former student, who helped with many details, offered constructive criticism of everything I wrote, listened to me complain, and sent out for hot pastrami sandwiches when things got difficult in the office.

James W. Leyerzapf, a friend from graduate school and now senior archivist at the Eisenhower Presidential Library, and Donald A. MacKendrick, professor emeritus of history and an exemplary former dean, read early drafts of the manuscript and made valuable suggestions. Richard Etulain of the University of New Mexico and Paul Fees of the Buffalo Bill Historical Center offered critical, judicious, and fair observations that improved the book.

A number of people helped with word processing, securing books, foreign languages, and European history. Jerry Nolan, Daniel Carroll, Donna Scott, Michael T. Larkin, and Frank Keller all came to my rescue when computer contrariness or operator ignorance led to difficulties. Jane M. Heitman of Mesa State's Tomlinson Library performed miracles by getting obscure publications on interlibrary loan. Several people willingly helped translate foreign texts into English. Nancy Longenbach and John Calmes did work for me in German, Rachel Marasco and John B. Genesio helped with Italian, and Harriet Bloom-Wilson, Hadassa Marvin, and Lewis M. Chere unraveled the mysteries of the French documents. I usually turned to Chere for guidance in European history.

A host of persons offered assistance and encouragement along the way. Gary Galanis, Deanna McBee Galanis, and their son Mason allowed me to stay with them while doing research at the Library of Congress. Supporters from my years at Adams State include Norma Peterson, who built a history program so strong that about ten percent of the graduates went on to earn Ph.D.'s. She served as my undergraduate mentor and then colleague and division chair for thirteen years. Carrol Joe Carter and the late Robert D. Compton both contributed significantly to my project at Adams State. Mike and Pam Masterson made my research trip to Cody enjoyable. Colleagues at Mesa State who assisted in various ways are Thomas D. Graves, Della Mottram, Barry Michrina, Christian J. Buys, Susan Moore, Charles Hardy, Laverne Mosher, and John McClain, a carpenter on the maintenance staff who always asked how the book was progressing. The Trustees of the State Colleges of Colorado granted me two sabbaticals to work on the project, and a cash award accompanying their Award for Teaching Excellence helped defray some research expenses. Theresia Holman, the departmental secretary, always found time to humor me, run off copies of the manuscript, and help with word processing problems. Jon C. Pigage from the University of Colorado at Colorado Springs took some photographs for me and Jerome O. Steffen from Georgia Southern University encouraged me with phone calls during the process of publication.

A special thanks goes to those at the University of Illinois Press. In particular, Elizabeth Dulany, associate director, has supported this project with good humor and valuable suggestions.

Former students assisted. Rita Eisenheim entered the entire manuscript on disk and offered editorial suggestions. Diana Jones helped organize the sixteen file boxes of notes accumulated while working on this project. Toni Chappell Wanebo read drafts of several chapters and discussed them with me.

I pressed family members into service. My late father-in-law, Harold Ingraham, lent a great deal of moral support to the project, and my brother-in-law B. J. Ellison devoted many hours to working with pictures. My daughter, Sue Ann Marasco, offered bibliographical suggestions and located some sources on Cody. When I had problems getting the words right, my son, Jed (a production potter), helped with philosophical discussions about the vicissitudes of artisanry and the creative process. My parents made a number of sacrifices to ensure my education and have supported my scholarship in many ways. My wife, Ann, helped with research at the Denver Public Library, the British Museum, the Library of Congress, and the American Heritage Center. I have concluded that she must be nearly as patient with her husband as Clara Catlin was with George.

# INTRODUCTION

In 1895 John Burke, a publicist for Buffalo Bill's Wild West show, wrote that "the amusements of a people are the best index of their character." Then he posited that the conquest of the frontier represented "the great epic of American history" and called the exhibition "America's National Entertainment." Burke asserted that the enterprise he represented was important and not "to be lightly dismissed or undervalued" because it was not "in any sense a trivial affair."[1] Pronouncements such as these reveal several things about Wild West showmen: their seriousness of purpose, their conviction that their exhibitions and ideas about the United States were inseparable, and their acknowledgment that their shows interpreted the western experience for Americans and Europeans. Reflecting the spirit of Burke, I regard Wild West shows as a form of entertainment, a vehicle for understanding the parent culture, and a catalyst for ideas about the West in the United States and abroad.

In this book I trace the history of four Wild West shows with reference to Burke's assertion that they reflected "national character" and therefore should not be "lightly dismissed or undervalued." I place the Wild West show phenomenon in a hundred-year perspective by beginning in the 1830s with the artist George Catlin, concentrating on Buffalo Bill Cody, and concluding in the 1930s with the Miller Brothers of the 101 Ranch and the movie star Tom Mix.

These men shared a goal: to create popular entertainments that replicated life on the Great Plains and afforded spectators an opportunity to witness and appreciate reproductions of frontier experiences. Despite claims of accuracy, Catlin,

Cody, the Miller Brothers, and Mix presented highly selective and subjective representations of the West and its people. I will investigate how these showmen interpreted the Trans-Mississippi West and how American and European audiences reacted to those depictions. My perspective is reflected in that somewhat unwieldy term *Wild West show.* Capitalizing *Wild West* acknowledges the importance of Cody and the ideas his enterprise represented, while adding *show* in lowercase reflects my determination to treat these events as entertainment and interpretations of reality.

Recreating the Plains experience in an appealing manner for ticket holders was a tall order. Wild West shows had to entertain and interpret happenings on the Plains in ways acceptable to most Americans. In doing this, showmen considered key cultural issues, such as progress, violence, the value of wilderness, depictions of Plains people as heroic, and gender and race issues. Put simply, to sell tickets the shows had to entertain and edify in ways acceptable to most Americans. Making this even more complicated was the fact that what pleased one generation often did not satisfy the next.

In addition to showing before their compatriots, Catlin, Cody, the Millers, and Mix traveled to Europe. Being abroad with uniquely American entertainments raised questions. Should they revere, reject, or remain aloof from Old World persons and surroundings? How could they and their entertainments remain self-consciously American and still curry favor abroad? And European nations differed. Whether England, France, Italy, Germany, or somewhere else, the showmen had specific ideas about each nation. So while abroad, they presented themselves and their shows as "American," watched European reactions, and then reacted to these new perceptions.

In the first two chapters of this book I explain how George Catlin entered show business in the 1830s to rally support for the Great Plains and the Indians and animals who lived there and then took his show to Europe. Chapters on Buffalo Bill detail his experiences before American audiences in the 1880s, his travels abroad, his triumphant return to the Columbian Exposition in 1893, and his promotion of imperialism and militarism until World War I. A chapter on the Millers' 101 Ranch show chronicles that entertainment's struggle for identity, direction, and survival from the early twentieth century into the Great Depression. In the final chapter on Tom Mix I discuss his apprenticeship in the 101 Ranch Wild West show, the transference of what he learned in that entertainment to silent western movies, and his eventual return to Wild West shows in the 1930s.

While I am selective in the individuals studied, those included are the most significant. In the interest of brevity and to focus on major themes, I limited this study to the largest and most representative Wild West shows. Other entertainments focusing on Native Americans existed in Catlin's time, Cody's show inspired legions of imitators, the Millers faced scores of competitors, and Mix was not unique in apprenticing in Wild West shows and rodeos and moving on to movies. Tim McCoy, revivals of the Buffalo Bill and Pawnee Bill shows, and other efforts represent valiant attempts to keep the Wild West show tradition alive.[2] However, in my opinion, other entertainers mostly mimicked Catlin, Cody, the Millers, and Mix. Americans of the time recognized the names of these four showmen, who offered carefully delineated images and ideas about the frontier. Each caused large numbers of people to react, favorably and unfavorably, and thereby created a forum on the meaning of the West.

All these charismatic men claimed extensive experience and intimate familiarity with the Great Plains. Because the shows bore the imprint of their principals, I have provided a brief biographical sketch of each person. Dramatic incidents introduce the showmen: Catlin meeting an Indian named On-o-gong-way, Cody's first seeing the Trans-Mississippi West, George W. Miller calling his family to his deathbed to give them his vision for the 101 Ranch, and Mix visiting the Buffalo Bill show. Perhaps each of these incidents happened exactly as related; perhaps they were embellished or even fabricated. The impossibility of separating truth from fiction reflects how these men mastered the art of storytelling by fusing the real and the imaginary. Whatever the veracity of the accounts, they encapsulate the personality, vision, and values of each man.

The book is not a business or theatrical history. This study does not relate what happened in the arena on a year-by-year basis or detail the development of the technical aspects of the shows. Nor is this volume an attempt to determine who within the Buffalo Bill, Miller, and Mix operations originated ideas. When I refer to Cody's ideas or Mix's pronouncements, I offer the party line; I have not failed to recognize that publicity agents stood behind these men. In my opinion, Wild West shows were not democratic organizations, and those who ran them did not speak for each and every performer; consequently, the words *showman, showmen,* and *showmanship* appear regularly in the text to denote and connote that males owned, managed, publicized, and determined the content of the shows discussed in this book. Also, words and expressions out of favor with many historians today—such as *conquest of the West, winning the West, frontier, frontiersman, the Old World,* and *civilization* and *progress* that refer to the white majority's view—remain in the text because they convey the spirit of Wild West shows.

In this volume I attempt to avoid duplicating other studies of Wild West shows. A book and doctoral dissertations provide understanding of music in

Buffalo Bill's productions and the evolution of his program on a year-by-year basis.[3] L. G. Moses, in *Wild West Shows and the Images of American Indians, 1883–1933*, emphasizes the Indians' place and experiences in these exhibitions. Don B. Russell's *The Wild West* provides a broad, almost encyclopedic, view of the phenomenon beginning with the Buffalo Bill show. Richard White, in "Frederick Jackson Turner and Buffalo Bill," interprets Buffalo Bill and his show in terms of "frontier iconography," while I stress the changing perceptions of the Plains and its people.

This study adds to the understanding of Wild West shows by placing them in a hundred-year continuum and offering new material and new interpretations of Catlin, Cody, the Millers, and Mix. The European experiences of all of them receive more attention here than in any previous work. The volume offers a new perspective on Catlin by explaining his intentional move into entertainment and his role as progenitor of Wild West shows. The chapters on Cody stress that he and his show evolved over time, always reflecting the dominant ideas in America. In the chapter on the 101 show I discuss the identity crisis that beset Wild West shows in the twentieth century, and in the Tom Mix chapter I chronicle the link between Wild West shows and silent western movies.

# WILD WEST SHOWS

# "The Raw Material of America": George Catlin and the Beginnings of Wild West Shows

s an old man, George Catlin fretted about his failure to generate enthusiasm for Plains Indians. Could he have done something differently during a lifetime of painting, writing, and presenting public shows? Perhaps, if he reached America's young people, he might change attitudes. To this end, Catlin wrote *Life amongst the Indians: A Book for Youth* (1861). In this book, Catlin related how, as a child, he gained an appreciation of Indians by meeting a warrior named On-o-gong-way. The account represented Catlin's worldview in microcosm, for it included everything that this first Wild West showman had tried to tell grown-ups in the United States and Europe for nearly thirty years.[1]

According to Catlin's retelling, as a ten year old, he spent an afternoon alone in the woods, hoping to kill his first deer. When he finally spotted a buck, excitement prevented him from pulling the trigger. Suddenly, a musket report from across the clearing shattered the silence. Curiosity about the other hunter turned to terror when an Indian stepped into view and claimed the fallen animal. The boy froze, afraid to move a muscle, yet thankful that the hunter had not seen him. In attentive agony Catlin watched the man advance to the carcass with gun and knife, cut its throat, hang it head down from a tree, and then take out pipe and tobacco to occupy his time while the animal bled. Afraid to watch, yet afraid not to keep his eyes on the Indian, the youngster peered from his hiding place. For an instant his eyes seemed to meet the hunter's, and the boy thought he saw the look of humanity in the supposed savage's eyes.[2]

Stories of massacres by Indians and tales of their villainy raced through Catlin's head. Convinced that if the warrior spotted him he would be scalped and his flesh eaten, the boy remained motionless. He considered shooting the Indian, but what if he missed or only wounded him? When the man finally shouldered the carcass and disappeared into the forest, Catlin sprung from the foliage and raced through the forest, losing his hat and gun in the flight for his family's cabin.[3]

Safely home, Catlin related the adventure to his family. Their house stood in a cluster of eight or ten farms in the Wyoming Valley of the Susquehanna River in southern New York, a locality that boasted a population of nearly two hundred farmers, laborers, hunters, and fishers. Clearly the valley was not heavily populated in these first years of the nineteenth century, but seeing Native Americans was not common. Still the youngster stuck to his story. The following morning a hired hand reported that a family of gypsies had camped on the farm, and Putnam Catlin took his son George with him to investigate. Instead of gypsies in the wheat field, they found the Indian George had seen the previous evening.[4]

The man's friendliness and the fact that his wife and daughter camped with him dispelled the youngster's fears. In imperfect English, the Indian explained that he was an Oneida named On-o-gong-way, which meant "a great warrior," and invited the visitors to make themselves comfortable. Learning of the episode in the clearing, he praised the hunting ability of the wide-eyed youngster and gave him a saddle of meat from the buck. As the day passed, George realized that his new acquaintance was a sensitive, complex, and admirable person. The Oneida talked freely, all the while turning the youngster's "alarm to perfect admiration."[5]

George Catlin listened particularly attentively to On-o-gong-way's account of the Wyoming Valley Massacre. The boy knew that it had occurred in July 1778 in the valley where they now sat, but he had not realized that there was another side to the story. On-o-gong-way explained that necessity, not cruelty, had driven his people to make a stand against those who had invaded their land. The Indians had ambushed the white men and then advanced to Fort Forty, where they took women and children prisoners. Catlin knew that his mother and grandmother were among those captives.[6] When more soldiers arrived, the Indians fled. On-o-gong-way explained that he had been a small boy and had carried, and then buried, a large golden kettle plundered from the whites. Now he had returned for the treasure, but settlers had cleared the land and he could not locate it. Hearing this, Putnam sent his son to get a brass kettle turned up while plowing. When George returned, the Indian recognized it. Putnam explained that the kettle was not golden, although it looked like the precious metal. Despite this disappointment, On-o-gong-way, his wife, and their daughter decided to stay on the Catlins' farm for a while.

In the days that followed, George became enamored of On-o-gong-way and absorbed stories and explanations of his lifestyle. The boy brought arrowheads from his collection of artifacts and watched in admiration as the man made arrows, constructed a bow, and fashioned a quiver from the hide of the buck shot in the clearing. All these the Indian presented to the boy. On-o-gong-way cut a handle for an iron tomahawk head that George had found and demonstrated his ability to throw it with unerring accuracy.

Then one day On-o-gong-way and his family disappeared. Most likely they began a return trip to their home between the Oneida and Cayuga Lakes. They left in the middle of the night, probably to spare George the ordeal of a tearful good-bye. In lieu of a farewell, the warrior left a gift in the Catlin's woodhouse: a saddle of venison adorned with a headdress of feathers. The premature departure worried Putnam, who had planned to send the Native Americans homeward by a safe route. His concerns proved well founded. Putnam learned that someone in the Randolph Valley had killed On-o-gong-way. In vain, the Catlins tried to learn the identity of the murderer and to discover the fate of the Oneida's wife and daughter.[7]

This story of an impressionable boy and an Indian mentor revealed much about George Catlin, the man who became the preeminent western showman of his age. Upon encountering On-o-gong-way in the clearing, ten-year-old Catlin was frightened because he saw the Oneida through the lens of white culture. However, through the ensuing friendship, Catlin transformed his stereotyped image into a flesh-and-blood human being, a family man, and a person of largess who took time from his life to give graciously to a child from another culture. On-o-gong-way provided material things such as bows, arrows, and tomahawks, a feather headdress, and venison, and shared nonmaterial treasures, such as explanations of the richness and subtleties of Indian life. As showman, Catlin would try to foster enthusiasm for the material, spiritual, and mythological aspects of Indian cultures. He collected material items and formed them into a museum-like aggregation he called his "*Gallery unique*," a collection so grand that an admirer designated it the "raw material of America."[8] As for the nonmaterial part, Catlin lectured and wrote in an attempt to enlighten others with what On-o-gong-way had shared with him.

The murder of the Oneida made a salient point: in the United States, white people destroyed Indians. In his writings and shows, Catlin reversed the roles of aggressor and victim seared into the psyches of mainstream Americans by sources such as captivity narratives. Throughout his career, Catlin said Indians, not European Americans, were victims. In his best-known work, *Letters and Notes on the Manners, Customs, and Conditions of North American Indians*, Catlin generalized: "Long and cruel experience has well proved that it is impossible for enlightened Governments or money-making individuals to deal with these credulous and unsophisticated people, without the sin of injustice."[9] Catlin raised a hue and cry about the imminent extinction of Native Americans. This message, which always involved criticism of the United States, did not endear him to his compatriots. Never would Catlin abandon his crusade, and while advocating the Indians' cause, the bug of showmanship bit him.

That bug linked Catlin with William F. "Buffalo Bill" Cody, whose Wild West show developed a half a century after Catlin's efforts in the 1830s. Those in Cody's show knew of Catlin. In fact, Cody's publicists compared their show and its purpose to Catlin's entertainment.[10] Certainly parallels did exist. These two men would inaugurate entertainments around the end of an epoch on the Plains. In Catlin's case, it was the end of Plains Indians' cultures built around family, ceremonial life, horsemanship, buffalo hunting, warfare, and other traditional pursuits free from outside influences. Catlin's premise was deceptively simple: because most Americans missed the Plains experience, they must be curious about it. Since he had witnessed Indian life, he would reproduce and interpret it for other Americans and make a living in the process. In doing this, Catlin pioneered much of the Wild West show tradition, including communicating the look and feel of the prairies, its people, animals that roamed there, the joy of the hunt and chase, colorful aspects of the frontier, extensive publicity, and trips abroad.

As a product of the age, Catlin conveyed his ideas through the reigning media of the day: paintings, museum-like collections, books, and the spoken word. Cody, on the other hand, lived in a time of great spectacles, high finance, well-paid publicity agents, and a vanishing Plains frontier. At that point, glorifying struggles and bloodshed and using a term such as *Wild West* was appropriate for an entertainment. Compared to the later show, Catlin's version of the "Wild West" was embryonic and restrained; he simply tried to tell the Indians' story and sometimes presented accounts "*a little too highly coloured.*"[11]

Like Cody, Catlin took a number of years to discover his calling. In fact, his life after meeting On-o-gong-way contained two halves: the first, in which he curtailed his interest in Indians, chose unrewarding professions, and resignedly followed traditional callings, and the second, when love of Native Americans propelled his work.[12]

Catlin was born on 26 July 1796 in Wilkes-Barre, Pennsylvania, as the fifth of fourteen children in the family of Putnam and Polly Catlin. A number of forces pushed George Catlin toward making a career of advocating for Native Americans. Childhood adventures outdoors, finding Indian artifacts, uninspiring careers as a lawyer and a portraitist, and perhaps seeing delegations of Indians arrayed in their finery on their way to negotiations in Washington, D.C., fueled Catlin's enthusiasm for the West. While a young man working in Philadelphia, he must have visited Charles Wilson Peale's museum and perhaps this inspired him to gather materials enough for his own collection. Catlin read every reliable source he could find about Indians, exploration, and the West. In a heart-to-heart talk about life, goals, and inspiration, Catlin and a brother named Julius decided to go West and begin collecting Indian items. Shortly thereafter, Julius drowned while swimming. Most likely, this tragedy convinced George to live his life meaningfully.[13]

On 22 February 1829, shortly after his brother's funeral, George Catlin wrote a letter to Peter B. Porter, the secretary of war. In it, Catlin detailed his aspirations and informed Porter how he could help. "Life is short," the artist explained, "and I find that I have already traveled over half of it without stepping out of the beaten path." Catlin told Porter that to the "attainment" of fame "I wish to devote the whole energies of my life." Porter could assist "without the least inconvenience" to himself or anyone else by awarding Catlin a professorship of drawing at West Point or by "an appointment to some little agency among the savage Indians, up the Missouri River, which would pay my expenses for a year or two." There, "among the naked savages," he "would select and study from the finest models in Nature, unmasked and moving in all their grace and beauty." After a few years painting "the principal Chiefs" and the "manners and customs" of the Indians, he could "open a Gallery first in this Country & then in London, as would in all probability handsomely repay me for all my labors, & afford me the advantages of a successful introduction beyond the Atlantic."[14]

In this unvarnished request for help, Catlin revealed much about his personality and goals. He often asked people, even strangers, for favors and expected them to recognize and support his plans. In addition to revealing Catlin's self-centered nature, the letter documented his ambition. His proposal would not cost the government much money, but he also made it clear that he would not remain an Indian agent: he wanted to stay in the wilderness only long enough to make a collection of paintings to launch a lucrative public career. About fifty years later, Cody wrote a letter before he entered Wild West shows in which he expressed his desire to visit England and do well there.[15]

Catlin's job-seeking effort with Porter failed, but this did not deter the artist from beginning his gallery of Indian portraits. Undaunted and somewhat embittered, he resolved to go West with "not one advocate or abettor," even though it meant separation from family and friends, financial expense, and danger. In his mind it was wrong that American Indians had "no historians or biographers to pourtray with fidelity their native looks and history." Consequently, he resolved to visit "every tribe of Indians on the Continent of North America," to paint the most important men and women in each tribe, and to provide "views of their villages, games, &c. and full notes on their character and history." In addition, he would "procure their costumes, and a complete collection of their manufactures and weapons, and . . . perpetuate them in a *Gallery unique* for the use and instruction of future ages."[16]

Catlin attacked the project with fervor. He called himself an "*enthusiast*" and wrote that the "predominant passion of my soul" was "to seek Nature's wildest haunts, and give my hand to Nature's men." And he must hurry because events pointed to the demise of traditional Plains Indian lifestyles. Fur traders pushed into the West and introduced smallpox, firearms, and liquor. National politics also caused alarm as President Andrew Jackson took land from eastern Indians and relocated them in the West.[17] Catlin believed this would irrevocably alter the cultures of those remote tribes who had thus far escaped the influence of European Americans.

The aspiring showman faced potential competitors; others also depicted Indians and traveled West. Charles Bird King held a government-sponsored position to paint Indian delegations that visited Washington, D.C. Samuel Seymour and Titian Ramsey Peale, who accompanied Major Stephen H. Long on his expedition to the West in 1820, had painted well over 150 western scenes and portraits, although only a few of them appeared in Long's report. The American Fur Company had allowed a German artist, Prince Paul of Württemberg, to paint Native Americans in 1832; and Peter Rindisbacher had depicted Indians and western scenes in the mid-1820s. However, most Americans knew little of these artists and their work, and none had traveled from town to town showing their paintings and lecturing about them.[18]

From 1830 to 1836, Catlin traveled, observed, painted, collected, gained notoriety, and eked out an existence with public exhibitions and lectures. During the summers of 1830, 1832, 1834, 1835, and 1836, at a time when Europeans and Americans knew little of the area or its peoples, he criss-crossed the interior of the continent, sometimes traveling by water, sometimes walking, and sometimes riding on horseback. Among his notable achievements were boarding the *Yellowstone* in 1832, the first steamboat to travel up the Missouri to the mouth of the Yellowstone River; canoeing the Missouri, Mississippi, Fox, and Wisconsin Rivers; and journeying overland in 1834 into present-day southwestern Oklahoma with the First Regiment of Mounted Dragoons searching for recalcitrant Comanches, Pawnee-Picts (Wichitas), and Kiowas. When not on the move, he often stayed in cities such as St. Louis, Cincinnati, New Orleans, and Louisville, which had waterway connections to the Mississippi River and the trans-Mississippi West. His mission meant sacrifices for his wife, whom he sometimes dispatched to live with relatives.[19]

Knowing that he could spend only limited time on the frontier, the artist-traveler worked frantically. Often he sketched persons and scenes quickly, planning to finish the works when he returned to a studio. Producing portraits amazed the Indians and earned him the status of a "great *medicine white man,*" and this reputation enabled him to move relatively freely among the Plains Indians. He visited more tribes (forty-eight by his count) than any white artist before him, painting Plains scenery, animals, and individuals from life, getting certificates of authenticity from reputable persons on the frontier who knew the Indians and scenes he painted, collecting Native American costumes and artifacts, and recording impressions in his notebook.[20] Catlin based a forty-year public career of painting, writing, exhibition, and expertise about the West on this limited observation. To make his experiences there appear more lengthy, he scrambled chronology in his writings and talks, measured his time on the Plains in yearly increments, and misrepresented his years spent there as a total of eight.

A series of enthusiastic travel accounts first brought Catlin's name before the public. Newspapers of this age often carried such narratives about experiences in exotic locales. The detailed discussions of geography, ethnography, history, and architecture in them delighted homebound Americans. Catlin's travelogues appeared in the *New York Commercial Advertiser,* a prestigious newspaper specializing in financial affairs. Its editor, William Leete Stone, admired Native Americans and sided with anyone who resisted or criticized the heavy-handed policies of the Jacksonians.[21] Sympathy for Indians and criticism of the Democrats made sense for a New York newspaper geared for the northeastern financial district that vilified the anti-bank Jackson.

Much of Catlin's public career in the United States transpired within the protective folds of groups of people who read such newspapers. However, outside safe environs like these, mainstream Americans supported Jacksonian Indian policy and admired Old Hickory for his energy and determination. Many people of this era embraced materialism, patriotism, nascent Manifest Destiny, and optimism. It was a practical and energetic age, a time of land clearing, canal and road building, steamships, staple crop production in the South, textile milling in the industrializing Northeast, and the emergence of railroads. Braggadocio was common, and Americans found themselves and their nation exciting, and sought praise for all they did.[22] Unlike Buffalo Bill Cody, Catlin failed to attune himself or his show to his age.

Catlin's travel account published on 24 July 1832, began a series of letters for the *New York Commercial Advertiser* that stretched over five years. Other newspapers reprinted Catlin's popular articles, making his name familiar to the "reading public" and establishing his reputation as a "celebrated Traveler" and "Historiographer of the Indian tribes." Catlin wrote enthusiastically about his love for the Plains and its people, demonstrated a flair for the dramatic, and told good stories about the grandeur and uniqueness of the Plains—its "*Soul melting* scenery," its romantic peoples, the colors and sunsets, and the savage fury of buffalo bulls.[23]

In addition to discussions of the beauty and power of the Plains, he wrote about adventures, such as buffalo hunting, peering across the Red River into Mexico, and seeing Plains Indians in their natural environment. He stood transfixed by "the splendid procession of a war party" and luxuriated in invitations to "sumptuous feasts of dog's meat" and "Beaver's tails and Buffalo tongues." Catlin also saw Indians perform. While at Fort Snelling, Indians "afforded" visitors "a fine and wild scene of dances, amusements, &c." He noted that the Native Americans appeared "to take great pleasure in 'showing off' in these scenes," and that those European Americans who watched, "both ladies and gentlemen," enjoyed such demonstrations.[24] Most likely, these impressions stuck with Catlin and would inspire him to include Indians in his shows.

Catlin's subject matter—Indians and the West—fascinated Americans. "Vagueness" and speculation shrouded the frontier. Catlin realized that for most in Jacksonian American "the West" was a inexact, protean, and intriguing concept. Maps during this time depicted the area as "empty land," although cartographers sometimes sprinkled a few sketches of Native Americans to fill voids in their drawings. Images of Indians excited many Americans and took a variety of forms: bloodthirsty savages of captivity narratives, "war-whooping" and sometimes tragic figures of James Fenimore Cooper's novels, and the "noble savages" of romantic writers.[25] Catlin claimed a grand and potentially lucrative subject matter for himself. Next he needed to establish himself as *the* expert on Indians.

Catlin's career as public entertainer began in April 1833 when several men visited his studio in Pittsburgh, where the artist finished canvases begun the previous summer. Their invitation to display and discuss his paintings undoubtedly pleased Catlin, particularly since the callers designated him "one of the most celebrated painters of our country." Catlin agreed, and the *Pittsburgh Gazette* promised the citizenry a show "full of interest and instruction" featuring Indians, "their mode of living, habits of war, &c," "sundry of the wild animals," and "Nature, in her wild and unsophisticated forms."[26] The invitation reaffirmed his "expert" status on Indians, and put him before live audiences. His career proceeded on schedule.

This first exhibition in Pittsburgh—and others in Cincinnati and Louisville in 1833, New Orleans in 1835, and a return to Pittsburgh in 1836—established a pattern for the rest of his career. First, he wrote a detailed advertisement, promising to show one hundred paintings featuring "the wildest tribes in North America." Lectures followed, and when interest in them waned, he displayed his collection of Indian portraits and objects in a museum-like manner.[27]

Lectures and exhibitions of paintings flourished in this age of modest public entertainments. Traveling shows remained small because railroads were still in their infancy, mud mired traffic on roadways, and myriad other factors made transportation difficult. Traveling entertainments included early circuses, equestrianism, acrobatics, music, puppets, oddities of all kinds, menageries, and other easily transportable features. Showman Catlin competed against attractions such as Ching and Chang, the "Siamese Twins," a five-hundred-pound man, Egyptian mummies, the "Albino Boy," and Herr Schmidt's stupendous fireworks display. The largest cities provided more varied fare, including theater, but much of the United States lacked commercial nighttime entertainments, and what was available was often limited to oration.[28]

In Catlin's time, people recognized names such as John C. Calhoun, Henry Clay, and Daniel Webster and associated them with powerful elocution. Schoolchildren read famous speeches in their textbooks, and teachers often required committing some of them to memory. Every Fourth of July celebration included one or more examples of sterling oratory; newspapers reprinted the best of these patriotic harangues. In many communities, lyceums brought a series of speakers to stimulate minds and uplift society with lectures on self-improvement, efficiency in the workplace, history, travel, geography, natural history, and reform. In addition, promoters hoped that lyceums would foster long-lasting enthusiasm for libraries, museums, and education. For a nominal sum, often less than two dollars, a person could purchase season tickets for a series of perhaps twenty lectures.[29]

Lyceum lecturers did not become rich, usually receiving between five and fifteen dollars above expenses for individual presentations. However, these speakers moved from town to town, so they could prepare one spectacular talk and use it again and again. Some in lyceums transferred their polished speeches to the written page and sold them as books. So, lyceum speakers often got respect, notoriety, a little money, and perhaps a publication or two. The movement attracted a variety of lecturers, some luminaries such as Ralph Waldo Emerson, reformers such as Wendell Phillips, the statesman Daniel Webster, the minister Henry Ward Beecher, the writer Oliver Wendell Holmes, and, for short stints, George Catlin. In 1838, for example, he lectured successfully for the Salem Lyceum. Catlin chose not to wed himself to the formal movement, probably because of his individualism, ambition, and the meager pay, but he followed its example: education was his goal, the spoken word was his form of communication, the Gallery unique was his museum, and the book was his ultimate format. Every city in which he spoke had a strong lyceum in place.[30]

The year 1836 and the early part of 1837 marked a critical juncture in Catlin's career. In his letter to Secretary of War George B. Porter in 1829, Catlin proposed to paint and collect and then show the Gallery unique in eastern cities. Catlin began this transition by bringing together the various parts of the collection, including items in storage in St. Louis. Putnam Catlin, the patriarch of the family, contemplated this development from afar and worried that something might happen to the Gallery unique as it traveled up the Ohio River to Pittsburgh, where George planned to organize the material for a show. When traffic in the waterways began moving in the late spring, George sent the collection to Buffalo, rented old church, paid for advertisements, got handbills printed, and prepared for exhibition. Then tragedy struck. Catlin's infant son died, and George returned to Albany to be with his wife.[31]

George Catlin's impetuousness caused another cancellation in Buffalo. With the paintings hung and the collection ready for exhibition, the artist-showman learned of a boat leaving for Sault Ste. Marie, a location close to the Indians' pipestone quarry. He departed, after instructing his brothers Francis and Henry, who now assisted him, to take down the paintings, pack everything, and await his return. Somehow the other Catlins could cover the unpaid bills. His family worried about the danger in visiting this sacred source of reddish stone for pipes that Indians guarded against outsiders. However, the excursion brought only a few tense moments. The artist painted pictures of the area and secured and studied specimens of the mineral eventually named catlinite in his honor. From the pipestone quarry, he wrote the last of his travel accounts for the *New York Commercial Advertiser*.[32] Odysseys to Indian country ended, at least for many years.

When Catlin returned to the East, winter weather prevented moving the collection. Making money meant transporting it, but railroad officials refused to move it because a clause in the railroad's charter prevented its "carrying freight." At this point, Catlin confided to his brother Francis that he was "too *poor* to do *anything*" and turned to his paintings and a manuscript on Indians. Finally Catlin moved the collection, and during the spring and summer of 1837, he successfully exhibited in Utica, Albany, and Troy, New York. In Troy and Albany, enthusiastic patrons wrote testimonials supporting Catlin and his work.[33] All this must have gratified a man preparing to take his show to the metropolises of the East.

The fall of 1837 and the year of 1838 were Catlin's most important months before American audiences. He tested his appeal in New York, Washington, D.C., Baltimore, and Boston. Facing high expenses and stiff competition from other entertainments, Catlin endeavored to increase the attractiveness of his collection. To do this, he wrote an explanatory catalog to enable patrons to view his paintings and artifacts with greater understanding. He experimented with his presentations and discovered that having Indians beside him on lecture platforms brought enormous crowds to his showrooms. Some of Catlin's admirers proposed that the U.S. government purchase the Gallery unique, and the showman talked openly about taking the collection to London.

Irony marked this quest to win the hearts and dollars of city-bound persons because these surroundings and people were the very ones he had fled by going West. Moreover, Catlin believed that these eastern city dwellers knew nothing of the Plains. About them he wrote: "there is scarcely any subject on which the *knowing* people of the East are less informed and instructed than on the character and amusements of the West." However, these stay-at-home urbanites, who had not seen Indians in their natural state, marveled at a prairie sunrise, or watched a buffalo lumber across the horizon, were those most inclined to look romantically upon the Plains and the people who lived there.[34] For Catlin and the Wild West entertainers who followed him, success in New York and other large cities of the East marked a rite of passage. There resided great masses of potential ticket buyers, cultural potentates to endorse entertainments, and powerful newspapers to spread the word about worthwhile entertainments. In the early years of his Wild West show, Buffalo Bill Cody would concentrate on playing in these cities, and the Millers would celebrate their first successful tour in the East.

When Catlin arrived in New York City in the fall of 1837, Indians and wilderness were in vogue. A work on which Catlin had refused to collaborate, James Hall and T. L. McKenny's *Illustrated History of the Indian Tribes of North Amer-*

*ica,* had appeared in February 1837. Many in the city savored Washington Irving's new works on the American West, *Tour of the Prairies* (1835) and *Astoria* (1837). For those wanting a blood-drenched thriller about the frontier, there was *Nick of the Woods; or, The Jibbenainosay: A Tale of Kentucky* by Robert Montgomery Bird (1837). The Indian melodrama *Metamora,* starring the popular Edwin Forrest, also attracted crowds.[35]

Determined to succeed in these surroundings, Catlin worked as feverishly here as he had in the West. Although he hired helpers such as his nephew Burr Catlin and a lively, talkative, and sometimes combative Irishman named Daniel Kavenaugh, the show remained essentially a fatiguing one-man operation. The collection required proper packing and shipping, sometimes by water and sometimes by rail. He found hotel accommodations, which cost seventy-five cents to one dollar per day, for himself and those with him. For exhibitions, he needed commodious, fashionable, and affordable rooms. Finding them proved difficult, so much so, that he was forced to cancel a visit to Philadelphia. In Boston, he moved his massive collection four times. Once he found suitable accommodations, Catlin often employed carpenters to build a platform for lecturing. All of this cost money, as much as ten dollars a day for rent, and two hundred dollars for construction costs. He searched for merchants willing to sell tickets in their places of business. With such a workload, it is not surprising that Catlin relaxed with a bit of brandy, punch, or wine in the evenings and ordered champagne sent to his room when his wife, Clara, joined him.[36]

For Catlin, advertising became a passion, and he inundated cities with newspaper notices, handbills, and broadsides. He apparently believed more was better in newspaper advertising and typically wrote long notices, bought space in several newspapers, and ran the ads daily. A receipt from Washington, D.C., for 1838 revealed Catlin's fondness for other printed material. He paid one printer $83.25 in a six-week period for 5,100 "advertisements," 350 circulars, 1,000 handbills, 200 prospectuses for his prints of the Seminole leader Osceola, and 2,000 copies of his catalog. This totalled 8,650 items, or about 206 pieces of printed material per day. In addition, publicity required talking with reporters and editors, issuing them free passes, and encouraging them to write about his show. Catlin sometimes feted special guests with get-togethers featuring buffalo tongues, venison, spring water, and peace pipe smoking.[37] Buffalo Bill Cody's Wild West show publicists would demonstrate this same penchant for advertising and staging western-style "rib roast" dinners for dignitaries and members of the press.

Those who attended shows probably came mostly from the middle and upper classes. Catlin's standard admission price of $.50 represented a hefty sum, equal to the daily wage of many working persons. This was a time when a kitchen chair cost $.30 to $.75, $2.00 bought a "Fashionable and Elegant Silk Hat," and $7.50 purchased a "Dress Coat, made and trimmed." Attendance at Catlin's shows varied—sixty patrons made a small audience, and several hundred a large one. Men constituted the majority in audiences, but women and children also attended, in part because, as reporters mentioned, women enjoyed seeing Indian clothing.[38]

When people arrived at the lecture hall, they found softly lighted and congested surroundings. Commodious quarters being scarce, Catlin settled for available space—saloons of law buildings, old chapels, an *old Theatre*," and other public buildings—and adapted them to his purpose. Pictures and artifacts crowded the walls, benches or chairs provided seating, and a lecture platform with an artist's easel on it stood at one end of the room. Candles, whale oil lamps, and gas lights provided illumination in that age, so some such contrivances must have hung from the walls and cast light on Catlin and the items he exhibited. Fall and winter weather most likely required a stove or a fireplace, but patrons noted that lecture halls were often too hot or too cold. Summers sometimes became sweltering, causing the showman to suspend lecturing until the weather moderated.[39]

In advertisements, Catlin urged people to be seated by the starting time of 7:30 or 8:00 P.M., and about this he was "punctual to the minute." His method of presentation was simple: he placed pictures, one by one, on the easel and provided "oral explanations." Catlin lectured in a "quick and unassuming" style about "several hundred pictures" each evening. To prove accuracy, he often displayed the actual clothing depicted on the human subjects in his paintings. Whenever possible, Catlin had purchased these items from the Native Americans after finishing their portraits. His prize exhibition was the regalia of a Blackfoot medicine man fashioned from the head, hide, and claws of a great "yellow bear," ornamented with all imaginable "anomalies or deformities" in the animal kingdom, and replete with the "skins of snakes, and frogs, and bats,—beaks and toes and tails of birds,—hooves of deer, goats, and antelopes; and, in fact, the 'odds and ends,' and fag ends, and tails, and tips of almost everything that swims, flies, or runs, in this part of the wide world." A large saucer-shaped rattle and a "medicine-spear or magic wand" completed the outfit. Sometimes Catlin appeared before his audiences wearing this costume. Sometimes he flourished tomahawks and held aloft other items from his collection to demonstrate his points.[40]

While wearing an Indian's costume and brandishing a tomahawk appealed to audiences, such actions may have subtly undermined Catlin's more serious purpose. His insistence on authentic costumes and objects from the West would establish a Wild West show standard. However, Catlin standing in a Native American costume and pretending to be an Indian blended authenticity and playacting. Throughout his career, Catlin experienced credibility problems, and perhaps he contributed to them by becoming an actor.

Lectures often stretched to two-and-a-half hours, and most listeners stayed for the duration and felt that they received their money's worth. Catlin allowed questions, and they ranged widely: some doubted his truthfulness, and others inquired about Indians' pictographs, their interest in Christianity, and a variety of other topics. His style of delivery required tremendous energy, kept him in a state of "constant agitation," and tired him, sometimes to the point of exhaustion and illness.[41]

In general, ticket holders found Catlin sincere, likable, knowledgeable, full of anecdotes, and possessing a "high wrought feeling of enthusiasm in favor of the Indians." Some felt he was an extraordinary man and called him a crusader for "truth and knowledge," a brave fellow with "extraordinary tact," a celebrity, and a man destined to win a place in history. To describe him, persons chose phrases such as "modest and unassuming," "enthusiastic and extremely agreeable and winning," and "most agreeably communicative." A number of visitors said Catlin painted word pictures so realistic that listeners felt almost transported to the grassy Plains and the circles of tepees he described. Many in his audiences appreciated his lively sense of humor and ability to pepper talks with "amusing anecdotes."[42]

While an engaging public speaker, he lacked the qualities that marked the great orators of the day. He was not physically imposing, standing a slender five feet eight inches in height; nor did he possess a voice powerful enough to elicit praise from reporters. He dressed well, although spectators seldom mentioned this, and he spoke without notes in a conversational style that sometimes became rambling and disorganized. One journalist commented that even after years as a speaker, Catlin lectured in an "artless manner" and another noted that when Catlin claimed not to be a good lecturer, he "told truly." When he failed to communicate ideas or expressed himself inappropriately, Catlin laughed along with his audiences.[43]

Catlin's lectures followed a predictable pattern. In introductions, he explained that he had undertaken a "noble, arduous, and original" task: traversing the vast interior of the continent, seeing its animals, visiting every Plains Indian tribe, and recording everything on canvas. Surely everyone could understand that the enormity of this task meant that many of his pictures were "hurried sketches" still "in an unfinished state." Although they were not finished works of art, he assured his listeners that "there was no deception practiced." In fact, many paintings carried certificates of authenticity signed by "different persons, to prove that the portraits were actually taken from the individuals whom they professed to represent, and that the costumes were really as represented."[44] Later Wild West showmen would display the same penchant for authenticity.

After introducing himself and his undertaking, Catlin spent about two hours developing what he had learned from On-o-gong-way: that Indians were flesh-and-blood humans with culture, emotions, artistry, and exciting and worthwhile lifestyles. Humanizing Indians was difficult because his fellow citizens drew their images and ideas about Indians largely from artistic and literary stereotypes. None of these depicted Indians as people with whom mainstream Americans could identify. Instead, they ranged from devilish red men illustrated in captivity narratives to smoothly stylized engravings of noble savages in works like those of James Fenimore Cooper.[45]

To discredit such stereotypes, Catlin emphasized that Indians differed from one another. They lived in separate groups—Sacs, Shawnees, Sioux, Crows, Arickaras, Blackfoots, Flatheads, Mandans, and others. Each formed a distinct cultural unit, and often they spoke different languages. Within those tribes existed family units with grandparents, aunts, uncles, fathers, mothers, and children, just as in white society. An observer concluded that the details and power of Catlin's lectures made observers feel as though they had seen an Indian "in all the phases in which he appears under the various forms of his national customs and manners, both in public and private, at home and abroad, in war and in peace."[46]

When Catlin discussed individual Indians, he began with names familiar to his fellow citizens, which, not surprisingly, revealed that America's most well-known Indian names were those associated with armed conflict against the United States. Although Catlin did not glorify warfare as those in later Wild West shows did, he found its presence inescapable, even in his pro-Indian entertainment. First on his easel were portraits of "Black Hawk, the Prophet, Na-Pope, and several other Sacs," painted while they were incarcerated at Jefferson Barracks near St. Louis. Most Americans recognized these names because of the Black Hawk War of 1832, which resulted from President Jackson's policy of Indian relocation. A thousand nearly starving Sacs and Foxes recrossed the Mississippi River headed to their traditional homeland in Illinois to plant corn when the militia and regular army met and defeated them en route.[47]

Catlin's conviction that Americans should leave Indians alone and allow them to live in their traditional manner emerged when he discussed a second kind of Native American, those "almost half civilized" like the Shawnees, Ojibways, and Sioux. In his opinion, contact with fur traders "tainted" these Indians. After listening to Catlin, a writer characterized this group of Indians as "depraved savages who linger upon the skirts of our advanced settlements, debased and emasculated by an intercourse with the whites." In sharp contrast to those "debased and emasculated" Plains Indians stood others: those like the Crows, who maintained their "noble and lofty bearing" because they lived beyond the influences of trappers, traders, and settlers. In Catlin's view, these were noble savages, the standard against which he measured other Native Americans, and his proof of the contaminating influences of "civilization." It was a tragic and unmistakable fact that, for Indians, "civilization" was "freighted with corruption and death."[48]

Catlin reiterated this message when he placed upon his easel his painting of Wi-jun-jon (the Pigeon's Egg Head or the Light). This particular canvas was divided into halves, one side showing the Assiniboine "dressed in his native costume, which was classic and exceedingly beautiful," and the other half depicting the man after he visited Washington, D.C., and "exchanged his beautifully garnished and classic costume for a full dress 'en militaire,'" which "strangled" his neck, and boots, "which made him step like a 'yolked hog.'" He carried an umbrella and a small keg of whiskey. Once back home on the Plains, the whiskey vanished, and his people ostracized and then killed him.[49] According to Catlin, as with On-o-gong-way, "civilization" destroyed Wi-jun-jon.

In this story, Catlin summarized his philosophy about the relationship between Native Americans and civilization. Although he did not encumber this story or his lectures with formal philosophy, the artist based his ideas on his reading of the "social contract" theorists, namely, John Locke, Thomas Hobbes, Jean-Jacques Rousseau, and Thomas Jefferson. For Catlin, the frontier was that place where civilization and savagery met or a condition suspended between a state of nature and civilization that brought out the worst in everyone. When settlers went there, the formally codified law melted away and they acted immorally. Products of a "state of nature," Indians lacked the moral restraints that came with civilization's rules.[50]

In Catlin's opinion, tragedy threatened all Indians because, one-by-one, so-called civilization would corrupt and then destroy every tribe. In expressing this view, Catlin reflected a romantic idea of "vanishing Americans" expressed by Michel-Guillaume-Jean de Crèvecoeur, the poet Philip Freneau, James Fenimore Cooper in *The Last of the Mohicans,* and those who would follow Catlin in Wild West shows. Unless Americans came to their senses, a "noble race" would "disappear from the face of the earth." This prospect moved Catlin to passion, outrage, and criticism of those he held responsible: traders, trappers, Indian agents, slaughterers of buffalo that fed the Plains Indians, and those who offered the "poisoned cup of intoxication." He even told audiences that all white Americans were "indirectly the cause" of the destruction of Indians. He usually avoided direct criticism of the U.S. government and the American Fur Company, but often an undercurrent of animosity toward them emerged in his remarks. While most Indian nations would die slow and silent deaths, he predicted that the Sioux would not. He warned of a great and bloody Sioux war in the making.[51]

Catlin's role as Indian advocate did not suppress an inclination for drama and enigma, particularly when he discussed the Mandans and their mysterious origins. The showman explained that this tribe looked different from other Plains Indians, and to illustrate this he exhibited paintings of two youthful Mandans "with silver grey hair and blue eyes," saying that such characteristics appeared in "every tenth or fifteenth family." Did their ancestry differ from other Plains Indians? This question intrigued an age that speculated endlessly about the origins of Native Americans. Catlin cultivated such interest by displaying pictures of the Mandan's O-kee-pa, or sun dance, which few white Americans had seen. This yearly ceremony, he explained, demonstrated knowledge of the Noacian flood because these people knew about a "big canoe," the "subsiding of the waters," and mourning doves that returned to the "big canoe" with a leafed bough signaling an end to the deluge.[52]

The showman moved to sensationalism when he discussed a part of the O-kee-pa, a rite of passage during which young men earned the status of manhood by enduring bloody and "terrible incidents." These involved piercing muscles of the chest or back with wooden pegs and suspending initiates from them until they lost consciousness. Catlin advertised these practices as "*cruel Religious Ceremonies and Tortures*" and lectured graphically about them. The news that smallpox decimated the Mandans in 1837 saddened Catlin, but, as his father observed: "unquestionably that shocking calamity will greatly increase the value of his enterprize & his works." Reflecting that attitude, Catlin urged people to see his show and get a "minute account" of the Mandans recently "extinguished by the smallpox."[53] The showman side of Catlin found ways to profit from the tragedy.

Another contrariety—this one between the conservationist and the showman—emerged when Catlin discussed buffalo. Most Americans knew little of these gargantuan creatures or how to hunt them. Catlin viewed them as valiant symbols of the Plains and painted them in all their savage beauty. Frequently, he decried the wholesale slaughter of them and predicted their extinction. Yet he exhibited "Twelve Buffalo Hunting Scenes" and celebrated the "exhilarations of the buffalo chase," which he had experienced on the Plains.[54] His emphasis on the bison foreshadowed the direction of future Wild West shows. Cody would rise to fame partly because of his legendary ability to kill these shaggy beasts.

To increase attendance and revenues, Catlin copied a technique from lyceums by sometimes organizing lectures into "courses," consisting of two or three presentations. One ended with the Mandan's O-kee-pa and the other with Catlin arrayed in the elaborate costume of the Blackfoot medicine man. An enthusiastic reporter who attended a course related that it portrayed "the wild prairies, the wild men, the wild sport, and the wild horrors of the west." He relished Catlin's accounts of the war dance, preparations for battle, ball play, buffalo hunts, smoking the peace pipe, Indians' propensity for "deadly, and unquenchable revenge," the "dog feast," and the mysterious shaman.[55]

As this account indicated, Catlin sometimes became a sensationalist. He peppered shows with stories of his own "hair-breadth escapes and curious adventures" on the frontier and sometimes concluded them with his own war whoops. In his gallery hung grisly trophies, including scalps, garments fringed with scalp locks and a Cheyenne knife with "the blood of several victims dried upon it." Certificates with the Cheyenne knife verified its sanguinary history. So much emphasis on blood made one observer wonder how Catlin could reconcile "the horrible scenes of cruelty and superstitions . . . with the virtues which he ascribes" to Indians.[56]

In 1837 in New York, Catlin seized the opportunity to add Indians to a performance. Sacs, Foxes, Iowas, and Sioux returning from negotiations in Washington, D.C., agreed to appear on stage. Long before the advertised opening time of 7:00 P.M., twelve to fifteen hundred persons arrived at Stuyvesant Institute. As many as possible crammed inside, and those unable to gain admission formed a mob outside. When showtime came, the Sacs and Foxes, some painted and stripped to the waist, entered the hall first because they planned to leave early to attend a theatrical performance. Among their number was the aged Black Hawk, whose portrait had been an attraction in the show from its inception. Next Catlin brought the Sioux into the hall. He began his normal routine of placing pictures on the easel and explaining them one-by-one, and beamed as Indians onstage recognized Mah-wee-re-coo, the wife of a Sac leader named Kee-o-kuk, and others depicted in Catlin's portraits. His triumph was that Mah-wee-re-coo wore the identical dress that appeared in Catlin's rendering of her. The artist-showman put a number of questions to the Sacs and Foxes, always to demonstrate to the listeners that he told the truth about Indians.[57] Such a concern suggests how many Americans must have doubted his veracity.

A "very spirited full length picture of Kee-o-kuk, in his richest costume, resting on his lance" brought approval from the Indians. While the audience admired this canvas, the Sac leader Kee-o-kuk arose and spoke through the interpreter, asking Catlin to exhibit the picture showing him on horseback. The showman responded that he would display it later because he always saved the best for last. This pleased Kee-o-kuk. When Catlin finally did place it upon the easel, he informed the Native Americans that audiences often questioned the accuracy of the painting by saying that no Indian owned such a fine animal. Filled with indignation, Kee-o-kuk addressed the crowd, assuring them that the horse was indeed as fine as Catlin had painted it. If the horse were not outstanding, he would not own it. He chastised the audience: why, he asked, were Indians not entitled to own fine horses, just like European Americans?[58]

Another portrait, that of Ha-wan-je-tah (One Horn), caused the Sioux onstage to place their hands over their mouths and to speak in low and reverent murmurs. Catlin explained that this leader had recently died in an extraordinary manner. Upon learning of the death of his son, Ha-wan-je-tah had, "according to a strange custom of the country . . . mounted his horse resolved to shed the blood of the first man or animal he met." That first creature was a buffalo bull, which he "fretted" with arrows "until he was perfectly enraged." Then Ha-wan-je-tah dismounted, tossed aside his bow, and attacked the animal with a knife. The furious encounter ended with the deaths of the man and beast. The Sioux onstage confirmed that Catlin told the truth.[59]

When he discussed buffalo hunting, Catlin made a standard remark: despite the smallness of their bows, Indians could sometimes "speed an arrow entirely through the animal, sending it to a distance beyond." This statement, the showman explained, had caused him considerable grief because doubters in his audiences had "discredited" it, and "some gentlemen have openly expressed their disgust of a statement which they have stigmatized as false and impossible." Would the Indians themselves wish to comment? Again indignation surfaced, and a young man arose, took a bow and arrows, and "showed how it was done." Kee-o-kuk also said that he had seen this many times among the Sacs and Foxes, and indicated that his hunters preferred bows and arrows to guns. The Sioux acclaimed their assent. Catlin concluded the first part of the show by saying that he had devoted seven years of his life so "that the white men might understand their noble natures and do them justice." The Indians shouted their approval of the man and his mission.[60]

As the Sacs and Foxes left the room, many in the audience surged forward to touch the Indians. One reporter noted that the women "seemed particularly anxious" to put their hands in the "palms of the Indians." After the departure of the Sacs and Foxes, an Iowa arose, reaffirmed that Catlin told the truth, bid all good-bye, and left the room. Then Catlin departed to arrange materials for the second part of the show.[61]

In his absence, William Leete Stone of the *New York Commercial Advertiser* arose and delivered a short discourse, thanking Catlin for his "energy and enterprise" in traveling to the far West and "affording a rich entertainment to the eye and mind." Upon Catlin's return, Stone then read a resolution thanking him for his work to "illustrate the character, manners and customs of our red brethren," and asserting that those present had "the fullest confidence in the veracity of Mr. Catlin, and in the truth of his delineations, both by his lips and his pencil." Choked by emotion, Catlin found it difficult to thank his supporters. After this, he showed articles of Indian manufacture: clothing, headdresses, bows and arrows, strings of beads and shells, and other items.[62]

The evening was immensely satisfying—and tiring. Exhausted by the heat in the overcrowded hall, lecturing, and the emotionalism of it all, Catlin suspended shows for a few days. However, he did not spend all the time recuperating. He planned another show—a grand one—in Chatham Street Chapel, where Native Americans would occupy an elevated platform, ensuring all spectators an unobstructed view of them. To add to the dramatic appeal of the presentation, Catlin would lecture from the entryway of his twenty-five-foot white Crow tepee beside a pole with real scalps attached. Kee-o-kuk would attend and receive a "magnificent present." The evening's festivities would conclude with pipe smoking and an Indian levee. Because the show would be so special, Catlin boosted the price of admission to one dollar and suspended free season passes, except to the press.[63]

This show may not have occurred. The newspapers that had covered the first one did not mention it. In addition, other things occupied Kee-o-kuk and his delegation, like going to Boston, visiting phrenologists, and seeing the American Museum, the Bowery Theater, and other attractions. Kee-o-kuk did receive his "magnificent present" from Catlin, the artist's rendering of the Indian on horseback.[64]

The show with Indians and the anticipated second one were significant. Catlin hoped to overcome his credibility problems by asking the Indians, over and over, for verification of his truthfulness. Additionally, the show proved the appeal of Indians: they attracted customers and enthralled them so much that people surged forward to touch them. The subject matter of the show—hunting, a duel to death between a determined man and an enraged buffalo bull, a demonstration with a bow, and Kee-o-kuk's horsemanship—centered on the prowess of the Plains peoples. Catlin's advertisement for the show with the Crow tepee, scalp poles, and other articles indicated his willingness to use items from his collection as theatrical props. These events and the others, filled with blood and adventure, all indicated the future direction of Catlin's show and foreshadowed much about Cody's approach.

Another visit by Indians to Stuyvesant Hall followed about a month later. An Indian agent whom Catlin had met during his travels on the frontier, Major John F. A. Sandford, accompanied about thirty Pawnees to the Gallery unique. Like other delegations at this time, they were in the East to negotiate a treaty and sightsee a bit along the way. When the Pawnees arrived to see Catlin's collection, a select audience watched. First, the Pawnees walked about the gallery, inspecting the paintings and enthusiastically expressing their recognition of leaders, buffalo hunting scenes, and the familiar prairie landscape. After examining the contents of the gallery, they retired to the interior of the great Crow tepee, where they smoked, sang, and beat out music on a drum while the spectators watched through the open flap of the tent. A reporter noted: "Mr. Catlin[,] like an old friend, was in the midst of them."[65]

The success of this event reassured Catlin. He and the Pawnees enjoyed it, the Indians confirmed the accuracy of the paintings, those in the audience relished watching the Pawnees, and the press endorsed the whole affair. And, it reaffirmed that live Indians had great audience appeal. But this show differed from the previous one because Catlin did not orchestrate or even prompt their actions. The Indians simply did as they pleased, and those in attendance watched admiringly. Several years later in England, Catlin would bring Indians into his show, confident that they would tastefully entertain and edify as had this group at Stuyvesant Hall.

In January 1838, two months after the Pawnees' visit, news came that the U.S. Army had captured Osceola and seventy or eighty of his followers and thereby ended the Seminole War. Catlin heard this report in New York, where many sympathized with the Seminoles. Some there even cried foul because rumors circulated that Osceola and his warriors were taken under a flag of truce and tracked by bloodhounds. These highly publicized reports of injustice set Catlin in motion. He made a "flying visit to the South, to paint the captive Osceola and his companions" incarcerated at Fort Moultrie, South Carolina. Back in New York, he added the portraits to his gallery and advertised them as attractions.[66]

His visit underscored his two-pronged relationship with Native Americans: he detested what happened, but used it for personal gain by commemorating it with paintings and providing information. His actions foreshadowed those of Cody, who would make his own "flying visit" to talk to Sitting Bull during

the Sioux war that Catlin had predicted. With the outbreak of the Spanish-
American War, Cody would send representatives to Cuba, secure participants
for the show, depict battlefield conditions, and provide the latest information
for audiences. The Millers would do the same when war threatened with Mexico. Warfare, it seemed, always attracted Wild West showmen.

For his part, Catlin painted the Seminoles gloriously. A reporter noted that
warriors appeared as "a group of as brave looking fellows as eyes have ever looked
upon," and "Osceola, at full length, with his rifle in his hands, is one of the
noblest figures that we ever saw." Also, the artist captured an ambience of "pen-
siveness," transmitted to him when the elderly leader supposedly poured out
his his heart to Catlin. He made a lithograph of the Seminole leader and offered copies for four dollars. Shortly after the sitting, Osceola died. In advertisements, Catlin promised to divulge details of their conversations.[67]

In lectures, Catlin depicted Osceola as a gentle and sensitive "hero," sometimes moved to tears during their talks. Moreover, he was a self-made man who
suffered "from abuses and neglect" as a boy, left home, and by "his native energy and talents, tho' not a chief, he became the acknowledged leader and master
spirit of his people." According to Catlin, the Seminole war stood as a "deep
and damning disgrace" for the United States, at least in part because the Seminoles had held off the large and imperialistic U.S. Army for so long.[68]

Painting ennobling portraits and praising Osceola vaulted Catlin into a tense
political situation. Southerners regarded the capture of Osceola as "gratifying
intelligence." The *Charleston Courier* condemned Catlin's portrait. To those at
the *Courier,* Osceola was no hero; in fact, he represented "the blackest stain upon
our national honor." The Cherokee leader John Ross offered a different view.
He studied the portrait for an hour and said: "That was a great man; his name
will go down to posterity as the bold resister of oppression, the defender of his
natal soil and the graves of his fathers."[69] However, southern members of Congress, not Ross, would eventually vote on whether the U.S. government would
purchase Catlin's collection.

Even with subject matter such as Osceola, the O-kee-pa, scalps, and buffalo
hunts, shows could not hold audiences' attention. When attendance dwindled,
Catlin ceased lecturing and opened his gallery to the public, so those who had
only glimpsed pictures and objects during his talks could return to inspect everything at their leisure. Visitors found pictures on three walls and the fourth
covered with "beautiful costumes, bows, pipes, and a variety of Indian nic-nacs,
all worthy of careful study." The artist-showman advertised his gallery as extensively as he did his lectures. The standard admission was fifty cents, although
sometimes it was twenty-five cents. Season tickets were usually a dollar, but that

fee might be only seventy-five cents. Family tickets could be arranged at the door. Normal hours were from 9:00 A.M. to 10:00 P.M. Usually Catlin left the collection in the care of assistants such as Burr Catlin and Daniel Kavenaugh, who would answer questions. Undoubtedly, Catlin instructed them to watch carefully for pilfering, but crowds of people made security difficult, and, on at least one occasion, valuable artifacts disappeared.[70]

A "full and explanatory" publication entitled *Catalog of Catlin's Indian Gallery of Portraits, Landscapes, Manners and Customs, Costumes &c.* accompanied the gallery. The 1837 edition listed five hundred entries divided into seven categories: portraits, landscapes, sporting scenes (mostly hunting), amusements, manners and customs, Mandan religious ceremonies, and Indian "curiosities" (Indian objects). Like the programs of later Wild West shows, this guidebook introduced the novice to the people and lifestyles found on the Great Plains. The gallery was a conglomeration commemorating Native American cultures. The twenty-five-foot white Crow tepee, "composed of the skins of buffaloes ingeniously dressed and ornamented," towered over everything. The enormity of the collection impressed people as a "copious" aggregation in the words of one reporter and "a perfect museum" in the estimation of another. Catlin covered all the wall space with pictures and the "several thousand specimens of Indian manufactures, costumes, weapons, &c." Calumets of catlinite, tomahawks, scalping knives, cradle boards, feathered headdresses, clothing, bows, arrows, quivers, shields, fourteen-foot iron-tipped spears, necklaces, tobacco pouches, strings of beads and shells, ornaments, whistles, rattles, flutes, and drums were among the items displayed. In advertising, he called the collection "immense," and those who saw it agreed. The Gallery unique prompted one reporter to call it "a rich treasure."[71]

For some, the gallery changed their image of Indians. Catlin's pictures reminded visitors that Plains Indian tribes included women and children, and the "domestic implements" in the collection revealed a home life usually obscured. "Exquisitely wrought" apparel, some splendid enough to "adorn any prince," proved Indian artistry. That Native Americans possessed a facility for design, detail, and artisanry surprised some Americans. Perhaps the most gratifying reaction of all were calls for the government to purchase the collection and make it a monument to the Indians.[72]

In 1838, Catlin savored rent-free use of Boston's Faneuil Hall, the historic building where American colonists held the first meetings to oppose England's tax on tea. In Catlin's day, only patriotic exhibits could appear there, and, much to his delight, the city government proclaimed his collection of "public and universal interest." Freed from the burden of rent, Catlin lowered the price of admission to twenty-five cents. The *Boston Morning Post* commended the show-man for his "liberality in throwing open the exhibition at a very low price, there-by bringing it within the means of a very large class of our citizens." Generos-ity was not new to Catlin. He sent money to family members, even when he could not afford to do so, and in New York, he had given some of his receipts to the "central committee for the benefit of the suffering poor." While at Fa-neuil Hall, Catlin invited public school students, including "pupils of the Fe-male Asylum, Farm School, and House of Industry," for a free visit.[73]

In Boston, five hundred grammar school children, teachers, and trustees viewed the gallery and heard Catlin lecture. Afterward, while they examined the artifacts, a war cry pierced the air and "the imposing form of a savage warrior . . . armed at all points, as if for the battle," appeared. Startled, some of the youths laughed nervously, and younger ones began to weep. However, the "terrifying apparition" turned out to be George Catlin, who began to speak again, explaining the "details of his personal wardrobe" from the grizzly bear claw necklace to his armaments. He demonstrated how Indians shot bows on horseback and how they speared buffalo and used their shields. Never, the show-man said, could he forget such an attentive audience.[74]

This show marked a milestone in Catlin's career. By this time he had presented four distinct kinds of public entertainments: lyceum-like lectures, exhibitions of Indians on the platform beside him, museum-like displays, and playacting as an Indian. Catlin discovered an idea with appeal to Americans, and he had been creative with it, but he was far from rich. In fact, family correspondence reveals his lack of cash, and newspaper articles documented sparse attendance at some shows.[75]

He took his collection to Philadelphia, where he lectured in the spring of 1839. Then he journeyed to the Stuyvesant Institute in New York, but did not lec-ture. Burr Catlin and Daniel Kavenaugh admitted visitors to the collection, while George finished paintings and worked on his manuscript. Such an arrange-ment produced little revenue. About this, his father fretted: "he will be fast spending money, instead of laying [it] up," and then he sent his son some cash.[76] All this work and financial sacrifice anticipated the next step in Catlin's career as showman: going to England. He had expressed this goal in his letter to Sec-retary of War George B. Porter in 1829, and the artist-showman stuck closely to that plan.

Catlin began openly discussing taking the collection abroad. He had men-tioned it to the artist Thomas Sully, who wrote Catlin in 1837 and asked: "When do you reckon upon taking your passage for old England?" Catlin encouraged people to see his collection as soon as possible because it would be going to

England. Sometimes he warned: "This collection is about to cross the Atlantic, and this is the only time it can ever be examined in this city."[77] Catlin did not call these final exhibitions "farewell tours," but that was the message. It would take Cody and his army of publicists to develop the idea of "farewell tours" into major publicity campaigns.

Several factors encouraged going abroad. Over and over people told him that he, his lectures, and his collection would create a sensation in England and make him rich. The apparently sympathetic English government added to such confident predictions. Catlin wrote officials there on 7 May 1838, asking that his collection be admitted in that country duty-free, and the "Lords of the Treasury," he learned, were "willing to allow Mr. Catlin the privilege he seeks." The *New York Commercial Advertiser* reprinted this epistle, and other newspapers copied it. Packet ships (vessels on regular schedules that carried mail, cargo, and passengers) made contact with England faster and more reliable. In Catlin's mind, England was also a good place to publish his book because the United States did not have an international copyright law, so American authors who published in their own country were "barred from securing a copy-right in England."[78] And surely he knew that a successful tour abroad would enhance his reputation and that of his collection in the United States.

Leaving had to be done graciously, however, since he was taking a uniquely American enterprise abroad, perhaps with the intention of selling it. To allay the fears of Americans and to answer the "loquiries" of his fellow citizens, Catlin wrote an open letter to the *New York Commercial Advertiser*. In it, he explained that he wished not to "expatriate" himself and that his stay in England would be short. There, he could publish his book and show his collection, but he did not want to sell the things in his collection: "I scarcely see how I could sell them, during my life, unless I sell myself with them." Yet, there was much talk about purchasing the collection in the United States. A resolution to that effect came up in Congress, only to be tabled. Catlin said he was not behind that movement and had not "tendered" the collection to the government. He hoped that he might return to the United States after the Panic of 1837 had subsided and have the collection "preserved under the protection of the government" and opened to the people. If that happened, and he were freed of the day-to-day care of the collection, Catlin hoped to be "let loose upon the unexplored regions of the great West," where he could study those tribes he had not yet visited. For now, however, he must go abroad.[79]

On 25 November 1839, Catlin sailed on the packet ship *Roscius*. Packed safely among his papers were letters of introduction from Henry Clay, Professor Benjamin Silliman of Yale University, the artist Thomas Sully, and perhaps

Washington Irving and President Martin Van Buren. With him were his nephew Burr, his assistant Daniel Kavenaugh, and the crated collection, which
weighed eight tons. For good measure, the showman threw in two young grizzly bears in stout cages. Philip Hone, a well-known New Yorker, commented
about Catlin and his departure: "He will show the greatest and most interesting collection of the raw material of America that has ever been on their side of
the water."[80] That phrase, "raw material of America" was an apt one for the cargo
in the *Roscius,* the manuscript Catlin carried with him, the persona of a rustic
he would adopt in England, and the knowledge about Native Americans the
artist-showman possessed. Nearly half a century later another entertainer, Buffalo Bill Cody, would also leave New York harbor bound for England with his
"raw material of America."

In this portrait William Fisk depicted George Catlin as an artist who had become so trusted by the Indians that they invited him into their tepees, where he painted them. Catlin wears a decorated tunic from his collection of Indian objects. (National Portrait Gallery, Smithsonian Institution, gift of Miss May C. Kinney, Ernest C. Kinney, and Bradford Wickes, 1945)

*Medicine Man, Performing His Mysteries over a Dying Man*, painting by George Catlin, 1832. Catlin sometimes adorned himself in this Indian raiment to entertain audiences at his Wild West shows. (National Museum of American Art, Smithsonian Institution, gift of Mrs. Joseph Harrison Jr.)

*Keokuk on Horseback*, painting by George Catlin, 1835. This picture of Kee-o-kuk caused many audience members to accuse Catlin of painting his subject too gloriously. (National Museum of American Art, Smithsonian Institution, gift of Mrs. Joseph Harrison Jr.)

An Iowa shaman named Se-non-ty-yah delighted a London audience with his accounts of deeds of valor and details of crossing the Atlantic and riding a train. He concluded with words of appreciation for the kind treatment afforded by the English. (Plate 10, George Catlin, *Catlin's Notes of Eight Years' Travels and Residence in Europe*, 1848)

This group of Iowas performed with Catlin in 1844 and 1845. 1. Mew-hu-she-kaw. 2. Neu-mon-ya. 3. Se-non-ty-yah. 4. Wash-ka-mon-ya. 5. Shon-ta-yi-ga. 6. No-ho-mun-ya. 7. Wa-tan-ye. 8. Wa-ta-we-bu-ka-na. 9. Ru-ton-ye-wee-ma. 10. Ru-ton-we-me. 11. O-ke-we-me. 12. Koon-za-ya-me. 13. Ta-pa-ta-me. 14. Corsair. (Plate 9, George Catlin, *Catlin's Letters and Notes of Eight Years' Travels and Residence in Europe*, 1848)

This drawing features a Crow tepee on display at the Louvre and indicates how unique Catlin's Gallery must have looked. Since Catlin's showrooms were usually smaller than this one, most of them must have appeared more congested. (Plate 22, George Catlin, *Catlin's Notes of Eight Years' Travels and Residence in Europe*, 1848)

# "Trembling Excitements and Fears": Catlin and the Show Abroad

"The nobility and others of the most distinguished people of the kingdom" entered the room and paused to write their names in the guest register. Nervous and exhilarated, George Catlin watched these elegant people. Dukes and duchesses, lords and ladies, bishops, earls, and editors of newspapers and scholarly and scientific journals gathered for this private showing of the Gallery unique in late January 1840. Many already knew about the artist-showman and his collection because English newspapers such as the *Athenaeum* had praised its exhibition in America.[1] At this opening, Catlin delivered no formal lectures, he just chatted and answered questions for the "distinguished" visitors who clustered around him and "listened with the utmost curiosity and interest." He related stories of his experiences on the prairies of North America, details about his collection, and discourses on the "abused and dying" American Indians.[2] Nowhere in America had he attracted so many notables.

Another man in the exhibition room, the Honorable C. A. Murray, Master of Her Majesty's Household, attracted his own throngs of admirers. Murray had engineered this social triumph by personally inviting most of the assembled dignitaries. Catlin could not have chosen a more valuable ally. In addition to direct connections with the royal household, Murray had traveled in the Amer-

ican West, lived among the Pawnees, met Catlin on the Plains in 1835, and recently published a popular two-volume work about his adventures entitled
*Travels in North America.*[3]

Catlin saw Murray take "Duchesses, Countesses, and Ladies" on his arm and
conduct personal tours. Murray often stopped before the portrait of Wee-ta-
ra-sha-ro and explained that this Wichita man had saved him from death at the
hands of the Pawnees, he took tomahawks and lassos in his hands and demonstrated their uses, and he escorted visitors inside the great Crow tepee standing
in the center of the room. Pointing to scalping knives and the scalps of those
"slain in battle," he made "lasting and thrilling impressions." Murray brought
guests to Catlin and introduced them. Frequently those meeting the American
artist asked that he visit their homes at his leisure. "Thus passed my first interview with the English aristocracy," he noted proudly.[4]

How should he react to being such a "*decided hit*"? Shortly after the private
showing, Catlin wrote his parents about life in this "great & splendid City." At
the wedding of Queen Victoria and Prince Albert, the royal party passed so
closely that he and his nephew Burr "could have touched them with our finger!"
And he had spoken "with great success" to over one thousand at the Royal Institution and received "greater applause . . . than any man ever before received
within its walls." Surely all this fanfare would produce a "snug little fortune,"
despite a lease on three rooms at Egyptian Hall for $2,700 per year and expenses
that ran $40 a day. All of this—social and scholarly recognition and the higher
financial stakes—created a feeling of "trembling excitements and fears" within
him. He was, after all, only "a green horn from the backwoods . . . making his
*Debut* & his bow to the most polite & fastidious part of the whole world."[5]

The "green horn from the backwoods" persona perpetuated his role as an
unaided and self-taught artist who had paddled his canoe and led his "pack-
horse over and through trackless wilds, at the hazard of my life." Therefore he
asked viewers to "be kind and indulgent enough to receive and estimate them
[his paintings], as they have been intended, as *true and fac-similie traces of individual and historical facts;* and forgive me for their present unfinished and un-
studied condition, as works of art."[6]

Labeling oneself as a American rustic was not a new idea: Ben Franklin and
others had plied it with great success while abroad. Catlin used it as a clever
device to exempt himself from meeting critical standards in painting and writing. The English apparently accepted the rustic status as willingly as Catlin
offered it because those who wrote about his gallery, publications, and lectures
usually excused his shortcomings and praised his accuracy. A writer for the
*Athenaeum,* for example, proclaimed that a man who "spent years some thou-

sands of miles beyond the limits of civilized life; who has dragged his weary way through the trackless wilderness, floated for days down unknown rivers . . . at the hazard of his life, with the pencil in one hand and the rifle in the other, is not to be questioned about minor matters."[7]

Reacting to Europe with "trembling excitements and fears" made Catlin a typical nineteenth-century American. In this time, American and Canadian artists and intellectuals admired European culture, dutifully made pilgrimages abroad, and relished acceptance there. However, these same persons often criticized Europe for its tiredness and decadence. Catlin fit this role: he savored approval abroad, but in letters home he criticized England for "the insolence of wealth and the wretchedness of poverty," "its wealth, its refinement, its luxuries—with its vices, with its incongruous mass of loyalty & disloyalty, Republicanism and Despotism—mixed & patched up together, soon to fall & crumble to pieces."[8] In his view, no place was as good as home.

After the private opening, Catlin made his exhibition available to the general public on 29 January 1840. The first wave of visitors saw "an exceedingly interesting exhibition." Extensive advertising—handbills, showbills in conspicuous places, lengthy newspaper notices, and men carrying signs announcing scalps and wigwams—apprised people of the show in newly scrubbed and whitewashed rooms in Egyptian Hall, Piccadilly. Having rented more than one room, Catlin could keep the gallery open during the day and lecture in a separate room in the evening. The exhibition impressed some visitors to the extent that they solicited their government to purchase the Gallery unique.[9]

The gallery attracted the most customers and revenues. Visitors found "thousands of specimens real as well as pictorial" and a thicker version of the 1837 catalog for sale. Its text contained more ethnographic information, large doses of primitivistic philosophy, as well as strong words about European diseases, whiskey, wars, and the U.S. government's policy of Indian removal. To add appeal for his audiences, he indicated which Indians were Canadians and, therefore, residents of "her *British Majesty's dominions*."[10] Making such a link was good for business and a precedent that later Wild West showmen followed.

Catlin's lectures reflected the pattern established in the United States. He organized them into "courses" and presented them at 8:00 P.M. in a room above the gallery. Admission for a single lecture was two shillings and two pence and about two shillings per lecture in the course offerings. During presentations, he placed pictures, one-by-one, on an easel and explained them. The showman covered a multitude of topics, including education, hunting, courtship, marriage, polygamy, feasting, scalping, and the O-kee-pa. As in the United States, some reporters likened his lectures to taking a journey into Indian country.[11]

In several ways, however, lectures departed from his established pattern. He moved at a slower pace, putting only about twenty or thirty paintings on his easel during lectures instead of the several hundred he had displayed nightly in the United States. Sometimes, too, his tone became vitriolic. He attacked his country by saying that Indians were doomed to extinction "under the civilising influences of fire-water, small-pox, and the exterminating policy of the Government of the United States, in which treachery has recently played a counterpart to the most gratuitous despotism." Nor had his views about traders moderated. An English journalist noted: "He shewed, with melancholy vividness, the polluting and destructive influence of the intercourse with the low dealers and trappers, who infest the frontier" and destroy the Indians with "ardent spirits." Catlin generalized that Americans "turn with disdain from the very name of an Indian." England fared better in his remarks. Many Indians, particularly those who had fought against Americans in the War of 1812, liked the British.[12]

Catlin found more enthusiasm for Native Americans here than in the United States. The people of the British Isles were an ocean away from explosive issues like Indian removal, often accepted the myth of the noble savage, and read the works of James Fenimore Cooper, Washington Irving, and John Heckewelder. In addition, Catlin's subject was novel because he concentrated on Plains Indians, who differed from those of the northeastern United States and Canada familiar to the reading public in England. Many Britons had followed the accounts of the Seminole War and sympathized with the Seminoles and Osceola. In fact, one of Osceola's nephews was in England, and when he learned that the American artist was in town, he paid him a visit.[13]

Sympathetic or not, many who came to Egyptian Hall lacked an understanding of Native Americans, and Catlin and his assistants answered the same puerile questions day after day. Do Indians have facial hair? Are they virtuous and amorous? Do they practice cannibalism? Do they run about naked and live on raw meat? Scalping intrigued Londoners, who inquired if Indians did indeed take scalps—and then eat them? Reason, intelligence, religion, love, marriage, and family life—do these exist among Indians? To spare himself answering such questions, Daniel Kavenaugh proposed posting questions and answers on a placard and making it required reading before viewing the collection, but Catlin rejected the request.[14]

For a time, Londoners talked about the show, but its newness wore off and attendance dropped. By March 1840, just over a month after Catlin began public shows, a writer for the *Quarterly Review* noted "empty" benches at Egyptian Hall, and by late summer Catlin began to worry. In a letter to his father, he discussed the "enormous" expenses, the number of exhibitions, and the competition among show producers for the shillings of the entertainment-seeking public. When levelheaded Clara joined her husband in London, she accurately assessed the situation and recited her concerns in a letter to George's parents. Yes, the show generated a lot of money, but it also incurred tremendous expenses. "Rent and provisions are just double what they are at home," she wrote. In addition, "the English grudge a shilling more than an American does fifty cents," a multitude of competing entertainments existed, and her husband gave too much money to down-on-their-luck Americans in London. During summers, well-to-do persons left the metropolis for the country, causing ticket sales to plummet. And expenses kept George from moving the collection out of London. Clara worried about her husband: "He is in a country where if any accident should occur, the harpies of the law would soon strip him of everything." Perhaps, she added, someone would purchase the collection and they could return home.[15]

The ledger validated her concerns: all of the $9,433 paid by 32,500 persons to hear the lectures and see the gallery that first year went to pay bills. An article in the prestigious *Quarterly Review* sounded the alarm by observing that Catlin's "means are slender," and his expenses oppressive. If someone did not purchase the collection, Catlin's efforts would end in "*ruin*" and his life's work "would hang as a mill-stone round his neck."[16] Despite the article, no buyer came forward.

Talk of "harpies of the law," "*ruin*," and the collection becoming "a mill-stone round his neck" caused Catlin to respond with energy, resolve, and imagination. London filled him with "trembling excitements and fears," but he could finish his magnum opus on Indians, move the collection out of London and before new audiences, and add crowd-pleasing aspects to his lectures. In these first years abroad, Catlin possessed a good deal of fight.

His long-awaited two-volume work came off the press in October 1841 bearing the title *Letters and Notes on the Manners, Customs, and Conditions of the North American Indians*. Although it did not bring a "snug little fortune," the books made money and attracted larger audiences to Egyptian Hall. The volumes received an enthusiastic reception in England but a lukewarm one in the United States, where the author's sympathy for Indians and criticism of Americans aggravated some reviewers.[17]

In addition to publishing an enthusiastic book about Native Americans, Catlin added dash and color to his lectures. Survival necessitated filling those empty benches; step-by-step, he moved ever closer to adding Indians to his show. More than in the United States, Catlin impersonated Indians. He adorned himself with "the costume of an Indian Chief," which included "a magnificent head-dress of the war-eagle's feathers," a bow and arrows, spear, and "deer-skin ha-biliments, profusely ornamented with scalp-locks, beads, porcupine quill, and various other decorations." And sometimes he put on that old standby—the Blackfoot medicine man's regalia. He became an actor and demonstrated the use of Indian weapons, sounded the battle cry, and illustrated the stalking and shooting of buffalo. Dances became a specialty. He provided "a delightful il-lustration of the mode in which an Indian dance is got up; the preparatory drumming for hours—the gradual excitement of the listening tribe—the kin-dling into animation of the haughty warriors." His performances were spell-binding, "for his enthusiasm renders him an excellent actor in those things." His reenactments brought applause from spectators.[18] Catlin apparently saw no contradiction between promoting the authenticity of everything in his show and role-playing.

Like the Wild West entertainers who followed him, Catlin recognized the publicity value of Indians—even fake ones—outside the lecture hall. Conse-quently, he, along with his nephew Burr and John Murray, dressed as a Sioux leader, a Sac warrior, and a motley half-Indian interpreter and crashed the fash-ionable Caledonian Ball, an event Catlin proclaimed one of London's "most brilliant and splendid affairs." Smeared with war paint and carrying a scalp reputedly fresh from the prairies of the United States, they made a dramatic war-whooping entry. Startled and intrigued, guests offered them jewelry, asked questions through the interpreter, and requested dances. Vigorous renditions of the war and scalp dances left spectators spellbound.[19]

However, droplets of perspiration ran down their faces, dissolved their make-up, and exposed them as impostors. According to Catlin, attendees at the Cale-donian Ball enjoyed the hoax, encouraged them to stay, introduced themselves, and made plans to see the paintings and collection at Egyptian Hall.[20] Despite its lighthearted aspects, the spectacle was intended to address a pressing issue: Catlin needed to sell tickets. Moreover, he had planted the idea that war-whoop-ing and war-painted Indians inhabited Egyptian Hall.

Other masquerades were deceptions, pure and simple. Catlin, along with Clara, Burr, and several friends, attended the Polish Ball in London in costumes from the Gallery unique. On that occasion, they hid their identities, and the interpreter informed the curious that these Indians could be seen at Egyptian Hall. This duplicity angered some who went there expecting to see authentic Plains Indians. Disgruntled patrons did not end the practice, however, because Burr Catlin wrote home that in a nine-month period he had been to "several Balls in Indian dress." About this, he said that he had shaved his head "except the scalp lock, and I pass for Simon Pure, & speak no English without an interpreter, i.e. at the balls." George felt guilty about such antics, particularly when they exposed his wife to stares and jostling, but he desperately needed to catch the public's attention.[21]

In 1840, Catlin moved closer to putting Indians on stage when he rented an additional room at Egyptian Hall and hired actors to present tableaux vivants. In this popular form of entertainment, people stood as living statues on stage to produce realistic but static scenes. Catlin capitalized on the fad and then moved beyond it by adding action and sound. English men represented warriors and boys dressed as women in his "Tableaux Vivants of the Red Indians." Catlin took musical instruments from his collection, and men played them, sang, and issued battle cries. Indian clothing from the Gallery unique adorned these "living and moving figures" and produced a "splendid effect." Burr Catlin wrote home about this: "we sometimes have 20 men in full dress, giving the Indian Dances, Songs[,] War-Parades—Battle & scalping, yells, signals—war whoop &c. all of which takes well here, as it is something new and novel."[22]

Catlin alternated two programs, one on warfare and one on domestic life. Eleven scenes constituted the warfare offering, which included the decision to attack, a war dance, an ambush, "dreadful" scalping of the fallen enemy, a victory dance, and reconciliation between the tribes. Such scenes brought "loud and repeated acclamation." The program of domestic scenes included a shaman's attempts to cure a patient, Catlin at his easel in a Mandan village, a wedding, the rescue of Captain John Smith by Pocahontas, wrestling, lacrosse, gambling, and dancing. Along with lectures and the gallery, these programs helped Catlin meet expenses for three years.[23]

"Tableaux Vivants of Red Indians" revealed Catlin's willingness to experiment, replace paintings with live performers, use materials from his collection in a theatrical way, and present a sequence of events. Catlin had progressed to "Wild West" showmanship by infusing his entertainment with action, bloodshed, and scalping on stage. Surely he noticed that warfare brought "loud and repeated acclamation" while the domestic scenes did not. Half a century later Cody would present an indoor show with a sequence of events similar to Catlin's tableaux vivants.

In May 1842, after about two years abroad, Catlin left London and began "a tour of the provinces," going first to the Mechanics' Institute in Liverpool, where he lectured and offered his tableaux vivants. After Liverpool, he embarked on an ambitious tour of sixteen other cities, which included Manchester, Stratford-on-Avon, Glasgow, Belfast, and Dublin. The excursion tired him, those "empty" benches sometimes appeared, and profits remained slim.[24] Despite small

returns, the show needed to move about the British Isles to find new customers. Perfecting the art of traveling western entertainment would have to wait
for Buffalo Bill Cody.

In 1843, immediately after his tour ended and while preparing to return to
the United States, Catlin received a letter from a stranger named Arthur Rankin,
a Canadian who had served as a British officer in the War of 1812 and opposed
slavery and dispossession of Native Americans in the United States. He suggested
that some of her majesty's loyal Indian allies in the Revolution and the War of
1812 be rewarded with a trip to the British Isles and a visit with the queen. Perhaps this argument convinced officials that nine Ojibways from Canada should
visit England with Rankin, despite laws that forbade such trips abroad for purposes of exhibitions.[25] Catlin accepted an invitation to meet with Rankin, and
in his own opinion, it changed his life, his "occupation," and his character.[26]
Perhaps Rankin turned Catlin's life in an unanticipated direction; but, given
how close he already was to putting Indians on stage, Catlin may have simply
yielded easily to temptation.

At the conference in Catlin's quarters, the Ojibways conversed with him
through their interpreter, examined the scalps, and signaled recognition of their
peoples' portraits with war whoops. These Indians had already met and danced
for the "leading citizens" of Manchester. They came prepared for exhibitions,
bringing with them complete wardrobes, "weapons of war and the chase, pipes
of war and peace, and a variety of other implements and articles." Catlin claimed
that the decision to include them in his show was problematic. He believed that
for the Indians, civilization was "freighted with corruption and death." He said
that he had even written the secretary of war, Joel Poinsett, expressing disapproval of Native Americans going abroad for show purposes.[27] But, when the
decision about the Ojibways came, he apparently thought more about Kee-o-
kuk at Stuyvesant Institute than On-o-gong-way or Wi-jun-jon and concluded that he could be a showman and a friend of Indians. Moving into performances with Indians placed Catlin squarely in the Wild West show school of
entertainment.

The Ojibways, Catlin rationalized, came to England without his knowledge,
of their own free will, and to make money. He could care for them and promote their cause better than anyone, and they had every right to go among
whites to make money since legions of traders had reaped profits from them.
Also he felt obligated to return the hospitality shown him when he traveled on
the prairies. That one of the Ojibways recognized him as the artist who had
visited their village several years earlier pleased the showman. Eschewing any
arrangement that made him directly responsible for them, Catlin agreed to

exhibit the Indians with his collection and to split the proceeds with Rankin.[28] He did not disclose what the Indians received.

The group contained nine Indians. Its patriarch was Ah-quee-we-zaints (the Boy Chief), a leader in his late seventies with a flair for oratory and a distinguished record in warfare. He claimed to have been "the friend and companion-in-arms" of the great Shawnee leader Tecumseh, who had united Indians and led them on the British side in the War of 1812. A second Ojibway familiar with armed conflict was Pa-tau-na-quet-a-wee-be (the Driving Cloud), a war leader with many scars from battle, which "he sometimes displays and speaks of." A third leader, We-nish-ka-wee-bee (Flying Gull), accompanied the troupe. The company included an Indian family: Gish-e-gosh-e-ghee (the Moonlight Night), his wife, Wos-see-ab-nuah-qua, and their ten-year-old daughter, Nib-nab-e-quah. The "Adonis of the party" was Sah-ma (Tobacco), who brought his young wife, Ne-bet-nuah-qua. An eighteen-year-old man of French-Canadian and Indian heritage named Not-een-a-aum (the Strong Wind, sometimes called Cadotte) served as interpreter and occasionally joined in the dances.[29]

The Ojibways appeared first in Manchester and then in London. Casting aside tastefulness, Rankin and Catlin headed advertisements in Manchester with: "Wild Enough! Nine Real Indians from N. America." Newspaper notices, handbills, placards, and broadsides in London promised the "War Dance with Other Dances, war-whoops &c." The notices alerted the public about the "chiefs," warriors, women, and a child who would "Display . . . their Dances, Songs, and warwhoops, and other Ceremonies in their rudest and wildest character."[30] Such tastelessness would continue to mark Catlin's advertising and that of Cody designed for the British public.

Outside the lecture hall, the Indians created a sensation. In Manchester, the chief of police asked Catlin and Rankin to keep them hidden, except during shows, to prevent the formation of unruly crowds. On the final evening of the Manchester engagement, Catlin needed police officers to restrain a mob that could not squeeze inside the hall. Once in London, reporters announced their "Extraordinary Arrival," declaring that "Indians from the wilds of America" were in the city. Catlin signed a six-month lease on rooms in Egyptian Hall, unpacked his collection, and prepared to stay for a while. To get publicity, the showmen needed only to put the Ojibways in public view. Morning omnibus rides and trips to ballets and other entertainments caught the attention of the public.[31]

Catlin and Rankin waited for Queen Victoria's invitation before beginning public exhibitions in London. Finally, the coveted request to visit Windsor Castle arrived. There Pa-tau-na-quet-a-wee-be expressed pleasure in meeting the queen and her guests, then Ah-quee-we-zaints began playing the drum and singing while the others danced. All this was a bit less refined than Victoria expected, and she reacted with "surprise, as well as amazement." Formality returned when everyone sat down to a roast beef luncheon. The visit was heady stuff for a self-proclaimed "green horn from the backwoods" and excellent material for the catalog and other advertising.[32] Over fifty years later, this same queen would summon Cody to give selected acts from his show, and he too would see its value for publicity.

"Real Indians" attracted turn-away crowds and generated profits for Catlin, perhaps as much as a thousand dollars a week after paying expenses and giving Rankin his share. The shows began with the Ojibways sitting silently in "their feathered head-dresses and cloaks of skin" on an elevated platform, which afforded everyone an unobstructed view of them. Catlin made a "few preliminary remarks" and interjected short extemporaneous explanations at other times, but action, noise, spontaneity, and personal contact with audiences characterized these new shows.[33] Catlin's willingness to let things happen naturally probably had grown from his success in the United States with Kee-o-kuk and the show with the Pawnees in 1837.

Sometimes the Indians played their musical instruments, mostly drums and rattles, and sang. When the time to dance came, an observer recorded: "they throw off their outer garments, and appear with the upper part of their bodies covered only with paint, their muscular forms, savage aspect, violent gestures, and shrill cries, have a formidable effect." Another reporter wrote that during the war dance, the young men were "barking like dogs, and hallooing like mad." The Ojibways danced so often and so vigorously that they sometimes felt "a little lame." In one instance, one of the Ojibways recognized the portrait of an enemy hanging in the collection, and he "raised the war-whoop; the others joining in it; and the war dance was commenced forthwith, the chiefs and warriors flourishing their war clubs with menacing gestures, directed to the portrait."[34]

In addition to dances, Ah-quee-we-zaints often addressed the audience through an interpreter, usually expressing his pleasure in visiting England and promising to speak well of its people on his return to North America. The shows often became hubbubs, where Ojibway men ran out into audiences, kissed women, and rewarded those who had brought a gift with a whoop of appreciation. If time permitted, Catlin or his assistant, Daniel Kavenaugh, fielded questions. After shows, all who wished to shake hands with a "real Indian" could do so.[35]

All of this ruffled the sensibilities of some members of the upper class, who preferred decorum and a government in which monarchy and aristocracy kept a tight rein on the commoners. Such people believed that democracy was dangerous because it could quickly slip into anarchy. Perhaps Catlin recognized this attitude, which may have prompted him to include as many "chiefs" as possible to convince people that he had brought an Indian aristocracy to England. If that was his purpose, he failed in the estimation of many, because his Indians did not act in a properly restrained and upper-class manner. They danced crazily, ran around kissing willing females, and solicited gifts. Not only did the Indians act badly but they might also encourage the uncouth among the English to do the same.

Charles Dickens, for example, found goings-on at Catlin's shows offensive. While in the United States gathering material for *American Notes,* he learned of the Gallery unique, so when Catlin came to London, he attended a show. About it he grumbled: "With his party of Indians squatting and spitting on the table before him, or dancing their miserable jigs after their own dreary manner, he [Catlin] called, in all good faith, upon his civilised audiences to take note of their symmetry and grace, their perfect limbs, and the exquisite expression of their pantomime; and his civilised audience, in all good faith, complied and admired."[36]

Another disgruntled observer found the performance disappointing and that "as soon as the Ceremony of *shaking hands* commenced, we retreated, as I had no ambition to grasp the palm of a dirty savage." A writer for the *Spectator* said the Native Americans were "both morally and intellectually . . . below the first chimney-sweep you may pick on chance," that the Ojibway's morning omnibus rides were transparent publicity stunts, and that the dances were "mere feats of animal vigor and dexterity" performed solely "for the sake of gain." Some observers asked pointedly: is it right to exhibit Indians?[37]

Some shows became so raucous that women ran screaming from the lecture hall. At one, a claustrophobic woman announced that she had to escape the crowd, came forward, and sat on the platform with the Indians. Seeing this, another woman announced that she too needed air; however, the size of the crowd prevented her from leaving, so she agreed to be lifted overhead and passed forward by many hands until reaching the platform. To the delight of the spectators, she arrived with her clothes disarranged.[38] Much had changed in the six years since Black Hawk and Kee-o-kuk appeared alongside Catlin at Stuyvesant Institute. Catlin had moved from being an educator of the lyceum mold to an entertainer whose shows became sensational enough to invite ridicule.

The English periodical *Punch* chided Catlin for bringing Indian dignitaries to England on a begging trip. This writer hoped that English royalty never found it necessary to exhibit broadsword combat and English-style dancing to earn money for passage home. The satirist referred readers, tongue-in-cheek, to the "announcements of Mr. Catlin, wherein it is stated that 'The Ojibbeway Indians exhibit daily. War-whoop at 12 precisely; Scalping begins at 3. Feeding time, 1 s extra.' "[39] Unfortunately, the shows worsened.

Rankin, probably sensing a fortune to be made, charged Catlin with taking the lion's share of the profits and broke the partnership. Rankin removed the Ojibways to Greenwich, then returned to London, where he rented a room in Egyptian Hall next to Catlin's, displayed the Indians, delivered his own lectures, and printed a thirty-page pamphlet entitled *A Short History of the Ojibbeway Indians Now on a Visit to England.*[40]

When the interpreter Not-een-a-aum, or Cadotte, and Sarah Haynes, an eighteen-year-old Englishwoman, decided to marry, Rankin publicized the wedding, and a gigantic crowd assembled at St. Martin's Church. Then Rankin advertised that the bride would appear on stage with the Ojibways to play the piano for their war dance. However, her father and new husband displayed better sense than Rankin and prevented her appearance. A groundswell of protest followed, and Catlin emphasized that he was not a party to this vulgarity. *Punch* lampooned the affair by publishing drawings of hideous-looking Indians, listing the names and ages of other Ojibways, and saying each wanted a wife to take back to North America. On the other side of the Atlantic, the *Detroit Advertiser* saw tragic humor in the Englishwoman's marriage to "a course, awkward, and booby looking Indian."[41]

Despite the unpleasantries with Rankin, Catlin brought another Indian into his gallery, a Sac leader named Joc-o-sot "in splendid costume, with the shaved and crested head peculiar to that tribe, giving the war song, the death song and various dances." Reporters paid little attention.[42] Catlin found himself with an expensive lease on rooms in Egyptian Hall and no attraction.

However, the opportunistic Catlin found a stellar performer in an adjacent room in Egyptian Hall—General Tom Thumb, brought to London by the American showman P. T. Barnum. The fifteen-pound Thumb had mesmerized Britons with songs and dances, met royalty including Queen Victoria and the queen mother, and attracted over two hundred of the nobility to Egyptian Hall in a single week. To Barnum's chagrin, Catlin persuaded Tom Thumb to come to his Indian Gallery to sing, dance, and "represent Napoleon musing the Grecian Statues & c." Joc-o-sot interspersed his acts among Thumb's.[43] Catlin had clearly strayed from his goal of championing American Indians.

Catlin quickly returned to standard fare, however. On 24 July 1844, the *London Times* announced that a party of Iowas—leaders, warriors, women, and children—along with a black linguist named Jeffrey Deroin (sometimes Jeffrey

Doraway) and their sponsor George H. C. Melody journeyed to England. A shipmate on the Atlantic called them "truly a wild enough looking company," claimed they possessed "strong athletic frames," and reported they enjoyed dancing and noise making. All would arrive in good health, having butchered a fat buffalo to provide suitable food for the ocean voyage. They were professionals, having performed in Hoboken, New Jersey, before thousands daily. With them came everything for a first-rate show: a "splendid wardrobe," tents, camp equipment, canoes, and weapons. They would live outside and give some open-air demonstrations.[44]

Perhaps some understanding existed between Catlin and Melody because even before their arrival, Catlin promoted the Iowas, calling them "the finest specimens of the Indian tribe that have ever visited Europe." Remarkable for their "extraordinary stature, their herculean strength, their skill in the use of Indian weapons and their knowledge of . . . varied and amusing games and diversions," they were "wilder" and "more primitive" than the Ojibways. After landing, Melody visited Catlin and they struck an agreement to exhibit the Iowas. Catlin maintained that Melody was the person responsible for bringing them to England and that they came with the approval of officials in the United States.[45]

Catlin now professed more enthusiasm for the Iowas than for the Ojibways. He claimed to favor them because they represented "the aristocracy of the tribe." Moreover, they had escaped most influences from "civilized" people because they hailed from an area between the Missouri River and the Rocky Mountains, a location fully a thousand miles farther west than the Ojibways' home near the Great Lakes. This troupe included two leaders: Mew-hu-she-kaw (the White Cloud), a thirty-five-year-old man who often wore an eagle feather headdress and a necklace of grizzly bear claws, and Neu-mon-ya (the Walking Rain), a fifty-four-year-old man who towered above nearly everyone because he stood about six-and-one-half feet in height. A shaman, or "great medicine man," Se-non-ty-yah (the Blistered Feet) was a forty-five-year-old bachelor and a natural entertainer who considered himself attractive to the opposite sex.

There were four Iowa warriors: Wash-ka-mon-ya (the Fast Dancer), No-ho-mun-ya (the One Who Gives No Attention), Shon-ta-yi-ga (the Little Wolf), Wa-tan-ye (the Foremost Man), and Wa-ta-we-bu-ka-na (the Commanding General, the ten-year-old son of Neu-mon-ya). Women with the group included Ru-ton-ye-we-ma (the Strutting Pigeon, wife of Mew-hu-she-kaw), Ru-ton-we-me (the Pigeon on the Wing), Koon-za-ya-me (the Female War Eagle Sailing), Ta-pa-ta-me (Wisdom, daughter of Mew-hu-she-kaw), and O-ke-we-me (the Female Bear That Walks on the Back of Another, wife of Shon-ta-yi-ga), who had an infant, Corsair, who often appeared in a cradleboard.[46]

According to Catlin's account, he talked seriously with them about alcohol. Governmental regulations prohibited Native Americans from consuming alcoholic beverages while abroad. On some occasions, such as the luncheon with Queen Victoria, Catlin had allowed the Ojibways to drink champagne. However, they had abused this privilege, drinking to excess at a brewery. Certainly, Catlin reasoned, the Iowas would not want to denigrate themselves like that. Probably because he was an ocean away from government officials, Catlin allowed the Iowas to drink moderately on special social occasions and to enjoy a tankard of ale under his supervision in the evenings after shows.[47]

According to Catlin, their arrival in late summer came at a poor time for exhibitions. To fill the empty seats, Catlin promoted the group aggressively by taking them out in public, advertising an "Unparalleled Exhibition," warning that people must see the Iowas soon because "they are on their way to the Continent," and making much of the striking appearance of the warriors, who shaved their heads, leaving only a jet-black scalp lock to which they added bright ornaments. This Catlin discussed "with all the enthusiasm of a craniologist," explaining that they left scalp locks to taunt their enemies. Those men in Melody's group appeared stripped to the waist, their upper bodies glistening with red paint and ornamented with blue and white streaks. About them, the *London Times* reported: "Their appearance is between the grotesque and the frightful; but to those who admire the incongruous, even in its disagreeable forms, a sight of them will be a high treat." Despite such remarks, the Iowas received a number of invitations from fashionable addresses, including that of former prime minister Benjamin Disraeli.[48]

Their first shows resembled those by the Ojibways. Catlin made introductory remarks, but he felt "obliged to let them arrange their performances just as they chose." Perhaps when he knew them better, presentations would change. Left largely to their own, the Iowas reportedly "shouted, and whooped, and flourished their tomahawks" in a number of dances, stopping periodically to smoke their pipes, and then "set to again with an awful tribute of lungs, stamping" through other dances.[49] Those desiring information about the Iowas could pay six pence for a program called *Unparalleled Exhibition: The Fourteen Ioway Indians Just Arrived from the Upper Missouri, near the Rocky Mountains, North America.*

After a time, Catlin arranged the program to provide a well-rounded representation of Indian life, including "Wigwam erecting" and dances of all kinds, including welcome, war, calumet, scalp, buffalo, and bear. The Iowas demonstrated amusements such as lacrosse, the game of the moccasin (in which one person placed a small stone under one of four moccasins and others bet on the location of the stone), and the game of the platter, which resembled casting dice. Music appeared in the form of war, death, wolf, medicine, burial, and farewell songs with instrumental accompaniment from rattles, whistles, and drums.[50]

However, among tepee erecting, game playing, and music came battle cries and "real Indian scalps." Scalps became props in the war dance, which Catlin said began with No-ho-mun-ya "waving his two scalps on the point of a lance" and demonstrating, with the aid of "his tomahawk and scalping knife . . . the manner in which his unfortunate enemies had fallen before him." About this, the showman noted: "This was probably the first time that the Scalp Dance, in its original and *classic* form, was ever seen in the city of London, and embellished by the presence of real and *genuine scalps.*" Perhaps the scene was "too much for the nerves and tastes of London people," but many attended the show "for the pleasure of receiving shocks and trying their nerves." After all, audiences gave the act resounding applause. Catlin concluded this part of the show with an explanation of the practice and meaning of scalping—something little understood among Europeans or Americans, he maintained. This, too, often brought approval from the audience.[51] Wild West showmen generally would warn that those squeamish about bloodshed might not approve of all acts.

A reporter for the *Era* appended a news article from the United States about a delegation of Iowas visiting Washington, D.C., with the comment: "Our friend, Mr. Catlin, must look to his laurels at the Egyptian Hall; or could he not induce them to visit London, and get up a real fight, with a practical essay on tomahawking?"[52] This journalistic jab came from a newspaper with a history of supporting Catlin, but the artist and champion of Indians had transformed his lyceum-like lectures into "Wild West" performances.

A writer for *Punch* wrote: "Real Scalps! Great Attraction." Mere Indians were passé, but scalps were something special: "Think of that ladies and gentlemen; the real skin and hair of a human creature. Is that not attractive!" Facetiously, the writer suggested actual scalping on stage. Surely "a few desperate wretches" could be found to risk their lives for such a noble cause and sufficient remuneration.[53] Despite such reproaches, Catlin stuck with features that sold tickets. Scalping would reappear in his show and in later ones, including those of Buffalo Bill Cody, who would turn a scalping into a grand spectacle.

The Iowas came with tepees and camped outdoors for a time. Catlin savored seeing this small Indian village with smoke rising lazily from tents, with the Iowas "darting into and about them during their various games and amusements." Catlin urged people to see "The Encampment" of "Wigwams, made of Buffalo-Hides, curiously painted." He advertised that for one shilling "the public will have an opportunity of witnessing for the first time in Europe illustrations of the stirring descriptions given by Cooper in his celebrated novels, The Last of the Mohicans, Prairie &c."[54] Camping outside and affording an opportunity to see an authentic Indian village was good entertainment, and something that Cody and the 101 Wild West show would offer as well.

In August and September 1844, while in camp, the Iowas gave outdoor performances, first at Lord's Cricket Grounds, St. John's Wood, and then at Vauxhall Gardens. Performed in roped-off one- or two-acre tracts, they included lacrosse, speeches, and contests of marksmanship between the Iowas and members of London's archery clubs. Like the tableaux vivants before them, these outdoor performances featured sequences of events illustrating war and peaceful endeavors. Warfare included the "approaching dance" (to ensure success in surprising the enemy), the attack, and an after-battle celebration with a scalp dance. In domestic scenes, the Iowas demonstrated the process of establishing a camp, beginning with a shaman's rites to ensure good health and luck there, women erecting tepees, and a welcome dance. The wild horse dance showed the chase, capture, and taming of those animals.[55]

Bringing English horses to Vauxhall Gardens enabled Catlin to put Indians on horseback, "fully equipped, with their own native shields and lances, and bows, and even the saddles and trappings." According to Catlin, "thousands flocked there to witness their powers of horsemanship and skill in prairie warfare." Danger lurked in these feats because the English horses were unfamiliar with Indian-style equestrianism. Among those who witnessed this were thirty-two thousand schoolchildren and their teachers, all admitted free of charge. Again, Catlin warned the curious not to tarry; he planned to take the Iowas to Paris.[56]

These outdoor performances featured Indians actually demonstrating horse riding, sharpshooting, and warmaking, things seen previously by most whites only in Catlin's paintings. Colorful and authentic costumes, and the danger and unpredictability of warriors riding galloping horses, added to the realism. This new kind of entertainment marked Catlin's last innovation as a showman. Much different than his early lyceum-like lectures, these open-air demonstrations foreshadowed the Wild West shows that Cody and the Millers would give. However, Catlin could not stick with the new format because these outdoor shows required the free use of public parks and borrowed horses.

Soon Catlin returned to his standard programs and sought new patrons in other cities in England and in Scotland and Ireland during a tour that began in the fall of 1844 and continued through the winter. During these travels, Catlin and the Iowas attracted good audiences and enjoyed attention inside and outside the show rooms. The same kind of rowdiness found in shows with the

Ojibways sometimes crept into performances. At one, a drunk man interrupted the proceedings to announce that the Indians' method of taming horses by holding them down and breathing into their nostrils did not placate animals; but it worked wonderfully well with women.[57] However, more serious matters than inebriated men plagued this trip.

The infant named Corsair died. Audiences had always responded enthusiastically when this baby appeared on a cradleboard during performances. Shonta-yi-ga, the boy's father, mourned grievously, and Catlin worried that he might stop performing for a time or even leave the show. While concerned about the grief-stricken parents, Catlin lamented that it hurt business and increased his problems. In a letter to his wife, he concluded: "So you will see that cares and anxieties are gathering on me while I am day and night working hard—hard—hard."[58] Producing a lavish volume of art prints called *Catlin's North American Indian Portfolio of Hunting Scenes and Amusements* contributed to the work load.

The portfolio, published in 1844, contained twenty-five large lithographs of his most popular pictures.[59] By expressing their preferences to Catlin, people at his shows had "voted" on what scenes they felt best represented the West to them. Those pictures "voted" into the portfolio anticipated much that would become standard fare in future western entertainments: buffalo, hunting, horses, and rodeo-style riding.

Pictures of buffalo dominated *Catlin's North American Indian Portfolio.* Thirteen of the twenty-five plates featured bison, with many of those drawings depicting gallant old bulls, sometimes locked in combat, sometimes dying, but always wild and glorious. Indians, buffalo, and buffalo hunting went together in Catlin's mind because these animals were the staff of life for these native people. For Catlin, the buffalo reflected the spirit of the untamed Plains.[60]

Horses and Indians on horseback symbolized the freedom and prowess of the Plains peoples to Catlin. In a painting called "Catching the Wild Horses," Catlin depicted the capture and breaking of mustangs and then wrote about it: " 'Taking the wild horse,' and 'breaking him down' is one of the proudest feats of the Indian, and requires the sudden rallying, and desperate use, of all his manly faculties." " 'Throwing the lasso' from the back of a horse at full speed" was the most common manner of catching the fleeing mustangs.[61] In the *North American Indian Portfolio,* Catlin immortalized those scenes that would become forever associated with life on the Great Plains—buffalo, buffalo hunting, galloping horses, bronco riding, and roping.

During this time Catlin looked across the English Channel to France, anticipating that "Frenchmen & foreigners" would fill his lecture halls. People there relished James Fenimore Cooper's *Leatherstocking Tales* in French-language editions and François-René de Chateaubriand's exceedingly popular romantic renditions of life in the American West. As a young man seeking a safe haven during the French Revolution, King Louis Philippe himself fled to the New World, traversed the Ohio and Mississippi River Valleys, and visited Native Americans along the way. Catlin knew the king, having recently met him while getting subscriptions for his *North American Indian Portfolio.*[62]

Catlin, with his wife and children, arrived in Paris in mid-April 1845. Touring the city with the Iowas, flooding Paris with advertisements, and hobnobbing with the social elite, led to a much publicized invitation from the Palace of the Tuileries. Afternoon and evening performances began at the Salle Valentino in rue St. Honoré in early June. The shows offered those same features seen by the English in indoor performances. Additionally, a 150-foot hall allowed the Iowas ample room to demonstrate their skill with bows and arrows. A pamphlet, *Catalogue Raisonné de la Galerie Indienne de Mr. Catlin,* made available details about the visiting Americans and the collection. A French observer compared Catlin's pictures to those of the old masters, and other visitors critiqued his collection gently, characterizing the paintings as field sketches, not finished works of art. More publicity came from a theatrical farce about Catlin and the Iowas wherein amorous French women pursued Indians. Perhaps Rankin's publicity about the wedding of Not-een-a-aum and Sarah Haynes in England inspired this.[63]

Parisians adored the Americans and their show. One observer called the Iowas people "cast in Nature's stateliest mould" and "fine specimens of the human form." Another said Catlin's remarks, paintings, artifacts, and the Indians' demonstrations provided "insight into the lives and history of this most interesting race, which has all the charms of the wildest romance, but which books can never supply." Persons "distinguished by science or philosophical research," including George Sand and Victor Hugo, attended performances. In addition, the prestigious Société Ethnologique elected Catlin to membership.[64]

Despite auspicious beginnings, disaster stalked the French tour. Social tensions were building toward the revolution of 1848, causing the government to impose strict regulations on public entertainment, to take part of Catlin's gate receipts to help the poor, and to scrutinize all printed matter sold with the show. Moreover, the police interrogated Catlin and stood at his doors equipped with bayonets to prevent possible public disorder.[65] But paranoia and harassment paled in comparison to the next round of difficulties.

O-kee-we-me, wife of Shon-ta-yi-ga and mother of the recently deceased Corsair, became ill and died shortly after public performances began. Financial records indicate that a cab driver had waited two-and-a-half hours for Shon-ta-yi-ga outside the "Woods of Boulogne," where the Iowa must have sought solitude to mourn the loss of first his child and then his wife. Shortly thereafter, the Iowas asked to return to the United States, and they left with Melody.[66]

In these troubled times, Catlin experienced his own grief from the death of loved ones. His wife, Clara, died from pneumonia on 28 July 1845. Without her support, objectivity, and mothering of their four children, Catlin's life grew even more complicated. Relatives in the United States worried about the children and that Catlin had stopped writing to family members. Then, in 1847, the "cruel hand of death" took "Georgie," his only son.[67]

For a time after the departure of the Iowas, Catlin gave shows without Indians, then eleven Ojibways under the management of a Londoner arrived in Paris on the day before Catlin's advertised closing date. This group also knew entertainment, having performed in the United States before going to England for the same purpose in March 1845. A bit of deception shrouded them. Their leader, George Henry—an Ojibway and a "well-educated former Methodist missionary"—had written that unconverted Indians reminded him more of orangutans than humans. Henry, or Maung-gwud-daus as he called himself, had organized his troupe of Ojibways, traveled with it in the United States, and had then gone to England to play in Egyptian Hall. While there, the program had become sensational, featuring such spectacles as Maung-gwud-daus shooting an apple off his son's head, a demonstration of scalping, and performances of a war dance.[68]

*Galignani's Messenger,* a English-language newspaper published in Paris, welcomed the group and noted their "singularly poetic names": Mang-groud-dans (this was Maung-gwud-daus, who said his name meant Great Hero), Say-say-gou (the Causer of Great Hailstorms), Mish-she-mong (King of the Lions), A-win-nwave (the Bird of Thunder), Wam-bud-dick (White Reindeer), Au-nim-muck-kurck-um (the Bird Who Travels with Hailstorms), Ke-che-us-sin (Mighty Rock), Noo-din-noo-kay (the Bird Who Directs the Raging Storm), Min-nis-sin-noo (Brave Warrior), Uh-je-juck (Pelican), and Uh-wus-sig-gee-zhig-goo-kway (Woman of the Upper World).[69]

Catlin explained their timely arrival by claiming that they were making public appearances in London when they learned of the Iowas' departure and decided to join him. Catlin advertised: "this party will be found far more exciting and picturesque than those of the Ioway Indians." With such hyperbole, Catlin hoped to dispel rumors that they were only second-rate imitations of the Iowas or perhaps just Frenchmen dressed as Indians. Probably to reduce expenses, Catlin moved his collection to new quarters, the Gallery of Beaux Arts.[70]

Catlin went, first alone and then with the Ojibways, to Saint-Cloud, a summer palace, where the Indians entertained the royal family. The Ojibways presented their standard acts, including dances, ball play, and archery. On the palace grounds, they found an authentic birch bark canoe from the United States and paddled it happily. Catlin advertised that the show would close on 30 October 1845, ten days after the visit to Saint-Cloud. After this he would pack the collection and leave France. However, Catlin and the Gallery unique so delighted Louis Philippe that he asked that the paintings hang in the Salle de Séance at the Louvre and wanted Catlin to make reproductions of his favorite paintings. Catlin remained in the Louvre about six weeks, enjoying visits from many distinguished persons and relishing the "flattering patronage of the King."[71] Hobnobbing with royalty and hanging his works in the Louvre delighted the "green horn from the backwoods."

Acquaintance with Louis Philippe led to an introduction to the Belgian king, who invited the artist to visit his country. This enabled Catlin to leave the collection rent-free and safely on public display and begin a tour with the Ojibways to Brussels, Antwerp, and Ghent. Financial prospects looked promising, but disaster struck in Brussels, where eight of the Native Americans contracted smallpox. Shows stopped while Catlin cared for them and secured medical attention. Despite these efforts, two died. In early 1846, when the survivors could travel, Catlin sent them to England with money and instructions for their return to the United States. Financial losses during this period exceeded a thousand dollars.[72]

These deaths by smallpox stunned Catlin. He hated the deadly disease and those who introduced it to Native Americans, and now it had felled those under his care. This struck Catlin's conscience full force, and he concluded that these events afforded "a shocking argument against the propriety of persons bringing Indians to Europe with a view to making their exhibitions a just or profitable speculation." In a letter published in the United States, he wrote: "Pray get some of the editors in the United States, whose papers reach the Western frontiers, to discourage any other parties of Indians from coming to England or France for the purpose of exhibition." Indians with him had failed "to realize more than expenses," and, if not for his own generosity, the Indians would have faced disaster. So far he had paid for six funerals for Native Americans. He urged, "for the happiness of the poor Indians," that people not bring them to Europe.[73]

Never again would Catlin exhibit Indians. His career as a showman, at least as a notable one, ended, and he returned to more private pursuits—painting, writing, caring for his three daughters, keeping his gallery open to the public, sometimes lecturing, and struggling to retain possession of his Gallery unique. Much of this he did at his gallery at number 6 Waterloo Place in London, but reporters gave him scant attention and few customers visited. Deeply in debt and down on his luck, he knew that he must sell the Gallery unique. Years of poor financial decisions, borrowing heavily against the collection, "unfortunate speculations," and a proclivity to spend his "last dollar" meant that "harpies of the law" were poised to strike.[74]

Catlin fought back as best he could. To inform everyone that his collection had grown substantially and to remind them that it was still for sale, Catlin prepared *A Descriptive Catalogue of Catlin's Indian Gallery* and filled it with information about his collection and reprints of laudatory newspaper articles from England, France, and the United States. He hurriedly wrote a two-volume work called *Catlin's Notes of Eight Years' Travels and Residence in Europe, with His North American Indian Collection* about his adventures abroad and the experiences with Indians in Europe. The idea was a great one: an American in Europe with Indians who confided their deepest feelings and reacted—often with disbelief—to the foibles of "civilized" people. It represented the reverse of all those Europeans who wrote about their travels in the United States and their observations about the "quaint" customs of the Indians. The books received mixed reviews, however, and did nothing to alleviate his financial crisis.[75]

Catlin rallied American artists in Paris and American citizens in London to petition the U.S. government to purchase his collection. He wrote influential persons, including Daniel Webster, to whom he confided that his financial affairs were in an "alarming state," causing him to "tremble for the security of my works."[76] Such efforts produced endorsements, committee reports, congressional paperwork, and votes, but no sale.

In addition to proffering the collection, from 1848 to 1852 Catlin pursued venturesome financial schemes. He knew of the money to be made in land speculation, having expressed interest in it while in Pensacola, Florida, in 1835, and having written his brother Francis in 1844 about making a "swell" in real estate speculation in Wisconsin. Those in the 1840s offering transportation to the United States and land on arrival could make money from Britons. Hunger, disillusionment, and political and social unrest in the British Isles during the midnineteenth century caused an exodus and spawned a rash of speculation and settlement enterprises promising escape and acreage to the discontented. A part of this movement, Catlin planned to raise money through the sale of stock, buy land, shepherd immigrants through the naturalization process, and otherwise ensure the success of a new agricultural community in the United States.[77] Financial exigencies had caused Catlin to stray from his first principles. His successors in Wild West shows would also discover that when bills came due, compromises were necessary.

To publicize his plan, Catlin published *Notes for the Emigrant to America* in 1848 to encourage "Anglo-Saxon" settlement on the Plains of North America. In this pamphlet, Catlin contradicted much of what he had written previously by praising pioneers such as Daniel Boone, saying that travel on the Plains had excited him about settlement there, and labeling Indians "cruel savages." Unscrupulously he promoted an area he alternately labeled Texas and the Mississippi Valley by praising its "superiority both in soil and climate over any other part of the United States" and calling it "one of the richest, most prolific, and best watered countries in North America," capable of growing cotton, wheat, rye, corn, tobacco, indigo, sweet potatoes, fruit, nuts, and other crops.[78]

In 1850 he lectured to London's Mechanics' Institution on the "Valley of the Mississippi, And Its Advantages to Emigration With Some Account of the Gold Regions of California," which he illustrated with "Colossal Maps and Paintings." Such lectures were free, and these and other things cost him a "catalogue of expenses." In the end the venture failed, and for his efforts he received only "kicks and curses." The episode cost him dearly: "two years of my life and £1200."[79] Cody would also squander time and money on the dream of a great agricultural colony, one in the Bighorn Basin of Wyoming.

In 1851 Catlin continued efforts to raise money by vigorously promoting a plan he had originally presented to the Royal Institution of London shortly after his arrival there. He proposed that his Gallery unique form the nucleus of a "museum of mankind" or "museum of history" to "perpetuate the looks, customs, history, and manufactures, of all the declining and vanishing races of man." Sometimes, he indicated that a ship would house this monument and sail about the world exhibiting it.[80] Obviously Catlin had vested interests in the project because it would have ensured the purchase of the Gallery unique and subsidized exhibitions and more ethnological pursuits.

The museum idea failed, but it linked him to later Wild West shows. Most likely, he realized that including a wide range of cultures would broaden the museum's interest to Europeans, particularly those in nations with colonies. Probably for the same reason, Cody would introduce a "Congress of Rough Riders of the World" featuring exotic horsemen.

Being in England surrounded by talk about the upcoming 1851 world's fair in London caused Catlin to wonder whether his collection would make money there. The press called for something really "American" in the Crystal Palace. Why, European critics asked, did the United States compete with them by displaying mostly manufactured goods? In this vein, a reporter for the *London*

*Times* wrote: "The peculiar greatness of their nation is that which cannot be represented in a 'glass house,' as they are pleased to call it." America represented things like "magnificent territory," "triumphs over the forest," and the power of the Mississippi River. Despite such pronouncements, Catlin failed to persuade exhibitors to include the entire Gallery unique and settled for sending two or three of his Native American costumes.[81]

His efforts at the Crystal Palace produced no money and little publicity. However, Catlin's instincts were right—and wrong. His collection contained the "raw materials of America," and anything representing itself as "American" should have included its natural wonders and its native peoples. However, Catlin's commentaries and collection would not have fit in a fair trumpeting "progress" and celebrating America's "triumphs over the forest." For too long, Catlin had protested the so-called progress this fair celebrated. Reconciling reverence for the past and enthusiasm for progress would come forty-six years later, when Cody took his show to Queen Victoria's Golden Jubilee.

When Catlin needed a spectacular success, he suffered failures—in finding a buyer for his collection, in land speculation, in the "museum of mankind" proposal, and at the world's fair. Consequently, in 1852, when creditors demanded their money, Catlin could not pay and was jailed for debt. His brother-in-law Dudley Gregory came to England, probably arranged for his release, and took his three nieces back to the United States with him. Still, Catlin hoped that the U.S. Congress would purchase his collection. When this proposal came before the House of Representatives, the members voted for purchase, but in the Senate it failed. Support came mostly from Whigs and northerners while southerners and Democrats voted against it. Catlin's championing of Osceola had alienated some southerners, which affected this crucial vote.[82] The final tally reflected what Catlin had known when he exhibited his collection in the United States: enthusiasm for him and his pro-Indian position existed mostly in the Northeast. Later Wild West entertainers would enjoy broader support.

After the vote, an auction of the collection began, and one of the creditors, an American named Joseph Harrison Jr., got possession of it, shipped it back to the United States, and stored it in the basement of a boiler factory, where much of it suffered water damage and disintegrated.[83] The fate of the Gallery unique symbolized national priorities. As a nation, Americans valued making powerful steam engines, the future, progress, and business, but showed indifference about a monument to Native Americans.

Catlin vowed to somehow regain possession of his treasure, but with the "millstone" no longer "round his neck," he became a free man. Or maybe he was not so free: he still owed creditors and could be sent back to prison. Whatever the motivation, he left Europe for seven years (the requisite number for the statute of limitations), took an assumed name, and returned to the unspoiled areas of the Western Hemisphere. This provided tonic for his soul—he "mustered courage yet to live—yet to love—and again to trust my luck in the wilderness."[84]

Searching for a lost gold mine in Brazil, visiting indigenous peoples, investigating geological features, prospecting, collecting topaz and amethyst crystals, and escaping the clutches of "civilization" motivated Catlin. Stopping in cities and villages to paint portraits provided a modest income. Accompanied by a six-foot-two-inch escaped slave from Havana named Caesar Bolla, Catlin traversed South America—the Amazon Basin, the high Andes, the pampas, and Tierra del Fuego—everywhere painting its native peoples. Then, probably in 1854, the two men went up the Pacific Coast of North America to the Aleutian Islands (and perhaps even to Siberia), traveled along the Rocky Mountains, and eventually returned to the Yucatan. Back in wilderness surroundings, Catlin recaptured the exuberance he had experienced in the North American West twenty years earlier. He particularly loved the Amazon Basin, which he christened "Nature's temple."[85] There and elsewhere in North and South America, Catlin found, admired, and painted Native Americans.

After his travels, the artist settled in Brussels in 1860, where he lived quietly and frugally while finishing his drawings and paintings. He contemplated his recent travels and recorded his remembrances in two impassioned books, *Life amongst the Indians: A Book for Youth* (1861) and *Last Rambles amongst the Indians of the Rocky Mountains and Andes* (1867). The books introduced no new ideas: in his view, Indians were still the noblest people on earth. What was different about the volumes was that he wrote them mostly for young people, whom he believed had the greatest capacity to understand Indians because he considered both innocent and open-minded, not yet corrupted by "society." Using stories such as On-o-gong-way's, Catlin wrote eloquently. His brother Francis, who came to visit, watched George paint indigenous peoples, listened to him talk about them, and concluded: "If the Indian has a friend, it is G. Catlin."[86]

In these books, Catlin attacked white Americans for their continued encroachment on Indian lands. In his view, the frontier movement was "a headlong stampedo of half-crazy adventurers flying to the gold fields of the Rocky Mountains." There and everywhere, "desperate men" threatened native peoples. He railed against "unprincipled men in the mountains and valleys of the Far West" and the "rich and powerful companies" they served. Settlers and soldiers preached "extermination" of Indians and offered a bounty of "twenty dollars for every Indian's scalp that can be taken . . . 'provided that both ears are attached to them!'" Given such circumstances, Catlin asked: "'Who is the *savage* and who is the *brute?*'" About the plight of Native Americans he concluded: "My heart bleeds at this, but I cannot prevent it."[87] Obviously advancing age did not dull Catlin's zeal, or his pen.

All this filled Catlin with a sense of urgency to record "the Ethnography and Ethnology of the two hemispheres of America," and inspired him to begin work on another Indian gallery featuring the groups observed in his most recent travels. Perhaps he could sell it to the U.S. government. Maybe Congress, an individual, or a group would rescue his first collection from storage, making it possible to combine the two collections into a grand monument to the disappearing Indians of the world. Why not take his collection on a grand tour to "Belgium, Italy, Prussia, Persia, and Russia"? He had another plan, a great leather-bound volume of writing and lavish illustrations on the Indians of the Western Hemisphere to be called "The North Americans in the Middle of the Nineteenth Century Fast Passing to Extinction, and Leaving No Monument of Their Own behind Them." To help get subscriptions for it, he summoned his brother Francis to Brussels. Catlin worked on too many projects; consequently, the book was never published. Oblivious to the limits of time and energy, he dispatched a string of letters to his brother, who had returned to the United States, instructing him to do publicity work for his book and exhibition, contact members of Congress, and otherwise prepare the way for his triumphant return to the United States with the new collection.[88] Catlin still dreamed great dreams and remained a showman at heart.

Eventually, Catlin returned to show business. After completing his new collection in the summer of 1870, he gave a moderately successful exhibition of his gallery in Brussels before returning to the United States in 1871. Then, he prepared a ninety-nine-page catalog called *North and South American Indians* and showed his paintings in New York's Sommerville Gallery, hoping to attract a buyer. Little came from this return to public life except the satisfaction of attracting a little attention and gaining another opportunity to champion Native Americans. When attendance dwindled, an old friend, Joseph Henry, invited the artist to hang his paintings in the Smithsonian Institution and to live in its front tower. Catlin enthusiastically explained the paintings to visitors. George Catlin died, probably of Bright's Disease, on 23 December 1872 in Jersey City at the home of his sister. He was buried beside his wife and son in Brooklyn's Greenwood Cemetery in a grave that remained unmarked for nearly a hundred years.[89]

This forgotten man accomplished much during his lifetime, including innovating much about "western" entertainment. He emerged as an exhibitor when the public accepted the spoken word, museum-like displays of artifacts, and paintings as adequate illustrations of the West. To add dramatic appeal Catlin wore Indian costumes from his collection and hired actors to do the same. He took his show abroad and brought Native Americans before the public, where they danced until their feet ached and war-whooped until hoarse. When he sensed that his audience wanted sensationalism, he pandered to their taste with scalps and scenes of warfare. When the opportunity to offer outdoor entertainments presented itself, he seized it. In these ways he pioneered the direction of future Wild West shows.

On his last visit to the Plains of North America, Catlin saw wagon trains headed to Oregon, but he witnessed this "almost frantic pilgrimage" without enthusiasm.[90] Had Catlin observed carefully, he would have noticed the white scouts for the wagons. These buckskin-clad guides who attracted none of his attention became for many Americans what the Indians represented for Catlin. In image, they would become stalwart Plainsmen in much the same way that Indians were Catlin's beau ideal. Perhaps Catlin lived too soon, for Americans forgot that he had already created Plains heroes and an entertainment featuring the "raw materials of America." Ironically, in 1872, the year that Catlin died, the nation set aside land for Yellowstone National Park in an attempt to preserve a portion of wilderness. In that same year, a Wild West show was being born. In 1872, a young Plainsman named William F. Cody, with the sobriquet "Buffalo Bill," began his stage career.

# "The Gladiatorial Contest Revived":
## Buffalo Bill's Wild West Show
## in the United States, 1883–87

Isaac and Mary Cody and their children found it difficult to wait for Kansas Territory to open for settlement. Isaac's brother Elijah had preceded them in the move westward, so when Isaac and his family arrived in Weston, Missouri, they stayed with Elijah. Although the Codys appreciated this, they wanted to begin life on the frontier. Finally, waiting frustrated Isaac Cody so much that he crossed the Missouri River on a "prospecting tour," visited the Kickapoo agency, and then established a trading post nearby in the Salt Creek Valley. When time permitted, he returned to see his family in Weston. On a visit in 1854, Isaac brought great news for his eight- or nine-year-old son, Willie. Would the youngster like to go into Kansas Territory with him? The news that two ponies awaited there fired the boy's enthusiasm.[1] The ensuing trip exhilarated young William Frederick Cody much in the same way that the youthful George Catlin's meeting with On-o-gong-way had inspired that boy. However, childhood experiences sent these youngsters in different directions. For Catlin, Native Americans became heroic and the westward expansion of the United States was "a headlong stampedo of half-crazy adventurers." For his part, Cody would identify closely with frontiersmen who fought against Indians and cleared the way for settlement.

Isaac and his son first stopped at Leavenworth, where the youngster watched a regiment of cavalry in dress parade. Never before had he seen so much dash, color, and skillful riding. After Leavenworth, they traveled toward the Salt Creek Valley. Pausing on a hill overlooking it, Willie spied perhaps a thousand white-topped "prairie schooners" and several thousand oxen. Willie Cody learned that some were pioneers and traders bound for places like California. Others were Mormons headed for Utah Territory. Those wagons parked in a defensive circle belonged to the Majors and Russell freighting enterprise and carried supplies to forts west of the Missouri River. From his lofty perspective, the boy watched a wagon train ascend a hill. So heavily laden that they nearly buckled, some wagons required fifteen yokes of oxen to pull them up the incline. Noise reverberated from the white-topped caravan as men yelled and cracked bull whips, filling the air with sounds like rifle shots. After savoring all this excitement, father and son descended into the valley.[2]

At a trading post run by M. P. Rively the youngster got a firsthand look at some of those going West. A rough-looking bunch, they carried "huge pistols and knives in their belts," tucked their pants in their boots, and wore "large broad-rimmed hats." Some looked "like a lot of cut-throat pirates who had come ashore for a lark." Here Cody saw his first Indians, whom he thought "dark-skinned and rather fantastically dressed." After observing westerners at Rively's establishment, the Codys moved on to the site of their own trading post, where the boy found his two ponies. That evening Native Americans visited and traded with the Codys. The day had been exhilarating for the boy and marked with "incidents . . . full of excitement and romance."[3]

This first trip West provided a kaleidoscope of images: cavalry, rough-looking men with weapons and big hats, colorfully dressed Indians, and the excitement of people headed West. Like many other Americans, the Codys had fallen under the spell of a powerful force called Manifest Destiny, which propelled millions of Americans to go West, seek their fortunes, and expand their nation. Unlike George Catlin, who had questioned this kind of so-called progress, William F. Cody embraced this doctrine, never questioned American expansion, and believed that men with "huge pistols" and cavalry units should spearhead this growth.

In fact, Cody and Manifest Destiny grew up together. William F. Cody's birth near Le Claire, Iowa, on 26 February 1846 and the coining of the term *Manifest Destiny* occurred within a year of each other. The doctrine postulated that the United States should expand to fill all or most of North America, preferably taking territory by peaceful means, but using force if necessary, supplanting native peoples and their societies with Anglo-Saxon institutions, Protestant

Christianity, and U.S. civilization. The concept encompassed two different moods, one stressing a sense of mission and a peaceful transformation of wilderness and another sanctioning force, violence, and killing Indians.[4] This youngster became one of America's most influential popularizers of the deadly arm of expansion.

The pull of the far West consumed Cody. William Russell, a principal of the freighting business Majors and Russell, the firm whose wagons the Codys had seen pulled into a circle in the Salt Creek Valley, offered the eager youngster a job. Cody found the rough-hewn freighters exciting companions, and they liked the spunky youngster and welcomed him aboard their wagons, where he listened to their tales and learned about life on the Plains.[5]

According to Cody's account, as a teenager and then as an adult, he experienced one adventure after another. His autobiography of 1879 detailed fourteen campaigns against Indians and fifteen fights with them, friendship with legendary men such as Christopher "Kit" Carson and General George Armstrong Custer, employment by the Kansas Pacific Railroad to kill buffalo to feed its construction crews, and service to the U.S. Army as a tracker of Indians and a man who could judge the lay of the land. During all this he earned several titles, "Buffalo Bill" for his skill at killing bison, "Chief of the Scouts" for his work with the army, and "Honorable" for his election to the Nebraska legislature in 1872, although he resigned his seat without serving. In addition to such noteworthy accomplishments, Cody claimed a multitude of other experiences: oxen herder, bullwhacker, wagon train commander, pony express rider, scout and guide, foe and slayer of outlaws, trapper, "jay-hawker" (horsethief for the Union side in the Civil War), hero of dime novels, Civil War soldier, hunter, detective, justice of the peace, prospector, and rancher. The degree of his honesty about these experiences is a question that still divides historians.[6]

This diverse background, combined with striking good looks and the ability to accomplish anything with a flourish, propelled Cody toward showmanship. Handsome and charismatic, he stood six feet tall, possessed an athletic build, had long flowing hair, and sported a moustache and goatee. Being on horseback magnified his commanding presence. A newspaper reporter who saw him after his Wild West show began commented that he was an "extraordinary figure and sits on a horse as if he were born in the saddle." Making him even more conspicuous was an inclination to "put on a little style" by wearing fringed buckskin, embroidered shirts, seven-league boots, and large soft sombreros.[7]

An instinct for theatrics enabled him to turn routine events into dramatic incidents. As the historian Paul Fees has noted, "style, independence, and the reckless gesture" characterized this man. In an alleged "buffalo killing match" with William Comstock, he rode his horse without saddle and bridle, drove a buffalo bull directly toward a group of female admirers, and killed the animal about fifty yards in front of them. Whether or not this contest occurred, the story demonstrates a great deal about the brashness of the man and the image he cultivated. As his reputation grew, he became a sought-after guide for notables who hunted big game on the Plains. When the Grand Duke Alexis of Russia came, Cody guided him and arranged for the Sioux to entertain him with a buffalo hunt and dances.[8] This exhibition for the grand duke foreshadowed Cody's Wild West show.

Buffalo Bill's rise to national prominence began when E. Z. C. Judson, a flamboyant dime novelist better known by his pseudonym, Ned Buntline, featured Cody in his works beginning in 1869. Other writers of the dime thrillers made Buffalo Bill a character in their writings, sometimes taking the liberty of signing Cody's name as author. About 550 of these novels about Cody eventually appeared. Although not the most respectable reading material, the ubiquitous yellow-backed books introduced Buffalo Bill's name to Americans and blended historical fact and mythology about him. In these thrillers, Cody emerged as a uniquely American person, a Horatio Alger–style hero, and a winner in the struggle for survival on the Plains. Mostly, these novels stressed physical achievements such as shooting and riding, rather than "moral and rational judgment."[9] The transformation into "nature's nobleman" would come later in Cody's career.

Portraying himself on stage before live audiences moved him closer to a career in Wild West shows. At Buntline's urging, Cody went to Chicago in 1872 to play himself in a stage production called *The Scouts of the Plains,* authored by the dime novelist. This began a period in Cody's life, which stretched to 1883, when he sandwiched a stage career between activities on the frontier and learned that eastern audiences would pay to see authentic Plainsmen depict violent aspects of life on the frontier. Adding real Indians pleased patrons even more. In addition, the plays provided experience before live audiences.[10]

Cody appeared in proletarian theaters like the Bowery, where men smoked cigars, drank beer, and demanded action. Physical strength and prowess, exhibited through a glorification of violence, appealed to these audiences, particularly when playwrights could ascribe them to an actual person. John M. ("Arizona John") Burke, a publicity agent who had replaced Ned Buntline in Cody's dramatic company, understood this dynamic. Burke's influence, added to that of Buntline and Cody's training in theaters, where cigar smoke mingled with gunsmoke, would mark the first part of Cody's career.[11] Physical prowess and bloodshed, encouraged by almost exclusively male audiences, distinguished Cody's productions.

An incident in 1872 during his first performance in *The Scouts of the Plains* indicated much about the man and his philosophy of entertainment. Cody forgot his lines, so he ad-libbed. At one point, he delighted the crowd by calling out to his wife, who was in the audience: "Hello Mamma! . . . Oh, but I'm a bad actor!" This remark was the same kind of ploy George Catlin had used when he argued that he was an American rustic and that his paintings were not finished works of art. Such a stance fended off criticism for Catlin and worked equally well for Cody. Reporters commented that Cody was not an actor and should not be held to professional standards.[12] Safely ensconced behind a protective shield that made westerners and western productions distinct from other entertainments, Cody took an important step as showman. His career on stage and in Wild West shows would be built on the foundation of western entertainment being the "raw material of America."

In a manner consistent with his productions, Cody sometimes acted like a frontier rustic and ruffian. He wrote to a friend that he was late in answering a letter because he had been on a "hell of a toot." In his autobiography he detailed social failings. He wrote that when he first went East in 1872, genteel men and women in Chicago and New York treated him as a celebrity and took him to a number of parties. However, he claimed to be "embarrassed and perplexed" by elegant surroundings, beautiful women, "being stared at," and "hundreds of questions." He accepted every invitation offered him, apparently oblivious to the fact that he could not be in several places at once; consequently, he failed to arrive at a formal dinner given in his honor. He apologized, saying he "had been out on a scout and had got lost, and had forgotten all about dinner." On another occasion, Cody attended the Liederkranz masked ball wearing a buckskin suit and performed an impromptu stomping dance. When he tried to dance in a more refined manner, he failed.[13]

According to Buffalo Bill's autobiography, life in the West failed to imbue him and his companions with high moral standards. He admitted that as a justice of the peace he had pocketed a twenty-five-dollar fine, explaining that he "didn't know any better just then." He added that he performed a wedding ceremony while drunk. The year that his autobiography appeared, Cody admonished a friend in a letter for being "like most of the prairie boys. tanglefoot gets away with you." So at this point in his life, Cody did not argue that frontier experiences brought communion with nature and enlightened moral values.[14] Later in his career, he would emphasize that living on the Plains made the inner person as exceptional as the physical one.

An incident occurred in 1876 that indicated Cody could, with a little coaching from Burke, masterfully combine myth, reality, bloodletting, and colorful costuming with a sense of the dramatic and give it all his personal flourish. The great Sioux war, which George Catlin had predicted, provided the setting for this *coup de theatre*. In that year, Cody closed his entertainment early and secured a position as scout for the Fifth U.S. Cavalry because he "was anxious to take part in the Sioux war which was then breaking out."[15] The war became even bigger news than Cody had anticipated, with the defeat of General George Armstrong Custer and his Seventh Cavalry at the Battle of the Little Bighorn. About a month later, Cody killed an Indian named Yellow Hand (or Yellow Hair).

Cody's party and a group of Cheyennes unexpectedly encountered one another in present-day Nebraska. Although the chance meeting startled everyone, Cody and Yellow Hand remained calm. The two adversaries fired at each other with rifles at close range, and Buffalo Bill's bullet struck his adversary in the breast. Then Cody bounded to his fallen foe, and, according to the account in his autobiography: "before he had fairly touched the ground I was upon him, knife in hand, and had driven the keen-edged weapon to its hilt in his heart. Jerking his war-bonnet off, I scientifically scalped him in about five seconds." As the force of soldiers who witnessed the fight rode forward, Cody waved the headdress and the scalp in the air and yelled, "*The first scalp for Custer.*" The incident moved a witness, who was both a soldier and a dime novelist, to call this duel "as plucky a single combat on both sides as is ever witnessed."[16]

Cody wanted every trophy from the fight; consequently, he stripped all the finery from the body. The scalp and headdress were placed in a storefront as advertisement for Cody's "noisy, rattling, gunpowder" play about the Yellow Hand incident called *The Red Right Hand; or, Buffalo Bill's First Scalp for Custer*. When some protested the public display of the scalp, Cody moved it to the theater. Cody's autobiography included an account of the Yellow Hand duel along with a full-page illustration of Buffalo Bill holding the scalp aloft. Ten years after the scalping, he still prized the top knot and reportedly would not part with it, even for a thousand dollars. He usually kept the scalp in his tent, sometimes showed it to reporters, and, if pushed, would retell the story of the duel with Yellow Hand.[17]

Cody used this "plucky single combat" to blend myth with reality. On the day of the duel, he wore his theatrical garb—a gaudy "Mexican costume of black velvet, slashed with scarlet and trimmed with silver buttons and lace." The costume had a premeditated purpose. He put it on that day so he could appear on stage the following year and say that he wore the actual getup of a prairie scout.[18]

By the end of his stage career, Buffalo Bill possessed a combination of qualities and experiences that would serve him well in Wild West shows. In addition to handsomeness and a showman's instincts, he knew a great deal about public performances and the extent of interest in the frontier. Dime novels and theatrical tours familiarized Americans with his name, and he made the acquaintance of John Burke, one of the best publicity agents in the business. Also, the plays in which Cody appeared were melodramas stressing action and spectacle, rather than plot, and stock characters to act out a conflict between good and evil. Consciously or unconsciously, Cody carried what he had learned, including the techniques of melodrama, with him into Wild West shows.[19]

Cody's career took a new turn when a man named Nate Salsbury told him to stop wasting his time with "dime novel thrillers." He suggested that they inaugurate a new kind of entertainment—a Wild West show—that would play in their country as well as abroad. An experienced actor and manager, Salsbury realized the potential in producing an outdoor entertainment depicting horsemanship and frontier life. Perhaps Buffalo Bill had been thinking along the same lines. His experiences as an actor had revealed popular enthusiasm for the Plains lifestyle. Working with a professional such as Salsbury may have appealed to him because he was tired of Plainsmen such as "Wild Bill, Texas Jack, John Nelson, Oregon Bill, Kit Carson [Jr.], Captain Jack," and others, who "just as soon as they see their names in print a few times they git the big head and want to start a company of their own." Also, in 1882 he served successfully as a grand marshall of a Fourth of July celebration in Omaha, Nebraska, where cowboys delighted spectators with feats such as roping and riding buffalo.[20]

Despite Salsbury's overtures, Buffalo Bill began his career as Wild West showman in 1883 with Dr. W. F. Carver, a pretentious marksman who billed himself "Evil Spirit of the Plains," "Champion Rifle Shot of the World," "Wizard Rifleman of the West, Conqueror of all America and Europe, and Cynosure of People, Princes, Warriors and Kings," and boasted that he played a vital role in winning the West despite any supporting evidence. Learning of Carver's involvement, Salsbury refused to join the venture. Another strong personality who would leave his mark on the show was Captain A. H. Bogardus, a trapshooter who billed himself as "America's Champion Shot" and "Champion Pigeon Shot of America."[21] The three men began the show without Salsbury's acumen.

The enterprise, called "The Wild West, Rocky Mountain, and Prairie Exhibition," opened on 17 May 1883 at the fairgrounds in Omaha and moved to St. Louis and then eastward to cities such as New York and Boston. The show included Indians, cowboys, Mexicans, a cowboy band to provide music, the notables Cody, Carver, and Bogardus, and individuals such as Frank North (Cody's ranching partner from North Platte) and John Nelson, whose Indian wife and their children intrigued patrons. Buffalo, elk, deer, wild horses, cattle, and a stagecoach added appeal to a program consisting of riding, shooting, roping, and a "Startling and Soul-Stirring Attack upon the Deadwood Mail Coach." This show, simple as it was, appealed to Americans. One enthusiastic reporter said the showmen had "out-Barnumed Barnum." Despite hard work and extensive advertising, Cody reported in letters to family members that "money is awfully scarce" and he had "not made much money." The partnership lasted only one year, partly because Cody's decision to return to the stage for the winter upset Carver, who wanted to produce the Wild West show year round. The men divided the show property and went their separate ways. Carver's departure enabled Cody to form a partnership with Salsbury and to build a show that would become famous.[22]

This was an ideal time to inaugurate an entertainment about the Plains. Present-day historians have explained why this age embraced Buffalo Bill's Wild West show so enthusiastically. According to David M. Wrobel, the 1880s marked the emergence of "frontier anxiety," or the "anxieties aroused in those who perceived that the frontier was closing or had already closed." Although this fear would not crest for a decade, anxiousness existed in the 1880s because of a growing perception that America's free land was gone or nearly gone and that its disappearance would change society. Richard Slotkin maintains that displaying Indians in the Wild West show demonstrated to other Americans that the fight for the Plains was complete and had ended in victory. Why else would Indians agree to appear as vanquished foes? Another scholar, L. G. Moses, argues that the belief that the frontier had ended created a nostalgic mood that spurred many Americans to ponder what they had missed by not going West. Cody's Wild West show addressed all these issues.[23]

Obviously, attitudes about the frontier had changed from George Catlin's time. His message that the first stage of Plains history had ended because "civilization" overran Indians aroused no frontier anxiety except in diluted form in the northeastern United States and Europe. However, by the mid-1880s frontier anxiety related to land, something tangible and worth money. Moreover, many Americans believed that an abundance of uninhabited land explained the exceptionality of their nation. Now they wondered how different the future would be without a frontier. Cody could capitalize on all these concerns. And, unlike Catlin, he would find receptive audiences everywhere in the United States, not just in selected eastern cities.

While the mood of the nation differed, Catlin and Cody shared some attitudes about showmanship. Both men worked themselves to exhaustion because they possessed a pride in ownership that made their shows intensely personal undertakings. Just as Catlin headed every advertisement with "Catlin's Indian Gallery," Cody put his name in the title of his show. Both believed that their names belonged there because they had earned that right by participating fully in the Plains experience. Concern for authenticity drove Catlin to get certificates to prove his "veracity," and Buffalo Bill insisted that when he advertised pony express riders in his show that they had actually been pony express riders, and that his "Deadwood Stage" had actually seen service on that route. While Catlin sometimes acted as a Native American during lectures and at social events in England, Cody did not impersonate Indians and allowed no one else to do so in his show. Typically, Buffalo Bill did not play other people, he portrayed himself.

In fact, Cody promised so much accuracy that he claimed his exhibition was not a show at all, but "reality itself." Those in his Wild West show were not actors or entertainers: "They simply appear just as they are; nothing more, nothing less." "The work done here is not the result of rehearsal, it is not acting, it is nature itself." Publicity agents called it the "Wild West" and avoided appending "show," because they claimed it was authentic in every way, and therefore not a "show" like circuses and other forms of entertainment.[24]

Cody introduced his show into a world of entertainment that differed from that in Catlin's age, when audiences accepted lectures, paintings, and museum-like displays as satisfactory representations of the West. By Buffalo Bill's time, entertainment was big business, and enthusiasm for spectacles, circuses, and outdoor amusements had reached its height. The industrial and technological boom of the late nineteenth century, which spawned intense interest in the West, also brought a network of railroads that bound together the metropolitan sections of the nation, making it possible to transport the show from city to city. As in Catlin's time, those in the urban United States were curious about the West, but typically knew nothing about it. Such viewers suspended disbelief, saw the show, and left convinced that they had seen an accurate picture of life on the Plains. These factors made the Wild West show a potent molder of ideas and images.

The show was tailored for American tastes and stayed before such audiences, except for an excursion into Canada in 1885. It became a big business by providing a simplified, patriotic, and believable national epic that blended history and mythology and legitimized the view of Manifest Destiny that sanctioned the use of force. Such an interpretation satisfied a cultural need because many Americans wanted to see the conquest of a continent as a grand accomplishment filled with drama and excitement. Characterizing the winning of the Plains frontier as easy and peaceful would have minimized something that Americans wanted to see as heroic. Even if the showmen had wanted to portray a peaceful settlement of the West, it would have been difficult to build crowd-pleasing acts around raising cabins and planting corn. The desiderata of the entertainment and the nation merged: both needed bloodshed, galloping horsemen, and conflict.

Moreover, Americans wanted one person to symbolize all this. The novelist Frank Norris, looking back at the Buffalo Bill phenomenon, called the conquest of the Plains an achievement of "epic proportions" that cried out for an epic hero. With his record of achievements in the West, publicity from dime novels, and a successful stage career, Cody was a logical choice. By wearing a gaudy *vaquero* outfit while killing and scalping Yellow Hand, Cody revealed himself to be a brash man perfectly suited to reenact legendary deeds. The man and the age fit each other. Publicity agents billed his show as "America's National Entertainment," and Cody's compatriots accepted that designation.[25]

A reporter observed: "It is a bold and original idea, this of reproducing, in mimic, the scenes which have been blood curdling realities." Others who saw the show made similar comments: "Buffalo Bill's 'Wild West' is wild enough to suit the most devoted admirer of western adventure and prowess"; the frontier was a place where "barbarism and civilization have their hands on each other's throats"; and that "one can easily understand the dangers which beset and checked the pioneers . . . and whetted their appetites for blood and strife."[26] All this formed a wonderful antidote for frontier anxiety.

Performers in the show cultivated images of battle-scarred fighters. At one time, Buffalo Bill claimed to have 137 scars on his body resulting from his fights with Indians. Burke, publicity manager for the show, mentioned that Cody had never killed a white man, but added: "This is not to his discredit, of course, especially as it is generally conceded that he had transacted some business in that line with Indians." Long Wolf, a performer with the show, boasted that he carried seven bullets in his body, as well as a dozen scars from knife wounds. Performers American Horse and Rocky Bear, too, claimed to "bear upon their persons the scars of many fights between the white and Indians." Wild West show reports billed the original Deadwood stagecoach as "the tomb of its passengers" in which over two hundred persons had died. The show wrote frontier history in blood.[27]

Wild West show publicity agents and reporters characterized the entertainment as "the gladiatorial contest revived." Such a comparison rested partly on the belief that Americans, like the Romans, had won a great empire and were similarly taking time to understand the methods and appreciate the hardihood that had won such a prize. Perhaps Cody thought in such terms, because the Colosseum in Rome held a special place in his heart: It was the location he most wished to stage a Wild West show.[28] The phrase "gladiatorial combat revived" reflected this early period when Buffalo Bill's Wild West show glorified frontier combat and those who excelled in it. Certainly, the image in the program of Cody standing over the vanquished Yellow Hand had a gladiatorial quality about it.

This enterprise's advertising rejected all subtleties. The publicity department produced dime novel–like "sensational, spectacular advertising" that fit the mood of the show. Posters, called "paper" by those in the business, were the most important part of advertising blitzes. Some years, a half million sheets of "paper" went in storefronts, on buildings, on fences, on specially constructed billboards, and in any number of other conspicuous places. These brightly colored posters ranged in size from a modest twenty-eight to forty-two inches to gargantuan ones measuring nine feet high and nearly 150 feet long. Large posters might cost fifteen or twenty dollars, but they were worth the money because so many people saw them. In fact, those who lived in areas where the show played found it impossible not to see them. More saw paper than read dime novels or attended the show. And these posters left strong impressions about the West in the minds of millions of Americans.[29]

Cody paid close attention to the paper and got superb products. He suggested ideas for posters, befriended those who drew and produced them, and made certain that the finished product reflected his ideas. The size, multiplicity, and artistic quality of the posters suggested the supremacy of this show. Posters varied from simple to complex. Some conveyed a single western scene, others an act or personage from the show, and still others a variety of western images and acts. A publicity agent wrote that their paper was "popular, sensational, melodramatic advertising" firing the imagination of viewers with images of "Indian Massacres, wild horse bucking, dare-devil riding, [and] hair-raising Indian dances." They advertised the "Wild West"—a place devoid of the mundane. Often Buffalo Bill appeared as the only figure on posters, a technique suggesting that he alone represented the "Wild West." The advertising process began when billposters arrived several weeks in advance of the show to paste paper in conspicuous places. While they worked, children gathered and listened to their stories of adventure on the road and tried to wrangle an arrangement whereby they could help those involved in the show in exchange for a free pass.[30]

After billposters came "advance men" who bought space in newspapers, filled their ads with "just the right touch of melodrama," and headlined them with phrases such as "The West at Your Doors" and "Practically a Tour of the Frontier." Publicity agents offered prepared stories about the show and distributed magazine-style publications called "couriers" with details about the West, the show, and its people. Many journalists reprinted such material with little or no alteration. Local reporters enjoyed talking to the entertainers, who offered a break from routine tasks. "Arizona John" Burke chatted with editors and reporters and told stories about Cody and frontier adventures.[31] When the show arrived, luminaries such as Cody, Annie Oakley, and Buck Taylor visited with journalists, who often filled their pages with stories about the show. In his day, George Catlin had been an advertiser par excellence, but Cody's organization indicated how far publicity had advanced in half a century.

Catlin would have recognized the promotional value of rib roast dinners. For journalists and local dignitaries, Cody and Salsbury sometimes hosted get-togethers at which the showmen roasted sides of beef over open fires and invited guests to spear a portion of meat, impale it on a stake driven into the ground, and eat without the benefit of table or silverware. Indians and cowboys served as waiters, talked to reporters, and sometimes entertained guests. George Catlin had served pure spring water at his dinners, but whiskey flowed freely at Cody and Salsbury's all-male gatherings. One participant noted: "There were three kinds of drinks—water, whisky, and whisky and water, and the greatest of these was whisky."[32]

These events indicated several things about the growing concept of westerners. Missing amenities such as tables, silverware, plates, and napkins suggested a certain crudeness about them. The emphasis on alcohol at these male gatherings implied that drinking was manly and that whiskey was the preferred beverage of rugged frontiersmen. These rib roast dinners were quaint western happenings, not events celebrating the wholesomeness of the western diet. Cowboys served as waiters, which indicated their separateness from genteel easterners. All of this would change when the show went abroad.

Like posters, newspaper advertising, and rib roast dinners, street parades called attention to the Wild West show. Whenever practical, the troupe gave one on the morning of its arrival. Some lasted for two-and-a-half hours, although most were shorter. Cody, in colorful dress, usually headed the parade. Following him were cowboy musicians of the brass band; Indians issuing battle cries and wearing "two coats of paint instead of a shirt," feathers, and beaded clothing; shouting cowboys in flannel shirts and broad-brimmed hats; *vaqueros;* festive western women; and sometimes soldiers. A New York journalist observed: "It was as if the wild regions of the West had mustered all of their queerest denizens, clothed in holiday dress and sent them forth."[33]

In addition to these "queerest denizens," townspeople often spotted the faces of prominent citizens and journalists peering from the Deadwood stage as it rumbled down thoroughfares. Whenever possible, the showmen recruited such persons as passengers. Street parades usually attracted crowds of curious and often vocal onlookers. Boys often returned the yells of the westerners, sometimes threw their hats in the air, and darted through the crowd in an effort to get a longer look at their favorite characters. When parades ended, throngs of children often surrounded Buffalo Bill and bombarded him with questions.[34] Undoubtedly, many of these youngsters used the several hours between the parade and the beginning of the show to make a pitch to their parents about the entertainment.

Deciding to attend the show meant weighing several factors. Escapist entertainment appealed to many urban Americans, who typically worked long hours at boring factory jobs and lived in crowded cities with few parks and limited recreational opportunities. News articles assured people that attending the show was a good investment of time and money, that it was perfectly suitable for women and children, that it was educational and realistic, that it was full of dash and color, and that it was "genuinely American." News articles warned that those who skipped the show might never be able to see anything like it again because westward expansion could destroy the people and animals living on the Plains.[35]

Against these arguments, Americans weighed reasons not to go. The United States was a work-oriented society still learning to accept leisure activities. People viewed traveling companies with suspicion because they sometimes attracted con artists and pickpockets, and local business leaders and civic-minded folks branded traveling entertainers as money-grabbers who impoverished the local economy by taking thousands of dollars out of town. Furthermore, attending Buffalo Bill's Wild West show was expensive, usually fifty cents for adults and twenty-five cents for children. The cost for a couple and four children was two dollars during a time when working men often earned between one dollar and a dollar fifty a day. Two dollars would buy a week's groceries, a kerosene lamp, a hardwood rocking chair, or a pair of dress shoes for an adult.[36] A family could easily spend more than two dollars at the show if they bought food, drink, programs, or mementos.

Nevertheless, crowds waited in line to buy tickets. Concession booths offering peanuts, "red lemonade," and a variety of other goods added to the congestion. Everywhere hawkers tried to sell programs for a dime. And there were other diversions, such as spending a nickel to throw three baseballs at a black man's head sticking out of a hole in a wall of canvas. After filing into the spec-

tators' area, patrons found seats, most under a protective canvas top, arranged
in a large horseshoe shape around an open-air arena. Next to the show ring stood
private boxes for the affluent or notable, and near the customer's entrance sat
the cowboy band. Publicity stressed that the uncovered arena separated the Wild
West show from lesser entertainments such as circuses, which required the protection of canvas. Hardy Plainspeople in this show shrugged off wind and rain;
and publicity agents said that inclement weather only added to the realism.
Arenas usually included several acres and a few props, such as a settlers' cabin.
The end without seating usually sported expanses of painted scenery large
enough to conceal mounted cowboys, Indians, and scouts, who rushed out from
behind these screens during performances. Pictures on canvases portrayed prairie
and mountain landscapes, adding a western aura to the grounds.[37]

While the stands filled, the cowboy band played. Before performers appeared,
Frank Richmond, the announcer, ascended a wooden platform and asked for
"silence and attention." He introduced the show, explained acts, made impromptu comments, and added touches of humor. His remarks were short:
action, not words, characterized the performance. Catlin-style lectures would
not have pleased these audiences. The formal spoken part of the entertainment
and some ad-libbing took something over thirty minutes during a two- or three-
hour program. Richmond reportedly possessed a "copious" command of the
English language and a powerfully prodigious voice. Without amplification, a
crowd of twenty thousand could hear him clearly. Richmond informed patrons
that vendors would circulate through the crowd with copies of *The Life of Hon.
William F. Cody, Known as Buffalo Bill, the Famous Hunter, Scout, and Guide:
An Autobiography* (1879), which would provide a fuller appreciation of the show,
the frontier, and Buffalo Bill.[38]

Richmond reiterated what the advertising proclaimed: spectators would experience something unique because Buffalo Bill's Wild West show was "not a
performance" but a rough-and-tumble exhibition that captured the "skill, courage, and individual excellence" of frontiersmen. To reinforce the idea of authenticity, he told listeners that the unexpected could happen because the entertainment mixed humans and wild animals. Then Richmond waved a flag, the
cowboy band set a properly patriotic mood with a spirited rendition of the "Star-
Spangled Banner," the "grand processional parade" began, and the Wild West
show company raced around the perimeter of the arena, stopped, and waited
for their introduction.[39]

Each group made a "grand entry" to musical accompaniment as Richmond
called forward groups including Indians, *vaqueros,* and cowboys and introduced
their principals. When announced, contingents shouted, raced across the are-

na, and brought their horses to sudden stops to form a long line in front of cheering spectators. Buffalo Bill received the final introduction, which was filled with accolades such as "servant of the government," "skill and daring as a frontiersman," "chief of scouts of the United States Army," and "one of the avengers of the lamented Custer." Performers cheered him, women in the audiences often waved their handkerchiefs, and men shouted their approval. He gave his introduction a typical Buffalo Bill flourish by tipping his hat, bowing, and saying: "Ladies and gentlemen, let me introduce you to the equestrian portion of the Wild West Exhibition." His short remarks often electrified those in the stands.[40] That salutation was significant because Cody was the only performer who spoke to the spectators.

Rapid movement; a kaleidoscope of color; smells of earth, animals, and gunpowder; and noise—all these set the mood of the Wild West show. Everything moved fast: horses always galloped and riders burst suddenly into view from behind the scenery. Cody's outfits set the standard for colorful costumes. A reporter commented: "in his embroidered magenta hunting shirt and white sombrero and with his long hair flying in the breeze he looks every inch the ideal scout."[41] *Vaqueros* dressed in outfits as bright as the one that Cody had worn in the duel with Yellow Hand; Native Americans, often stripped to the waist, adorned themselves with feathers, beads, and paint; and cowboys sported colorful regalia.

The aural aspect of the show was powerful, even intimidating at times. The cowboy band played "most of the time" and added dramatic impact to happenings in the arena. The hooves of fast-moving horses pounded the earth. In addition there was "tremendous noise of the blank cartridge . . . the terrific whoops of the painted warriors" and cowboys intent on proving that "they could fire blank cartridges more quickly than the red man and could yell louder too." In this age of vocal audiences, spectators added to the tumult with cheering, shouting, and "deafening applause." The smells of gunpowder, animals, and dampened earth permeated the air, giving the Wild West show a pungent odor. These elements—movement, color, sounds, and smells—bombilated audiences.[42]

Performances that followed the introduction varied from year to year, and, even during individual seasons, programs changed as the showmen experimented and juggled acts to find those with the most appeal. Despite alteration, five primary categories of acts characterized the entertainment: horsemanship, marksmanship, Plains animal exhibitions, variety acts, and Plains Indian acts, which usually featured conflict between them and white frontiersmen. Although no plot bound these vignettes together, the management argued that the show conveyed a complete and accurate rendition of life on the frontier.

About one-fourth of the acts focused on horses. They appealed to Americans because many had personal experience with these animals. Horses in the Wild West show were extraordinary, however—not plowhorses, swaybacked mounts, or pullers of peddlers' wagons, but glistening, galloping, and ornamented steeds and truculent buckers. These animals raced around the arena, and like the people atop them, looked wild and free.

Horse races illustrated that westerners prized fast horses and spent a great deal of time on that pursuit. Native Americans often appeared in these contests; those from different tribes raced against one another, and against cowboys and *vaqueros.* One race pitted an Indian on foot and one on horseback and the contestants dashed fifty yards, turned around a pole, and sprinted back. White women, billed as "lady riders," raced. During contests, each person rode a horse characteristic of his or her group and used the tack of that culture, allowing spectators to compare styles of riding.[43] All this speeding around the area left the impression that westerners never walked or rode their mounts at a normal pace. Also, such scenes conveyed the image of the typical Native American as a war-painted Plains Indian on horseback.

"The Wonderful Pony Express" offered more galloping horses and linked Buffalo Bill with frontier history. The announcer explained that Cody's old employer, William Russell, started the business to move mail quickly across the West before railroads and telegraph wires spanned the continent. Billy Johnson, an authentic pony express rider, demonstrated how quickly an adept westerner could change mounts.[44] Galloping horses added romance to Indians, "lady riders," and pony express men, but cowboys won the hearts of audiences.

When Buffalo Bill's Wild West show began, most Americans knew little about cowboys and cared less about them. Writers used the terms *herdsman, vaquero,* and *cowboy* interchangeably. Fiction about cowboys was atrocious. In some quarters lurked a distrust of people who lived beyond the reaches of civilization. William Holmes McGuffey, moralist and influential author of the *McGuffey Readers,* taught children to fear such people. President Chester A. Arthur in 1881 spoke of cowboys as "armed desperadoes" and held them responsible for terrorism and bloodshed in the Arizona Territory. Five years later the *New York Times* still carried articles about the violent nature of cowboys.[45]

In his pre–Wild West show days, Cody saw nothing spectacular about cowboys. Even though he owned cattle and worked with them on his ranch in North Platte, his autobiography contained only two pages on roundups and cowboys. In them, he noted their riding skills but he did not lionize them or praise their character. About cowboy life, he commented that it was a great deal of "hard work" and that he "could not possibly find out where the fun came in." Although he claimed to have been involved in a number of occupations during his frontier years, Cody never claimed to have been a cowboy.[46]

Although cowboys attracted attention in the Wild West show, their tarnished image remained in some news articles. In 1885, a journalist praised Cody for starting the Wild West show because it removed cowboys from the frontier, where they would be constantly in mischief. Another felt the need to ameliorate the image of "American frontiersmen and cowboys," who were often "grossly misrepresented and as often abused." The writer maintained: "They are not cheats, nor drunkards, nor rioters; but honest, temperate, and of quiet and gentle behavior."[47]

Those in the show worked on the image of cowboys. The program for the first Wild West show carried an article entitled "The Cow Boys" that called for recognition and respect. The piece said that they were not popular or familiar to Americans and were "falsely imagined," "greatly despised," "little appreciated," and often assumed to be cattle rustlers. The Wild West show was the "advent" of cowboys before easterners that would improve their image. Cody and his partners asked patrons to recognize that these hands worked hard and helped to extend American civilization.[48] Adding these qualities helped make more Americans consider cowboys respectable.

Such publicity and action in the arena worked wonders. Audiences grew to love cowboys, and soon a number of them joined the troupe. The most striking was Buck Taylor, a man of "great strength, nerve, endurance, and skill," billed as the "King of the Cowboys." In addition to handsomeness, he stood over six feet tall and appeared as a hero in dime novels.[49] He remained with the show for a number of years and set the standard for cowboy appearance. The Wild West show made cowboys and horses appear inseparable. Posters with captions such as "Bucking Bronco," "Bucking Steer," "Steer Riding," and "A Bucking Mustang" put captivating pictures of these men before the public. Programs explained that cowboys excelled in "feats of horsemanship, riding bucking mustangs, roping cattle, throwing buffalo, etc." An act designated "Cowboy Fun" featured these colorful westerners riding bucking ponies and mules, roping and riding "Wild Texas steers," and "Lassoing and Riding the Wild Bison of the Plains." Early in his career, Cody occasionally joined "Cowboy Fun" and demonstrated his roping and riding skills.[50]

Much that cowboys did in Wild West shows would eventually come to be known as "rodeo." In this age before chutes and other apparatus, cowboys and *vaqueros* chased and roped broncos and steers, tied them up, mounted them, and then released the infuriated animals, which tried to hurl the riders from their backs. To dislodge their whooping tormentors, horses sometimes laid down and rolled over. Ferocity, danger, and unpredictability made these contests exciting. Predictably, injuries did occur in the show, mostly in the rodeo-style acts. Features such as bronco riding impressed spectators and added bravery, tenacity, and toughness to the image of cowboys. Trick riding illustrated dexterity on horseback. Lanky Buck Taylor rode at full speed, leaned from the saddle, and plucked his hat and handkerchief from the ground. Sometimes in these early programs, western women demonstrated fancy riding.[51]

In the first years of the show, cowboys were a rough conglomeration of riders chosen on the basis of skill. Most were Anglo-Americans, but Bill Bullock was half Sioux, Voter Hall was black, and sometimes the line between cowboys and *vaqueros* blurred when the two groups joined forces to rout Indians and rope and ride broncos and Texas steers. As the cowboy's popularity in the show grew, working cowboys evolved into show cowboys who reflected what audiences wanted to see. In addition to possessing cowboy skills, the new breed of cowboys would reflect Buck Taylor's looks and ethnicity.[52]

As with horses, these shows presented firearms as essential for life on the Plains. Acts featuring marksmanship constituted about one-fourth of the show. Programs explained that, on the frontier, the rifle found its "greatest use" as "a necessity for the preservation of life and the defense of home and property." Bullets served as "the forerunner of growth and development." The program summed up the show's emphasis on weapons and violence: "the bullet is the pioneer of civilization, for it has gone hand in hand with the axe that cleared the forest, and with the family bible and school book. Deadly as has been its mission in one sense, it has been merciful in another; for without the rifle ball we of America would not be to-day in the possession of a free and united country, and mighty in our strength."[53]

Posters for the show bristled with images of rifles and pistols and made them appear as a standard item of dress. Advertising depicted cowboys wearing revolvers, even while riding bucking horses and steers, when weapons were an encumbrance. In scenes featuring warfare between white men and Indians, rifles and revolvers were much in evidence. In many of those depictions, cowboys fired revolvers from the backs of galloping horses. Poster art, then, left the impression that weapons were everywhere in the West, that frontiersmen shot their way across the Plains, that six-shooters were a standard part of the cowboy costume, and that people with revolvers on running steeds did much of the fighting. Revolvers were much more common in the Wild West show than they were on the frontier.[54]

Those who attended Wild West show performances learned that westerners not only shot often but also shot well. The show always carried several expert shooters, including Dr. W. F. Carver, Captain A. H. Bogardus and his four sons, Seth Clover, Dr. David Franklin "White Beaver" Powell, and Johnny Baker. Their acts included a variety of specialties: firing from horseback; breaking clay pigeons; hitting objects such as marbles, composition balls, and coins thrown into the air; shooting with their bodies contorted; and firing with the sights of firearms obscured. Rapid firing during the acts often produced near-deafening noise that sometimes overwhelmed audience members. Although they were excellent shots, "special bullets especially designed to scatter shot within a small area" improved their odds of hitting targets. Disintegrating bullets afforded safety to the audience, as well as persons and property close to the showgrounds. Shooters took the added precaution of firing their weapons toward the open end of the horseshoe-shaped arena. According to some accounts, such acts made it impossible for Wild West shows to be presented under cover, because bullet fragments would have perforated a canvas top.[55]

Publicity touted Buffalo Bill as the preeminent marksman. Introduced as the "Hon. William F. Cody, champion all around shot of the world," he provided a memorable demonstration using a shotgun, a rifle, and a revolver. The act began with Cody breaking clay pigeons with a shotgun. He pulled the traps himself, thereby demonstrating his dexterity. After this, he used a Winchester rifle and then a revolver to break composition balls in midair. In portions of this act Buffalo Bill fired from horseback as an assistant, often a female or an Indian, rode alongside him tossing balls into the air. The message was clear: as the consummate western man, Cody excelled in the use of firearms.[56]

Annie Oakley similarly impressed people by firing shotguns and rifles, hitting stationary targets, and shattering airborne clay pigeons and composition balls. She played an important role in the Wild West show. Most Americans viewed expertise with firearms as a male role, yet this woman displayed obvious ability while remaining conventionally feminine, always making her entrance a "pretty one." A publicity agent noted: "She never walked. She tripped in, bowing, waving, and wafting kisses." When she started shooting, it often "brought forth a few screams of fright from the women," but soon Oakley had "set the audience at ease." Sometimes she demonstrated her skill in horseback riding, doing such things as picking objects from the ground while riding her mount at a gallop. In a show extolling manly arts and physical prowess, she represented grace, dignity, and familial ties. Poster art depicted "Little Sure Shot" wearing dresses, and she always wore them in the arena. She emphasized her closeness to family by including her husband, Frank Butler, and their pet dog in her act. In her riding, she used a sidesaddle—considered the right choice for a proper lady of that day.[57]

Oakley drew admirers from many quarters. According to a widely circulated story, she so impressed Sitting Bull that he "adopted her into the Sioux tribe." After she spent a number of years with the show, the *Police Gazette,* a publication crammed with gruesome stories of criminal activity, details about brawny pugilists, and titillating pictures of actresses in tights and models in swimming suits, awarded her its "female shooting championship of America." The publication reflected conflicting attitudes about her role by praising her as a "modest little girl" and also as a woman who "Shoots Like a Man."[58]

While Annie Oakley enhanced Buffalo Bill's enterprise, her presence in the show did not result from a determination by the show's management to recognize the role of frontier women. She auditioned in 1884, but the showmen had no place for her, in part, because they already had the well-known Captain A. H. Bogardus. When Bogardus unexpectedly left the following year, Oakley demonstrated her ability and impressed Nate Salsbury, who immediately offered her a job. Including a woman in the show, then, resulted from an unplanned hiring rather than a predisposition of Cody, or anyone else in the managerial ranks, to include white women in the show. Those who purchased Cody's autobiography found little in it about the contributions of women.[59]

Perhaps because of Annie Oakley's success, other women joined the show. In 1886 the sharpshooter Lillian Smith, called "The California Girl" and "The Champion Girl Shot," and trick riders Della Ferrell and Georgia Duffy performed regularly. Even in later years when more women performed in the show, their presence in the troupe rarely exceeded ten percent, however. Reflecting the winning of the West as a male accomplishment fit the mood of the age, which stressed separate spheres for men and women. One historian has argued that western films would emerge as the uniquely male "antagonist" to the considerable influence of women writers in domestic literature. Perhaps the same can be said about Buffalo Bill's Wild West show.[60]

In addition to acts demonstrating riding and shooting skills, the entertainment also featured Plains animals. Like George Catlin, Cody made wildlife an important part of the image of the West. Cody's early shows included buffalo, elk, wild horses, Texas steers, Mexican burros, mountain lions, coyotes, deer, antelopes, and mountain sheep. The 1883 program included "Lassoing and Riding the Wild Bison of the Plains," a demonstration of hunting elk, deer, and wild horses, and a "A Grand Hunt on the Plains." In these acts, Cody and cowboys chased the animals and shot blanks, and Indians assaulted the shaggy beasts with blunted arrows. However, the thrill of buffalo hunts, which both Catlin and Cody had experienced, proved impossible to replicate because the buffalo eventually became accustomed to milling around in the arena and mostly ignored their pursuers.[61]

That buffalo faced possible extinction made them interesting to audiences, and the showmen advertised having "The Largest Herd of Buffalo on the Continent" as well as a rare Mexican (Zacatecan) buffalo. However, the show emphasized hunting bison more than preserving them. The Wild West show was an accurate barometer of the age in this regard. Americans knew that buffalo and other big game animals might become extinct, and some—romantics, in particular—advocated protection of them. But Cody exemplified the prevailing mood: progress required dominion over wilderness, its people, and its animals.[62]

Miscellaneous variety acts constituted another identifiable category in the show. Patriotism emerged in the 1886 program when Sergeant Bates and his son Master Bates made a feature of displaying the American flag. That same year, Gabriel Dumont, a Canadian who had allied himself with Louis Riel's movement to prevent incorporating the Northwest Territories into Canada, joined the show. The Dumont act was a rare attempt during this period to include international affairs, which would become a focus in years to come. "Mustang Jack" demonstrated athletic ability by high jumping over animals in the arena. First he cleared a single burro, then an Indian pony, and finally "Doc. Powell," a white horse that stood "nearly six feet" at the shoulders. Athletic events, of all kinds, were increasing in popularity because Americans of this period devoted much of their free time to sports.[63] All these features—patriotism, international affairs, and athletics—would become more important in future seasons.

Some variety acts belittled minority groups, which many white Americans openly scorned during this period. In one the exotic-sounding "Feejee Indian from Africa" rode a saddled "wild elk." The joke was that the man turned out to be Voter Hall, a black cowboy. "An exciting race between Mexican thoroughbreds" featured uncooperative burros that the announcer explained were "bred with great care, and at considerable expense, their original cost being sixteen dollars per doz." While riders attempted to get their stubborn mounts to move, the band played "We Won't Come Home till Morning." In another act, a "Mexican thoroughbred" performed acrobatic tricks designed to keep it from being ridden. On a more serious note, an article in one show program suggested that cowboys and *vaqueros* shared some qualities, but that a tendency to overdress and become dangerous when drunk separated *vaqueros* from cowboys. In his autobiography, Cody found little good to say about most minority groups and journalists writing about the show sometimes referred to the Mexican performers as "greasers."[64]

Although Cody's Wild West show reflected attitudes prevalent in the United States it was somewhat more enlightened in this regard than society at large. Antonio Esquibel, "Champion Vaquero of Mexico," and "Wallupi—Champion Vaquero Rider" were treated respectfully and enjoyed favorable publicity, and *vaqueros* sometimes joined scouts and cowboys in routing Indians in scenes such as the attack on the settlers' cabin. The ambiguity evident in the portrayal of Mexicans probably reflected a general feeling that white men had won the West, while others served as the supporting cast.[65]

Native Americans performed throughout the show, and, like Catlin, Cody respected them. In interviews, Cody often sounded like Catlin, calling Indians "kind and true-hearted people," who "if properly treated by whites would give our government little or no trouble." Both showmen believed that understanding the Plains required appreciation of the Indians who lived there, and these two men gave them conspicuous places in their entertainments. Like Catlin, Cody believed that Indians had the right to defend their homelands. Cody took seriously the responsibility for those in his employ, often personally selecting those hired for the entertainment, buying new clothes for them when seasons ended, and making certain that they left the show with money.[66]

Despite some similarities, however, Catlin and Cody viewed Native Americans as different in many ways. Catlin made a sincere effort to see things from an Indian perspective. In this regard he had carefully recorded and presented phonetic spellings of the names Indians themselves used. Publicity for Cody's show and those that followed, however, typically presented only white people's translations of Native American names. An artist, ethnographer, and philosopher of sorts, Catlin saw Indians as vulnerable, frail, and "vanishing Americans." On-o-gong-way and Wi-jun-jon, after all, had both died because of civilization's touch. While Catlin went among Indians with notebooks and oil paints, Buffalo Bill traveled the Plains with rifle in hand. Cody's autobiography brimmed with stories of shooting buffalo and fights with Indians. Never did he question Manifest Destiny, and he killed Indians because his survival required it.

From this came a hard-nosed respect for Native Americans. Buffalo Bill believed that they possessed enough toughness and resilience to survive in the modern world. Unlike Catlin, the question of taking Indians on tour presented no great moral dilemma for him. They were adults who should have the opportunity to make money, to travel around the United States and Europe, and to learn about these cultures. Cody respected Indians as fighters—that was how he got to know them. In this way Cody fit a pattern noted by the historian Richard Slotkin: those who fought against Indians often became the recognized experts on them. For his part, Buffalo Bill saw no paradox or irony here:

he knew Indians well, respected them, and in the past had killed them when necessary. A program appearing after the turn of the century summed up his perspective: you really do not "fully appreciate a man" until you have "fought with him" and learned "respect for the war-like qualities of his foe." His was a kill-or-be-killed gladiatorial worldview that included admiration for worthy adversaries and caused him to say that he "never shot an Indian . . . but I regretted it afterwards."[67]

The acts in Buffalo Bill's Wild West show did not reflect the subtleties of his beliefs. George Catlin's regard for Indians got lost among battle cries and scalps, and action in Cody's arena turned Plains Indians into war-painted aggressors to be met, defeated, and killed. The showmen were, after all, showmen, and their entertainments were as much a reflection of mainstream society and its values as they were of the ideas of their principals. Audiences voted by purchasing tickets and applauding, and they demanded action, simplicity, and excitement—not a show that raised thorny issues like degrees of rightness and wrongness resulting from two different civilizations meeting and fighting on the Plains.

As in Catlin's day, many Americans believed that Indians and their cultures might disappear. However, Cody's compatriots remained woefully ill-informed about Native Americans because stories of warfare were still the most common source of information. However, in Cody's day a debate about the "Indian Problem" raged among reformers, politicians, bureaucrats, and others.[68] This dialogue about the place of Indians in modern America generated a great deal of interest but contributed little substance to the understanding of Native American cultures. One place where Americans could get more information was Buffalo Bill's Wild West show, which promised to educate and entertain with an authentic picture of the West and its people. What they got, however, was what white Americans wanted to see.

Poster art depicted Indians as fiendish descendants of those from the captivity narratives of Catlin's day, except that these people rode horses and dressed more colorfully. Paper with captions such as "A Close Call" and "Congress of American Indians" bombarded the American public with images of fights between frontiersmen and Indians. One called "To the Rescue" showed Buffalo Bill saving a settler about to be burned at the stake. Some publicity accentuated the fierceness of Native American performers in Wild West shows by saying that Indian agents often selected the most hostile ones to tour with the show as a means of separating the troublemakers from their more peaceful comrades.[69]

Not surprisingly, the most memorable acts in Buffalo Bill's Wild West show depicted frontiersmen fighting and defeating ferocious-looking Indians. A journalist noted that the Indians appeared "stripped to the waist, in paint, feathers, wampum, armed to the teeth . . . and fight with thrilling realism their battles on foot, on horseback, and with fire, dart, spear and hunting knife." In the arena, Indians scalped fallen adversaries. For a time, the show included "the massacre of a tribe of wandering red men and women by nomadic warriors of their own race." How could any people be so bloodthirsty, one reporter wondered?[70]

Colorfully dressed scouts and cowboys, superb horsemanship, hairbreadth escapes, daring rescues, and the roar of gunshots often brought cheering crowds to their feet. Such enthusiasm represented more than appreciation of good entertainment; by cheering the show, Americans applauded their nation and the gladiatorial approach to Manifest Destiny. The Wild West show reduced the western saga to a morality play in which Cody, along with scouts and cowboys, represented the forces of good and civilization and Indians and a few errant white road agents symbolized evil and barbarism. Enhancing the heroic qualities of white frontiersmen required presenting the struggle for the frontier as difficult and dangerous. In a fast-moving, open-air program with few props and very little dialogue, human opponents were the way to dramatize conflict. Natural forces such as hurricanes, droughts, and blizzards could not be depicted; consequently, the Plains Indians provided the danger.

One act—"Duel between Buffalo Bill and Yellow Hand"—reduced westward expansion to gladiatorial combat. In introducing it, the announcer informed listeners that the showdown actually occurred during the "Sitting Bull war," and that it produced "the first scalp taken in revenge of Custer's fate." The "wonderfully realistic representation of the duel" showed cowboys and Indians riding toward each other, Yellow Hand's challenge to Buffalo Bill, the two combatants galloping forward, each man stopping his mount and firing, hand-to-hand combat (Cody with a knife and Yellow Hand a spear), and Cody knifing his opponent. Then "the supposed scalp of Yellow Hand was triumphantly exhibited by the invincible scout of the Plains." Following this, the Indians charged "and the Liveliest kind of engagement ensued between the Indians and cowboys, the Indians finally getting the worst of it."[71] In a period when the Wild West show stressed frontier bloodshed, the act enhanced Buffalo Bill's reputation by demonstrating his bravery, patriotism, and his role in clearing the way for "civilization."

Another act featuring the Deadwood stage depicted white frontiersmen facing the fury of "fierce and warlike Indians" determined to stop the advance of civilization. The announcer explained the stagecoach was an authentic and historical relic, having made the run between "Deadwood and Cheyenne," thereby earning it "an immortal place in American history, having been baptized many times by fire and blood." Real westerners appeared in the act: John Higby, who had driven stages on the frontier, piloted the conveyance; John Hancock, the "Wizard Hunter of Platte Valley," rode shotgun; imposing Con Croner, "Cowboy Sheriff of the Platte" and inveterate foe of rustlers and the "hoodlum element" in Nebraska, positioned himself on top of the coach; and "Broncho Bill" was alongside it to provide additional firepower. To fill the Deadwood stage with passengers, the announcer asked for volunteers. Those selected were usually prominent people in the community, reporters, and celebrities.[72] The act combined elements typical of Buffalo Bill's Wild West show: authentic equipment from the frontier, real westerners demonstrating before audiences what they had actually done on the Plains, the message that westward expansion was violent, and good public relations as represented by those local potentates riding in the stage.

Also making this act typical were rapid movement, noise, skillful riding, color, excitement, and the timely arrival of cowboys. The feature opened with the stage, drawn by a four- or six-mule team, beginning a quiet trip, and then a "band of marauding Indians and road agents" attacking it. A furious chase ensued, wherein the rickety old coach careened around the arena and Indians were "swerving around on their horses' necks to avoid the shots from the occupants of the coach and discharging their rifles in the most unheard of positions." Sometimes Indians fired flaming arrows, and a smoke machine in the coach made it billow great clouds. Impressed with the act, a reporter commented: "Hundreds of shots were fired in a minute, and the air was thick with smoke and men dropped from their horses and bit the dust in the most lifelike or deathlike fashion." "With mighty savage yells," the Native Americans prepared to scalp or burn their victims at the stake, but "just in the nick of time, came the rescue party of dashing, dare-devil cowboys, headed by no other than Buffalo Bill himself, in all of his colorful, flashy attire." "The yipping, madly riding cowboys" then killed most of the Indians and sent the remainder fleeing for their lives.[73]

A mad chase, flaming arrows, and smoke made the act memorable, but splendidly mounted Plains Indians provided the essential dramatic element. Increasing the number of Indians in such acts enhanced the illusion of danger. The number of Indians in the show grew from about fifty in 1885 to eighty or one hundred the following year. In cowboy-versus-Indian scenes in Wild West shows, Indians always outnumbered their opponents.[74] Hollywood's western movies would eventually copy such scenes and their dramatic effects. Both Wild West shows and movies exaggerated the typical number of Native Americans in actual battles, since the real ones involved small groups of warriors, guerrilla tactics, and few casualties.

Buffalo Bill's Wild West show included acts called "spectacles," which shared

characteristics with the Deadwood stage act and usually filled the final spot in
the program. In one of these, "Grand Buffalo Hunt on the Plains," performers
captured and feigned the killing of buffalo, elk, deer, and wild cattle. Both Indian and white hunters joined in the chase, then hostilities occurred, and the
scene ended with a "grand realistic battle scene, depicting the capture, torture
and death of a Scout by the savages. The revenge, recapture of the dead body,
and the victory of the Cow-Boys and Government Scouts." The victors sometimes scalped the fallen Indians.[75]

Another spectacle the announcer called an "attack upon a settler's cabin by a
band of marauding Indians" portrayed an isolated pioneer family attacked by
"nearly a hundred" Indians, who usually set the cabin on fire. Sometimes the
settler husband died in front of his wife. When all seemed hopeless, Buffalo Bill
thundered into the arena at the head of a group of scouts and cowboys (and
sometimes *vaqueros*) as audiences roared their approval. A journalist described
the battle: "Indians, cowboys, horses, and powder smoke were flying in confusion all over the field at the end of the sham battle. The more there was of bang-
ing pistols and scurrying Indians the better apparently the spectators like it."
Soon, the "field was left strewn with the dead and dying" and the Native Americans fled. Journalists often remarked that the Wild West show and its spectacles brought to life scenes like those in dime novels.[76]

This act differed from others because it struck at the heart of what made the
idea of the frontier so special to Cody's fellow citizens. As the historian Richard White has demonstrated, to Americans of this day, the settlers' cabin was a
cultural icon representing the most basic values—"self-reliance and a connection with place," individual energy, progress, and family.[77] While most audiences liked the other acts, more Americans could identify directly with a settlers' cabin because it represented family, Manifest Destiny, and the American
Dream. The possible disappearance of free land and the settlement frontier was,
after all, what created frontier anxiety and attracted many people to the Wild
West show in the first place. Their rescuing of settlers portrayed Cody and cowboys as heroic defenders of Americans' most cherished values.

With Native Americans cast as attackers of settlers' cabins, it proved difficult
to get audiences to venerate Indians and their culture. When introduced to
audiences, individuals such as White Eagle of the Pawnee, Dave of the Wichita, and Little Brave of the Sioux did not receive the same enthusiastic cheering that greeted Cody or Buck Taylor. Domestic scenes featuring Native Americans did not generate much enthusiasm either. Some reproduced those same
acts that George Catlin had presented: music, a shaman curing the sick, and
dances. In 1885, Pawnee, Sioux, and Wichita Indians demonstrated war, grass,

corn, and scalp dances. One journalist critiqued the act: "The Indian dances were grotesque and funny, but rather tame. The warriors gathered in a circle, stamped their feet and jerked their bodies in time to the monotonous music from a couple of tum-tums, keeping up a continuous falsetto squeaking, and looking as hideous as possible." Sometimes audiences saw the dances as humorous, and spectators shouted "such sallies as 'Rats!' 'Whoop'er up ther, Jim!' 'Dosy-do' at the most critical points in their performance," evoking "obvious disgust" from the Pawnees.[78]

Knowing how Indians felt about much that occurred was difficult to ascertain because many relied on interpreters during interviews, and even a publicity agent with the show doubted that interpreters always gave full and accurate translations of their remarks. Complicating the issue were opposing groups that used Indians' pronouncements to support their positions. Some government officials and humanitarian groups opposed Native Americans appearing in shows because it perpetuated stereotypes of them and exposed them to "corruption." Those in Cody's organization wanted no hint of mistreatment, unhappiness, or impropriety made public. A Sioux named Black Elk did speak out and seemed to enjoy performing and receiving pay for doing things he considered exciting, but questioned why cowboys and scouts always won the mock battles and focused attention almost exclusively on their own skills.[79]

A case study of another Indian's reaction to performing came in 1885 when Tatonka-i-Yotanka, or Sitting Bull, traveled with the show. Almost everyone in the United States knew his name because of his involvement with the Battle of the Little Bighorn. Tatonka-i-Yotanka began his career as a showman in the fall of 1884, when he, along with seven other Sioux and two interpreters, toured twenty-five cities with the "Sitting Bull Combination." The group attracted little attention, but when Sitting Bull joined Buffalo Bill, he rivaled Cody in popularity. His impact was so profound that Sioux replaced Pawnees as the most popular choice for show Indians.[80] Obviously, Cody's enterprise already had strong publicity and a reputation as a good place to see Indians, which generated more interest in Sitting Bull than when he had appeared independently.

The showmen made a great deal of Sitting Bull. Buffalo Bill, for his part, made conciliatory remarks about Indians while Sitting Bull was in the show. The 1885 program carried an article entitled "History of Sitting Bull," which called him the *"Napoleon of the Indian Race"* and praised his bravery. According to it, Sitting Bull desired to meet William F. Cody, "the noted frontiersman who had contributed so largely to his defeat in 1876." When Tatonka-i-Yotanka joined the show, he and Cody solemnly smoked the peace pipe, much to the delight of the crowd gathered to witness the occasion. The showmen used the shaman for publicity purposes, introducing him to the president of the United States, and inviting reporters to smoke the peace pipe with him. Sitting Bull did not perform, but appeared in parades, usually in "war costume of paint and feathers," and attended the rib roast dinners for celebrities and the press. Sometimes he participated in the grand review and rode around the arena. Sitting Bull received fifty dollars a week and the "sole right to sell his own Photographs and Autographs." He apparently sent most of his earnings back to the reservation for the care of children.[81]

The Battle of the Little Bighorn, which had occurred nine years earlier, generated animosity toward Tatonka-i-Yotanka, as did the ongoing Indian wars. Consequently, during this season many Americans, and to a lesser extent Canadians, saw little to admire in Sitting Bull. Hisses and boos greeted him in the grand review. Attendees sometimes yelled from the stands that he should be hanged, and when a man came to his tent, planning to do him bodily harm, Sitting Bull defended himself and left a three-tooth-sized hole in the attacker's mouth. One reporter branded him a "murderous old fellow." Another said that it was better that Sitting Bull was in the show "than leading scalping expeditions in the West." The press sometimes trivialized the man, calling him "Sedintary Taurus" and "Bull."[82]

Predictably, Sitting Bull's role in the Battle of the Little Bighorn intrigued Americans, and reporters plagued him with questions. What were his views of the massacre? Had he masterminded it? Who had actually killed Custer? Why had the Indians failed to scalp the golden-haired general? Sitting Bull detested discussing the battle and often refused to speak of it at all. Once when asked to make a speech, he avoided talking about anything of substance by pointing out a soldier in the crowd who had rolled cigarettes for him while he was incarcerated at Fort Randall. He sometimes refused to appear in public because of the incessant questions and the staring of spectators.[83]

As the season wore on, Sitting Bull became less and less patient with audiences, and by the end he had vowed to return home and not become involved in any more entertainment ventures. In an interview late in the season, Sitting Bull assessed his reaction to the questioners, especially reporters: "Some were light frivolous men. Some were bad men. I know not any of them. . . . They were all the same to me . . . but to my ears it was like the noisy waters, which man cannot stop." When he left the show, publicity agents reported that he suffered from homesickness, and he probably did. But the barrage of questions and the intense interest in the bloody aspects of the West probably contributed significantly to his desire to return home. When he departed, he took two presents from Buffalo Bill: a white hat and a gray horse trained to begin a Wild West show act when gunfire started. Cody wanted him to return for the next season, but an Indian agent named James McLaughlin opposed it, so the showmen abandoned the idea.[84]

Much about the show glorified violence, however, the entertainment ended on a softer note: would patrons like to see the Wild West show camp located on the showgrounds and see "domestic life, in all its romantic and stirring features," and perhaps chat with scouts, cowboys, *vaqueros,* and Indians? Newspaper articles and show publicity assured visitors that although cowboys, scouts, and Indians were wild on the Plains, they were gentle in the camp, so women and children could safely visit them. The entertainers asserted that a Christian spirit pervaded the camp. Performers reportedly spent Sundays, not in the show ring, but attending church services and reading the Bible. According to the publicity, the Native Americans took Christianity seriously. In church they always sang hymns with such fervor that their voices rose above the rest of the congregation. The only misfortune that might result from a Sunday visit to the Wild West show camp was that spectators could disturb the Indians, who would be found devoutly singing psalms.[85]

Only minor scandals occurred in the camp. Indians let it be known that they wanted whiskey and sometimes obtained it. A nineteen-year-old white woman in Newark "made a conquest" of a Pawnee named Pushaluk. The couple fled to New York and married, but were found and returned to the Wild West show camp, where they set up their own tepee.[86]

The show's camp was important, but it was not the major symbol of America that it would become in later years. In this early period, Indians preempted the image of outdoor people. In 1886, for example, when all the show's personnel camped in a New York park, local reporters commented that Native Americans enjoyed getting back to nature, but they failed to credit other members of the troupe with the same sentiments. While other performers stayed in Columbus, Ohio, hotels in 1885, Indians camped outdoors because they could not stand such confinement, according to a newspaper account.[87] The Wild West show camp would eventually take on added significance when show publicity postulated that camping outdoors rejuvenated the physically and morally superior westerners.

Visiting the camp completed a day of entertainment at Buffalo Bill's Wild West show. For most, the experience was memorable. Cody's childhood remembrances—Manifest Destiny, rough men with "huge pistols," and Indians—came to life and intrigued patrons. "America's National Entertainment" fit the mood of the country in the 1880s by making the conquest of the Plains appear fun-filled, glorious, simple, and patriotic. Certainly the show would continue to evolve, but western features remained at its heart.

Even in this early period, the showmen experimented with the format of the show. Typically, this traveling entertainment operated only during the summer months; however, in January 1885 they gave winter shows in New Orleans. Here they offered their standard fare, except for the final evening spectacle, "a grand pyrotechnical representation of the 'Battle of New Orleans.'" The *New Orleans Daily Picayune* reported: "The cowboys did not draw their idea of battle from history, but they did make the scene exciting if not exact." In it, Buffalo Bill played the part of Andrew Jackson. Cody rarely played another person and probably limited his roles to ones that complemented his views. His portrayal of Jackson was appropriate because Jackson's popularity rested, in part, on his reputation as an Indian fighter and opening the frontier regions to settlers. In addition, an elaborate mythology existed about Andrew Jackson and the Bat-tle of New Orleans. According to a view popular in the United States, Jackson was an instrument of Providence, a nature's man, and a person of iron will.[88] Certainly Cody would have had no problems with any of those ideas. More-over, Cody exuberantly associated himself with things military, especially with victories as stunning as the Battle of New Orleans.

Another bit of experimentation came at the end of the regular season in 1886 when Nate Salsbury and Buffalo Bill transformed their outdoor show into an indoor one and moved it into Madison Square Garden for a winter season. They hired Steele Mackaye, a famous actor, playwright, and producer known for using theatrical inventions, to convert the Wild West show into an extravaganza for the stage. Elaborate lighting effects and sophisticated machinery made it pos-sible to stage cyclones and prairie fires. Thus, frontiersmen in the show could struggle against the forces of nature as well as Native Americans and outlaws. Preparations for the indoor show cost sixty thousand dollars.[89]

A street parade, an Indian encampment, a "Grand Introduction," and other standard Wild West show scenes remained in this engagement. Cody and Sals-bury dubbed it "The Drama of Civilization," told everyone that it would have unity and not be "a series of detached exhibitions, as formerly," and promised "a great historical, educational, pictorial, and dramatic spectacle."[90] Now the show had a narrative underpinning spelling out the process of transforming wilder-ness into civilization in a series of identifiable steps. The show was moving from a "gladiatorial contest revived" to one championing westward expansion.

According to the *New York Times*, "The Drama of Civilization" brought on stage nearly two hundred mounted persons, including "Buffalo Bill, several dozen cowboys, cowgirls," *vaqueros,* and "a hundred and fifty Indians of various tribes in full fig and feather." Between acts, or "epochs," appeared standard Wild West show offerings, such as Indian dances, and Lillian Smith, Annie Oakley, and Cody demonstrating sharpshooting.[91]

The first scene, or "epoch," "The Primeval Forest," offered a nighttime view of wilderness prior to the arrival of white Americans. A bear, a pair of deer, and a herd of elk drank from a spring. As dawn lit the sky, Native Americans appeared and sent a volley of arrows toward the animals. Then bands of Sioux and Pawnees met, talked, danced, and fought "a rough and tumble massacre."[92]

Scene two featured the prairie and opened with Cody yelling and shooting at buffalo gathered at a waterhole, followed by him meeting scouts and sharing whiskey with them. After this, white settlers appeared in prairie schooners, settled down for the night, and were driven from their camp by a prairie fire and a stampede of animals fleeing the conflagration. The next scene portrayed a cattle ranch, with "the rowdy and athletic cowboy . . . in his glory, with bucking horses and obdurate cattle." Then "torturing and scalping" Comanches and Kiowas appeared "led by Seven-Fleas, Son-of-a-Gun, Loaded-for-Bear, Busted Flush, Peach-Blow-Spittoon, Two-Buckets-of-Red-Paint, and other famous Chiefs." Cowboys arrived and sent the Indians "to the happy hunting grounds in a body."[93]

Next, attention turned to a boisterous mining camp, where viewers saw a "'Wild West' Tavern," "a duel to death with revolvers," the arrival and departure of the pony express, exhibits of marksmanship, and the arrival, departure, and holdup of the Deadwood stage. The fourth "epoch" ended with a cyclone destroying a U.S. cavalry camp somewhere on the Plains. As in outdoor performances, the acts were altered throughout the season. Sometimes the "Drama of Civilization" concluded with a spectacle, a battle between the cavalry and Indians, and late in the season, the Battle of the Little Bighorn ended the show. For part of the Madison Square Garden engagement, Cody "wore a wig to represent Custer's auburn locks" and played the fallen general. So for a second time, Cody played a recognized hero; however, after this Cody generally avoided such roles.[94]

The acts, like the show itself, were in a state of transition. "The Drama of Civilization" featured those things which had worked in open-air arenas, like horsemanship, marksmanship, Plains animals, variety acts, and spectacles where white men defeated Indians. Some "rawness" still clung to the show as evidenced by denigrating names for Indians, scouts routinely consuming alcohol, and

Indians who tortured and slaughtered settlers. However, the "Drama of Civilization" looked forward because it carried a carefully articulated theme of progress which would grow in importance in the show.

New York had overwhelmed Cody on his first visit in 1872, but now he was a successful showman. Those in the entertainment business came to admire Mackaye's theatrical paraphernalia, and other New Yorkers thronged to see the great show from the West. Advertisements warned patrons that the "Drama of Civilization" was so popular that "Thousands [Were] Literally Turned Away" and that it was "The Biggest Triumph Ever Known." The press confirmed the full houses. Two performances on Thanksgiving Day, for example, brought a total of 19,800 attendees.[95]

By 1887, Cody's show was an American success story: it had begun as an obscure entertainment, but now stood preeminent, nearly monopolized the western theme, and easily withstood threats from the multitude of small shows that tried to imitate it. Other kinds of entertainments, such as commercialized rodeos and movies, had not emerged to compete for audiences. In addition to the run at Madison Square Garden, other factors indicated the show's success. Persons connected with the show reported that a million people saw it in five months during 1885. The show stayed on Staten Island the whole summer season of 1886. While there, the seating capacity of twenty thousand proved inadequate, and the showmen added another ten thousand seats. In this year, Cody wrote to a friend that he was making "about $40,000 a week." Journalists often commented on the size of the show, giving numbers of railroad cars, people, and animals, and remarking that the Wild West show must be a lucrative venture.[96]

In addition to success with the public, Cody and Salsbury's show garnered praise from other entertainers. P. T. Barnum, Catlin's old antagonist, paid it a great compliment by attending—the only competitor's show he had ever seen—and pronouncing it a great success. Captain A. H. Bogardus, who had quit the enterprise and opened a shooting gallery in Bloomington, Illinois, attested to Cody's success by telling a tongue-in-cheek story. He claimed that every year when the show came to town, "he hired a Negro to kick him up and down an adjacent alley" to bring home his stupidity for selling his part of such a successful venture.[97]

The showmen had achieved tremendous success before audiences at home, but could "America's National Entertainment" do well abroad? Like George Catlin, Salsbury and Cody encouraged people to see their exhibition before it went overseas. Salsbury traveled in Europe in 1885, and John Burke went to London in 1886; both reported interest in the show abroad. Buffalo Bill was the man to capture the imagination of the Old World because dime novels had fanned enthusiasm for the American West in England and Cody's name and his entertainment intrigued the English. In addition, Cody had made important friends such as Henry Irving, a popular British actor, who had seen the show in the United States and assured Salsbury and Cody that Europeans would enjoy it. In 1887, talk about a foreign tour became a reality when the Wild West show received an invitation to become a part of the American exhibition at the Golden Jubilee, a celebration of Queen Victoria's fiftieth year of reign. Nate Salsbury promised that the show would retain its "thoroughly American character" and that he would "keep the stars and stripes always floating above the exhibition."[98]

On 31 March 1887, a crowd filled with reporters gathered to give an enthusiastic send-off to the ship *State of Nebraska* transporting the Americans to London. The press provided interested readers with details about who was on board and the number of animals making the trip. The journalists saw more to the story than just a catalog of equipment and personnel; they too reflected the hope that the entertainment would impress Europeans. One reporter had predicted in 1885, when talk about Cody's trip abroad started: "when he takes the show to England next year, the blarsted Britons will go wild over it."[99]

Mark Twain added his support to the venture and penned an open letter to Cody declaring: "It is often said on the other side of the water that none of the exhibitions which we send to England are purely and distinctively American. If you will take the Wild West show over there you can remove that reproach." According to a *New York Times* reporter who witnessed the enthusiastic departure, the purpose of the trip abroad was "to show effete Europeans just what life in America is like." He added about Cody and the probable impact of the show: "The demonstration he expects to make when he arrives on the other side will give the stolid Britishers new ideas of the magnificence of this Western Hemisphere."[100] Everyone agreed: the show must educate Europeans and impress them with the grandeur of America. With this in mind, Cody and Salsbury would make their entertainment more than just a "gladiatorial contest revived."

Tatonka-i-Yotanka (Sitting Bull) poses with Buffalo Bill Cody during his tour with the show in 1885. (Buffalo Bill Historical Center, Cody, Wyo.)

Annie Oakley, ca. 1889, a celebrated sharpshooter, impressed nearly everyone who saw her perform. (Western History Collections, University of Oklahoma Library)

Lillian Smith retained proper Victorian dress and deportment when she demonstrated her skill with a rifle. (Western History Collections, University of Oklahoma Library)

This strip of cowgirl stickers demonstrates how the Miller Brothers 101 Ranch Wild West show emphasized the physical attractiveness of its female performers. (Buffalo Bill Historical Center, Cody, Wyo.)

Wild West posters typically did not feature minority women. This one from 1908 stressed Arrow-head's appearance more than cultural diversity. (Circus World Museum, Baraboo, Wisc.)

*To Mr. Dean* · *Joan et Jean* · *J. John*

John Burke, press agent for the Buffalo Bill Wild West show, inscribed this photo of himself taken in front of Rheims Cathedral by the statue of Joan of Arc, "Joan and John." Such whimsy reflected the intention of the showmen not to take European monuments too seriously. (Neg. 28139, American Heritage Center, University of Wyoming)

IL SUCCESSO DI BUFFALO BILL A FIRENZE

This cartoon from the 15 March 1890 issue of *Il Vero Monello* captured the confrontational mood of Italians and those in Buffalo Bill's Wild West show. (Buffalo Bill Historical Center, Cody, Wyo.)

Patrons could purchase mementos like this watch fob at Wild West shows. The companion busts of Buffalo Bill and Pawnee Bill became the trademark of the "Two Bills" show. (author's collection)

Joe Esquival, Jim Kid, Jim Mitchell, Dick Johnson, Billy Bullock, Antonio Esquival, Tom Duffy.
Lying down in front is Johnny Baker, and Billy Johnson.

GROUP OF COWBOYS WITH THE OLD TIME BUFFALO BILL'S WILD WEST SHOW

Buffalo Bill Wild West show cowboys, 1886. (Western History Collections, University of Oklahoma Library)

This poster entitled "Westward the Course of Empire" (1898) made a strong statement that Americans should remain committed to Manifest Destiny. (Circus World Museum, Baraboo, Wisc., and Poster Photo Archives, Posters Please, Inc., New York City)

In 1901, the Buffalo Bill Wild West show act "The Rescue at Pekin" encouraged the use of military force to expand U.S. influence abroad. (Circus World Museum, Baraboo, Wisc.)

# "To Esteem Us Better":
# Buffalo Bill Cody before International
# Audiences, 1887–93

Upon arrival in London on 16 April 1887, the Americans flew into action designed to impress the British. When the *State of Nebraska* docked, Wild West show personnel quickly got the animals and equipment off the ship and aboard the train transporting everything to the showgrounds. By six that evening, the troupe had accomplished a prodigious amount of work: the animals were fed and safely resting in the stables, tents for the performers were up, and Indians had erected their tepees. Then, everyone sat down to a thoroughly American supper of "beef, mutton, corn-bread, ham" and other wholesome fare. All around—on rooftops, on walls, in the streets, and from any other place that offered a suitable vantage point—thousands of enchanted Londoners watched the activities in the camp. When the flag was hoisted overhead, the Americans swelled with pride and the cowboy band played the national anthem. At the urging of the throng around the camp, the musicians then offered a rendition of "God Save the Queen." The crowd roared its approval.[1]

While all this appeared spontaneous, the showmen had carefully orchestrated it to impress the English. About this, Cody explained: "Trivial as these details may appear at first sight, the rapidity with which we had transported our stuff from dock to depot, and depot to grounds, and made our camp . . . had an immense effect." These first activities had Londoners saying: "By St. George, the Yankees mean business." Cody intended to make a lasting impression because, for a number of years, he had wanted to go to England and "be treated like a gentleman." Perhaps Cody knew that his nation's ambassador to England, James Russell Lowell, did not approve of the show's visit to England.[2] This, too, may have motivated the showman to succeed abroad.

In the days that followed, feverish activity at the Wild West show camp continued. With New World enterprise and determination, the Americans converted their portion of the metropolis into a suitable wilderness environment. A location adjacent to the railroad tracks enabled them to receive seventeen thousand carloads of rock and earth to construct hilly terrain on which to live. Then they planted trees. Ten days of diligent labor completed the project, after which the Americans took time to appreciate their life in a "state of nature." The flurry of activity had its desired effect: the English noted the efficiency of Americans, and the *London Observer* urged readers to visit the camp and study "the wilful ways of the children of the prairie before popular favour and superfluous luxury render them civilised and effeminate." Another journalist remarked: "We are, perhaps, suffering a little from over-culture just at present." A visit to the Americans might teach people "that there may be something else worth living for besides scandal, social supremacy, and sensuous sentiment." Cody noted: "The sight of the Indians, cowboys, American girls, and Mexicans living in their primitive simplicity, was very attractive to them."[3]

Nearby, other Americans assembled the official U.S. exhibition at Queen Victoria's Golden Jubilee. Like Cody, they intended to impress the Britons. As part of a young nation seeking respect from the rest of the world, Americans approached international expositions in the nineteenth century with resolve. At the center of their exhibition stood a giant iron and glass edifice measuring 400 yards long and 150 yards wide that housed the "American Exhibition . . . Of the Arts, Inventions, Manufactures, Products and Resources of the United States of America." This massive collection of art, articles and tools of manufacture, and other products heralded the nation's material and cultural progress. Symbolizing the closeness between the official exhibit and the Wild West show, seven stuffed bison on loan from Cody stood at its gate. The *London Times* made an obvious point: the official exhibition of the United States and the Wild West show "supplemented each other."[4]

Another part of the exhibition, "The Gardens," demonstrated the beauty, diversity, and importance of American flora. Reflecting the same spirit as the Wild West show camp, the official guidebook explained that understanding their nation required appreciating Americans' special relationship with nature. To illustrate this, the Americans planted a twelve-acre exhibit that they called a "Garden." It contained two sections: one illustrating the importance of cultivated plants in the United States and the other featuring a "natural style" that showcased the grandeur of New World forests still untouched by civilization. Another exhibit was a diorama depicting urban scenes, such as New York Harbor, the Statue of Liberty, the Hudson and East Rivers, New York, Brooklyn, Jersey City, and the Brooklyn Bridge. All these—the "American Exhibition . . . of the Arts, Inventions, Manufactures, Products, and Resources of the United States," "The Gardens," scenes of bustling urban life, and the Wild West show camp—heralded America's multiformity and progress. Interestingly, many at the jubilee would find Buffalo Bill's Wild West show the most instructive part of the U.S. exhibit.[5]

Cody wanted his entertainment to improve the image of the United States. In *Story of the Wild West and Camp-Fire Chats* (1888), which appeared after the trip to England, Cody noted the impact of the Wild West show abroad: "I am convinced—and I say it in no boastful spirit, but as a plain statement of fact— that our visit to England has set the population of the British Islands reading, thinking, and talking about their American kinsmen to an extent before unprecedented. They are beginning to know of this mighty nation beyond the Atlantic and consequently to esteem us better." That phrase—"esteem us better"—explained the goal of the trips abroad. Cody saw it as an accomplishment that would be a "source of comfort" to him until his "dying day."[6]

"Esteem us better" propelled much that these Americans did on the other side of the Atlantic, and it defined a new role for Cody. Abroad he became an unofficial ambassador for his country. In this capacity, he did what formally appointed ambassadors do: present one's country as positively as possible, defend one's native land when challenged, serve as a repository of information, help fellow citizens abroad, win the respect and approval of foreign leaders, point out areas of similarity between the host country and one's own, and return home happily with a solid record of accomplishment and no hint of having compromised one's principles.

In this period, Cody and those around him became cultural ambassadors by going before international audiences and calling attention to the United States and its achievements. Action in the show ring was the magnet that attracted people to see the westerners, but Americans interacting with their foreign hosts characterized this time abroad. "America's National Entertainment" became a crucible of cultural interchange. In the years from 1887 to 1893, the show visited England, France, Spain, Italy, Austria, Germany, and Holland and appeared at three international expositions: Queen Victoria's Golden Jubilee, the Exposition Universal in Paris, and the Columbian Exposition in Chicago. When the show returned to the United States for the Columbian Exposition in 1893, it had added a "Congress of Rough Riders of the World," which included members of the European military and horsemen from around the world.

Combining entertainment and instruction made the show conspicuous abroad. As for the entertainment part, the showmen brought to England a proven program of acts honed before American audiences. The instruction part showcased America's uniqueness and progress. Thirty-six years earlier in London, when Catlin had hoped to include his Gallery unique in the 1851 world's fair, a reporter for the *London Times* had urged Americans to stop trying to duplicate European exhibits and instead celebrate the American landscape and the "triumphs over the forest."[7] At the Golden Jubilee, Cody did exactly that. His Wild West show chronicled the winning of the West and championed U.S. accomplishments.

These Americans both followed and departed from Catlin's pattern abroad. Like Catlin, they sometimes characterized Europe as old and tired and used its shortcomings as a foil to glorify "nature's men." These showmen, however, differed from Catlin in several ways. Catlin called himself a "a green horn from the back woods" and reacted to London with "trembling excitements and fears"; but Cody went abroad confidently and embarked on a "grand tour" of Europe. Also, Catlin had limited his show to Native Americans and a specific depiction of them, but Cody represented a nation with an exciting frontier history, many different kinds of people from the Plains, and a country comfortable with progress.

Since Catlin's arrival forty-seven years earlier, England had changed in ways that benefited Cody's show. Politically the ascendancy of liberalism meant fewer privileges for the elite and more democracy for the common folk. Prosperity from foreign trade, iron, coal, shipbuilding, and textiles brought jobs, so the working class had money to spend on entertainment. To city dwellers, the show offered escape to an imagined simpler world across the sea. Much information about the United States still came from dime novels and the works of James Fenimore Cooper, but now the financial sections of British newspapers paid respectful attention to the United States. Cheap American wheat grown on the Great Plains, carried eastward on newly built railroads, and transported abroad by ships had flooded the British Isles, causing a crisis among farmers. In addition, American industry was flourishing, the former colony had begun building a new steel navy, and the country was making imperialistic moves in Samoa and maneuvering to gain control of the Hawaiian Islands.[8] All this spurred the British to learn more about this nation across the Atlantic.

At Cody's camp, everyone wanted a first-rate exhibition. Show participants and workers, about three thousand in all, labored on proper showgrounds. The troupe rehearsed seriously, and those in the publicity department plastered flamboyant posters on nearly every conspicuous location in the metropolis. The showmen hosted "Indian breakfasts" and rib roast dinners. Frontiersmen wearing western garb appeared regularly on the streets of London, and Indians went to churches, theaters, and other public places. Journalists flocked to the camp and issued detailed reports.[9]

A procession of distinguished visitors focused attention on the Americans. Former Prime Minister William Gladstone and his wife toured the camp and enjoyed a preview of the show. Albert Edward, the Prince of Wales (who would become King Edward VII), the Princess of Wales, and other guests visited the official American exhibits and then climbed into the grandstands for a preview of the Wild West show. In an unfinished arena, the performers gave the grand processional review and eight selected acts filled with shooting, riding, and screaming. What the royalty saw impressed them, and even the unfinished nature of the arena added appeal. The enthusiastic prince asked to meet performers, and upon leaving, he complimented Cody on the entertainment and wished the show success.[10]

When opening day arrived on 9 May 1887, people thronged to the showgrounds. The Americans had invested about $165,000 in the enterprise, with approximately $130,000 spent on stands replete with "Refreshment bars" and able to accommodate forty thousand patrons. Show publicity called them the largest ever constructed in England. Once seated, spectators looked down on a mostly dirt arena about a third of a mile in circumference with the side farthest from the crowd sloping upward. From this sculptured earthen incline rose painted scenery of "great height" and five hundred feet in length that blocked out the urban landscape. Rocks and trees hid those places where the scenery met the ground. The visual image of the far end of the arena was a "rocky pass in the mountains." From there, riders would burst into view. Directly behind the painted mountains, out of sight of the spectators, stood the Deadwood stage, corrals for the horses, burros, Texas steers, elk, and deer. Show statistics boasted 200 performers, including 90 to 95 Indians, and 250 animals, including 35 buffalo.[11]

The official program proclaimed the entertainment "new, startling, and instructive," and noted an impetuousness that came from mixing cowboys, Native Americans, and *vaqueros* with wild beasts. A reporter who had seen the show in the United States described it as "a combination of a sort of savage circus, and a rough and ready theatre" and likened it to taking a tour of the wildest parts of the country "under the personal conduct of Buffalo Bill." Jubilee goers saw a time-tested program featuring the "Grand Processional Review," horse races, "Cowboy Fun," the Pony Express, sharpshooting, Indian dances, a buffalo hunt, *vaqueros,* and an attack on a settlers' cabin. Acts with Indians remained vital. "Phases of Indian Life" demonstrated a village on the move and women setting up tepees. An additional spectacle, an assault on a wagon train, also appeared on the program. These popular acts filled the arena with shooting, battle cries, color, and action. The cowboy band provided music, and Frank Richmond followed a script much like the one he used in the United States.[12]

This show included more female performers, perhaps a dozen now, and posters often included images of them. The sharpshooter Lillian Smith impressed viewers, as did Annie Oakley. Women appeared more frequently on horseback, and news articles often designated them "cowgirls," a term suggesting they were worthy counterparts of cowboys. Wearing long colorful dresses and western hats, they participated in a "Ladys' Race by American Frontier Girls" in which some rode sidesaddle and others astride, and women joined in a "Virginia Reel" on horseback. At least one woman "gained great applause" for riding an "accomplished bucker."[13]

Only minor criticisms of the show surfaced. Injecting more vigor in the buffalo hunt would improve it. Could someone make the *vaqueros* treat the wild Texas steers more kindly? Find a new way to clear the "dead" from the arena after battle scenes, because watching them get up and walk away at the conclusions of spectacles ruined the realism. A writer for *Punch* lampooned the whole affair, commenting that if the Wild West show truly represented life on the Plains, it must be "a theatrical, circus-like sort of existence" where "everyone dresses in a fancifully embroidered costume" and lived among "highly-coloured canvas mountains." The writer also urged Cody to let the Indians win once in a while, lest they refuse to play any more.[14]

While those at *Punch* poked fun at the Americans, Cody remained steadfast in his goal of winning respect. Early visits by William Gladstone and others helped in this regard, but something momentous occurred when Queen Victoria commanded a performance for herself and friends. They saw standard Wild West show acts, which concluded with the cowboy band playing "God Save the Queen." Victoria met Cody, who, in turn, introduced Annie Oakley, two Indian women with babies, and Red Shirt, chief of the Sioux. Publicly, her highness expressed "her entire satisfaction with all she had seen." On 20 June, the queen returned, bringing with her European royalty in London for the jubilee. The group numbered perhaps three hundred and included kings from Belgium, Denmark, Greece, and Saxony; crown princes from Austria, Germany, and Sweden; and a grand duke from Russia.[15]

Poster art commemorated these royal visits by portraying Cody, Annie Oakley, and others in the troupe at ease with distinguished guests. Posters depicted Buffalo Bill's image surrounded by portraits of kings, queens, grand duchesses, lords, princes, and princesses who had visited the show. In addition, publicity proclaimed that the queen's attendance at the Wild West show marked her first public appearance since the death of Prince Albert. According to American accounts, the exhibition was simply too large to take to Windsor Castle, forcing Victoria to go to the showgrounds. Cody claimed that the queen bowed before the American flag when it passed, and that this constituted the first formal recognition of the Stars and Stripes by a British sovereign since the Declaration of Independence.[16]

An often-repeated story about trading witticisms with royalty enhanced Cody's reputation as a man able to hold his own against anyone. According to this account, Cody asked kings from Belgium, Denmark, Greece, and Saxony and the Prince of Wales to ride in the Deadwood stage. This prompted the prince to joke that a royal assemblage of four kings constituted "four of a kind," a hand hard to beat in poker. Cody retorted that four kings plus the prince serving as a "royal joker" made a royal flush, an unbeatable hand.[17] Such tales, accurate or not, led the public to believe that Cody and his frontier entertainment garnered royal approval and that he acted successfully as an envoy for his country.

Now Cody played two roles—representative frontiersman and cultural ambassador—and moving between them required constantly "jumping from his buckskins into a full-dress suit." He learned, by trial and error, that acceptance as a gentleman required downplaying violence. At first, he discussed the duel with Yellow Hand and displayed the scalp, which sometimes "excited the wonderment of the ladies." However, this did not impress everyone; in fact, some considered such stories and displays "self-puffery."[18] Consequently, newspaper accounts about the scalp abated. Buffalo Bill found that if he wanted to "be treated like a gentleman," he could not act like a gladiator toting grisly trophies.

The Yellow Hand duel disappeared from the program in England, and Cody spoke out against scalping. An English reporter suggested "the introduction of a little scalping" and asked: "Why should not the Indians overcome a party of scouts, and 'raise their hair'? Wigs and scalps are not very expensive, and carmine is decidedly cheap." Buffalo Bill thundered back: "Sham scalping" would not satisfy "gentlemen of this reporter's gory turn of mind. Nothing but a real massacre, with genuine blood flowing and a comfortable array of corpses" would satiate this armchair adventurer's lust for gore. Had this fellow actually been involved in frontier warfare with "red Indians," perhaps "he would not be so zealous for realism."[19] Cody wanted the world to believe that he had a more serious purpose than sensationalism. However, the duel with Yellow Hand would reappear in the program after the show left England.

The Americans won acceptance in England. Cody became the "lion of the London season." The *London Times* called him "the hero of the London season," and affirmed: "he found time to go everywhere, to see everything, and to be seen by all the world." A journalist characterized Cody as "A man of lofty and exalted ideas, refined, in spite of the rough frontier life he has led, he is as courtly and as polished in the society of ladies as some cavalier of the medieval ages." Obviously, foreign travel polished his image. Unassuming Annie Oakley impressed Queen Victoria, the Prince of Wales, and others. From the prince, she received a medal and an autographed picture, and he arranged a match of sharpshooting for her against Grand Duke Michael of Russia, whom she beat easily. Londoners copied her equestrian techniques, sent her flowers, and requested her presence at shooting clubs. She personified simplicity by claiming to be most happy in the rural United States and indicating that modesty prevented her from wearing medals won in shooting matches.[20]

Cowboys and scouts—something new in London—drew attention wherever they went. At first, some worried that jubilee-goers might find these frontiersmen brutish. A reporter observed that "the uninformed nose will be elevated at the word 'cowboy,'" and Cody urged Britons to see more than "uncouth language and grizzly garb" in them. However, reporters warmed quickly to these Americans and explained their dress and style of life and praised their bravery, prowess, and riding and shooting skills. In news accounts they were generally described as men hardened physically by life on the frontier, but perfect gentlemen in refined society. One reporter called them "usually a fine, full-grown specimen of Nature's aristocracy" and "quiet men of gentle manner and speech." Journalists explained that educated men often became cowboys because they needed the challenges and adventures the frontier offered.[21] Calling cowboys educated and "Nature's aristocracy" helped these cowhands shed some of their dime novel roguishness and encouraged those in England's upper classes to look more favorably on them.

Enthusiasm ran so high that Londoners claimed these colorfully dressed Americans as a part of England's extended family. Former Prime Minister William Gladstone visited the Wild West show camp, said that he enjoyed reading American history, and declared: "God Almighty made Englishmen and Americans kinsmen, and they ought to have affections for one another." The *Illustrated London News* urged readers to support the American exhibition and to attend the Wild West show because the United States was "intimately connected with us by social sympathies, by a common language and literature, by ancestral traditions and many centuries of a common history, by much remaining similarity of civil institutions, laws, morals and manners," and other factors.[22]

Some of the British saw reflections of themselves in these people who had settled the New World in precisely the way vigorous Anglo-Saxons should do it—with a combination of prowess and refinement. One reporter wrote approvingly: "men of our own blood . . . tempered and sharpened by more stimulating conditions . . . have achieved in raising a wonderful fabric of modern civilization." Another journalist noted that Americans visiting London provided "a just gratification in seeing what men of our own blood" have done to extend English-style civilization "across the whole breadth of the Western continent." The show's publicity agents exploited this perceived similarity and explained that the show was "an exhibition intended to prove to the center of old world civilization that the vast region of the United States was finally and effectively settled by the English-speaking race."[23]

Such sentiments fit well in Britain, where imperialism was gaining force. Enthusiasm for it sparked sympathy for a show chronicling a kindred nation conquering a continent. Perhaps the Wild West show was evidence that Americans followed Britons' example by spreading their culture across North America. These British, who themselves subjugated other peoples, criticized U.S. Indian policy much less than those of Catlin's day. Queen Victoria spoke for this age by commenting publicly that she enjoyed meeting the show's performers, but confiding in her journal that, while she admired the cowboys, "the painted Indians, with their feathers, & wild dress (very little of it) were rather alarming looking, & they have cruel faces."[24]

As for white cowboys and scouts, the historian Paul Fees suggests that people, like the English, linked these "nature's noblemen" with the "cavalier" and the chivalric past. Their knightly features included individualism, traveling on horseback, colorful and almost armor-like clothing, prowess in warfare, and riding about the countryside performing deeds of valor. The resemblance to Sir Gawain and Ivanhoe was striking. In this view, then, cowboys were important, not because they created a new image, but because they "codified the familiar" by reaffirming old romantic heroes.[25]

The Americans ended their summer season in London on 31 October 1887. The *London Times* reported that the Wild West show complemented the official exhibit, helped to promote kinship between the two nations, and perhaps contributed to the signing of a treaty of arbitration between them. That he might have influenced international relations pleased Cody. Another man with the show concluded that it promoted friendship between Great Britain and its former colony. A poem about Cody in an English newspaper concluded: "You came, you conquered, now you take your leave." About 2.5 million persons had seen the show, making "barrels of money" for its owners. After closing, Cody took a two-week vacation to Italy with his daughter Arta. The Colosseum in Rome interested him because the British press had suggested it as a site for a future show. Meanwhile, these Americans followed Catlin's strategy by touring provincial cities, going first to Birmingham, and opening there on 5 November and remaining for four weeks.[26]

The winter season opened on 17 December at the Manchester race track, where workers constructed the New Colossal Building, an enormous edifice with steam heat and electrical lights. The facility combined the lighting and elaborate sets characteristic of stage performances with the immensity and grandeur of outdoor spectacles. Tiers of seats reaching a height of forty feet, arranged in a crescent shape, held ten thousand persons, and from them, spectators looked down on an enormous stage backed by great panels of scenery. The stage—more an arena with its great earthen floor—would accommodate 250 performers on horseback. The orator Frank Richmond explained the action, and music from the cowboy band dramatized it.[27] In these impressive surroundings, audiences saw "A Depiction of American Pioneer History," an enhanced rendition of the "Drama of Civilization" given at Madison Square Garden in the winter of 1887.

Seven episodes in "A Depiction of American Pioneer History" traced the development of the frontier from the "Primeval Forest, peopled by the Indian and Wild Beasts only," to the triumph of civilization. Native American dances and battles, the landing of pilgrims, the rescue of Captain John Smith by the "beauteous Indian princess, Pocahontas," a buffalo hunt, an immigrant train, a prairie fire, cowboy skills, "Western Girls," the Battle of Little Bighorn, scenes of Deadwood and the coach named for it, and the fury of a hurricane highlighted the program. As in London, Cody busied himself with social obligations and impressed people to the extent that they named three thoroughfares after him: Buffalo, Bill, and Cody Streets. On 1 May 1888, the troupe gave its last indoor performance, proceeded to Hull for a single show, and then boarded the *Persian Monarch* for the trip home.[28]

The group arrived at Staten Island on 20 May 1888, when ten thousand enthusiastic people greeted them. Cody told reporters that "he had nothing but words of the highest praise to speak for the English people," that "he had been honored by royalty and nobility," and that "the whole undertaking had been a great success in every way." More information appeared in a new book: *Story of the Wild West and Camp-fire Chats, by Buffalo Bill, (Hon. W. F. Cody). A Full and Complete History of the Renowned Pioneer Quartette, Boone, Crockett, Carson, and Buffalo Bill . . . Including a Description of Buffalo Bill's Conquests in*

*England with His Wild West Exhibition, Where Royalty from All the European Nations Paid Him a Generous Homage and Made His Wonderful Show the Greatest Success of Modern Times.* The volume, as the title suggested, detailed Cody's time in England. In addition, it underscored his patriotism. He maintained that although the elites of both London and Manchester befriended him, the groups represented different values: London's reflected "long descent" and "the glamours of inherited wealth," while Manchester's leaders were "coal and cotton lords and self-made millionaires." Buffalo Bill said Manchester's productive capitalists were a "sublimer royalty" because their industry, service to humanity, and productiveness reminded him of the American spirit. Cody reassured everyone that he was glad to be home.[29] Like a good ambassador, Cody went abroad, praised his country, won the respect of European leaders, and returned full of accolades for his native land.

During the 1888 season, spent before American audiences, the entertainers emphasized their success abroad and their undaunted patriotism. An 1888 advertisement, for example, encouraged people to "welcome home the typical Americans of Buffalo Bill's Wild West." Perhaps to reaffirm the values espoused in England, they lived in primitive simplicity in the Wild West show camp. When reporters came to his tent, Cody talked about his warm reception in England and conspicuously displayed pictures of Queen Victoria, the Prince of Wales, and the Princess of Wales. Poster art confirmed that this show had pleased European royalty. The program remained basically unchanged, yet still made money. An eleven-week stay at Staten Island, for example, produced profits of $100,000. That Annie Oakley left to join a rival show run by Pawnee Bill concerned Cody and Salsbury; fortunately, she would return to the fold the following season.[30]

The next year, 1889, took Buffalo Bill's Wild West show to a world's fair in Paris called the Exposition Universal to celebrate the centenary of the French Revolution. That Cody would be there pleased the French, and Americans approved of the show going abroad to "delight and instruct" Parisians.[31] The stay at the Exposition Universal followed the pattern established in England of presenting a romanticized view of the West at an international exhibition where crowds sought entertainment. Since Catlin's visit, French politics had normalized, so this visit proved mostly enjoyable.

The Americans located themselves in Neuilly, a suburb of Paris. Securing this site near the exposition involved "great expense," persuading the city government to close two streets, and negotiations with thirty-two different shopkeepers with businesses along those avenues. After this, construction began on grandstands for twenty thousand, workers painted scenery, and a "delightful" Wild

West show camp appeared in the Parc de Neuilly. Bill posters plastered Paris with images of a running buffalo with Cody's likeness in a circle in the center of the animal's body. Emblazoned on the posters was the simple message "*Je viens*" (I am coming). Never before had Parisians seen such an advertising blitz, and some found it offensive. Despite some displeasure, everyone knew the Americans were in town.[32]

This trip to France differed from the one to London. American schoolbooks of the period questioned the wholesomeness, industriousness, morality, and political stability of the French, and other sources contrasted American purity and innocence with French decadence. Reflecting their parent culture, Cody and his troupe approached Paris determined to remain untainted and anticipating differences between themselves and their hosts. For their part, the French perceived the United States—and its frontier, in particular—as a vigorous and "open-ended" society offering freedom, adventure, and opportunity. Enthusiasm for Indians and America's adventure-filled frontier came, in part, from French-language editions of James Fenimore Cooper's works and novels about the American West written by the popular French author Gustave Aimard.[33] So the French and Americans agreed that their nations differed, and much that happened concerning the Wild West show verified their preconceptions.

To handle the language barrier, the Americans hired secretaries, interpreters, and press agents fluent in French, but they did not hire a French-speaking announcer. Frank Richmond, "who couldn't say beans in French" when he arrived, prepared for reading his script "by hollering French at the natives for two hours and a half although he didn't understand a word of what he was saying." This generated conflict at a season-opening, invitation-only affair for "the most noted personages of France," including President Sadi Carnot and his wife, the members of the French cabinet, sundry other French politicians, the social elite, scholars, and the American minister Whitelaw Reid. When Richmond began the show with a harangue about the life of Cody, he butchered the language, "every syllable being hammered out as if with a spade." The audience endured it for a time, then raised a tumult of hoots, shrieks, and pounding of canes and umbrellas on the grandstands. Finally, Richmond abandoned his text, and the show started. Fortunately, the exhibition itself featured crowd-pleasing action, not mastery of the French language.[34]

The incident marked the first of several that would generate conflict abroad. In this case, as in the others, the showmen defended themselves. American reporters called Richmond a natural linguist who spoke the language "with a genuine Parisian accent." Another characterized these French plutocrats as skilled in "fault finding" and said they had "behaved like so many unruly school

children." This journalist asked: did it not take the French Revolution for any
new ideas to "penetrate the French skull"? Since these complainers represented
the jaded leisure classes, Americans should ignore them. After all, how seriously could anyone take a crowd where the men wore patent leather shoes and had
"pearl gray finger tips"? The common people of France would behave better.[35]

After this invitation-only affair, the show opened to the public. Newspaper
advertising provided tantalizing details: it included about 250 persons and an
equal number of animals, visitors could find American food at the show, and
patrons could visit the camp. Cody offered shows of about two-and-a-half hours
twice daily, with evening performances illuminated by an electrical light plant
of two hundred thousand candle power. Single seats were priced similarly to
those for the shows in Great Britain and ranged from one to four francs each.
The total for two-franc seats for a family of four about equaled a day's wages
for a working man. Those wanting to see the show in style could rent boxes for
six or eight persons for forty and forty-five francs, respectively. Well over 25
million saw the Exposition Universal, and a large number of those attended the
Wild West show. In fact, often two or three thousand individuals at a time were
turned away from the sold-out shows. Most reporters lauded the entertainment
as the greatest attraction at the Exposition Universal. The Americans noted
happily that royalty such as the shah of Persia, the imperial family of Russia,
and the Prince of Wales attended shows. Some honored guests, including Queen
Isabella of Spain, even rode in the Deadwood coach.[36]

The official printed program carried a cover in English that read *Buffalo Bill's
Wild West* and inside included standard illustrations and articles translated into
French. The performances themselves differed little from the earlier ones for
American and English audiences. The French accepted the sharpshooting, rugged horsemanship, and bloody battles as valid depictions of the frontier. News
accounts touted the amount of gunpowder exploded in the arena, praised scenes
such as wagon trains going west, called cowboys "forerunners of civilization,"
and said that when Indians attacked, everyone knew "each bullet must hit a man
or it is death and pillage" at the hand of Indians.[37]

The showmen had altered the program somewhat to add appeal for the
French. The cowboy band played "La Marseillaise," the French flag appeared
alongside its American counterpart during the grand entry, and scenes and
peoples illustrated French activities in Canada. Two trappers—Ambrose Lepine
and Maxime Goulet, participants in a pro-French movement in Manitoba called
Reil's Rebellion—appeared in the arena. The printed program explained that
when the rebellion failed, these French Canadians escaped death by fleeing to
the United States and joining the Wild West show. Viewers got a look at an

Eskimo driving a dogsled in one act.[38] While the tricolor, music, and Canadian displays added to the appeal of the show, little specifically French appeared in it.

Buffalo Bill caught nearly everyone's attention. *"Guillaume Bison"* or *"Guillaume le Buffle"* acted as a gracious host. About ninety thousand Americans came to Paris for the exposition, and some found his tent. Buffalo Bill gave a breakfast for seventy-five of the most distinguished visitors, and he and Whitelaw Reid gave short orations. The inventor Thomas A. Edison received special recognition and a standing ovation at a show. The camp also attracted the French. Couples found it chic to marry there and then touch Indian children, an action that supposedly ensured fertility. Buffalo Bill invited commoners and celebrities into his tent and chatted amicably through interpreters with French speakers. Rosa Bonheur, the French artist, visited regularly and painted a romantic rendering of Cody on horseback. She even asked for the head of his horse, Tucker, when that animal died, and took this and other mementos from the Wild West show to adorn the walls of her studio.[39]

The French accepted Buffalo Bill with enthusiasm rarely shown a foreigner because of his "poetic and heroic" reputation and because he looked and acted like a frontier hero. For many, he personified a New World man hardened and made handsome by "physical force and exercise" and a lifetime of subjugating "savage people and ferocious animals."[40] This, along with the plethora of posters with his personal promise of *Je viens* made Buffalo Bill the sole representative of the frontier in the eyes of many in France.

Others in the show attracted attention, too. In statements that tied cowboys to a romantic chivalric tradition, the press heaped praise on the cowboy, calling him an "incomparable cavalier" and explaining that he "lived only for the protection of virtue and the prevention of horse thefts." The French counted six white women in the show: two sharpshooters, Annie Oakley and Lillian Smith; riders Bessie Ferrell, Della Ferrell, and Georgia Duffy; and "Marm Whittaker," who played the wife in the attack on the settlers' cabin. Marm Whittaker's performance drew favorable comments, and her novel American-style sunbonnet attracted considerable attention. Journalists noted the skill of the Ferrell sisters and Lillian Smith, but audiences liked Annie Oakley best. One journalist underscored her prowess by calling her a "young Amazon woman," and another reported that when she or another sharpshooter missed hitting a glass ball, "everyone felt individually grieved."[41]

To a greater degree than in any other nation's, sensuality crept into French accounts of principals in the show. About Buffalo Bill, a reporter rhapsodized: "He is a James Fenimore Cooper type of hero; tall and slim, of irreproachable proportions, his Herculean body is surmounted by a superb head, illuminated by deep set, flashing eyes, and when he appears on his horse, letting his long, shoulder length hair wave in the wind, one experiences an indefinable sensation and one feels oneself transported to another hemisphere." Likewise Annie Oakley set many hearts atwitter, but journalists warned admirers that she preferred guns to suitors.[42]

Such comments probably reinforced the troupe's perception of the French as hedonists and strengthened the Americans' resolve to remain wholesome. Annie Oakley served as a model for American-style simplicity and modesty by expressing preference for a backwoods life to that of an entertainer and wearing simple dresses to social functions. An American reporter in Paris adulated the troupe by contrasting the purity and morality of Wild West show performers with the decadence of Parisians. Even the Europeans respected the men and women in the show for their high moral standards. Ladies could visit the showgrounds and circulate freely among the frontiersmen without concern about unwanted attention, annoyance, or suggestive remarks. By contrast, the journalist saw the French aristocracy as jaded, stubborn, and despicable.[43] The showmen wanted others to "esteem us better," and while in France they added wholesomeness and morality to their list of virtues.

The 102 Indians in the American camp fascinated Parisians. Queen Victoria had found them uncouth, underdressed, and a bit scary; but the French viewed them as romantically as they had in Catlin's day because of enthusiasm for the works of James Fenimore Cooper, a continuing fascination with "noble savages," reports that the warriors were among the fiercest in the United States, sympathy for them as "vanishing Americans," and antipathy for the spread of Anglo-Saxon civilization across the globe. When the artist Rosa Bonheur lunched with Buffalo Bill, Indians, and some of the other performers, she waxed philosophically about what she saw: the Indians represented humanity's ancestry, and Cody stood for civilization, and the two dining together indicated that savagery and civilization had made peace in the United States. Others shared her enthusiasm and called the show the "most marvelous ethnological exposition that anyone has ever seen." Ethnologists visited the showgrounds, measured the skulls of Native Americans, and recorded other physiographic features to advance knowledge about primitive peoples.[44]

Anything the Native Americans did made the newspapers. It flattered the French, for example, that they climbed to the top of the Eiffel Tower. Reports from the United States that the Indian commissioner might stop allowing them to go abroad caused a writer to lament: "Goodbye feathered warriors who gave us so much joy during our childhood. Goodbye legendary heroes of Fenimore

Cooper and Gustave Aymard." When Red Shirt and his wife became parents
of a baby boy, the French press celebrated the event and expressed pride that
the child would be "Parisian in part." In a journalist's opinion, Red Shirt's wife
typified the hardihood of Indian women, who delivered babies with less difficul-
ty than Europeans or Americans. To substantiate this, the press reported that
shortly after the earlier birth of a baby in the United States, the mother walked
a hundred miles.[45]

Despite their enthusiasm for Native Americans, Parisians applauded their
defeat and any other acts during which blood flowed freely. While in England,
Cody railed against those who wanted to see scalping. Now, in October 1889,
he reintroduced the duel with Yellow Hand. Newspaper accounts detailed the
event and one reporter commented: "The act is well played, and the vast audiences are daily thrilled by its actuality." The press reported that Buffalo Bill
brought the actual scalp of Yellow Hand with him on his trip to Paris, kept it
hanging in his room, and used the identical bowie knife from the duel every
day in its reenactment. Another popular, sensational act demonstrated the hanging of a horse thief. In it, a deserter from the U.S. Army steals a horse from a
sleeping cowboy, who, along with his companions, captures the culprit. "Then
they stretch him up by a rope, and when his body has been riddled with balls
they ride away." Cavalrymen searching for the deserter find the bullet-riddled
body, cut it down, and return to the fort with it.[46]

In England, Buffalo Bill had personified propriety, but perhaps he sensed a
different mood in France. As a people, the French believed that they needed to
strengthen and invigorate themselves, in part because of lingering embarrass-
ment from their defeat in the Franco-Prussian war (1870–71). In addition, the
nation reflected a mood of growing militarism in continental Europe, as well
as admiration for athleticism and "physical culture." Consequently, the French
saw the Wild West show as an object lesson in physical force, exercise, and *la
jeunesse,* a phrase describing fresh demeanor and youthful vigor. French soldiers
attended regularly to observe and learn from demonstrations in the arena.
Moreover, journalists admonished the public for becoming soft and urged them
to attend the show to foster appreciation for physical exercise, discipline, horsemanship, camping outdoors, and sharpshooting—all necessary in warfare.[47]

The show inspired some. Three young boys from respectable families ran away
from home, fled to Bois de Boulogne (the largest park in Paris), made a tent
from bedsheets, and pilfered sardines, fruit, chocolate, wine, and liquor from
local merchants to emulate the "nomadic life of the American West." One boy
stood guard at night with a bayonet attached to a broomstick. Most other youngsters simply settled for finding bits of rope and lassoing their siblings. The show

"seduced" adults and stimulated interest in the American West, causing fairgoers
to seek books and information about it and buy Indian relics, cowboy hats, and
American-style saddles. Social trendsetters clamored for Cody's attention. The
French liked the Native Americans so much that a stray feather or trinket from
a costume became a prized possession. One reporter even suggested that the
big western hats in the show and the patterns and color combinations of paint
worn by the Indians could inspire fashion trends in Paris.[48]

After their stint in France, the Americans could point to indicators of success, such as large crowds and the approval of royalty. While England had offered themes of commonality, in France the Americans mostly contrasted themselves with the French. Americans emerged from the Exposition Universal
viewing themselves as moral and upright, particularly when compared with
France's idle and effeminate aristocracy. By defending their announcer's less-
than-perfect French, the Americans proved that, when provoked, they would
defend themselves. In Paris, the showmen kept "the raw material of America"
pretty raw by exploiting the bloodiness of the frontier experience and highlight-
ing Americans as more vigorous, more hardened, and more prepared for war
than the French. In doing all this, they amplified notions about Americans
beyond those fashioned in England and prepared themselves for touring more
of continental Europe.

At the end of the stay in Paris, Cody offered the president of France a cus-
tom-made American lamp valued at £250. The ornate piece must have been
quite a sight. The nine-foot lamp was fashioned of carved brass resting on a
"plate of Mexican onyx." Mounted on the lamp was the head of a bison, killed
on the Plains by Cody himself. A lampshade of scarlet silk covered with green
tulle and ornamented with embroidered brightly colored flowers topped the
piece. President Carnot, whose predecessor had been embarrassed by corruption in the palace, refused it, saying he did not accept gifts of any kind. The
refusal "chagrined" Cody, who had apparently failed to familiarize himself with
the president's well-known conservative tastes. These Americans had opened
their tour with their orator "butchering" the native language, and they departed indignantly because a French leader had refused a tasteless gift. Apparently,
these showmen had learned nothing about the nuances of French culture during their stay in Paris.[49]

While Cody wrapped up things in Paris, Salsbury arranged for the show to
visit other places, including Lyons, Marseilles, and Barcelona. The troupe visited Spain during the six-week holiday season, opening in Barcelona on 21
December 1889. Little impressed them there, perhaps because Americans of this

period typically did not take Spain seriously. Instead of achievements, the show
members saw corruption and ignorance. In Spain, they said they received a lot
of counterfeit money, but since their banks regularly dealt in bogus currencies,
Americans disposed of it easily. In speaking of this incident and others, a representative for the Wild West show explained: "Of course one has to excuse a
great deal, as they have not much education." In this man's view, Americans
were better educated, more honest, but still shrewd enough to handle any situation in Spain. Christopher Columbus was an obvious link between the nations, so Cody and Salsbury publicized that he had sailed from Spain for the
New World and now, nearly four centuries later, Cody returned from there.
Photographs of Indians in front of a statue of Columbus made news. According to one account, an Indian man contemplated the statue for a moment and
then said in English: "It was a damned bad day for us when he discovered
America."[50]

Ten thousand spectators saw the first performance, but an outbreak of influenza resulted in a quarantine of Barcelona, and fear of the disease cut attendance to handfuls. Members of the show succumbed: Annie Oakley sick-
ened for a time, and Frank Richmond was so weakened by the disease that he
contracted pneumonia and later died. In addition to influenza, a misunder-
standing soured relations between the Americans and Spaniards. When a man
inquired about the ferocity of steers in the Wild West show, Buffalo Bill down-
played the danger. The press reported that Cody claimed the bulls were not
dangerous and this enraged the Spanish, who assumed Cody was maligning
bulls and denigrating bullfighting. Cody argued that his remarks had been
misinterpreted.[51] However, his attitude would change; during the Spanish-
American War, Cody would claim that he had intentionally lambasted Spain's
national sport.

From Barcelona, the troupe traveled to Italy for a tour that lasted from 28
January to 16 April 1890 and included performances in Naples, Rome, Florence,
Bologna, Milan, and Verona. The Americans enjoyed less success here than in
England and Paris. Cody would learn that ambassadorship became difficult in
countries where hosts and guests regarded each other warily. Some animosity
originated with the Wild West show troupe, who reflected attitudes prevalent
in the late nineteenth century, when many Americans believed that poverty and
indolence characterized southern Europeans. Of course, Americans admired
Italy's art, music, and antiquity. In this age of the "grand tour" of Europe,
Americans dutifully stopped in Italy because it represented the quintessence of
Old World culture.[52] Those in the Wild West show responded to Italy in pre-

dictable ways: they saw all the sights, alternately praised and criticized the nation's antiquity, bemoaned its social conditions, and peppered their remarks with a dose of American cockiness.

Italy differed from England and France, lacking those nations' industry and prosperity and facing problems with national unity and political radicalism. Italians had less romantic views of the United States and did not celebrate its accomplishments. In fact, many Italians knew little about the United States. A report that George Washington had made Cody a colonel dismayed an American journalist and prompted him to say that this typified a "prevailing ignorance concerning America." Italians who read about the United States usually took their perceptions from the fiction of James Fenimore Cooper, Mark Twain, Mayne Reid, Bret Harte, Amédée Archard, and Gustave Aimard.[53]

In Italy, publicists prepared the way for the show by blanketing cities with colorful posters and filling newspapers with advertisements and articles, sometimes accompanied by action-filled illustrations taken from printed programs. When the show train arrived, crowds gathered and watched the unloading and erection of the camp. The size of the show—its one hundred Indians, one hundred other performers, and two hundred animals—fascinated the press. Admission remained affordable, at one, two, three, and five liras. The seventeen-act program featured standard fare, which publicity likened to "a real page of history" and "an ethnological study." At most shows, people applauded enthusiastically, and women waved handkerchiefs and threw candy to the performers. The Italians particularly enjoyed watching Indians participating in the grand entry and performing their dances, Annie Oakley's shooting, Buck Taylor and "Cowboy Fun," the pony express, and attacks on the immigrant train and the Deadwood stage. Italians noted the western women, Marm Whittaker, Georgia Duffy, and Della Ferrell. Before walking through the Wild West show camp, many Italians purchased something novel—a bag of American popcorn. It pleased the troupe that prominent Italians and other dignitaries found their way to the show.[54]

Italians celebrated Buffalo Bill in particular. Newspaper accounts mentioned him by name, indicated that audiences applauded him, described his life in glowing terms, and often printed his picture. Using illustrations such as the duel with Yellow Hand, journalists reported that he had "risked his life a hundred times on the Prairie." They noted *"Boofela"* or *"Buffa Bill's"* attractiveness to women in reports that ranged from claiming that "dark-eyed Bolognese beauties" found him the "handsomest man ever seen here" to a cartoon in which two women talked as they passed a poster bearing his likeness. In this, one woman commented on his handsomeness and added that he domesticated wild animals and made them "sweet as lambs." To this, her companion responded that she would send her husband to see him. While many accounts mentioned Cody's handsomeness, Italian comments lacked the sensuality of those in France.[55]

Most who met Buffalo Bill liked him. They noted the elegance of his tent and that he kept cherished objects there, such as a gold cup from the Grand Duke Alexis, a picture of Rosa Bonheur, and a photograph of Indians before Mt. Vesuvius. Italian dignitaries invited him to their gatherings, including a "grand reception" given by Count Primoli for Prince Jerome Napoleon. A reporter commented that this man who impressed the Roman elite deserved more respect at home.[56]

More than in any other country, the Wild West show troupe acted like tourists, visiting the Pantheon, numerous basilicas and shrines, the Colosseum, and Mt. Vesuvius and taking a gondola tour of Venice. Members of the American press followed the sightseeing carefully and reported details for the folks back home. The showmen commemorated their travels with poster art depicting them near Vesuvius, in the Colosseum, at the Vatican, and in gondolas. Indians participated in many of these activities, and in addition, placed a wreath at the grave of Victor Emmanuel in the Pantheon and took the sacrament at churches.[57]

A blessing by Pope Leo XIII generated considerable publicity. Cody requested a private audience for the troupe; however, the pope deemed the company too large for this and instead invited them to join the crowd on 3 March 1890 in the celebration of the twelfth anniversary of his coronation. Picking out the Americans there was not difficult. Eschewing swallowtail coats, they appeared as in the arena—Indians "in full war paint and their sleek skins were dazzling with every hue of the rainbow" and cowboys "spattered with mud and picturesque beyond description." The pope stopped before the troupe, and they presented him with a cushion bearing the pontifical arms. The splendor impressed the Native Americans, who fell to their knees and received the pope's blessing. The fact that the only Indian to miss the ceremony died that night added import for them. The visit was "perhaps the very acme of William F. Cody's (Buffalo Bill's) honors." He and his troupe had gotten Leo XIII's blessing and received much publicity—all while wearing frontier garb. A reporter writing for a French newspaper wondered whether "curiosity, religion, or business" prompted the visit, but added that whatever the motivation, P. T. Barnum could not have done it better.[58]

Newspapers informed readers that Buffalo Bill was a Catholic, as were some of the cowboys and almost half of the Indians. About the papal visit, one reporter noted that Buffalo Bill "clinched the matter by saying that he had been the means of conversion of several of the heathen Apaches, Nez Percé's and other native Americans in his Wild West." The bemused writer, perhaps realizing that no Apaches or Nez Percés traveled with the show, said that he wanted to rush this information about "Bison William" into print to dispel ignorance of his "missionary line" in the English-speaking world. If Cody was really a Catholic, this information had been kept secret too. Interestingly, no one mentioned that Cody's wife, Louisa, received her education in a convent.[59]

In addition to professing Catholicism, the entertainers did other things to win support in Italy. A *vaquero* carried the Italian flag during the grand entry, and the cowboy band played the royal march. Cody designated the "Roman aristocracy" as "great lovers of horses and sport" who really understood the show and appreciated it so much that they sat through entire performances in rainstorms. He said that "without exception, we had a better class of people at Rome than in any city we have visited." When Americans and Italians in the prestigious Florence Club feted him, he said all the right things. After a banquet of "turtle soup, salmon, and York ham" washed down with champagne, Pauillac, and other fine wines, the crowd toasted the visiting American and shouted: "hip, hip, hip, hurrah." Cody responded with a short speech in which he explained that rains in Rome had made for soggy performances and mud-covered "trappings and equipment." However, he delayed cleaning them because the mud represented "a bit of the Eternal City."[60]

While such public pronouncements flattered the Italians, the Americans often glorified themselves by using Italians as bad examples. Cody praised the "Eternal City," but those in the show sometimes interpreted the age of Italy negatively by saying that it represented "hoary antiquity," while the United States embodied "bounding youth." The prospect of giving a Wild West show in the Colosseum intrigued Cody, but he pronounced it too dilapidated and too small. A *New York Times* reporter compared cowboys to gladiators of old and suggested that the Wild West show revived the original purpose of the Colosseum by glorifying combat and testing the prowess of people against animals, in this case, "American bison" and the "Texas steer." Perhaps Americans invigorated this old nation, because one reporter observed: "All the excitement of Rome of ancient days seems to have been aroused here by the Wild West troupe." Cody claimed that the American entertainment recaptured the vigor and excitement lost to the Italians since the glories of the Roman Empire: "The Italians were delighted with the show. They said they had not seen so great an excitement in Rome since the days of Titus."[61]

In the Americans' view, Italy's prosperity had disappeared along with its vigor. Cody contrasted the extremes of wealth and poverty in continental Europe with American abundance. To illustrate this, he commented on the small denominations of European coins, including one worth one-fifth of an American cent. According to Cody, in the American West the quarter dollar was the smallest coin generally circulated and westerners called it a "bit." However, that "bit" was worth 135 times as much as the Italian one. He asked, if westerners called twenty-five cents a "bit," "What would the boys call this?"[62] His point, of course, was that Italians must be very poor.

Life in the Wild West show camp also differentiated Italians from Americans. An Italian reporter compared the camp to scenes from the works of Bret Harte, Mark Twain, and James Fenimore Cooper. A spokesman for the show explained that Westerners "live here just as they do on their native prairies" and that "modern improvements are just so many obstacles to their ideas of comfort." He added: "They prefer to camp out wherever they go, Europe or no Europe." There the troupe ate "the identical fare of the Western ranch," such as beef, pork, beans, and potatoes. Rich and exotic European cuisine offended the western palate; indeed, "sad experience had taught the managers that it was better to make no innovation in the accustomed menu" because European food made the Indians sick. Such remarks made good publicity, but privately the troupe enjoyed Europe's refinements. Annie Oakley and some of the Native American women lived in hotels for a part of the stay in Verona, and several white performers in the Wild West show carried with them fine gowns purchased in Paris.[63]

Some of the Indians complained about Italians. Small boys followed them through the streets, mocked them, and, according to the Sioux Rocky Bear: "Everyone holds out his hand for money here." The Sioux found Italian tobacco so repugnant that they threw it on the ground. After performances, the Indians fled to their tepees and closed the flaps to avoid the crowds who came into camp to touch them, pinch them, and pull their hair to make certain that it was real. Rocky Bear consoled the others with the observation that ruins filled this country, which obviously signalled its decrepitude. Moreover, those troublesome boys would grow old and die.[64]

Other incidents aggravated the Americans. In Rome, the entertainers discovered that the "wily" Italians had passed many "spurious tickets," so Cody protested, but got no satisfaction. In fact, one report said that the cleverness of the counterfeiter impressed the magistrate more than the showman's complaint. Also, Florentine officials, mostly in the city's police department, hounded the show. They weighed each of the buffaloes and taxed them as food items, stopped a performance because the rope barrier between the arena and seats might offer insufficient protection for spectators, and suspended another because the number of tickets sold exceeded seating capacity. However, less zealous officials helped rectify each of these annoyances.[65]

Italians complained in kind about their guests. They packed crowds of eight and ten thousand into seating designed for five thousand. The Americans did not hire enough people to direct traffic and oversee parking to end the problem of a nearly impenetrable tangle of carriages on the showgrounds. Petty and unreasonable complaints surfaced: the Indians wore faded costumes, looked poor, and brought ugly women. The shooting and riding were unexceptional. An actor would better portray Buffalo Bill and a first-rate director would improve the production. Perhaps, too, these Americans received preferential treatment and made too much money. In Bologna, Cody's show paid only five hundred liras for eight days' rental of showgrounds. No Italian company could have tendered such a deal. The press noted that the show made twenty thousand liras in Bologna and fifty thousand in Florence. A cartoonist captured the antipathy with a depiction of a dour Buffalo Bill seated on a chianti bottle, which served him as a rocking horse. According to the caption under it, Florentines had given this man fifty thousand liras in three days, but these ticket holders would not have contributed more than one thousand liras for a "worthy" project like building houses for the poor.[66]

A reporter in Verona said cowboys and Indians deserved no one's respect. Of "independent, warlike, and of unsettled temperament," the slightest provocation prompted Indians to "destroy everything with fire and arms" and "commit any atrocity." As proof, the author listed gruesome tortures practiced by Native Americans. Further, white people's arrival on the Plains exacerbated bloodshed in events such as the slaughtering of six hundred Indians at Sand Creek in Colorado by Colonel John M. Chivington's troops and the massacre of General George Armstrong Custer and his soldiers by Sitting Bull and his followers. According to this reporter Indians eventually lost the struggle and sunk to "vulgar drunkards" who beat and sometimes killed their wives. Cowboys herded cattle, worked for pittances, subsisted on a diet of salted pork and moldy flour, and often came from the ranks of the irresponsible and unemployed. Many had no choice but to accept these miserable conditions because they were debtors and fugitives from the law.[67]

An account from Milan listed a litany of complaints: Why did the Americans plaster everything with their posters and sell more tickets than the arena would hold? Why should Italians have to endure the cowboy band's "barbaric" rendition of Italian music? The reputedly ferocious buffalo behaved like lambs. Who could muster excitement for cowboys picking up objects from the ground while riding a horse? The broncos did not buck much, and American lasso work impressed no one. The most interesting thing about the act featuring the Deadwood stage was watching to see if the rickety coach would disintegrate into rubble before the scene ended. Cody came to town with nothing more than a circus, and all nations had these. About him, the fellow wrote: "Buffalo Bill may have tamed Black Heart, Yellow Hand, Red Nose, Crooked Mouth, or Dirty Face. He may have won against the Sioux. He may have knocked down a hundred others; fine and dandy, but he has nothing more or better than one of the brave directors of the equestrian companies." Those wanting to see a Wild West show should patronize Mariani's Equestrian Company, an Italian group that reproduced the American entertainment in Rome.[68]

Two incidents in Italy—both involving bronco riding—created more ill will. One began when Duke Don Ontorio Huzog of Sermone declared that no one could ride the wild horses on his estate, and the cowboys from the show accepted this as a challenge. A judge moved to stop the showdown because of possible danger to spectators, but this publicized the event even more. While stands and sturdy wooden barriers went up, people debated the outcome of the event, asked if one or more of the Americans might die, and backed their opinions with bets. Before a cheering crowd of about twenty thousand, the cowboys rode the animals, despite pouring rain. Then some Italians asked: could some of our *buttari* return at a later time and ride Wild West show buckers? James Creelman, an American not connected with the show, stirred emotions by offering one hundred dollars to any Italian who could ride a bronco for five minutes. At least one Italian rode an American horse, Jubilee, after a lengthy struggle. When time expired, Cody stopped further efforts, causing spectators to hiss and boo.[69]

A propaganda war erupted between some Italian- and English-language newspapers. Each contingent charged the other with acting unfairly and reneging on bets. American and English sources claimed that the cowboys rode the animals quickly (five to thirty minutes) and that the Italians failed or succeeded only after excessive amounts of time (thirty minutes to one hour and fifty minutes). The Italians said that their *buttari* performed well. Each side charged the other with mistreating the horses. An Italian reporter protested the Americans' ruthless horse-taming methods, and an English-language paper reported that the Italian riders used chains and "brutal cruelty." One American said that the *buttari* stuck iron rods down the horses' windpipes to prevent them from arching their necks and bucking with their usual vigor. This, according to a man with the show, "nearly killed two of our horses," and even then the Italians failed to stay atop them.[70]

The incident prompted some Italians to call Buffalo Bill "a buffoon, a cheat, and a swindler" who refused to pay his "debts of honour." Others saw him as a loudmouthed American who bragged about the superiority of cowboys. A reporter from Florence retorted that the Wild West show folks had created a "fiasco," that Buffalo Bill had lost a bet and had been humiliated, and that he should refrain from saying stupid things. In the United States, the *New York World* published a laudatory poem entitled "Buffalo Bill's Riders" and another journalist called the event "well worth beholding" and claimed "the accomplishments of the gladiator sink into insignificance when compared with the feats of the American cowboy." He concluded that the Wild West show performers "would mount and ride one of those gladiators as easily as he conquered Sermoneta's brutes." Those in the show propagated their version of the event in printed programs for a number of years.[71]

The second acrimonious incident also involved bronco riding. When William Badini, a rider for the Mariani organization that copied the Buffalo Bill show, appeared as a spectator, Nate Salsbury asked if anyone in the crowd wished to ride a bucker. When Badini did not volunteer, Salsbury singled him out and challenged him to attempt it. Badini replied that he had already done this, so repeating it was pointless. Then Salsbury offered to bet half the day's gate receipts that he could not do it, and still Badini refused.

Imitators and impostors plagued the Americans. An Italian who called himself *Buffalora Bill* also patterned a Wild West show after the American one.[72] Hostile reviews, the actions of Badini, and "*Buffalora Bill*" all indicated the same thing: Italians believed they could perform Western feats as well as the visiting Americans.

Their experiences in Spain and Italy differed from those in England and France. Because they encountered less industrialization than in much of northern Europe, Spaniards and Italians cared little about the Wild West show's reproduction of life in the pre-industrial past. For their part, Americans saw these Europeans as backward, poor, undereducated, and untrustworthy. In such surroundings, those in the show turned European attributes such as antiquity into foils to promote themselves as youthful, vigorous, prosperous, and honest. The Spanish and Italians saw offending braggadocio in these Americans who said bulls were mild mannered, proclaimed themselves the world's greatest riders, and bragged about their nation's accomplishments.

From Verona, the Wild West show moved to Munich, where it opened on 19 April 1890, then went to Vienna, and finally returned to Germany, where it played in Dresden, Leipzig (with a contingent in Magdeburg), Hanover, Braunschweig, Berlin, Hamburg, Bremen, Cologne, Dusseldorf, Frankfurt, Stuttgart, and finally Strasbourg, where a heavy snow in late October sent the company into winter quarters. The entertainers enjoyed success, except in Vienna, where only about fifteen hundred persons attended, a number that did not pay expenses.[73] The showmen discussed an excursion to St. Petersburg, but did not go.

Cody reflected the perception of Germans that prevailed in the United States by saying that he admired the order, respectability, and honesty of his audiences. Americans grew up with schoolbooks that characterized Germans as industrious, thrifty, mechanically inclined, and trustworthy. Americans associated Germany with Anglo-Saxon and Teutonic hardihood, the beginnings of democracy, and philosophy and education, which attracted American scholars to German universities. Many Americans believed that the great numbers of Germans who immigrated to the United States in the midnineteenth century had become good and industrious citizens. Only minor reservations about German Americans remained: a tendency to retain their language and culture, sometimes remain Catholic, congregate in saloons, and drink beer on Sunday. Those in the Wild West show did not condemn enthusiasm for beer; in fact, in Germany they endeavored to prevent good brews from going to waste.[74]

Conditions in Germany favored the Wild West show's visit. The novels of James Fenimore Cooper, Bret Harte, Mayne Reid, Gustave Aimard, and Karl May fanned enthusiasm for the American West, and Germans knew about Buffalo Bill's exploits on the Plains and his success in Europe. In addition, Germany's zeitgeist set a mood of acceptance for the show. In 1890, Germany and Austria industrialized rapidly and generally enjoyed prosperity, but modernization made many people nervous and some felt they suffered from overcivilization. This was not the frontier anxiety found in the United States, but their nations teetered between an old agrarian way of life and a modern industrial one; consequently, many people looked nostalgically to things romantic and historical. In a climate of neo-romanticism, enthusiasm for the "uncivilized" flourished, and many regarded former ages as somehow more wholesome and comfortable than their own.[75]

The Wild West show, with its vigorous depictions of pursuits in a romantic place called the American frontier, benefited from these circumstances. An Austrian journalist concluded that the show captured a fresh and virile kind of "Romanticism" that made the European variety seem "faded" by comparison. He said that the show brought to life scenes from the works of Bret Harte and reenactments of struggle on the frontier that everyone found irresistible. This stay for the Americans, then, differed significantly from those in England and France, where world's fairs championed progress. In Austria and Germany, few mentioned American progress; instead, "Romantic," "romantically," and "nature's men" appeared regularly in descriptions of the show, as did mention of the demise of Indians and buffalo.[76] George Catlin would have responded favorably to much that these Austrians and Germans said.

While the Wild West show fed a desire for the romantic, efficiency in its operation also attracted attention. Germans admired the Americans' ability to load and unload railroad cars quickly, set up and dismantle camp effectively, feed large numbers of people and animals, and transform an unoccupied area into a city "with astonishing rapidity." One reporter commented that this almost instantaneous erection of a tent city reproduced, in microcosm, America's transformation of the West from wilderness to civilization. Masterful use of railroads to transport themselves, animals, and mountains of supplies interested the Germans because they knew that Americans had learned to use railroads for military purposes during its Civil War. Journalists and military officers watched and took notes on every aspect of camp life—the details of unloading, the kitchen facilities, the positions of workers, and the time everything took. How much the Germans learned became evident during World War I.[77]

The showmen used their standard techniques to get attention, ingratiate themselves, and make money. Germans noted the plethora of posters, variously described as "truly American advertisements," "adventuresome representations in words and pictures," and "giant posters and all forms of advertising." Newspapers often devoted front-page coverage to the show, reproducing illustrations and copy from programs. Other factors helped win acceptance: rib roast breakfasts, the Wild West show camp, a program like that given for other Europeans, royal visitors, ethnological features, and regional flags, such as those of Saxony in the arena in Dresden and that of Bavaria in Munich. Affordable admission prices of one, two, or three marks corresponded roughly to prices in the United States. In both cases, taking a family of four to the show cost about the daily wage of a working person. Light for nighttime performances, refreshments at the "American drink stand" and "cigarette temple," references to the many Germans who had migrated to America's Far West, and other Wild West show staples ensured the success of the show. As in other countries, sportsmen and soldiers found the show particularly appealing.[78]

Cody met with skepticism because Dr. W. F. Carver, his old partner, preceded him in Vienna and Berlin with a mediocre entertainment called "Wild America." Buffalo Bill, however, won over the doubters with a show dubbed "true to nature" that brought to life "all those dreams about the American West." Attendance ranged from fifteen hundred in Vienna to five thousand enthusiastic persons in Munich, audiences much smaller than those in London and Paris.[79]

To the Germans, "*Büffel-Wilhelm*" was a romantic hero whose appearance in the arena brought "roaring applause." They boasted that Germany accorded him the warmest welcome in continental Europe. In *Büffel-Wilhelm,* many Germans saw James Fenimore Cooper's Leatherstocking. Others praised his rugged demeanor. One journalist rhapsodized: "His exterior appearance alone evidences the boldness, defiance of death, the courage and resoluteness of this weather-hardened American." Another praised his muscular body and described him as a "picture of manlihood in its fullest form." Germans looked to the past for comparisons, saying he resembled a knight, and that his reenactment of the duel with Yellow Hand revived combat like that of "Homeric heroes."[80] Cody, who had eschewed his dime novel background in England, found that Germans liked gladiatorial combat.

In cowboys and western women, Germans saw hardihood almost as exceptional as Cody's. Their colorful costumes and riding skills produced favorable comment, but the image of "natural" and "untamed" men and women appealed most to Germans. A journalist explained that these individuals "came from the plains with no abundance of discipline" and called them "two legged lions and tigers." Another writer said they were refugees from regimentation—people who found it impossible to live in settled areas and had fled to the West. These freedom-loving individuals knew nothing of comfort, lived in their saddles, always carried rifles and revolvers, and faced "constant struggle."[81]

Five western females, variously called "lady riders," "squatter-women," "spirited Amazons," and "American backwoods women," received praise because they could "ride and shoot in an exceptional manner." An advertisement announced that some "female riders" would appear on "wild horses," a statement suggesting they rode bucking broncos. Also, in one act, a woman played the banjo and sang "sentimental melodies." Most accolades went to Annie Oakley, however. One German writer called her "a true Nimrod in petticoats."[82]

Many Germans found Indians irresistible for similar reasons. Scalping, war making, their frightening appearance, dances, and horsemanship enchanted Germans. Those connected with the show promoted Indians as warlike people by referring to their language as "scalp language" and presenting the Yellow Hand duel as a major attraction. The idea that they, along with the buffalo that sustained them, would vanish because of the advance of settlers added appeal. One man criticized the show for celebrating this "battle of annihilation," and another charged the Wild West show with demonstrating the "full bestiality of racial war."[83]

In these surroundings, a reporter in Berlin asked Buffalo Bill a series of leading questions about Indians. "Is the best Indian a dead Indian?" "Are not squaws treated like slaves?" Exactly what happened in the Yellow Hand duel? The interrogation riled Cody, and he defended Native Americans vigorously. He called their character the "most worthy and most respectable to be found in the world" and praised them as a deeply religious group. They were so trustworthy that their society required no prisons and no locks on their doors. The scout expressed regret for leading so many campaigns against them, calling them the "original Americans" and defending their right to oppose a government that systematically dispossessed them. Cody announced that injustice prevailed in the United States, where Indians became "wanderers in their home land." Rocky Bear corroborated Cody's remarks before the Munich Anthropological Society. In an emotional speech, the Sioux upheld his people's right to defend themselves and proclaimed: "The American people have done us a great injustice."[84] Had he been there, George Catlin would have nodded his approval.

Germans and Austrians welcomed Indians wherever they appeared, including taverns and inns, where Indians became a "great friend of firewater." At the highly publicized rib roast breakfasts, Indians smoked cigars, drank along with the others, and offered "colorful toasts," even though show policy forbade Indians from drinking alcohol.[85] While Buffalo Bill did not condone drunkenness among Indians, he did attend the rib roast dinners, and newspaper articles about Native Americans in taverns and inns appeared so frequently that Cody and others in the show must have known about their activities. Perhaps Cody did everything possible to stop it or perhaps his attitude reflected that of George Catlin, who, despite his hatred of alcohol's influence on Indians, had allowed his charges to enjoy a tankard of ale after performances.

The stay in Germany did bring problems. A Sioux named Wounds One jumped from a moving train car near Braunschweig, crushed an arm and a leg, and died from his injuries. The funeral services, conducted by a Sioux chief, attracted a crowd of people. In another incident, some Indians complained of "bad handling," saying, for example, that accommodations for the trip to Europe were cramped "between or middle deck" quarters. The year 1889 brought five other Indian deaths: Uses the Sword died during a Wild West show performance and disease claimed four. Buffalo Bill sent five others who were ill back to the United States. Once there, one of them, Kills Plenty, died, and another, White Horse, complained to the press about treatment abroad. The *New York Herald* reported this and indicated that one-third of the Indians in the show had "straggled" home.[86]

Adding to the difficulties, Thomas Jefferson Morgan became commissioner of Indian Affairs. A forceful man of the Christian-humanitarian tradition, he opposed any vestiges of "savage" culture among Indians, as well as civilized vices like drinking and smoking cigars. Under his guidance, he foresaw the day when Native Americans would be educated, peaceful, and productive proponents of the Protestant ethic. Wild West shows, in his view, denigrated Indians because they offered only "temporary" employment, brought Indians "into association with some of the worst elements of society," and depicted them as "incapable of civilization." In short, the process enriched showmen, exploited Indians, and perpetuated negative stereotypes, so Morgan resolved to remove Indians from Wild West shows. He asserted his authority by preparing a list of questions for Cody and demanding documentary proof that the Native Americans were well treated. He made all this very formal by having the American consul general in Berlin deliver the paperwork.[87]

Cody, Salsbury, and the other show organizers defended themselves against the charges. Native Americans should be able to educate others about their own cultures. Moreover, the Wild West show experience benefited them by providing employment, travel, and exposure to white culture. Such experiences enabled Indians to return to their peoples with this new knowledge. As for sentimentalists and bureaucrats such as Morgan, Cody called them "cranks" and woefully ignorant about Indians. He also reminded Morgan the he had nearly started a war by keeping Indians "cooped up on their reservations" and refusing to let them keep the hides of cattle butchered there. Cody and Salsbury invited the consul general, the secretary of the delegation at Berlin, and the consul of Hamburg to visit the camp and see the Native Americans for themselves. After the inspection, these men reported that the Indians were well, and the *New York Herald* printed a retraction of its earlier story in its Paris edition. With no winter season in Germany, Cody and Burke took some Indians back to the United States as living proof that they were healthy and happy. There, show Indians refuted all charges by claiming they were well fed, happy, and, contrary to some reports, they never appeared naked in the arena.[88]

The return occurred when many anticipated a great Sioux uprising. Attention focused on a volatile situation in South Dakota, where Sioux performed the "Ghost Dance," a revitalization movement Native Americans believed would make game return, European Americans disappear, and ancestors rejoin those living on earth for an Indian millennium. At Standing Rock Agency, the Sioux danced and announced they would defend their right to do so. Commissioner Morgan remained determined to stop the ceremonies. Rumored to be at the center of the conflict was Sitting Bull.[89]

The veteran Indian fighter Major General Nelson A. Miles contacted Cody as soon as he reached the United States and gave him a card inscribed with a succinct message: "You are hereby authorized to secure the person of Sitting Bull and deliver him to the nearest Commanding Officer of U.S. Troops, taking a receipt and reporting your action." Cody headed for the Standing Rock Agency, leaving John Burke to take the Indians to Washington, D.C., and argue the show's case. Three companions who had frontier and Wild West show experience accompanied Cody: Dr. David Franklin "White Beaver" Powell, the former pony express rider Robert "Pony Bob" Haslam, and G. W. Chadwick. Dubious about Cody's involvement, officials at Standing Rock Agency detained him until word came from President Benjamin Harrison prohibiting Buffalo Bill from seeing Sitting Bull. Future Wild West show publicity would speculate that if Cody had reached the Sioux shaman, tragedy might have been averted.[90]

In these troubled and confused times, the Sioux debated the Ghost Dance among themselves, and U.S. troops nearby exacerbated matters. Sitting Bull died on 15 December 1890 in a shoot-out between his supporters and the Indian police. A much larger conflict occurred on 29 December 1890, when U.S. soldiers slaughtered Indians at Wounded Knee. While Cody did not participate directly in either event, a remnant of the Wild West show was at Sitting Bull's cabin. When his horse, a gift from Cody and a veteran of the show, heard the gunfire, it took this as its cue and started performing its show act of sitting and lifting a hoof. Somehow the animal survived the cross fire. The next season the horse would return to the show.[91] Sitting Bull's horse, the shaman's death, the Ghost Dance, the cabin, and Buffalo Bill's attempts to become involved in the happenings—all became part of the Wild West show's publicity.

Even though Cody did not reach Sitting Bull, the incident put him back in the national spotlight and made excellent publicity. His trip west resembled Catlin's "flying visit" to Osceola, and, like Catlin, Cody used it to publicize his show. When he returned to Germany, a sizable contingent of Sioux, including twenty-three of the Ghost Dancers, accompanied him. What better way was there to end the Ghost Dance than to take Kicking Bear, Short Bull, and their followers abroad and thereby separate them from their people? Even most officials in the Bureau of Indian Affairs could appreciate this logic.[92]

During these tumultuous times, Nate Salsbury expanded the show from its exclusively frontier focus to include military and international acts. Thus the show became decidedly bifocal, including a "Wild West" portion plus a "Congress of Rough Riders" that featured military men and cowboy-like horsemen from around the globe. The question of whether Indians would be available for the show undoubtedly affected Salsbury's decision, but changing the show made sense for other reasons. In continental Europe, particularly France and Germany, the showmen sensed a new spirit of militarism. Cody's background as scout for the army would fit easily into a military-focused format. From the beginning,

Salsbury saw the Wild West show as an opportunity to offer an international exhibition of horsemanship. Adding a Congress of Rough Riders would make the show more cosmopolitan, attract old customers back to the show, and reflect the current mood of internationalism. Russian cossacks, gauchos from Argentina, as well as soldiers from Germany, England, and the United States joined the show in 1891.[93] Perhaps, too, Salsbury anticipated the world's fair in Chicago. Travel broadened this show, just as it had for Catlin, who visualized a "museum of mankind."

In 1891, the reorganized entertainment toured German cities, beginning with Strasbourg on 19 April, going then to Karlsrhue, Mannheim, Darmstadt, Mainz, Cologne, Dortmund, Duisburg, Krefela, and closing in Aachen on 27 May. Then it went to Brussels and Antwerp, where it stayed from 28 May to 16 June. After this, the show proceeded to Leeds, England, and toured the British Isles. The troupe wintered in Glasgow, giving the indoor pageant developed by Steele Mackaye. Buffalo Bill left the show during the winter for a trip home to Nebraska, then rejoined it for the 1892 season.[94]

In 1892, the entertainment, now billed as "Buffalo Bill's Wild West and Congress of Rough Riders of the World," returned to Earl's Court in London, its starting point for the European tour in 1887. Queen Victoria commanded a performance, mostly to see the cossacks. The western artist Frederic Remington also visited it and found the Congress of Rough Riders appealing, pronounced its western acts authentic, and sketched the colorful characters in camp. The additions to the show, cossacks and gauchos in particular, intrigued him.[95] These, along with the brightly uniformed soldiers from England, Germany, and the United States, and *vaqueros,* cowboys, cowgirls, and Indians, made a colorful and cosmopolitan group. Such a troupe made 1892 a successful year.

At the end of the season, the show returned to the United States and prepared for the upcoming world's fair in Chicago. Called the Columbian Exposition, the fair commemorated the four hundredth anniversary of Columbus's landing in the New World. The United States took this grand event seriously, seeing it as a "rite of passage" during which the nation might win recognition as a world leader. The midwestern novelist Hamlin Garland reflected the high degree of enthusiasm by moving to Chicago for the occasion and instructing his parents to see the fair, even if it meant selling the family cookstove to finance the trip. Interest ran so high that some families actually did mortgage their farms to bankroll their excursions. About 27 million Americans crowded into the Windy City.[96]

Americans built a "White City" to house the fair and advertised its size: the grounds were three times larger than those for any previous world's fair, the area under the roofs was twice as great, the Manufactures and Liberal Arts Building was the largest roofed structure ever built (four times as large as the Colosseum in Rome), and it cost $1.5 million to build. In addition, the Columbian Exposition was more international than any of its predecessors. Sixty nations, states, and colonies sponsored exhibits, and nineteen nations had their own buildings. The United States scored a triumph when Russia broke from its isolationist stance and sent a large exhibit.[97]

Complementing the fair, a broad street six hundred feet wide and a mile long called the Midway Plaisance contained about three thousand persons from forty-eight nations who hawked their goods and entertainments. It represented one of the most colorful aggregations of peoples, scenes, handicrafts, and amusements ever assembled. W. G. Ferris's giant Ferris wheel stood there, as did numerous ethnic "villages," such as Irish, German, Javanese, and Dahomey exhibits, where fairgoers could visit, purchase mementos, and observe different cultures. Using Darwinism as an organizing principle, the Columbian Exposition officials arranged exhibits along the Midway in a "'sliding scale of humanity,'" placing American Indians low on the scale. Another attraction, the "Street of Cairo," offered glimpses of the Middle East and the opportunity to rent a camel or donkey and join wedding and birthday processions winding through the village. In one theater, an alluring woman billed as "Little Egypt" created a sensation by gyrating to Arabian music. The Persian Palace of Eros advertised a sensational dancing woman called Fatima, and the Algerian village offered a third female dancer whose act American reviewers pronounced "animalistic." Such features indicated that people found titillation as well as edification at the Columbian Exposition.[98]

Most prominent of the unofficial entertainments clustered near the fair was Buffalo Bill's Wild West and Congress of Rough Riders of the World. Their request to be an official part of the Columbian Exposition having failed, Cody and Salsbury chose to compete with it. They secured a fourteen-acre lot, set their entrance near the main gate to the fair to attract customers away from it, and started performances a month before the fair opened. Electrification made possible evening performances. Cody shrugged off bad weather, maintaining that the Wild West show's covered grandstands made this an excellent place to spend a rainy afternoon or evening. Such factors made the show's success phenomenal. Nearly six million persons paid to see it, including many who saw it several times. Seating for twenty-two thousand proved insufficient, so performances often started before the advertised time once the stands had filled to capacity. Thousands missed it because of a lack of room. One reporter estimated that crowds spent $150,000 a week at the entertainment, and Cody and Salsbury made $1 million in Chicago.[99]

Perhaps because they competed with the fair and a mile of exotic entertainments on the Midway, the showmen's publicity sometimes exceeded the bounds of good taste. Among the attractions at the main gate to the Wild West show appeared relics of the massacre at Wounded Knee. The bullet-riddled cabin where Sitting Bull died stood there as an attention-getter and as a place to entertain officials of the fair, members of the press, and distinguished visitors, sometimes with a "sumptuous spread" of food and drink. The curious could also see Sitting Bull's sweat lodge and the pole that he had purportedly used in the Ghost Dance. In addition, two Sioux women, claiming to be his widows, sold baskets and moccasins to visitors. Those who asked about the Ghost Dance and Sitting Bull learned that his horse led the American contingent in the show and that many of the Ghost Dancers appeared in the performance. Although the Ghost Dance was not presented, the printed program discussed it, called it "weird and peculiar," and said that its origins lay in Christian teachings "distorted to conform with Indian mythology." Others at the fair also claimed connections with Wounded Knee: the North Dakota State exhibit also claimed to display Sitting Bull's cabin, and the Indian village on the Midway included lodges from Wounded Knee sprayed by fire from Gatling guns.[100]

The Wild West show's program offered time-tested standard western acts and ones new to Americans. Syrian and Arabian horsemen, gauchos from South America, and cossacks from Russia demonstrated their styles of horseback riding. Act twelve featured "Military Evolutions" performed by the Sixth Cavalry of the U.S. Army and detachments of German, French, and British armies. Such additions offered Americans an opportunity to compare their riders and soldiers with those from other parts of the world. According to Wild West show publicity, never before had such a colorful congregation assembled.[101]

Like the "villages" on the Midway, the Wild West show camp afforded the opportunity to see a variety of peoples living in harmony. Fairgoers streamed there to study various lifestyles and marvel at the goodwill among cowboys, Indians, cossacks, gauchos, Arabians, Syrians, and soldiers of many countries. An advertising poster bearing the title "A Factor of International Amity" commemorated all of this by depicting a serenely competent Buffalo Bill leading contingents of respectful soldiers from various nations. At the bottom appeared the explanation that President Carnot of France had used this phrase to describe the show. Added to this was the *London Times*'s comment that "Buffalo Bill has done his part in bringing America and England together."[102] The message in all this was that the world was a friendly place, particularly with an American in charge.

Such pronouncements made it appear that Cody and his Wild West show had succeeded so well as ambassadors that they now packed an international wallop. Those who doubted it could check the most recent biography, whose very title, *"Buffalo Bill" from Prairie to Palace,* documented his success. Perhaps taking his cue from the title, one reporter called Buffalo Bill the man who conquered "two worlds," the American frontier and Europe, and said: "Everyone knows how he took the scalp of Europe and wears the glittering trophy at his belt." Some journalists treated the visits of European royalty and nobility to the Wild West show as national triumphs. For such dignitaries, Cody played the part of a gracious host.[103] On the international scene, then, much about the Wild West show—travels abroad, Buffalo Bill's image as a leader, and amicable relations in camp—suggested success.

Cody's image now included two distinct roles, one as the representative frontiersman, and the other as a person of international import. His bifurcated show reflected the duality of its principal. Buffalo Bill's place at the head of the Congress of Rough Riders proved to Americans that the rest of the world did "esteem us better." Likewise, the western part of the show struck a responsive chord in Americans who experienced frontier anxiety. Cody's fellow citizens wanted assurance that everything was in order at home in this era when industrialism and urbanization replaced agrarianism and traditionalism.

At the Columbian Exposition, Americans self-consciously considered their country's prospects. Material objects such as rows of tools and paintings in official exhibits provided answers for some; a series of officially sponsored symposia called the World's Congress Auxiliary brought together intellectuals to cogitate the meaning of America. At one meeting, the Congress of Historians, Frederick Jackson Turner read a paper entitled "The Significance of the Frontier in American History" in which he explored the implications of the disappearance of the frontier on American society. In it, he suggested that the existence of free land had made the United States exceptional, and that the disappearance of the frontier meant major changes. It represented a scholarly rendition of frontier anxiety.[104]

Cody lacked the scholarly credentials of those at the Congress of Historians, but those in the Wild West show aggressively proffered their figurehead and their entertainment as an important interpreter of American history. In fact, they said that understanding the significance of Columbus's voyage required attending their show. After all, Buffalo Bill completed the process of settlement begun by

Columbus's journey four hundred years earlier. A giant banner at the main gate made this point. On one end appeared a portrait of Columbus, "Pilot of the Ocean, the First Pioneer," and on the other end was a picture of Buffalo Bill on horseback labeled "Pilot of the Prairie, the Last Pioneer." Cody offered a reassuring perspective about all this. Instead of spouting Turner's pessimism, he claimed that the frontier experience made Americans tough, resilient, and adaptable, and while they should venerate the past as he did, they should also look confidently to the future.[105]

In Cody's opinion, the United States was the best place in the world. Abroad he saw problems: decadence in France, corruption and ignorance in Spain, poverty and tiredness in crumbling Italy. Cody predicted that Europe's animosities would produce another senseless war. At the fair, Cody saw exotic foreign dancers exuding sensuality and contrasted this sharply with respectable Americans in the Wild West show. Certainly, wholesome Wild West show women did not writhe half-naked before spectators for profit.[106]

In addition to wholesomeness, Cody stressed American progress. At two previous world's fairs, Buffalo Bill had promoted his nation as progressive, and he reassumed this stance at the Columbian Exposition. There, he equated American progress with the frontier by postulating that the westward movement inaugurated a cycle of national growth and material development, and that America's place in the world was secure if the nation remained committed to progress and competition. As for the future, Cody expressed optimism: "It occurs to the writer that our boasted civilization has a wonderful adaptability." The showman contemplated prospects for Native Americans in similar terms, saying that they too must recognize that "the inevitable law of the *survival of the fittest*" required that they must "march cheerily to the tune of honest toil, industrious peace, and placid fireside prosperity" to survive.[107]

Such Darwinian phrases had crept into accounts of the show during the European tours. The showmen argued that their mustangs resulted from a highly selective process. In their view, conquistadors had brought the best horses to North America, some had escaped, and while living free on the Plains the impartial laws of nature had weeded out those with any weakness. A journalist in 1893 concluded: "the bronco is an evolution, one that Charles Darwin should fall to his knees and worship were he alive and down at the Wild West show to-day." Impressed by the hardihood of cowboys, an English journalist wrote: "Whether it is 'the survival of the fittest' which is the cause or not, the breed produced under these conditions is a fine one." So removed from "city clerks," these men appeared to be of different "species." Those in the Wild West show believed that such a process also explained the exceptionality of westerners. In their view, only the most hardy went west, and once there the best of this already select group rose to the top.[108]

As the leader of such people, Cody exemplified the highest example of manhood. The printed program at the fair, for example, called him "a natural man of the highest order" and proclaimed his physical superiority to all in camp. In addition, while abroad, he demonstrated the capacity to adapt to civilization. The biography of Cody, *"Buffalo Bill" from Prairie to Palace,* which appeared in the year of the Columbian Exposition, proclaimed this man at home on the frontier or in the palaces of Europe. One observer called him one of America's "most imposing men" and remarked that foreign travel had polished this frontiersman: "In his earlier days a hint of the border desperado lurked in his blazing eyes and the poetic fierceness of his mien and coloring. Now it is all subdued into pleasantness and he is the kindliest, most benign gentleman, as simple as a village priest and learned as a savant of Chartreuse. All the gray that has been thrust into his whirlwind life has centered itself on the edges of his beautiful hair."[109]

This poetic assessment reflected how many people felt about the man who had gone abroad in 1887 to make others "esteem us better" and to fulfill his personal goal of being "treated like a gentleman." It was the zenith of his career and the grandest moment in the history of Wild West shows. Crowds enthusiastically cheered Cody when he appeared; reporters listened intently to tales of his exploits; and news accounts routinely attributed the success of the show to Buffalo Bill's unmistakable attractiveness to Americans.[110]

William F. Cody occupied the spotlight at a critical juncture in history, when Americans believed that the frontier had ended and a modern country was emerging. He entertained, excited, and reassured his compatriots about the basic goodness and soundness of their nation. He answered fundamental questions about the future of the United States and its ties to the past. Cody and his show proved the vitality and prowess of American men and women and assured Americans that their nation possessed dynamism and adaptability developed in its frontier period that would enable it to move confidently into the future. The well-traveled and mature Cody equally personified international respect. And validating all of this was a popular and scientific theory that explained why and how plants, animals, people, and societies competed and became the best.

The stay at the Columbian Exposition successfully concluded a stage in Cody's life and his show when he had endeavored to make others "esteem us better." As a cultural ambassador, he went abroad, won respect for himself and his nation, defended the United States, and returned home full of praise for his country. He succeeded in Chicago in 1893 by convincing Americans that they enjoyed international respect and that their nation would prosper in the future. The next phase of the show would also focus on America's place among the nations of the world and life in a country leaving behind its frontier past. However, the new mood would rely more on conquest and militarism than ambassadorship.

# "Resplendent Realism of Glorious War" and Decline: Buffalo Bill's Wild West Show after the Columbian Exposition

**A** man wearing the stripes of a major general appeared in the twilight, visually surveyed a clearing among palm trees, and then signaled others to come forward. Black soldiers of the Twenty-fourth Infantry appeared singing "There'll be a Hot Time in the Old Town To-night." Then more African-American soldiers appeared, these from the Ninth and Tenth Cavalries, followed by brown-clad Rough Riders. Next came an artillery battery, Cuban scouts, and a train of pack mules laboring under great mounds of crates. Everyone pitched tents, built fires, and set up night watch. Exhausted but enthusiastic, the military contingent burst into a stirring rendition of "My Country 'Tis of Thee" as campfires died and the intense darkness of the Cuban jungle swallowed the camp.[1]

When dawn flooded the tented field with blazing tropical sunlight, a bugle blast shattered the silence, and soldiers prepared for battle. The enemy's seemingly impregnable defenses—a blockhouse surrounded by sturdy breastworks and rifle pits—loomed above the encampment. Seeing the activity below, the foes unleashed a "torrent of shrapnel and Mauser bullets." The Americans returned fire with rifles and a Gatling gun, but their forces were trapped: they could not retreat, and an advance would expose them to the full force of the enemy's firepower. The Spanish continued their deadly barrage, felling soldiers, medical doctors, the wounded, and members of the Red Cross.[2] The situation called for heroism.

A stocky man on horseback wearing a Rough Rider's uniform rushed forward and called for the brave to follow him. Shouts of approval greeted his actions, the troops sprang from their hiding places "yelling like tigers," and everyone confidently charged "straight up and to the fortressed foe." Unnerved, many blue-coated Spanish abandoned their stronghold and fled in the direction of Santiago. Hand-to-hand combat quickly dispatched the remainder. Amid much shouting, down came the Spanish flag, that "gold and crimson emblem of ruthless oppression," and soon the Stars and Stripes lofted in the breeze.[3] The battle of San Juan Hill ended, and Americans sensed victory in the Spanish-American War.

This was not the actual charge up San Juan Hill, but an act in 1899 that publicity for Buffalo Bill's Wild West show called "Resplendent Realism of Glorious War" and "a vivid, truthful, thrilling, heart-stirring, dioramic reproduction" that "supersedes the imagination," "raises the gooseflesh," and "enriches literature." Reporters wrote that the presentation captured the mood of the United States, and one observed: "Considering the spirit that prevails during these war times, no more appropriate or interesting exhibition could be presented than that led by Col. Cody." Other journalists noted that the entire program was "up-to-date" and "suggestive of war"; that this was a time "when the blood is heated" and Americans wanted to see "spectacular exhibitions of daring" and "simulation of conflict"; and that war had "a peculiar charm and military drill a fascination."[4]

The sham battle awed spectators. About six hundred performers participated in it, and they fired perhaps ten thousand shots, burning about five hundred pounds of gunpowder in the process, creating a nearly deafening roar, and filling arenas with smoke. Sometimes showmen issued carbines to members of the press and dispatched them to guard the Gatling gun. A reporter declared this assignment nearly broke his eardrums and made him feel "lust for combat." The act impressed patrons, particularly in Madison Square Garden, which provided good lighting effects and an area large enough to construct a hill. "GENUINE PARTICIPANTS in the FAMOUS BATTLE" appeared in the arena, including Rough Rider Tom Isbell, a red-headed cowboy from Muskogee, Oklahoma, whom the publicity claimed had "fired the first shot" in the actual charge and "received eight bullets, two of which he now carries." Other Rough Riders, "more or less wounded," appeared alongside the Oklahoman.[5] However, those looking for Cody did not find him in the act.

Everyone in the show proclaimed hatred for the Spanish and refused to portray them. The onerous task fell to Filipinos, Hawaiians, Mexicans, and Arabs, who all protested the assignment. More money finally convinced them to don the light blue uniforms. Native Americans joined the outcry against the Spanish, expressing special contempt for Columbus, who had sailed under the Spanish flag, "discovered" America, and began its European settlement. Eventually, however, even the Indians acquiesced and put on the Spanish garb.[6] All this made excellent publicity for a show promoting nationalism.

"Resplendent Realism of Glorious War" helped a variety of businesses. Journalists such as William Randolph Hearst and Joseph Pulitzer fanned the flames of war to sell bales of the *New York Journal* and the *New York World*. Entertainers of all sorts displayed the flag and supported the war to sell tickets. Even the fledgling movie industry exploited war fever with short productions such as *Tearing Down the Spanish Flag*. No enterprise, however, supported the war more vigorously than Buffalo Bill's Wild West and Congress of Rough Riders. John M. Burke, general manager of the show, went to Cuba to get firsthand information, returned, and urged war. In his view, that island's proximity made it strategically important for the United States, the Monroe Doctrine applied to it, Cuba possessed rich natural resources, and its people would stop speaking Spanish and quickly assimilate into American society.[7]

Before the United States declared war, the Wild West showmen glamorized Cuban guerrillas, who fought to free themselves from colonialism. The entertainers found and exhibited a "colored guard" of Cuban guerrillas, "each . . . wounded from twice to eleven times in the cause of freedom," who brandished machetes and made spirited cavalry charges. Posters depicted them as brave freedom fighters who attacked Spanish fortifications, despite heavy casualties. Publicity announced that these men would remain in the show only until their wounds healed, then they would rejoin the fray. Cody himself said he wanted to fight the Spanish, and would do so when the United States declared war.[8]

War came, and Major General Nelson A. Miles, senior commander of the U.S. Army stationed in Puerto Rico, cabled Cody to report for duty. At first, he probably did plan to go, but then decided not to disband the show and "entail a big loss," about $100,000 as he figured it. He stalled by assuring that he would serve if the war proved long and grueling. Instead of fighting, the showman capitalized on the war by having telegrams from the front read to audiences, purchasing thirty of the Rough Riders' horses, and contemplating taking fifty of Roosevelt's Rough Riders to Paris for a show. Subsequent Wild West show programs explained that Cody had supported the war effort by supplying horses, but that the "brevity of the campaign rendered his presence unnecessary."[9]

Show publications informed readers that Buffalo Bill had already waged a private little war against the Spanish. Patrons who turned to "Buffalo Bill and the Bullfighters" in their printed programs learned that he had angered the Spaniards with remarks about their bulls when the Wild West show visited Barcelona on their European junket. The publicity recast this affair into an inflammatory incident. The new version said that Buffalo Bill offered to "wager any amount" that his cowboys could "lasso and ride any bull in Spain," that he faced an angry crowd, and that he withdrew his offer only when the American consul and Spanish police asked him not to "ruin the national sport" of Spain.[10]

In this period of "Resplendent Realism of Glorious War" Cody brought a squad of Roosevelt's Rough Riders and U.S. Cavalry, including some African-American detachments, before Wild West show audiences. These men demonstrated precision riding and kept the Stars and Stripes prominently before the public, causing audiences to cheer with patriotic fervor. Other soldiers fired Napoleonic-style brass cannons, historic Civil War cannons, and modern machine guns. Such artillery, Wild West show publicity boasted, could "blow you clear over the next vacation."[11]

The world's military powers—Great Britain (sometimes represented by Irish Lancers), France, Germany, and Russia—sent detachments to the Wild West show. The colorful regalia and complicated maneuvers on horseback intrigued audiences. In a "grand musical military ride and drill," members of the U.S. cavalry came into the arena to perform with the others. Americans enjoyed seeing their servicemen alongside those of other great armies, and applauded most vigorously for their fighting men. Even after the Spanish-American War, Buffalo Bill displayed soldiers, weapons, and battle scenes. In 1901, a reporter commented that in the street parade, people could see representatives of "every war that has occurred on this globe during the past thirty years."[12]

Zouaves added more colorful soldiers to the proceedings. Dressed in billowing red trousers, blue vests adorned with gold braid, and red fezzes, they performed precision drills and scaled walls. Americans knew that troops like these had participated in the Civil War. In the postwar United States, Zouave units became popular as entertainers. During the Spanish-American War such "armies" pledged to defend the United States.[13]

Also, representatives from possible colonial areas appeared in the Congress of Rough Riders. Wild West show material explained that "the fate of war, the hand of progress and the conquering march of civilization" placed these peoples "under Old Glory's protecting folds." Americans responded enthusiastically to Hawaiians or "Sandwich Islanders," who appeared wearing grass skirts. The group included former bodyguards for Queen Liliuokalani and "the private Hula-Hula dancers of the late King Kalakaua." The show's printed program said that cattle ranching flourished on the Sandwich Islands, so these men and women demonstrated their "cowboy" skills. After the Spanish-American War, Filipinos and Puerto Ricans joined the troupe to provide a look at peoples from lands controlled by the United States. In addition, the entertainers enlisted others exotic to the majority of Americans: Costa Ricans, Siamese, Japanese, Chinese, Persians, Greeks, Cubans, Turks, Hungarian *chikos*, Syrians, and Mexican *rurales*. Some of these may have appeared only in street parades, and some may have actually been Americans playing the parts.[14]

Arabs, cossacks, gauchos, and *vaqueros* performed in their own separate acts, probably because their abilities on horseback fit the Wild West show format. Americans had seen all of these people before except the gauchos, who had joined the show in London in 1892 but had not appeared in 1893 in Chicago. The press characterized them as "a mixture of cowboy and soldier," and show publicity explained that these "primitive horsemen are of Indian and Spanish descent from the interior plateaus and pampas of the Argentine." The gauchos threw bolas, demonstrated their manner of riding, and added "color and contrast and motion."[15]

At the Columbian Exposition journalists' accounts and publicity about the show had characterized its camp as harmonious, but the racial attitudes of the "nationalist nineties" were becoming more obvious. Now, when some reporters looked at the aggregation of people in the Wild West show camp, they saw potential for conflict. Although it may not have reflected actual conditions, a journalist commented that Cody ruled his troupe with an iron fist, something necessary because of the ill will among the nations represented in the show. A courier for 1895 explained that a horse race between a cowboy, a cossack, a *vaquero*, a gaucho, and an Indian was a *"race between races"* and that "national pride," personal distinction, and *"the glory of his Race"* motivated each contestant to win. A reporter noted: "All the races are for blood." Americans cheered their fellow citizens, and it pleased audiences that American cowboys nearly always won such contests. A journalist reflected the ethnic stereotyping of the times when he commented that *vaqueros* were "as reckless and as daring" as cowboys, but "Spanish descent" meant the Mexicans did not have "the open, free-and-easy countenance of the cowboy." Consequently, audiences did not "'take to him' instinctively" as they did to the cowhand.[16]

Aggressive masculinity prevailed in the entertainment and in its camp. A courier called it the "manliest exhibition of our day, and probably all the days since the birth of Adam." A reporter who watched a street parade noted "a

grim genuineness" and that the men were "muscular, hardy and stern-faced
. . . accustomed to hard knocks and strenuous wear and tear." At sessions with
reporters, Rough Riders vied with one another in telling stories of bloodshed:
an Indian told tales of scalping; an Arab related how he had won his wife by
decapitating a rival suitor; and *vaqueros,* gauchos, cowboys, cossacks, and others added their gory stories. This emphasis on vigorous manliness reflected
many Americans' desire for evidence that physical prowess survived in the
modern world.[17]

An act in the 1901, "Heroes of Storm and Wreck," emphasized saving lives,
rather than taking them, by demonstrating rescues at sea. It consisted of setting up a ship's mast, shooting a rocket to carry a line to it, and having a man
walk to the mast, climb it, secure the line, and get into a breeches buoy, where
sailors drew him to an imaginary shore. All the while, the cowboy band played
"Sailing, Sailing, over the Bounding Main." Rounding out the entertainment
were standard Wild West features such as sharpshooting by Annie Oakley,
Buffalo Bill, and others; rodeo features and "cowboy fun"; buffalo hunts; horse
races; the attack on the Deadwood stage; and spectacles such as the "Battle of
the Little Big Horn" and the "Attack on a Settler's Cabin." Audiences liked the
"Wild West" features best, although people occasionally complained about their
lack of novelty.[18]

All of this—glorification of war and military men, emphasis on international competition, exotic people from around the globe, rescues at sea, and prov-
en western features—made up the Wild West show after the Columbian Exposition. This array, disparate as it appears, reflected the values of a new age.
"America's National Entertainment" and Buffalo Bill himself remained attuned
to the mood of the United States in the 1890s and confidently asserted that their
enterprise represented "*a great factor in the development of the national character.*"[19]

"National character" became complicated in the 1890s, when "a new urban
industrial thrust in American society challenged the older mentality of a rural,
agricultural America." The nation moved from one worldview to another and
Americans worried about many things, including economic depression, radi-
cals like the Populists, corruption in cities and politics, labor unrest, robber
barons who flaunted the power of their great trusts, and a world dominated by
machines. Cody's fellow citizens, including Theodore Roosevelt, Frederick Jackson Turner, John W. Burgess of Columbia University, Brooks Adams, and some
in the political and business communities, believed that the frontier's bounty
of raw material had fostered prosperity and stability. Such people hoped to regain frontier benefits with expansion into "underdeveloped" parts of the world.

A persistent national depression in the 1890s buttressed the belief that the nation's vitality required territorial growth.[20]

In addition to an unsettled domestic front, the international scene became competitive, causing nations to spar for supremacy and expand armies and navies. The winners received economic rewards, international trade, and empires. Many Americans accepted the ideas of the military theorist Alfred Thayer Mahan, who combined Social Darwinism with Anglo-Saxon greatness and postulated that the future belonged to countries with strong navies. Another thinker, Josiah Strong, linked expansionism, patriotism, Anglo-Saxon superiority, and Christianity by advising Americans that a God-given duty required them to spread civilization and the "true religion" everywhere. Theodore Roosevelt, above all others, personified the bellicose spirit by advocating war to rejuvenate frontier aggressiveness, promoting the fight with Spain, and then leading Rough Riders up San Juan Hill. For many, this encapsulated how the world should be: the United States ejected Spain from the Western Hemisphere, ensured Cuban independence, acquired the territories of Puerto Rico and Guam, and sent American troops to occupy the strategically important Philippines, which could serve as a stepping stone to Asia. The Wild West show celebrated all this with an entertainment "peculiarly apropos to these days of 'grim-visaged war.'"[21]

According to the historian David M. Wrobel, the belief that free land in the United States was gone caused a "crisis in the nineties," forcing Americans to look for solutions to the "closed frontier." Wrobel suggests that they found two categories of remedies—"external" and "internal"—to find more land and opportunity. External responses meant looking outside the United States, and, if necessary, wresting territory and resources from others. Less dramatic internal solutions included finding more usable land within the United States by such means as using irrigation to convert arid or otherwise marginal land into productive farms and ranches.[22] Buffalo Bill's Wild West show from this period clearly supports Wrobel's thesis. In acts such as "The Battle of San Juan Hill," military maneuvers, and rescues at sea, the show offered external answers. Cody would also support internal solutions by promoting irrigation in Wyoming's Bighorn Basin. Celebrating external and internal solutions to the closed frontier when times demanded it revealed Cody's genius for adjusting his show to fit the changing mood of the American public. Earlier, when the nation had wanted evidence that the conquest of the Plains was a fait accompli, Cody had verified this with a gladiatorial rendition of his show. In the next phase of the entertainment, he had gone abroad as a cultural ambassador seeking to make others "esteem us better" in an era when Americans wanted respect for their nation and the progress it had achieved. Now, in the final stage of his career as show-man, Cody promoted growth and progress in forms appropriate for that age—in expansionist external forms and the more moderate internal ones.

As for the external solutions, combining militarism, expansionism, and internationalism was natural for this man, whose life encompassed them all. As a child, Cody watched a cavalry drill at Fort Levenworth and then saw wagons headed west from the Salt Creek Valley. After this, he scouted for the U.S. Army, earned military titles, and, while abroad, attracted attention from professional soldiers. As for internationalism, the Congress of Rough Riders of the World brought together many nations on horseback, and Americans admired Cody for hobnobbing with "European potentates," taking "a stein or two with German nobles," and "hypnotizing the British lion."[23]

Adding militaristic features to the program required no rethinking of the old formulas. In the show, as in the United States, the theme of Manifest Destiny evolved into the "New Manifest Destiny." The Wild West show had always portrayed "the bullet as the pioneer of civilization," and putting weapons in the hands of soldiers as well as cowboys did not change the commitment to the use of force.[24] The acts themselves remained basically the same: shooting Spaniards in the "Battle of San Juan Hill" resembled routing Indians in the "Attack on the Settler's Cabin"; displaying Hawaiians differed little from exhibiting Native Americans; and rescues at sea were not unlike saving people on the prairie.

Buffalo Bill lectured that progress required risk-taking. He enjoyed relating how friends cautioned him against touring Europe but that he stuck by his principles, went abroad, and took the continent by storm. The United States, Cody believed, should follow his example by ignoring the naysayers, taking some chances, and broadening its horizons. He scorned all "Mossbacks," or those who did not enthusiastically advocate progress.[25]

For Cody, territorial growth stood at heart of U.S. history because the nation had "expanded under the Louisiana purchase and since." About the United States, he asserted: "The farther it would reach out and the more territory it would acquire the bigger and better a nation it would be. I say never take down the American flag after it has been once hoisted, and hoist it over all the territory that it is possible and profitable to take in." Journalists called him an "expansionist of the broadest type" and "an imperialist in every sense of the word." Cody prophesied that those who "howled against the government" because of expansionism "would be ashamed of the position they have taken in the matter." In politics, Cody supported Republicans, who promoted imperialism and business.[26]

Buffalo Bill viewed growth as good, whether it occurred in the West or abroad.

Consequently, as a frontiersman who had brought civilization and progress to the West, he believed that he could defend national interests anywhere. In his mind, non-whites everywhere resembled Native Americans. When asked about fighting Filipino insurgents, he anticipated no problems because he claimed that, like Indians, they used guerrilla tactics. In the arena, non-Caucasians became Indian-like. When Filipinos joined the show, they were put on horseback, even though they had never ridden these animals.[27]

Cody believed all American fighting men—cowboys, scouts, and soldiers—worked to extend U.S. civilization. The year that he introduced the Congress of Rough Riders to America, the biography *"Buffalo Bill" from Prairie to Palace* written by John Burke appeared. Here, in his typical flowery style, Burke called these servicemen "Those Pioneers of Progress Who Have Led the Advance of Civilization into Savage Lands, Defying Danger, Suffering Every Hardship, Overcoming All Obstacles, Offering Life as a Sacrifice When Called Upon."[28] Such a view endorsed the belief that weapons served as tools of civilization, in the hands of pioneers as well as soldiers.

The show's publicists worked to strengthen Cody's image as a military leader. *"Buffalo Bill" from Prairie to Palace* abounded with portraits of American military officers and included a fourteen-page chapter of testimonies about how Cody valiantly served the U.S. Army as a scout. One of the strongest messages about him emerged in the act depicting the Battle of the Little Bighorn. In some renditions of it, Buffalo Bill arrived after its completion, surveyed the carnage, and then remorsefully exclaimed: "Too Late! Too Late!" It was a powerful message: if only Cody had arrived a bit earlier, he could have prevented this tragedy. Journalists usually depicted Cody as an experienced warrior. One called him "a prominent feature in the war history and literature" of the United States and another remarked that "fighting has been his business."[29]

Poster art also emphasized that Cody was a natural leader by depicting an amicable mingling of respectful westerners and soldiers. In one, flags of a dozen nations appeared, and Buffalo Bill rode among the international group "Reviewing the Rough Riders." Another trumpeted his style of wholesome militarism by contrasting him with Napoleon. On this poster were the French artist Rosa Bonheur at her easel, Napoleon mounted on horseback to the viewer's left, and Buffalo Bill on horseback on the right. Napoleon appeared "flabby, beaten, and despondent," while Cody looked "straight, tall, and sure of himself." The message was that Napoleon represented the past, while Buffalo Bill was the man of the 1890s, who triumphed in frontier struggles and won the respect of cultured Europeans like Bonheur.[30] Cody, then, represented an American hero—

in his ascendancy, admirable, vigorous, wholesome, and fundamentally differ-ent from dangerous Europeans.

Americans readily accepted Cody as a warrior of considerable ability, but he had no experience in international warfare. Consequently, acts like "The Bat-tle of San Juan Hill" offered no place for him. Instead of Cody, "The Battle of San Juan Hill" focused attention on Theodore Roosevelt. Even the song in the act, "There'll be a Hot Time in the Old Town To-night," lionized Roosevelt because everyone knew of its popularity in the Cuban campaign. Admiration for Roosevelt and other celebrities became the focus in a feature where the show-men projected stereoscopic portraits to see which one received the loudest ap-plause. Audience members responded warmly to likenesses of Ulysses S. Grant, William McKinley, William Jennings Bryan, and General Joseph G. Wheeler. However, patrons reserved their loudest endorsements for Admiral George Dewey and Theodore Roosevelt, heroes of the Spanish-American War.[31] Buf-falo Bill's portrait did not appear among the images.

That audiences cheered Roosevelt's picture related most directly to his role in the war, but other activities probably appealed to those who approved of messages in the Wild West show. He advocated the "strenuous life," or self-in-vigoration through bodybuilding and challenging outdoor activities. In his most recent works, *Ranch Life and Hunting Trail* (1888) and *The Winning of the West* (1889–1896), he praised America's frontier history, which he claimed "fostered the 'Pioneer Spirit' and produced a 'rugged and stalwart democracy'" and "'vig-orous manliness.'" These books, combined with an interlude as a cowboy in the Dakota Badlands, made him an authority on the West in the eyes of many Americans. His acceptance as such represented a trend of upper-class eastern-ers like Roosevelt, Owen Wister, and Frederic Remington going West, learn-ing about it, and becoming respected interpreters of it.[32] In the future, such "experts" would gain more and more credibility, even though their achievements in the West paled before those of Cody.

That the Wild West show merchandised his accomplishments and claimed the term *Rough Rider* displeased Roosevelt. He had applied it to his First Vol-unteer Cavalry, then tried to drop it because it called up the image of a "hip-podrome affair," an obvious reference to Buffalo Bill's Wild West show. The showmen pointed out that the term was theirs, saying that they had used it for a number of years, and that Roosevelt had taken it from them. Despite such squabbling, Roosevelt went to Madison Square Garden in 1899 to see Cody's show. After watching "The Battle of San Juan Hill," he pronounced it "accu-rate," shook hands with his former Rough Riders, and verified them as ones who had stormed up the hill with him. Performers and spectators alike enjoyed Roosevelt's attendance, and many crowded around him to talk and shake hands.[33] His change of heart probably resulted from the presence of the Rough Riders, since he would do nearly anything to support them.

The focus on militarism and contemporary international affairs brought problems because the showmen tied their fortunes to nations and events beyond their control. One day those brightly bedecked soldiers might be heroes, but the next day they could be villains. In 1898, for example, Americans hissed German soldiers or allowed them to pass in silence because of events in the Philippines. Germany had a small fleet in the area to protect its citizens, and the German commander may have intentionally maneuvered his ships to interfere with the activities of the Americans. Admiral Dewey called for war. The English fleet in the area worked with the Yankees to stop German meddling. This renewed Americans' enthusiasm for the Britons, causing audiences at Wild West shows to cheer them.[34]

Attitudes toward Third World peoples could also change overnight. When Cuban freedom fighters appeared, they "created the most intense enthusiasm," but when reporters alleged that they were poor fighters, spectators at Wild West shows gave them chilly receptions. Americans called Filipinos "intelligent, courteous," and "daring" when they first joined the show because they had fought against the Spanish. When American troops arrived to occupy the archipelago, however, the Filipino nationalists considered them colonialists and launched bloody raids; consequently, Wild West show audiences began to snub, hiss, and boo Filipinos. At this point, one disenchanted American reporter remarked: "Kipling knew his business when he described the Filipino 'half devil and half child'—it fitted the tawny dull eyed creatures perfectly."[35]

The changing perception of the Filipinos entangled Buffalo Bill in the question of their place in American society. Anti-imperialists such as William Jennings Bryan, Andrew Carnegie, Samuel Gompers, William Dean Howells, Carl Schurz, and Mark Twain asked difficult questions. Should the United States, which fought a war for its own independence, now build an empire and have colonial subjects? Would these peoples get full rights of citizenship? Does the Constitution allow for the annexation of territory not intended to become states? Will the creation of a large standing army to defend American interests abroad mean that this same army might endanger the liberty of Americans and suppress striking workers? Others raised the specter of racism: do we want more dependent colored people in our society?[36]

For a time, Buffalo Bill advertised "Strange People from Our New Possessions" as "future fellow-countrymen." However, when Filipino guerrillas turned against American troops, he advocated that the United States crush them. When asked about Filipino trustworthiness, he expressed doubts. No more talk of them as citizens came from the Wild West show's principals, although Buffalo Bill remained an "avowed expansionist insofar as controlling the islands is concerned, until the natives are able to govern themselves."[37] Eventually, Filipinos disappeared from the show.

Some international incidents produced no clear-cut consensus among Americans. Both sides in the Boer War (1899–1902) were appealing: the English represented the forces of settlement and empire, while the Boers represented the citizen soldier, a desire for independence, and "nature's men." Americans found it difficult to choose between them, so Cody did not stage mock battles.[38] He simply brought representatives from both sides into the arena.

In 1901 the show concluded with "The Battle of Tien-Tsin," a scene from the Boxer Rebellion of 1900. Americans generally supported international efforts to crush the Chinese traditionalists, known in the Western world as "Boxers," for reasons that ranged from avenging the deaths of westerners to supporting Christian missionary activity to controlling the lucrative "China trade." Most Americans had no enthusiasm for China because they had grown up with schoolbooks that usually criticized Asia and its people. Nativists in the United States called Chinese immigration to their country a "Yellow Peril."[39]

The Wild West show act, sometimes billed as "The Rescue at Pekin," lasted a full half hour. It began with a camp scene showing the gathering of Sikhs and foot soldiers and cavalries from the United States, England, France, Russia, Germany, and Japan, who demonstrated camp life and military maneuvers. Part two featured these soldiers attacking the city, colorful zouaves scaling its walls, and the wild-looking Boxers—played by Native Americans—scurrying for safety with their pigtails flying.[40]

While most audiences cheered such scenes, not everyone agreed that the United States should be empire building. When the show was strictly a western entertainment, Mark Twain had esteemed it and had even urged Cody and Salsbury to take it abroad in 1887 as a truly American enterprise. Now, however, he quarreled with his nation and the Wild West show. In two articles, "To a Person Sitting in Darkness" and "The Chronicles of Young Satan," Twain berated his compatriots for their greed and conquest. He attended the inaugural performance of the 1901 season at Madison Square Garden largely to protest imperialism. A reporter who watched him enter described him as "sour as a German pickle." Surveying the audience probably worsened his attitude, because it bristled with high-ranking military officers in uniform. When the show began and Cody appeared, Twain "clapped his hands feebly." With the introduction of the contending forces in the Boer War, Twain ignored those fighting for extending England's empire and applauded loudly for the Boers. With the announcement of "The Battle of Tien-Tsin," Twain "expressed his disapproval of our foreign policy by abruptly leaving the Garden."[41]

Like Twain, many others questioned the wisdom of an American empire. In fact, by 1901 even Theodore Roosevelt said that he had no more desire to add territory than "a gorged boa constrictor might have to swallow a porcupine wrong-end-to." Shortly after the turn of the century, commentators called for changes in the program, specifically: "more of the Wild West and less of the effete East"; replacing foreigners and the military with more cowboys, Indians, and bronco riding; and substituting something more palatable for imperialism and militarism.[42] The "Battle of Tien-Tsin" disappeared from the program, but soldiers from the world's military powers remained.

While battles, soldiers, exotic peoples, and weaponry glorified external solutions, many Americans supported the other remedy for the closed frontier—internal solutions, such as restricting immigration, protecting land with conservation, and bringing irrigation to arid places. In keeping with this philosophy, Cody continued to trumpet progress and his belief that exemplary westerners adapted and changed. A show program carried an article entitled "The Wave of Progress at the Foothills of the Rockies," which asserted that the "spirit of Progress moves when the energetic sons of toil rally in her wake, to wrest from Nature the riches she has stored in abundance for those who seek the comforts that come from well-directed industry." Another program called progress and settlement an "irresistible force" that "turned this primitive, savage, wild, yet picturesquely romantic, unknown region into a rapidly settled, fruitful field for the world's overteeming millions of the white race, . . . adding to the world's economic value."[43]

The most poetic celebration of internal expansion appeared in a 1898 Wild West show poster entitled "Westward the Course of Empire," a stupendous piece of publicity that measured twenty-eight feet wide and over nine feet high. It drew upon powerful symbols of expansionism, a painting with the same title by Emanuel Leutze that hung in the House of Representatives, and "Westward the course of empire," a line from a poem celebrating America by the Irish philosopher George Berkeley. The poster conveyed an "almost Biblical approach to the subject matter," with Cody standing at the edge of a cliff overlooking lush soil, almost like "a modern-day Moses leading his people to the promised land." About him clustered disciple-like followers.[44]

The poster linked the Judeo-Christian tradition and expansion with force, signaled by the rifle in Cody's hand. In addition, Cody leading settlers into a garden-like West linked the agricultural frontier with religion. Everything about the poster—its size, its relationship to national symbols of expansion, its powerful slogan, and its biblical imagery—indicate that the showmen wanted to make a strong statement. One aspect of that, of course, was that the West still offered opportunity.

Cody promoted such ideas, in part, because he headed an irrigation project. Water diversion became popular in the late nineteenth and early twentieth centuries. The work of John Wesley Powell on this subject, the Carey Act (1894), and the Newlands Act (1902) indicated growing support for such policies. Reflecting this spirit, Cody worked to overcome the "difficulties of Nature and climate" by bringing water to the Bighorn Basin of Wyoming. In the mid-1890s he leased three hundred thousand acres of land from the government, hired two thousand workers to dig irrigation canals, and endeavored to turn the arid land into productive farms. Letters to family and friends brimmed with enthusiasm for the project.[45]

Buffalo Bill flooded his showgrounds with information about his farming scheme. Determined to "do a world of advertising" and make the Bighorn Basin "the most talked of place in America," Cody filled booths at the entrance to the show with promotional literature. Brochures entitled *Ideal Western Lands Selected by the Famous "Buffalo Bill"* explained that water from the "Cody Canal" ensured ample harvests of vegetables and grains and a "paradise" for ranchers. Mineral resources, such as gold, silver, coal, and iron, abounded, and evidence existed of oil deposits. Furthermore, one could remain comfortable while making a fortune, because "Chinook" winds warmed the area.[46] Such hyperbole sounded like Catlin, about half a century earlier, promoting his agricultural colony in the Southwest.

In interviews, Buffalo Bill maintained that irrigation could transform this part of Wyoming into a garden, that he would rather discuss water and agricultural settlement than the Wild West show, and that he wanted to be remembered as a man who brought a large-scale water-diversion project to Wyoming. Programs encouraged readers to write for more information, and brochures asked: "Are you dissatisfied with your present surroundings? Have you a desire to better your conditions?" He designated the project for America's common people, saying that he eschewed "trusts" and "millionaire purchasers" and offered tracts of land to small-propertied individuals, whom he called "the Man With The Hoe."[47]

With his talk of "the Man With The Hoe" and the Bighorn Basin as a "garden," Cody used powerful symbols and myths of the agricultural frontier suggesting the unlimited potential of western farmland cultivated by the yeoman farmer or the ideal democrat. Mainstream Americans found both myths appealing, but they represented something different from the "Wild West" of adventure and romance found in Buffalo Bill's show. Undoubtedly, Cody recognized the differences between the agricultural West and the "Wild West" because he did not attempt to present acts about digging ditches, hoeing corn, planting oats, or harvesting wheat. The public struggled with his roles as Wild West showman and agriculturalist. A reporter noted that it seemed incongruous to talk of irrigation and farming with the man who represented the Wild West. Americans would accept no one, not even Cody, as the spokesman for both frontiers.[48]

While Cody blithesomely promoted land sales, his private correspondence revealed deep concerns. Digging a great ditch proved slow and expensive work, often delayed by leaks and washouts. He invested his own money and worked to raise capital, but bankruptcy often threatened the undertaking. When the election of 1896 pitted William Jennings Bryan against William McKinley, Cody wrote a friend that "the blooming free silver Democrats" had ruined the bond market and this imperiled his irrigation project. Management from afar proved frustrating, and he penned angry letters demanding better on-site supervision, requesting more information, and asking if he was being fleeced.[49] Most likely, Cody was the victim of fraud and mismanagement.

In addition to irrigation and farming, Buffalo Bill promoted Cody, Wyoming, and built a hotel there named the Irma in honor of his daughter. His military bent led him to plan a school called Cody Military College and International Academy of Rough Riders in the Bighorn Basin. He proposed to teach young men cavalry skills as they lived outdoors and thereby gained strength, health, and high moral values. The old scout believed such qualities were no longer being stressed because so many young men spent their time dancing the tango and generally "act[ing] like girls."[50] The academy did not materialize, but his planning indicated his continuing enthusiasm for the military ideal.

Cody's commitment to progress and money-making spawned other projects: coal mining, promoting tourism and dude ranching, bringing a branch line of the Burlington railroad into the Bighorn Basin, bottling mineral water, owning a newspaper, and heading a company to search for oil and gas deposits. He poured money into an unsuccessful gold mine in Arizona and purchased land in Wyoming on which he developed a cattle ranch called the TE, which became a refuge and his "only ray of pleasure," as he called it in one letter. In that same epistle, writing about family squabbles and a possible divorce, Cody remarked that his personal life had become a state of "war." Furthermore, the Wild West show business was "just wearing the life out of" him.[51]

While Cody remained a forward-looking, but sometimes unhappy, businessman, the western acts in the show encouraged some Americans to look backward in time. During this period when the nation seemed to be rushing headlong into an industrial and urban style of life, many looked nostalgically to the frontier past. The western artist Frederic Remington observed that the Wild West show encapsulated a spirit of freedom missing in contemporary society. He characterized Buffalo Bill's entertainment as a "poetical and harmless protest against the starched linen—those horrible badges of our modern social system, when men are physical lay figures and mental and moral cog-wheels and wastes of uniformity—where the great crime is to be individual and the unpardonable sin is to be out of fashion." The Wild West showmen endorsed Remington's remarks by reprinting them for a number of years.[52]

Cody himself often became an idyllic reminder of the past. One reporter characterized him as "the connecting link between the wild, rough frontier past, with all its glories of physical manhood, and the present, with its machine action and emasculating commercialism." Another saw him as "the representative of nineteenth century chivalry."[53] Wild West show arenas offered an alluring vision of a time when individualism still counted and Americans solved problems directly and decisively by drawing six guns and chasing Indians. No one needed to fret about the outcome, for everybody knew that cowboys and scouts—those who represented the true American spirit—would triumph.

The huge number of horses—five to eight hundred—contributed significantly to a portrayal of a simpler preindustrial time. Observers saw equestrianism as the heart of the Wild West show and praised its variety: "beautiful, high strung animals ridden by Colonel Cody," "fine chargers" belonging to soldiers, "bucking broncos," trained animals that feigned death in battle scenes, and draft animals that pulled equipment from depots to showgrounds. After seeing the entertainment, a reporter designated Buffalo Bill "the greatest living exponent" of horses.[54]

When the show traveled to England after the turn of the century, people there appreciated the horses and equated them with independence. A journalist wrote that the Wild West show portrayed freedom, and that views of "untrammelled freedom . . . invariably include a horse—not a motor-car." Another observed that the show offered escape from " 'the miserable life of the cities' " and represented "an apotheosis of the horseman." A reporter watched workers use horses to erect canvas and queried: Would not traction machinery be better for that heavy work? A press agent quickly explained that machines "would take all the aesthetic and sentimental interest out of the show."[55] Such a statement indicated that nostalgia, and perhaps even a little antagonism toward the machine age, had crept into the show after the world's fairs.

The western part of the program also appealed to patriotism because it reassured Americans about the uniqueness of their nation, the glory of their heritage, and the glamor and admirability of Plains peoples. No new explanations for such greatness appeared; instead, the showmen repeated familiar ones, like the frontier provided a proving ground that elevated truly outstanding individuals and life in nature promoted healthfulness and uplifted people morally. Cody reflected such views by arguing that cowboys and members of the U.S. Cavalry could beat all the other riders in feats of endurance because "Blood tells them." A journalist proclaimed "the Anglo-Saxon cowboy of North America" as "the best of all the rough riders." "These knights of the Western plains" were "more pleasing to the eye" than other groups. One observer characterized Buffalo Bill as a "splendid specimen of a handsome, vigorous and skillful Anglo-Saxon who had emerged with honor and glory from the most trying tests possible for men to endure."[56]

About Native Americans, Cody continued to offer kind words. The "Introduction" to the 1907 program divided his career into three stages: the first as a frontiersman, the second as an entertainer who educated the world about the West, and the third and present one as an advocate for Indians. To build respect for these peoples, Cody discussed their legends; extolled their goodness, honesty, virtue, and intelligence; sometimes called them "Nature's Noblemen"; and blamed white men for corrupting them. He confided in an interview that he felt "a bit ashamed" for the part he had played in defeating the Indians, and show programs said that there was "something touchingly pathetic" about the demise of many Indian civilizations.[57]

A Catlinesque quality marked Cody during these years—in fact, publicity linked the men. John Burke looked back to the roots of the Wild West show tradition and observed that Buffalo Bill's show revived Catlin's goals. Burke called Catlin a "great historian and Indian painter" who spent his life trying to depict accurately the West and Indians, celebrating nature, and trying to preserve it. The 1907 program noted that Buffalo Bill "regarded the Indians with feelings of fraternal sympathy, and like Catlin the Great Indian painter and chronicler of aboriginal life of that period, he has endeavored to preserve the picturesque identity" of Native Americans. Despite sounding like a reformer at times, Cody did not change what Americans had come to expect from the Wild West show. His exploits as Indian fighter still remained an important part of the show, and publicity often depicted Indians as warlike, misguided, and frightening opponents.[58]

Many acts featuring Native Americans brimmed with violence. Some years, audiences saw Indian dances followed by the "Battle of Little Big Horn," which illustrated how Indians "with strategic cunning ambushed the gallant Custer . . . and remorselessly annihilated the entire command," and were "scalping and gloating over their captives" and "a heap of dead soldiers and horses." Adding more realism, the person playing Custer rode the "favorite war horse of the late Chief, Sitting Bull." Publicity claimed the act featured actual participants in the battle, including an old chief "having had his left jaw shot away, he says, by Gen. Custer himself."[59]

During this period Americans discussed women in new ways. Victorian culture with its emphasis on "separate spheres" for men and women was beginning to yield to a new view of the sexes. Victorian standards emphasized women's frailty and their duty to marry, bear offspring, and devote their lives to care of their children, husbands, and homes. The new view proclaimed women as robust individuals who could participate in traditionally male activities such as politics and work outside the home. Americans watched the "new women" move into the workplace, demand the right to vote, and fight for Progressive reforms in prostitution, child-labor laws, and prohibition. Many Americans applauded such movements, but others viewed them with trepidation.

As a product of the age, Cody reflected uncertainty about the status of women. Sometimes he praised the "new woman." The 1899 Wild West show program, for example, said that he endorsed their right to vote, form their own organizations, live alone without restrictions, and enjoy the same employment opportunities and pay as men. He told a female reporter that American women possessed more self-determination, and consequently "more style and good looks," than those in any other nation. Women, he concluded, should vote and have "absolute freedom."[60]

Once, he invited twenty female journalists to his tent for lunch and endorsed woman's suffrage. However, during much of this discourse he related in "tender tones how his mother's little talks" had guided and inspired him while performing acts of prowess. This, clearly, was praise for the "cult of motherhood," and characteristic of the Victorian era. In another interview, he declared that women should not wear "bloomer pants" or ride bucking horses. A 1902 program stated that frontiersmen had "signalized themselves by performing prodigies of valor, while the women, in their heroic courage and endurance, afforded a splendid example of devotion and self-sacrifice."[61] Such comments revealed that Cody sometimes espoused traditional views of "woman's sphere."

A similar bifurcation marked the Wild West show's advertising art. On some posters, women wore revolvers, whirled lassos, and rode bucking broncos. Others stressed Cody's endorsement of female performers by placing them close to him: in one a woman rode directly behind him, and in another that ranked performers by status, women appeared near the middle of the troupe. While such paper endorsed the "new woman," others pictured helpless women needing men for protection. In "Westward the Course of Empire," a man helped a woman up a hill, and women appeared in traditional dress and held babies. In posters featuring Indian attacks, men did the fighting.[62]

In 1894, the year that Cody invited the women to his tent for lunch and advocated more rights for them, a female reporter noted that Annie Oakley was the "only white woman" listed as a performer and fumed: "Only one woman in the show! I gasped and read through the list of attractions again." Then she asked: Did not "brave women" participate in "emigration to the far West"? The next year, a reporter noted that Oakley was the "only white woman in Buffalo Bill's camp." Rosters in newspaper articles and Wild West show route books for 1896 and 1899 listed no other white female performers. Although these reporters focused rightly on women's absence from most of the acts—or at least their billing in them—their emphasis on white women revealed the racism of the age. Most likely, the show always included Native American women, and, in some years, there were Arabian, Hawaiian, Mexican, and Filipino female performers.[63] Granted, their roles were minuscule compared with those for cowboys and Native American men—or even white women—but the press paid them little attention.

Usually, white women did appear in the western part of the show. However, features such as "Resplendent Realism of Glorious War" offered no place for women, since they had not assumed combat roles at San Juan Hill or in the Boxer Rebellion. In acts such as the attack on the settlers' cabin and the rescue of the Deadwood stage, they played victims. Often they appeared on horseback, in street parades, in the grand entry, and in horse races. After the turn of the century, they received more visibility, however, perhaps because women made gains everywhere in American society during this period. An act called "Perils of the Prairie" included a scene in which women and men demonstrated a Virginia Reel on horseback. The entertainers offered a variety of billings for the female performers, including "cow-girls," "broncho-riding women," "Wild West Girls," "Western Prairie Girls," "Western Girl Rough Riders," and a "Bevy of Beautiful Rancheras" (probably Hispanic women riders).[64]

Annie Oakley's expert shooting kept her the most conspicuous woman. Her "modest, quiet, lady-like appearance" was Victorian, but much about her was not traditionally Victorian. She expressed opinions on gender issues, particularly about physical culture, stressing female hardihood and saying that she would welcome the opportunity to ride broncos in the show. Her own fitness routine included horseback riding, bicycling, swimming, walking briskly, sprinting, fencing, and workouts with dumbbells. One reporter called her the "prototype of the 'New Woman.'" Annie Oakley left the show in 1901, perhaps because of injuries from a train wreck, a head of hair that turned gray rather quickly, or the failing fortunes of Buffalo Bill's Wild West show.[65] Whatever the explanation, Oakley's departure left a void in the show.

After the turn of the century journalists often commented about women in the entertainment. In England in 1903, western "girls" riding both sidesaddle and astride interested audiences, and, two years later in France, references to "cowgirls" became standard in Wild West show advertising. Back before American audiences, a woman led the bandits in a train robbery scene in 1907. Another act that year depicted the "characteristic nonchalance of western ranch life" by having women appear "in the side saddle and the more modern method of riding astride, while some of the girls don the 'chaps' of the typical cowboy." A courier described these "girls" as "strikingly graceful and charming representations of physical and equestrian beauty."[66]

Those who attended the Wild West show saw an entertainment in metamorphosis, with its mixture of western acts, soldiers and scenes of battles in faraway lands, and stands sprouting brochures about irrigated farmland in Wyoming. In addition to obvious alterations in programming and personnel, changes—good, problematic, and bad—occurred behind the scenes at Buffalo Bill's Wild West show.

The year of the Columbian Exposition ushered in a crushing depression. During economic downturn, giant trusts formed in tented entertainment, competition became ruthless, and survival for independent operations such as Buffalo Bill's Wild West show became difficult. To compete, Cody and Salsbury kept their entertainment large and impressive. In 1894, for example, they spent "a cool million" on showgrounds for a season at Ambrose Park in Brooklyn; the show employed about eight hundred persons; expenses ran about eleven hundred dollars a day; and show bills alone required five thousand dollars a week. For tickets, Cody charged fifty cents for general admission and one dollar for reserved seats—steep prices during hard times.[67]

During this difficult period, Salsbury's health failed. In the spring of 1895, Cody wrote that "Salsbury is still dangerously sick—can't sign a check." Although incapacitated, Salsbury remained part owner. Needing a new arrangement for managing the show, Cody and Salsbury entered into a partnership with the circus tycoon James A. Bailey, of the Barnum and Bailey Circus, and another entrepreneur, W. W. Cole, to furnish transportation and equipment, aid in routing the show, manage its business aspects, and share in the profits. Cody, with limited help from Salsbury, ran the entertainment part of the show. In practical terms, this meant that Buffalo Bill lost a partner with whom he worked well, faced an increased workload, and forfeited much of his control.[68]

With new management, the philosophy about routing changed. Whenever practical, Cody and Salsbury had found permanent locations; but the new managers, with circus backgrounds, sent the show across the nation with a schedule marked by many one-day stands. In 1896, for example, the show used 42 different railroads, traveled 10,787 miles in a 190-day season, made 132 stands, and gave 332 separate performances. In 1897, it appeared in 104 cities and visited Canada, and in 1898 the show traveled 10,253 miles while visiting 133 cities and gave 345 performances.[69] Buffalo Bill's Wild West show still played metropolitan areas, but now it also visited many smaller cities, affording many Americans their first opportunity to see it.

Towns in rural areas often virtually closed down for the Wild West show. Citing its educational benefits, superintendents sometimes declared a school holiday so students could spend a day there. Buffalo Bill gloried in this veneration, particularly in western towns where old-timers endorsed the show as authentic and "almost talked a lung out" of him. He enjoyed a trip to the Trans-Mississippi Exposition in Omaha in 1898 when Nebraskans honored him with a special "Cody Day." Despite appreciating many aspects of travel, he confided to a friend: "I am so busy with these long runs and many thousands of old Western timers who bore me to death."[70]

Cross-continental scheduling changed the show and sometimes complicated management. In earlier years, permanent locations assured slack periods for relaxation, leisurely talk with reporters, and time for visitors to stroll through the camp. Now hurriedness marked days that stretched from 5:00 A.M. to midnight and included caring for livestock, parading through the streets, erecting seats and preparing arenas, performing in afternoons and evenings, dismantling the show's property, hauling everything by wagon back to the train, and loading it. Sometimes only one performance could be given daily, and audiences in smaller cities saw abbreviated shows. Extensive travel brought problems, such as breakdowns of rolling stock, gasoline explosions in railroad cars, licenses and fees required in each town, arrival in agricultural communities during planting or harvesting seasons, inadequate lighting from the portable light plant, confrontations between the Wild West show troupe and locals, tight money, cyclones, snowstorms, and train wrecks.[71]

While running the show became more taxing, Cody aged. By 1896 he wore a wig, and, once, while sweeping off his hat, he accidentally removed his toupee and bowed, thus exposing his "shining bald head" to the audience. A performer in the show claimed that once Buffalo Bill left his tent without the wig and that the experience angered and embarrassed him so much that it took "two tumblers of hi-power egg-nog" to salve his bruised ego. The press department worked feverishly to keep such stories out of the papers. In 1900 a newspaper article mentioned that Buffalo Bill required eyeglasses to do his shooting act from horseback. Other journalists commented on his graying hair and rounder body. One reporter even gave the old scout's weight, saying it was 215 pounds in 1900, and 200 in 1901. After the turn of the century, publicity agents with the show often avoided mentioning the date of Cody's birth. Looking back on the history of the show, one member of the troupe said that Buffalo Bill's age contributed significantly to its decline.[72]

The rigors of travel and an aging Cody subtly changed the show. Being on the move meant that the Wild West show camp, which symbolized the troupe's desire for natural surroundings, was not a regular feature, and this impacted Cody's image. In 1899, a journalist noted: "William F. Cody is no longer the rough ranger, who sleeps with the horn of his saddle for a pillow. Mr. Cody has grown to be a fastidious creature of comfort. He was resting on a downy bed at Hotel Cadillac." In the late nineteenth century, Cody began riding in a carriage during the street parades. The press commented that this detracted from his appeal. Some criticized the aging Plainsman, but others' remarks were kindly, such as one that characterized him as "portly but dashing and debonair."[73]

Cody needed something to put magic back into his life and his show. A scintillating book would have filled the bill nicely. Instead, he got a biography called *Last of the Great Scouts* (1899), a vapid book written by his admiring sister, Helen Cody Wetmore, who cluttered the text with sentimentality, accounts of Cody's tenderheartedness, stories of devotion to his mother, and a sterling pedigree for the family—a Spanish king on the paternal side and "the best blood of England" on the maternal side. In addition, Wetmore claimed their forebears won the American Revolution nearly singlehandedly and performed other patriotic feats. The book was doubly damning: written by someone outside the Wild West show tradition, it contained none of the themes the showmen had worked to develop and, making matters worse, Cody endorsed the overblown work and hurt his own credibility by saying: "There is only one true book about me, and it was written by my sister; all the rest is fiction."[74]

While Cody failed to get good publicity, the publication of *The Virginian: A Horseman of the Plains* (1902) by Owen Wister signaled the end of the Wild West show's control of the mythical cowboy. Cody legitimately took credit for elevating the cowhand to the status of folk hero, claiming: "Until the advent of Buffalo Bill's Wild West introduced the cow-boy to the world at large, the great majority of people had altogether wrong notions about him."[75] Despite his possessive pronouncements, the cowboy no longer needed Wild West shows.

*The Virginian* enhanced the physical and intellectual image of the mythical cowboy. The protagonist, known simply as "the Virginian," earned respect with superior western skills, then became the intellectual equal of the schoolteacher Molley, married her, and proved his mettle by donning a dress suit and going East, where he impressed his wife's genteel parents. Near the end of the novel, the Virginian disassociated himself from Wild West show cowboys by asking people not to confuse him with them.[76]

Despite this declaration of independence, the Virginian owed his birthright to Wild West shows. In appearance, he replicated Buck Taylor, "King of the Cowboys." Physically imposing, both handsome men had dark features, towered above others, possessed great physical strength, and excelled in rodeo features. The action sequences in *The Virginian*—riding, shooting, and bringing outlaws to justice—mirrored Wild West show scenes. Furthermore, the novel reflected the show's themes: Wister stressed the Virginian's hardy Anglo-Saxonism and characterized the West as a Darwinian crucible in which the best triumphed. Like the show's "The Rifle as an Aid to Civilization" philosophy, the Virginian explained to his bride that he must engage in a gunfight, not for a love of bloodshed, but because the extension of civilization required hard men willing to eliminate evil. In addition, Wister made the Virginian a man of "shrewd intelligence" who understood the importance of irrigation and achieved financial success when the railroad built a branch line to his land, which contained coal deposits.[77]

Thus, Owen Wister imbued his hero with adaptability, devotion to progress, and success in business, but the book ended before the details of ranch management, railroads, farming, or other mundane tasks occupied the Virginian. Most likely Cody and his show inspired much of what Wister wrote, but as a novelist he could give his work a happy ending. Cody would not be so fortunate. His business ventures often turned sour, and Americans did not find glamor in his farming ventures or plans for coal mines.

The year that *The Virginian* appeared marked the last of a series of financially successful years (except for 1894) that stretched back to 1893. The Wild West show was an institution more suited to the nineteenth than the twentieth century. About the turn of the century, frontier anxiety decreased and Americans felt more comfortable with their country and its prospects. Perhaps Cody sensed the change, because he talked openly of retirement, saying 1900 seemed a reasonable date, particularly since he had a "hankering for one more World's Fair," specifically the one planned for Paris that year. A successful visit there would bankroll his retirement. Perhaps, he speculated, he would visit other places in Europe, but he did not plan to continue his career much into the twentieth century.[78] He failed to find a comfortable niche, but he did get another opportunity to go abroad.

His partner, James A. Bailey, decided that bringing the Barnum and Bailey Circus back from Europe and sending the Buffalo Bill Wild West show there would benefit both entertainments. Cody hoped a European tour would be profitable, even though he had already missed the world's fair in Paris. He left for the British Isles in December 1902. On 24 December, two days before the show's scheduled opening in London, Nate Salsbury died. This, Cody wrote, gave him "more work and responsibility." The show would remain abroad until 1906, and, while there, followed a route similar to that of the first European tour: London, Wales, Scotland, Paris, provincial France, Italy, Austria-Hungary, Germany, Luxembourg, Belgium, the Netherlands, and then returning to England. Urgency marked Cody's letters during this time. Was this his last great opportunity for a windfall? In 1903, he wrote to his sister Julia: "No rest this winter. I am going to organize a ten million dollar Company and make the boldest dash I ever dreamed of attempting." That same letter also discussed problems with the show, and perhaps fatigue prompted him to sign it "old Brother." Other letters documented expenses and indicated that sundry business ventures in the United States kept him broke.[79]

Despite talk of the "boldest dash," this visit lacked the vigor of the previous one. The entertainers worked hard, but no great unifying themes such as "esteem us better" and cultural ambassadorship motivated them during this tour. Instead of linking their show to grandiose goals, they stuck with time-tested techniques like extensive advertising, street parades, invitations to their camp, and rides for celebrities in the Deadwood stage. Royalty attended, and the show's advertising posters carried this good news. The showmen touted the enterprise as wholesome and educational entertainment that instructed observers about frontier life, the military tradition, and ethnology and recited figures about the size of the enterprise. However, Cody failed to become the "lion" of London's social scene as in 1887, and the Wild West show did not create a sensation. In fact, attendance was sometimes sparse.[80]

Reporters inquired about the statement in his latest biography that linked him to royalty and wrote that he symbolized the vigor of the Anglo-Saxon race. Publicity urged people to see the show because Cody planned to retire and would not return to this part of the world again. In interviews, Cody talked about the West and discussed his irrigating, mining, and town-founding enterprises. He presided over a twenty-two-act program much like that previously presented

to Americans. Western features remained popular, and people carefully watched
the horses. The "Battle of San Juan Hill," "Ranch Life in the West," or "Attack
on a Settler's Cabin" concluded performances. In addition, English ticket holders
enjoyed features tailored for them, such as "Military Exercises by Veteran English Cavalrymen."[81]

The outbreak of the Russo-Japanese War in 1904 provided new subject matter. Great Britain and Japan had become allies, in part, to prevent Russian expansion into Manchuria and Korea. Many Britons watched with approval when
the Japanese attacked Port Arthur and the war began. Admiration for the Japanese grew when they bottled up the Russian fleet and scored a series of quick
victories. Capitalizing on a new brand of "Resplendent Realism of Glorious
War," the entertainers brought Japanese performers into the arena. A reporter
noted: "the smart-looking Japs came in for the greatest amount of cheering,"
except for that which greeted Cody himself. Another journalist designated them
"those sturdy little 'Britons of the Orient.'" To capture the spirit of the military engagements, cossacks and Japanese soldiers demonstrated their modes of
fighting. Samurai, clad in their distinctive armor, illustrated that ancient warrior tradition, and the Japanese cavalry presented "the modern and successful
evolutions" that ensured victory against the Russians. The press explained that
the English approved of the Japanese because "their country has emerged from
its condition of semi-barbarism into the light of Western methods as regards
military tactics." Act fifteen brought Arab and Japanese acrobats before audiences.[82]

Another new feature provided escapist entertainment, with no connections
to international affairs, militarism, Rough Riders, or the Wild West, except that
its principal called himself "Carter, the Cowboy Cyclist." In a "Wonderful Bicycle Leap through Space," he sped down a seventy-five-foot arched ramp that
shot him upward and outward to a second elevated ramp and finally to a net
that caught him and the bicycle.[83] The act indicated two things: bicycles were
replacing horses in recreational activities and the Wild West show now offered
novelty scenes without relevance to the Wild West or the Congress of Rough
Riders.

In 1905, the show traveled to France, where it played in Paris at the Champs
de Mars (a military field) from 2 April to 4 June, and then toured other cities.
Royalty attended, and Cody enjoyed a moderately successful visit. The 1905
season ended on 12 November in Marseilles, where the troupe wintered and then
opened the 1906 season. Buffalo Bill fascinated the French, partly because advertising claimed he did not plan to return to that country. Western features
and riding skills in the program generated enthusiasm, and patrons enjoyed

seeing the Wild West show camp. The efficiency with which the Americans unloaded and erected camp, the plethora of posters, and the supposed look at typical America brought people to the showgrounds. Those with a real interest in Cody could purchase a French-language edition of *The Last of the Great Scouts*.[84]

The Americans reacted to the French much as they had in 1890. One of the troupe characterized Paris as a city with two social classes: one intent on making windfall profits by overcharging for everything and another determined to spend money as quickly as possible. This same American admired the beauty of Paris, but said that it attracted the idle rich from all over Europe, who turned the city's focus almost entirely to sensual pleasure. The observer noted people of provincial France, on the other hand, resembled wholesome and hardworking Americans. While Americans believed they remained more salubrious and temperate than the French, their moderation slipped when the troupe entered the champagne-producing region of France and found that elegant wine abundant and inexpensive.[85]

The entertainers modified the program to accommodate French tastes. That nation, along with other continental European powers, disapproved of American actions in Cuba because of investments there, sympathy for the Spanish monarchy, and disapproval of American expansionism. Probably for these reasons, "Custer's Last Stand" replaced "The Battle of San Juan Hill" as the concluding spectacle. Perhaps the generally militaristic mood in France caused the entertainers to emphasize carnage in the "Battle of the Little Bighorn." The showmen continued to capitalize on the Russo-Japanese war by presenting samurai and "an imperial Japanese troupe." Cossacks, as usual, represented the Russians. The Wild West show personnel camped in regulation army field tents, which gave a decidedly military appearance to the congregation.[86]

The 1906 season opened at Marseilles on 4 March, and then the Americans moved to Italy. About this country they expressed doubts, seeing it as "a land of anarchists, with bombs and stilettos." In Rome, an American reporter named Julian Street met Cody and accepted an invitation to travel with him. Street's accounts echoed familiar themes: the show's motley collection of peoples interested Europeans, Wild West show posters appeared everywhere, performers ate wholesome American food, Cody reminisced about life on the Plains, the Deadwood stage carried passengers across the arena, and Americans reacted negatively to poverty in Italy.[87]

Street called broncos in the Wild West show the most ferocious in the world and related that an Italian count, considered one of his nation's best horsemen, decided not to try to ride an American bronco after seeing one buck. Perhaps that decision benefited everyone, given the controversy created by the bronco-riding contests during the first tour. Italians often aggravated Cody, who wrote from Rome: "these people are so d— crazy wild to see something for nothing they run all over us. I am going to kiss the first New York policeman I see." From Italy, the group traveled to Austria-Hungary, Germany, Luxembourg, Belgium, and the Netherlands. The Wild West show presented its final performance in Europe in Ghent, Belgium, on 21 September 1906.[88]

Everyone returned home exhausted. The last year of the tour alone took the show into nations with sixteen different languages. James A. Bailey died on 22 March 1906, and Cody's work load again increased. Even more difficult times loomed ahead, because Bailey's heirs would complicate ownership and management and hound Cody for payment of a $12,000 note, which he claimed to have already paid.[89]

The years 1907 and 1908 were the last ones for the Buffalo Bill Wild West show as an independent production. With Salsbury and Bailey dead, Cody became the general manager, a position that drained his strength but allowed him to control the content of the show. Much of it remained the same, including emphasis on the military and foreign peoples. Soldiers from the "armies of America, England, Germany, Japan, Russia, Arabia, and Mexico" remained, as did the artillery act featuring the firing of Civil War cannons, Devlin's zouaves demonstrating "the adaptability of Citizen-soldiery in warfare," and standard western acts such as marksmanship and the Deadwood stage.[90]

Cody experimented a bit with the western theme, including adding "A Holiday at T-E Ranch," which featured his Wyoming spread.[91] By illustrating rodeo features, an Indian attack, and their defeat by cowboys, it followed a time-worn format, but it cast Cody in a new role—as the owner of a particular ranch, not a scout who wandered the extent of the Great Plains. The act foreshadowed the future glorification of ranchers by the Miller Brothers.

Other "new" western acts reworked features from previous shows. At Madison Square Garden, with its capacity for elaborate spectacles, "The Mighty Avalanche" depicted hunters and a stagecoach trapped by a blizzard and a snow-slide covering a village. Publicity called this new, but it presented the destructive forces of nature similar to those in the "Drama of Civilization" of 1887. "The Battle of Summit Springs" put Cody in his familiar role as scout and Indian fighter. In it, he shot Chief Tall Bull from his horse and led in the rescue of captive white women. Like "The Duel with Yellow Hand," it reproduced an actual occurrence in Cody's life. The act combined familiar features such as Native Americans in their village, a war dance, a battle between the U.S. Cavalry and Indians, and removal of the dead from the field of battle. Wild West show publicity called it *"The Greatest Savage War Spectacle,"* and in it Native Americans behaved like fiends from captivity narratives by mistreating their prisoners.[92]

Some acts added a contemporary air to the western theme. "Football on Horseback" melded a western motif and Americans' growing interest in sports. Participants played with gusto, making these games bone-bruising contests "little less than murder." Singing appeared in "Perils of the Prairie" with "songs by the emigrants octette" in a camp scene. This anticipated a future trend in western movies to feature singing cowboys. "The Great Hold-Up and Bandit Hunters of the Union Pacific" contained painted scenery with Pikes Peak dominating a sylvan landscape and an authentic-looking locomotive fashioned over a truck that pulled replicas of railroad cars. The locomotive puffed, emitted "immense volumes of black smoke," whistled shrilly, and even sported "an electrical head-light of great power."[93] This act heralded a transformation in the entertainment.

To this point, Cody had venerated technological progress primarily outside the arena. Locomotives transported people between engagements and also hauled earth and stone for the Wild West show camp in London in 1887. The showmen touted the electrical plant that illuminated their entertainment. As for steam, it had heated their Manchester theater and moved the steamships that ferried them across the Atlantic. In Wild West show arenas, however, people on horseback reigned. Now, with "The Great Hold-Up and Bandit Hunters of the Union Pacific," a steam-driven locomotive that belched smoke and found its way with an electrical light had invaded the arena. The issue of modern technology and its place in western romanticism would remain a major concern for future entertainers such as the Miller Brothers and Tom Mix.

"The Great Hold-Up and Bandit Hunters of the Union Pacific" revolutionized the Wild West show's subject matter. The entertainers suggested the act featured something new—authentic train robbers. It opened with outlaws, including a woman bandit dressed as a cowboy, waiting for the train. They stopped the locomotive with a danger signal, boarded it, rousted passengers from the cars, threw the safe from the baggage car, and blasted it open with dynamite. The racket attracted a sheriff and posse, who engaged the bandits in a gunfight and subdued them. Posters depicted heavily armed outlaws, passengers lined up beside the train, and the explosion in the baggage car in scenes reminiscent of those in *The Great Train Robbery,* a popular movie from 1903.[94]

*The Great Train Robbery,* while not the first western or the first movie with a plot, energized the infant moving picture industry by bringing together plot, a chase on horseback, gunplay, and justice triumphing. Americans loved it, and those in the Wild West show must have noted its popularity. Although the showmen claimed they "intended to describe in a general way any of the scores of train robberies which have formed a part of the history of Western development," the act reproduced the movie. In one sense, borrowing a feature was poetic justice because early filmmakers took from Cody sequences of western action and subjects such as the Spanish-American war, the Boer War, and the Boxer Rebellion for dramatization.[95] However, by copying the fledgling movie industry, the Wild West show had abandoned its position as leader and innovator in western romanticism.

Cody tried his hand at appearing before movie cameras, but little came from his efforts. In 1894, he and some of his performers visited the Kinematic Studio of Thomas Edison, where they were photographed. Others took a sequence of a street parade and portions of a Wild West show performance in 1902. Letters from 1908 and 1914 indicate that Cody believed he could make authentic movies about the West and educate Americans with them. Could this be the key to his fortune? In 1913, he founded Cody Historical Picture Company and began a documentary called *The Indian Wars,* which included material on the Ghost Dance, the Battle of Wounded Knee, and the death of Sitting Bull. Wanting accuracy, Cody included original participants and authentic locations, but the movie generated little excitement.[96] As a product of the nineteenth century, he understood live audiences, not clicking cameras.

In 1908, he formed a partnership with another showman named Gordon W. Lillie, known in the entertainment world as Pawnee Bill. By this time, ownership of Buffalo Bill's Wild West show was complicated. When Cody, Salsbury, and Bailey worked together, they divided the entertainment into thirds. With the deaths of Salsbury and Bailey, their shares had passed to other people. Cody retained ownership of his portion, but mortgaged it. The heirs of the Bailey estate held the controlling interest and informed Lillie that he should cooperate with them, not Buffalo Bill. Lillie responded by purchasing the Bailey interests and making Cody his partner. Perhaps altruism moved Lillie to treat Cody as an equal; but, most likely, Lillie recognized that becoming his partner and putting his name beside Buffalo Bill's elevated his own status and enhanced his chances of become Cody's successor in the Wild West show business.[97]

Lillie recognized the potency of the name "Buffalo Bill," because, as a child, he read dime novels, idolized Cody, and perhaps saw him, along with Wild Bill Hickok and Texas Jack Omohundro, in the play *The Scouts of the Plains.* Eventually, Lillie became a hero in dime novels and owner of and attraction in his own Wild West show. Like many others, Lillie's entertainment resembled Cody's show. The 1900 program, for instance, included the pony express, a stage coach robbery, cowboy skills, sharpshooting, Arabs, gauchos, cossacks, a detachment of "Roosevelt's Rough Riders," a "Grand Military Tournament, Introducing the Tactics of the Great Military Powers of the World," and a concluding spectacle called "The Burning of Trapper Tom's Cabin."[98]

Pawnee Bill's wife, "Miss Mae Lillie, the World's Greatest Lady Horseback Shot," filled the need for a female sharpshooter. Lillie spiced his program with sensational acts such as "Catching and Hanging the Horse Thief by Cowboys and Mexicans," "A Realistic Representation of the Atrocious Mountain Meadow Massacre," and a "Mohaje" Indian cremation. In 1904, the captured Geronimo joined the show, and Lillie borrowed a quote from General Miles and billed the Apache: "The Worst Indian That Ever Lived."[99]

Pawnee Bill's reputation never equalled that of Buffalo Bill's, and, with the exception of Annie Oakley, who joined Lillie's show for a time in 1888, he lacked well-known performers. However, Lillie always found a way to survive in the ruthless world of tented entertainment. Lillie took his show abroad, and despite difficult times there, kept it solvent. A publicist who worked for both Cody and Lillie said of the latter: "He had little of the dash and color of Buffalo Bill but, unlike Cody, he could unflinchingly face a crisis in the show business and fight his way out of it."[100]

Publicity for the combined show, including a volume sold in the stands for a dollar entitled *Thrilling Lives of Buffalo Bill and Pawnee Bill,* detailed the exploits of both men. About Lillie, *Thrilling Lives* related that as a teenager, he had crossed "a genuine bad man" named "Trigger Jim." During the first two meetings, Lillie thrashed the outlaw with his fists but the third prompted a gun duel wherein Lillie shot and killed the desperado. Other adventures included trapping, befriending Jesse James and his gang, forming a posse and capturing bank robbers, becoming a friend to Native Americans, delivering a contingent of Pawnees to the Buffalo Bill Wild West show in 1883, and leading settlement into Oklahoma. Like Cody, he considered himself a businessman, and *Thrilling Lives* explained that economic opportunity, as well as adventure, drew him to the West. Visual imagery stressed the similarity of the two men. The hallmark of the show—companion busts in three-quarter profile—appeared in poster art, in illustrations in programs and couriers, on watch fobs, and on the cover of *Thrilling Lives.*[101]

Business skills, experience with tented entertainment, a reputation as a tenacious fighter, and a high level of energy made Cody regard Lillie as a good partner. Pawnee Bill believed that with proper management, the combined shows could turn a profit. Cody expressed his optimism in a letter to a friend: "Lillie is a close conservative manager. Allways on the job and it wont be long now until I am on easy avenue again." The official name for the combined show was "Buffalo Bill's Wild West and Pawnee Bill's Far East," although people in the entertainment business simply called it the "Two Bills Show."[102]

In 1909, the grand review of the combined show included cowboys, Native Americans, Mexicans, Singhalese, Dahomeans, scouts, guides, U.S. Cavalry members, Wild West women, Australian aborigines, Arabians, Japanese, and cossacks. Wild West acts included the pony express, rescue of the immigrant train, Buffalo Bill shooting from horseback, the attack on the Deadwood stage, "Battle of Summit Springs," Johnny Baker's marksmanship, the train holdup, Mexican lassoers, cowboy fun, and cowboys versus Indians in "Football on Horseback." Military aspects were the "U.S. Cavalry Artillery Drill" with Civil War cannons, Devlin's zouaves, and a U.S. Cavalry drill. The showmen satisfied interest in the recent Russo-Japanese war by hiring Japanese performers to commemorate their victory against the Russians. In addition, Boy Scouts displayed the U.S. flag, and "Auto-Polo" celebrated the internal combustion engine with two automobiles, stripped down to bare essentials, "wide open" mufflers, and "uncovered" engines. Each vehicle sported a driver and a helmeted partner who wielded a mallet and struck an oversized white polo ball in an attempt to drive it to the opposite end of the arena.[103]

The "Far Eastern" section offered "A Dream of the Orient" that began with a camel caravan at the base of the pyramids. Tourists, taken captive by a band of Bedouins, waited there for friends to ransom them. When this occurred, the sheik ordered a celebration. "Rossi's Musical Elephants" pounded out recognizable tunes, and then came a parade of "strange" people from around the globe: Arabian acrobats, "Hindu Fakirs, Illusionists, and Wonder Workers" who performed magical acts. "Australian Boomerang Throwers" demonstrated their amazing weapons, and Singhalese danced to ward off evil spirits.[104] Such spectacles must have impressed the Miller Brothers of the 101 Ranch because after World War I, their show would offer similar attractions.

Lillie used phrases such as "romantic, historic, and alluring" to describe the Far East and called those who lived there "picturesque," "strange," "unfamiliar," and "mysterious" peoples who practiced unusual "combats, weird dances and strange religious ceremonies and incantations." Advertising described American Indians "as strange, incongruous and out of date" in the modern world as a "five toed salamander of the carboniferous era." Show publicity said patrons could study these "HOWLING, YELLING, JUMPING, RIDING, AND TOEING-IN" anachronisms, and that "Australian boomerang throwers" were "the lowest type of humanity . . . little removed from the dumb beast in matters of intelligence."[105] The combined show exuded an exotic allurement reminiscent of the midway at the 1893 Columbian Exhibition.

In this regard, Lillie stressed the physical attractiveness of women in the show. No one as shocking as Little Egypt appeared, but publicity announced that this show offered "FAIR MAIDENS FROM MANY TRIBES," a "buxom and swarthy senorita from Mexico," "carefree and healthy queens" from North America's prairies, "olive-skinned representations of Oriental beauty," and "Arrowhead," a Native American identified as "the belle of the lot." A courier featuring Arrowhead's picture explained that Americans might hate male Indians, but all "right-thinking men" would appreciate this beautiful Indian woman.[106] All of this varied significantly from the beginnings of the Wild West show, when George Catlin worked to convince Americans that Native Americans were noble and that nature was worth preserving.

During 1910, the second year of the combined show, the cover of the printed program carried the message "Buffalo Bill Bids You Good Bye," and inside the publication appeared a "Valedictory" by Cody saying: "I here announce the inevitable close of my public career." He wrote: "this farewell visit will positively be my last appearance in person, in the towns and cities of the present tour." This brilliant piece of publicity turned Cody's age and talk about leaving show business into good advertising copy and money. Cody, however, dallied, arguing that farewell tours meant saying good-bye to everyone and visiting all locations on previous tours. The public and press became disenchanted with interminable "Farewell Tours." The old man, obviously, resisted quitting.[107]

By 1913 the entertainment lacked gusto. A performer speculated that the merger had added a few years of life to the enterprise, but that both men were past their prime and the demise of the show was just a matter of time. To keep it going, members of the troupe took pay cuts. Adding to already difficult circumstances, personal problems plagued Cody: money shortages severe enough that he sold Scout's Rest Ranch in North Platte, Nebraska, to Lillie; lawsuits; impractical generosity; and spells of bad weather. The old scout, who had electrified audiences when he galloped his horse into arenas, now appeared in shows in a carriage. Posters pictured the aged Cody with his bald head clearly visible.[108]

Tragedy struck in Denver, Colorado, in July 1913, when law enforcement officers appeared during a performance and attached the equipment. Buffalo Bill had borrowed $20,000 from Harry Tammen, owner of the *Denver Post* and the Sells-Floto Circus. Tammen knew that breaking up the Cody-Lillie partnership and then contracting Cody for his entertainment would strengthen it. In addition to Cody's indebtedness, Tammen claimed that Buffalo Bill had agreed to join the Sells-Floto Circus in 1914. It was all legal; Cody had signed such a document, but probably without having read it. So Tammen and his partner, F. G. Bonfils, closed the show with the goal of bringing the patriarch into their own circus.[109] Like Catlin, Cody learned about "harpies of the law."

Despite Cody's and Lillie's efforts, they saw their property auctioned. Three relative newcomers to the Wild West show business—Joe, Zack, and George Miller of Oklahoma's 101 Ranch—bought livestock and equipment. The bargain prices pleased them, but Joe Miller wrote: "Was very sorry indeed to see such a grand and big outfit like that finish as it did."[110] After this, Lillie left the Wild West show business and returned to his ranch and business interests in Oklahoma.

Cody appeared in the Sells-Floto Circus during 1914 and 1915. The show began with "THE INITIAL LAUGH," wherein a female impersonator named Fred Briggs "caricatured the feminine sex." Then came the grand entry, followed by Buffalo Bill in the ring alone to greet the audience. After this, interspersed among circus acts, appeared standard Wild West show features: trick roping, Australian whip crackers, Virginia quadrilles on horseback, Indian equestrianism, war dances, rodeo events, horse races, the attack on the Deadwood stage, Devlin's zouaves, and horseback maneuvers by the U.S. Cavalry. Cody found the circumstances nearly unbearable. Missing a single performance might bring a lawsuit for $100,000, and he believed his employers would avoid paying his full salary. All in all, it was his "all fired darkest summer."[111]

In 1916 he joined the Miller Brothers' 101 Ranch Wild West show, which combined western and military features. To promote U.S. "Military Preparedness" for World War I the Millers included a pageant entitled "Preparedness" in their show and put Cody in charge of "a big realistic military display" to give audiences a firsthand look at U.S. armed forces and "to arouse public interest in the enlargement of the army."[112] With scenes of camp life, deafening displays of weaponry, arenas filled with smoke, and audiences bursting with patriotic fervor, it was "Resplendent Realism of Glorious War" reborn.

Despite a new war to promote, Cody's career and quality of life deteriorated. The old man had become a commodity shuffled from one show to another. Dexter Fellows, a press agent for Buffalo Bill during his heyday, saw Cody about a year before his death and reported that the seventy-year-old man's greatest fear was dying during a performance. But the old scout still talked of producing his own entertainment the following year. Cody, like Catlin, could not quit the business. He died at the home of his daughter, May Cody Decker, in Denver, Colorado, on 10 January 1917. His death, the result of "a complication of maladies attendant upon old age," caused an outpouring of grief throughout the nation. A journalist who had followed his career revealed that "a great depression came upon me. To me . . . he represented the last of the links connecting the present with those glorious frontier days."[113]

The Miller Brothers fancied themselves the successors of the old scout. These Oklahoma ranchers possessed those things Cody sought in the years after the Columbian Exposition: large holdings in real estate, leadership in agriculture, enthusiasm about ranching, and money to lavish on a show. With all these advantages, could they rekindle America's love affair with Wild West shows?

Cover art for a 101 Ranch Wild West show program. (Western History Collections, University of Oklahoma Library)

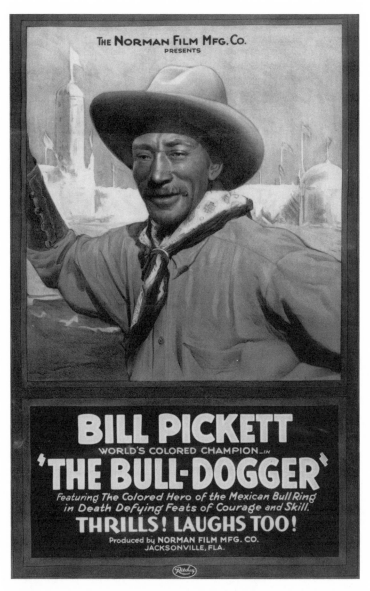

Bill Pickett ranked among the best known of the performers in the 101 show and sometimes appeared in movies. (Buffalo Bill Historical Center, Cody, Wyo.)

When the Millers presented one of their first Wild West shows in 1905, Geronimo entertained guests by driving this auto and then shooting a buffalo, which was barbecued for the guests. By this time, the Apache leader had become a celebrity. (Western History Collections, University of Oklahoma Library)

In the 1920s the Miller's Wild West show featured dancers in scenes from antiquity. Such acts failed to generate much excitement among spectators. (Western History Collections, University of Oklahoma Library)

A scene from Tom Mix's *Son of the Golden West*. (Archives and Manuscripts Division of the Oklahoma Historical Society)

Tom Mix apprenticed in Wild West shows and transferred what he learned in live entertainment to silent western movies. Here he demonstrates daring horsemanship with Tony. (Archives and Manuscripts Division of the Oklahoma Historical Society)

# "An Empire within Itself":
# The 101 Ranch and Its Wild West Show

When Colonel George W. Miller, founder of the 101 Ranch of Oklahoma Territory, realized that he was dying, he summoned his
family to the bedside. All assembled and listened carefully, particularly his three sons—Joe, Zack, and George. The old man reminisced about
his early life as a cattle trader and pioneer rancher and said that he wanted his
holdings to remain intact; therefore, he was leaving his property to his family
as a group because it would be a mistake to divide it and let it "dribble away."
He encouraged his survivors to complete a large Southern style white house to
replace the dugout headquarters beside the Salt Fork of the Arkansas River,
where they now talked. The dying man urged his family to buy land to increase
the fifty-thousand-acre spread leased from the Ponca Indians. Miller had recently
negotiated with them for the purchase of some real estate, including the section where the headquarters now stood. Money was available because the farming and ranching operations grossed as much as half a million dollars in good
years. Miller's life and this last talk "fired his sons with his ambition to make
the 101 the largest, the best, and the most far-famed of all the ranches."[1]

Miller's hunches were right on all counts: he died shortly thereafter on 25 April
1903, and his advice about owning land led to a huge enterprise. The family
collected $30,000 from a life insurance policy, bought six sections, and contin-

ued to lease and to purchase all that the Poncas would sell. The Millers planned well, leasing and buying in a checkerboard fashion that prevented small farmers and ranchers from interfering with their plans to consolidate an empire.[2]

In keeping with Colonel Miller's request, the 101 remained a family enterprise, and his sons became known as the "Miller brothers." They cooperated to build a ranching and farming showplace that eventually encompassed 110,000 acres. Orchards, large-scale farming, ranching on grand proportions, and the discovery of oil all contributed to the family's fortune. Consequently, the Millers prospered in the early years of the twentieth century, a time when fluctuating markets for cattle, high interest rates, disease, and other problems drove many out of the livestock business.[3]

The ranch, however, symbolized more than success, because the Miller brothers possessed a nostalgic side. They vowed to make the 101 "a monument to their father's love of the West of pioneer days," praised the "West of romance and adventure," and saw themselves as "Titans of the trail, keeping gallantly alive the memories and customs of the old days." Joe claimed that the Poncas made him the "White Chief" and invited him to participate in their sun dance. In addition, show publicity maintained that the tough cowboys who remembered the early days on the frontier respected him because "he never drew a six shooter" back then except when "necessary" and "he never asked a another fellow to ride an outlaw horse that he had not ridden himself." Likewise, Zack was a "wholehearted, broad-minded, clean-cut westerner, the best type of the picturesque cowboy," "the highest specimen of the western rancher," and the kind of person Theodore Roosevelt had chosen to be a Rough Rider.[4] In many ways the ranch did become a monument to the Old West. The Millers employed "the old time cowboy with his picturesque costumes," protected Native Americans from modern influences and allowed them to live as they wished, preserved longhorn cattle, set aside a special "buffalo pasture" for those shaggy beasts, kept herds of deer and elk, and maintained cages of bears and monkeys. With so much unique about the ranch and those who lived there, the 101 became, in the words of a local journalist, "an empire within itself—the dream of its founder."[5]

Such verbiage conveyed how the Millers felt about themselves and the 101. It was almost a magical place, both forward-looking and backward-looking, managed by an extraordinary family, and separate and distinct from mundane life. The Millers considered themselves exceptional—patrician, different from "ordinary" Americans, and a cut above the cowboys and other workers on the ranch. The Millers wanted to call the most attention to themselves as ranchers. Certainly they expected everyone to admire the grizzled cowboys and other western characters, but in their view, everyone should recognize that ranchers—not cowhands or anyone else—were the most important people on the 101. Always, the Millers exhibited a little arrogance.

They believed that Americans admired them and clamored to learn about them and their ranch—after all 100,000 visitors a year came to see the 101 first-hand, admire its enterprises, and savor the lingering spirit of the frontier. The Millers made these people feel comfortable by inviting as many as possible to their dinner table, by constructing accommodations called Riverside Camp alongside the Salt Fork, and even by staging a mock holdup at the local train station for one tenderfoot who arrived by rail.[6]

In addition, the Millers claimed that they began the demonstrations of western life that evolved into rodeos and Wild West shows. According to their account, while on a cattle drive in 1882, Colonel Miller and his son Joe provided cow-boys and cattle to entertain the folks of Winfield, Kansas, a demonstration they believed marked the beginnings of rodeo as a spectator sport. Further, in 1883, the year that Cody began his Wild West show, Joe Miller took a group of Na-tive Americans to the state fair in Alabama to perform dances. They also attended a Baptist church service, where White Eagle, with Joe Miller interpreting, ex-plained the general tenets of his religion to an overflow crowd. Impromptu rodeos thrived on the 101, and cowboys from the ranch regularly entered con-tests in cities such as Wichita, Kansas, and Enid, Oklahoma. The Millers said that the 101 cowboys garnered the prize money so often that others considered them professionals and barred them from some competitions.[7]

Enthusiasm for exhibitions of Western skills and pride in themselves and their ranch moved the Millers closer and closer to professional showmanship. After a dress rehearsal in 1904, the Millers staged their first large Wild West show in 1905 when the National Editorial Association, the National Association of Millers, and the National Association of Cattlemen held conventions nearby. These groups, in addition to throngs of other spectators, arrived at the ranch on 11 June 1905. At about two o'clock, a parade, stretching nearly two miles, began to pass before the grandstands constructed especially for the event. Vis-itors faced a thirty-acre natural arena with a hill that provided a backdrop and a barrier over which entertainers could appear dramatically and dash before spectators.[8]

This show encapsulated much about the Millers. The free entertainment reflected their generosity and hospitality. The production showcased about five hundred cowboys and a thousand Native Americans, a fitting testimony to the size and spirit of the "empire within itself." The show was a local product, pre-sented by 101 Ranch employees, Ponca Indians, and other Oklahomans. It offered established Wild West show acts: cowboys riding bucking broncos, Lucille Mulhall demonstrating her equestrian abilities, and Indians hunting buffalo, playing ball, dancing, demonstrating camp life, and attacking a wagon train. By presenting a standard set of acts, the Millers followed the trend in Wild West entertainments, instead of developing a new one. Most likely, Buffalo Bill's show provided their pattern, because Zack saw it with Will Rogers in 1901 and with Tom Mix in 1904.[9]

However, the 1905 show gave a realistic twist to buffalo hunting and introduced something new in rodeo. It featured Willie M. Pickett, known in Oklahoma simply as Bill Pickett, and a bull. A short, muscular man, mostly of black and Indian ancestry, Pickett learned to subdue bulls single-handedly by observing pugnacious bulldogs follow cattle into brush patches where cowboys could not ride. There, bulldogs harassed cantankerous cows, causing them to lower their horns for protection. Once a cow's head neared the ground, bulldogs clamped vise-like grips on bovine lips or noses, and then held the animal motionless until a cowboy slipped a rope around its neck. If a dog could render an animal helpless like this, why not a man? For the crowd at the 101, Pickett demonstrated "bulldogging," his technique of sliding from the back of a running horse and subduing bulls by sinking his teeth into their lips or nostrils.[10]

Pickett's act was not for the squeamish, and neither was the one featuring Geronimo. By 1905, this old Apache leader qualified as a veteran showman with an impressive record of appearances: the Trans-Mississippi and International Exposition in Omaha (1898), the Pan-American Exposition (1901), the Louisiana Purchase Exposition in St. Louis (1904), Theodore Roosevelt's inaugural parade (1905), and many local celebrations in Oklahoma. When a request came from the Millers, Geronimo obliged. He either drove or rode into the arena as a passenger in an automobile, raised a rifle, and shot a buffalo bull to be cooked for editors.[11] The acts by Pickett and Geronimo, as well as the less sanguinary ones in the program, delighted the crowd. At this 1905 affair, the Millers learned that they could give a successful Wild West show for a large audience and that they enjoyed doing it.

The following year brought about fifty thousand persons, including many of Oklahoma's "Boomers," to the 101 to commemorate the opening of the Cherokee Strip thirteen years earlier. The entertainment included a battle between cowboys and Indians, rodeo skills, Bill Pickett's bulldogging, and a reenactment of the opening of the Cherokee Strip. That same year, the Millers took cowboys to the convention hall in Kansas City to demonstrate rodeo events. While there, the Millers decided to take a show to the Jamestown Exposition scheduled for 1907 in Norfolk, Virginia.[12]

The 101 Ranch show opened there on 20 May 1907 with a status like that of Cody's at the world's fairs. The show stood next to the official U.S. exhibit and drew many visitors, including President Theodore Roosevelt, who pronounced it a realistic portrayal of ranch life. Encouraged by this, the Millers sent a second show to Brighton Beach, New York, and then routed the one in Norfolk to the Georgia State Fair before returning home. From this, the Millers learned that they could put more than one show on the road at a time, a pattern they would continue. The commitment to a permanent traveling Wild West show came in the winter of 1907–8 when Edward Arlington, who saw the show in Virginia, approached the Millers and told them they had the makings of a good entertainment. Arlington was a young but experienced showman, having worked with the Ringling Brothers and Barnum and Bailey circuses and the Pawnee Bill Wild West show.[13] Persuading the Millers to become entertainers proved easy, and they struck a deal with Arlington, purchased circus equipment, and prepared for the upcoming year.

The Miller brothers opened their 1908 season at Ponca City, Oklahoma, on 14 April with a street parade followed by afternoon and evening performances. The mayor declared a holiday, and enthusiastic townspeople thronged to the Millers' production. A local writer pronounced the show a first-class operation with the "finest circus train in the history of tented amusements." Reporters pointed out that it represented the only real Wild West show left in the nation, that it would "winter" near Ponca City and thereby bolster the local economy, and that the entertainment, filled as it was with Oklahomans and carrying the name of the 101 Ranch, would advertise the state.[14]

Becoming professional showmen enabled the Millers to promote themselves and to venerate the ranchers' frontier. Just as Catlin praised Plains Indians and Cody celebrated the conquest of the Plains, the Millers wanted to promote their view of the West and its era of great ranches. After all, the 101 was the "Last of the Big Ranches Left in America."[15] Unlike Catlin and Cody, the Millers had an independent source of income to finance their entertainment.

The Millers championed their show as "a reproduction of life as it is seen at the Miller Brothers' big tract in Oklahoma." A cowboy in the show declared that the performance was "just as if the Miller boys had shifted their ranch to Boston for a time." It was a "true glimpse of ranch life" illustrating how westerners "work, and play and fight out where the buildings arn't so thick as they are in the East." One article emphasized that the Millers constantly shuffled cowboys and cowgirls between the ranch and the show, with many 101 employees trading the Oklahoma prairies for the show ring "for the fun of the thing" and to see the rest of the United States. Publicity noted that those few individuals not from the ranch itself came from Oklahoma's smaller ranches and farms. The Millers pointed proudly to the fact that the governor of Oklahoma's son traveled with the troupe and rode in its street parades. While all of this made good publicity, many of the performers were actually professionals hired specifically for the show.[16]

The Millers, it appeared, represented the best hope for the survival of Wild West shows as a distinct type of entertainment. There was no shortage of them; in fact, they had become commonplace, but mostly remained small, low budget, traveling shows that eked out an existence by reproducing on a limited scale what Buffalo Bill had popularized. County fairs, carnivals, and circuses all sported "Wild West" exhibitions.[17] By contrast, the Millers wanted something big and impressive associated with their ranch. Moreover, they eschewed the international emphasis that prevailed in Buffalo Bill's Congress of Rough Riders and in Pawnee Bill's Far East. The Millers were wealthy men on a mission to rebuild and redignify Wild West shows by concentrating solely on the West and focusing attention on themselves and their ranch.

However, ensconcing themselves and their ranch as new symbols of the mythical West was a tall order. Such a focus resulted in playing down the role of others, such as Native Americans, whose place in Wild West shows went back over seventy years to George Catlin's time. This stance fit these Oklahomans, who had not marveled at classic Plains Indian cultures or engaged in bloody battles with them. In that last talk with his family, Colonel George W. Miller discussed cattle trading, ranching, and building an empire, not exploits involving Indians. The Millers gained much of their land by convincing the Poncas to sell it and then assuming a paternalistic role toward them—actions that reflected little respect for Indians. Native Americans appeared in the 101 show, but the Millers did not feature them, or discuss them, with zeal equal to that of Catlin or Cody.

Another problem with promoting the ranchers' view of the West was that the cowboy already represented the cattle kingdom, and in no way had the public indicated a desire to diminish the cowboy's appeal by adding another representative figure from the same frontier. Nor was there popular support for ranchers. Unlike Catlin, who lived in a time when *Leatherstocking Tales* popularized Indians, and Cody, who benefited from dime novels, the Millers could not draw on imaginative literature to generate special interest in ranchers. In fact, fiction usually portrayed them as either stodgy old men or ruthless cattle kings.[18] Even Cody failed to develop much enthusiasm for himself while promoting the agricultural frontier and the TE Ranch.

Furthermore, ranchers were businessmen, a group whom Americans resisted valorizing, particularly in the early twentieth century when Progressives and others railed against the excesses of robber barons and their irresponsible corporations. During the first years of the Millers' show, two influential books appeared, Herbert Croly's *The Promise of American Life* (1909) and Walter Weyl's *The New Democracy* (1912). Both authors argued that opportunity on the frontier had created an aggressive, individualistic, acquisitive, and "monopolistic" side to Americans, but that with the end of the frontier, such values needed to be replaced with concern for the good of all Americans.[19]

Disregarding (or unaware of) the views of Progressives, the Miller Brothers filled their Wild West show publications with stories of their cattle-trading on a grand scale, immense wealth, vast herds of cattle, shrewd business deals, and even praise for their accounting practices.[20] These documented their success but certainly did not curry public favor or transform them into popular heroes.

Making the 101 the representative institution of the Plains also proved impossible. Trying to restrict the concept of the West to one identifiable place departed from the thinking of earlier Wild West showmen. Catlin called the West vague, expansive, and something as undefinable as appreciating seas of prairie grass, buffalo bulls locked in mortal combat, the mysterious O-kee-pa, and "noble savages" beyond the reaches of "civilization." Cody linked the West to protean terms and ideas such as "the gladiatorial contest revived," "to esteem us better," and "Resplendent Realism of Glorious War." So, the Wild West show tradition had stressed vagueness and a host of colorful characters performing soul-stirring deeds in unspecified Plains locations. Now the Millers planned to restrict all this to themselves and their 110,000 acres in Oklahoma. The public would attend their Wild West show, but they would not accept the Millers and the 101 as the sole embodiment of the West. And the Millers, for their part, failed to support their assertion about the uniqueness of themselves and their ranch with anything really new about the West. Their shows simply replicated those western acts pioneered by Catlin and Cody.

Despite their failure to redirect thinking about the West, enthusiasm for Wild West shows still existed, and the Millers managed to make money in the years before World War I in the face of inexperience, cutthroat competition, and inclement weather. Annie Oakley, then retired, saw the show, enjoyed it immensely, and pronounced it a success. In 1908, Cody confided to a friend that competition with the Millers cost him dearly. Often, they sent more than one show on tour, including small groups to Trinidad, Brazil, Uruguay, and Argentina, and larger ones to Mexico and Canada. Posters, impressive street parades, Indians living in Wild West show–style camps, and sideshows all caught people's attention. The Millers praised their "straight wild west performance" and disparaged competitors like circuses, Cody, and Lillie. The Millers called circuses "tawdry" and believed that Cody and Lillie sullied themselves with the circus-style segments of their show.[21]

In these first years, the 101 Ranch Wild West show offered standard western features. Performances that stretched to nearly three hours began with a grand review of cowboys, cowgirls, Native Americans, cossacks, and *vaqueros* led by Joe or Zack Miller, followed by sharpshooting men and women, horse racing, the pony express, a quadrille on horseback, bronco riding, trained horses, and cowboys galloping their mounts and plucking handkerchiefs from the ground, bulldogging steers, and demonstrating lariat tricks. This show also contained a feature, much like one in the Pawnee Bill show, in which westerners apprehended a horse thief and dragged him to death behind a mount. The Millers filled their own Deadwood stage with spectators, which Mexican bandits promptly attacked. Sometimes, a man rode a bucking buffalo. The Millers touted the "Pat Hennessey Massacre" as a new and authentic spectacle because it depicted an actual event in Oklahoma's history. However, it followed the pattern of the Battle of the Little Bighorn from Cody's show, even to the Millers claiming that it contained combatants from the actual event—Chief Bull Bear, the leader of the Cheyennes, and W. E. Malaley, the U.S. marshall who discovered the carnage after the massacre.[22]

Presentations by Native Americans followed the pattern established in Buffalo Bill's show. Joe Miller wanted Plains Indians with long hair who rode well. In the arena, they attacked white settlers, played football on horseback, rode in horse races, and sometimes performed "Indian dances and other weird aboriginal rites and ceremonies." Like George Catlin, the Millers sensationalized the war dance by describing it as "fantastic, savage evolutions, in which the old Indians feign war, pretending to attack and scalp their enemies, and entering into the spirit of the stage-battle as though it were grimly real." As in Cody's show, publicity claimed that government officials prohibited Indian children from watching such a dance because it was so dangerous. The Millers purported that their show included four participants in the "Custer massacre," Charlie-Owns-the-Dog (a cousin of Geronimo), Standing Cloud, Long Bull, and Flat-iron, whom old cowboys in the 101 show claimed "harangued the Indians before they went into the Custer fight." The Millers pointed out that their aggregation included representatives from as many as twelve tribes, not just Sioux as in Cody's show.[23]

Beginning with Bill Pickett and Geronimo in 1905, the 101 show offered a bit of sensationalism. The Millers continued this with lurid descriptions of scalp dances and recreations of massacres. Like George Catlin's accounts of the O-kee-pa and Cody during his "gladiatorial" period, Joe and Zack believed that western life sometimes included gore and that their role as showmen obligated them to provide accurate representations of the West, even if such depictions shocked some. The Millers insisted that none of their features exceeded the bounds of good taste, because their mother and Edwin Arlington's mother reviewed them all, monitored the degree of violence, and watched for any other improprieties. In 1914 in New York, the show even boasted an "official chaplain," a position filled by the Reverend Robert Rein, an evangelist who took it upon himself to become the guardian of morality for the troupe.[24]

The Millers included patriotism on their list of virtues. Like Catlin and Cody, they viewed life on the Plains as uniquely American and beyond reproach. A journalist reported that the Miller Brothers followed "the idea of patriotism to the highest possible degree." Their brand of Americanism often lacked appreciation for foreigners, however. A 1909 courier informed readers: "Every performer—cowboy, cowgirl and Indian—is a product of the prairie, except the contingent of Cossacks" and then added: "relations between the cowboys and the Cossacks are formal, even strained." Show publicity noted that many people considered cossacks the best riders in the world but then called them acrobats on horseback rather than superior horsemen, since they avoided bucking broncos. So cossacks served as a point of comparison with the cowboys, not to win the hearts of spectators. The 101 entertainment included Mexican riders and ropers; however, Wild West show publicity contained faint praise for them. Other foreigners, such as Arabs, who applied for positions got terse replies saying that the Millers planned to keep their show "strictly wild west."[25]

Such attitudes fit the overall national mood of the period, because interest in foreign affairs had diminished since the late nineteenth century when Cody had introduced the Congress of Rough Riders. These days, Theodore Roosevelt, the old Rough Rider and imperialist, talked less of war and more of progressivism, conservation, and regulation of trusts. His successor in the White House, William Howard Taft, a 350-pound man who sometimes fell asleep in front of his guests after eating prodigious meals, inspired few Americans. Entertainers could not build acts around this genial and low-key man who avoided the limelight, longed to resume being a judge, promoted industrial growth and business, contemplated the tariff, and practiced "Dollar Diplomacy." The other president to serve between the turn of the century and the outbreak of World War I was Woodrow Wilson, a bookish and idealistic man who did little to excite Wild West showmen either. Quiet diplomatic efforts had replaced the bluster of the earlier years, and Europe seemed peaceable, despite the imminence of World War I. Relations with Latin America revealed that the United States and its presidents could be heavy-handed. Roosevelt swinging the "Big Stick" in Panama, Taft positioning American bankers to direct Nicaragua's finances, and Wilson flexing America's muscle during the Mexican Revolution set a mood that infused the Millers' show.

Although nationalism in Wild West shows increased with the Millers, it obviously did not begin with them. Privately and in *Notes of Eight Years' Travels and Residence in Europe,* Catlin grumbled about much in Europe. Nor was Cody above praising Americans at the expense of others. He presented *vaqueros* and gauchos as pale copies of cowboys, nearly caused a riot in Spain when he disparaged bullfighting, encouraged his cowboys to humiliate Italian *buttari* in a bronco-riding contest, and denigrated foreigners in depicting the Battles of San Juan Hill and Tien-Tsin. The Millers, however, outdid their predecessors during a trip to Mexico after the regular season in 1908.

When the Millers crossed the border, they entered a nation seething with frustration and anti-Americanism.[26] Mexicans remembered the loss of territory after the Mexican war, resented the "Big Stick" that Theodore Roosevelt yielded to get the Panama Canal, and regarded the Mexican president Porfirio Diaz as a puppet. The pent-up anger that would sweep Diaz from office and begin the revolution in 1910 was strong when the show visited Mexico in December 1908. The time and place were wrong: most Mexicans did not want to see an American entertainment, particularly an overtly nationalistic one like the 101 Wild West show. Things started poorly for the Oklahomans and progressively worsened.

The show arrived in Monterrey on 6 December 1908, traveled to San Luis Potosi, and then moved to Mexico City. Because of poor attendance, the Millers lost about a thousand dollars a day, but they could not leave because Mexican law required that shows stick exactly to their advertised dates of departure. Mexicans criticized nearly everything about the performances, including Pickett's bulldogging, which they said lacked grace and required no courage. To spark controversy and thereby create interest in the show, Joe Miller declared that bulldogging required more skill and fortitude than bullfighting, and that Pickett could upend the fiercest beast the Mexicans could find. This certainly caught the attention of the country.

On 23 December 1908, twenty-five thousand persons paid to see the contest. Although the bull gored Pickett's horse to death, Pickett did not throw the animal and it failed to kill its tormentor. Pickett managed to survive for 38.5 agonizing minutes, including 7.5 of them holding on to the animal's horns. Angered by the stalemate, the audience members pelted Pickett with whatever they could find, including a beer bottle that broke three of Pickett's ribs. He and the others in the show managed to escape, thanks to an escort of two hundred men. Pickett, for his part, wanted no more to do with Mexican bulls, saying that Zack Miller could handle the bull wrestling assignments in the future.

Back in the United States, the showmen used the event to blacken the reputation of Mexicans. They turned the spectacle into an act and advertised it with a poster entitled "Barbarous Mexico" that depicted a white cowboy wrestling a Mexican bull to the ground. A 101 publication explained that Pickett "had belittled the boasted prowess of every professional toreador." In the 101's account, the danger to the "Brave Cowboy" came not from the bull, but from the spoilsport Mexicans, who bombarded him with "Fruit, Bottles, Canes, and Even Open Knives." The publication explained: "Every visitor to Mexico knows the native has no love for Americans." For Joe's part, he admitted only that his "Americanism was running rampant."[27]

Joe Miller's disdain for Mexicans resurfaced in 1910, when the Mexican Revolution erupted and strained relations between Mexico and the United States. He wrote to a friend that the only way to solve the problem was to "kill all the Mexicans." "Killing Mexicans" became the order of business in the show's arena through reenactments of Mexican rebels fighting the Federalists and a "sham battle between Mexicans and Texas Rangers." The showmen promised that the combatants would "continue to use blank cartridges" even in the "event of war." Participants in these acts wore authentic equipment taken in January 1914 when Federalists had fled across the Rio Grande to Presidio, Texas, where American troops seized their goods and horses. Zack purchased everything, and he would produce the bill of sale for anyone who doubted his story about buying an entire Mexican army.[28]

Should war come, Joe Miller planned to be its "Rough Rider." He telegraphed President Wilson, asking to be commissioned a colonel and offering to raise, train, and equip a regiment of "Rough Riders." Miller said he knew the terrain where the fighting might occur, offered five hundred burros to the government, and argued that the horses purchased from the fleeing Mexican army would be excellent for any campaign that might occur. The War Department expressed some interest in using the 101 Ranch as a base in the anticipated war and instructed Congressman William Murray to get precise information about it, including the location of water supplies and the number of troops and animals that could be kept there.[29]

The show prompted statements like those about Buffalo Bill's show on the eve of the Spanish-American War. A journalist entitled his article "Wild West Smacks of War" and wrote, "The Mexican war situation happened just in time for the 101 Ranch Wild West show." He commented that problems with Mexico made "people ready to appreciate the taste of gunpowder and the roar of guns," and that when the show ended, the audience was in a "fighting mood." Mexicans in the street parades became the "center of attraction," and, fearing an incident, Miller forbade them to carry their flag.[30]

A cowboy named Guy Weadick predicted that Mexicans would use guerrilla tactics in the upcoming war, capture Americans by roping them, and mistreat prisoners because Mexican "blood thirsts for torture." Weadick claimed that he had watched them "lasso one of their number for some minor depredation and then torture him." He concluded: "these 'Mex' are a bad lot, and to me they always reminded me of cats playing with mice."[31]

The 101's cowgirls clamored to fight Mexicans as well. Should hostilities begin, Edith Tantlinger hoped to lead a "regiment of women sharpshooters." Already twelve cowgirls in the 101 show had volunteered to join her. Tantlinger claimed to know about Mexicans and declared that they hated the United States. In an event said to have happened in the 101 camp, a cowgirl named Rocky Mountain Kate waged a one-woman war against an ill-behaved *vaquero* reportedly nicknamed "Greaser Joe," who abused his Native American wife. According to the story, the gallant cowgirl gave the offending Mexican a thorough beating with her fists, after which she drew her six-shooter and ordered him to kiss his wife in front of the Wild West show troupe. Thereafter, Rocky Mountain Kate returned daily until the *vaquero* mastered the art of kissing and learned to be a good husband.[32]

In addition to talk about them, Mexicans became scoundrels in the 101's arena. They played bandits in stagecoach holdups, and reporters wrote that such acts ended happily because cowboys "put the Greasers to flight."[33] Thus, happenings in and out of the show ring made Mexicans appear to be nefarious, anti-American, and cruel. This negative view would continue in the future, particularly in western movies, where Mexicans appeared as villains for many years. The 101 had done its part to promote antagonism toward Mexico and its people.

War with Mexico, however, did not materialize; and, lacking great battles to reproduce, the show's militarism abated. This entertainment, despite its bellicose stance, offered a different view than that in Cody's Congress of Rough Riders. Cody had direct ties to the professional military, had an appreciation for soldiers of other nations, and included professionals from other world powers in his Congress of Rough Riders. The Millers, however, had no military credentials or enthusiasm for the outside world and instead centered attention on themselves and their ranch and praised westerners as citizen-soldiers, even to the extent of endorsing Edith Tantlinger's plans for a "regiment of women sharp-shooters."

During this time when Americans talked of war, the Millers took their show to New York's Madison Square Garden. There they hoped to "succeed the Buffalo Bill show in the affections of New Yorkers" with an entertainment that "adheres to the spirit of the plains and the real wild west." Publicity posters called attention to the recently issued buffalo nickel, for which a bison from the Millers' herd and an Indian named Iron Tail supposedly served as models.[34]

The 101 bunch immediately succeeded in attracting attention in the metropolis. Upon arrival, they gave a traffic-snarling, "illuminated parade" down Broadway. When the show opened, many New Yorkers praised it, noting the realistic scenery, bright and attractive costumes, and interesting Indian village set up in the restaurant room of Madison Square Garden. Longhorn cattle, with horns that spanned six to seven feet, fascinated New Yorkers, and the Millers maintained that these represented some of the last of the breed. The show spurred a cowboy craze, causing a run on cowboy hats and other articles of western dress.[35]

Performances offered Wild West show standards: a grand entry, cowboy skills, sharpshooting, Native American dances, Mexican bandits attacking a stage-coach, and an Indian assault on a wagon train. The troupe punctuated the entertainment with a "continuous volley of shots." "An Indian dropped dead" with every firing until "the great hall was filled with powder smoke." Mixed with traditional offerings were horseback football games between cowboys and cowgirls and Indian men and women. Vern Tantlinger, an American cowboy who had lived in the "wilds of Australia," demonstrated use of the boomerang.[36] Acts such as these marked a search for novelty that continued throughout the life of the 101 show.

Such innovations failed to attract much attention, but New Yorkers doted on the fifty cowgirls in the show. Advertising made "a special feature of its cowgirls," calling them regular ranch employees who worked for wages and routinely performed cowboy skills such as roping, riding bucking broncos, and tending cattle, and the women made their own publicity by talking about fighting Mexicans.[37]

One reporter credited the engagement in New York with enabling Native American women to enjoy greater equality within the show. In truth, all the women in the show probably benefited because New York was a center of the suffrage movement. In these supportive surroundings, the 101 cowgirls became the West's answer to "the bachelor girl and independent women of the East,"[38] spokespersons for women and the western way of life, and critics of the "over-civilized" East.

These women claimed not to "ape" men and proved they could vie with cow-boys in performing daring stunts on Indian broncos and bucking horses. Ap-parently, the more dangerous the action, the more cowgirls enjoyed it because they "whooped away joyously as they perched on top of the plunging beasts." A reporter remarked that a glance at these women proved they were the "sauc-iest, happiest, loveliest assemblage of femininity imaginable."[39]

Advertising posters praised cowgirls and emphasized their vigor. One depicted Theodore Roosevelt waving to 101 women and exclaiming: "That's Fine! That's Bully!" He also was pictured shaking hands with Lucille Mulhall and praising her as "The Bravest Girl in All the West," an accolade he had bestowed several years earlier after watching her entertain former Rough Riders at one of their reunions. Another portion of the same poster indicated that Will Rogers ad-mired Mulhall and designated her the "first Cowgirl," although of course she was not the first. The poster also portrayed cowgirls in strenuous activities: riding buffalo, playing "Equestrian Football," and firing from the backs of their horses. "Wenona, Indian Princess" could shoot so well because she was really the sharp-shooter Lillian Smith. After leaving Cody's entertainment and appearing in other shows and exhibitions, Smith darkened her skin and called herself an Indian.[40]

In New York, 101 cowgirls became the symbols of and spokespersons for the salubrious western way of life. A *New York Tribune* reporter called them "natty, healthy, sinuous-looking girls." Edith Tantlinger informed reporters that the strenuous life of cowgirls gave them "healthy chests, excellent breathing and physical endurance." Tantlinger asserted that life on the Plains made cowgirls so healthy that they could overcome any injury, regardless of its severity. Those speaking for the 101 said cowgirls possessed remarkable endurance because they could "execute an equine quadrille or Virginia reel, and then gallop twenty miles without feeling a suspicion of fatigue." Show publicity and news accounts de-picted these physically fit women as beautiful, and some news accounts sug-gested that they were sexy.[41]

Everything about these women—their demeanor, vigor, western skills, health-fulness, and appearance—grew naturally from their simple and wholesome way of life. The women criticized what they saw as artificial, particularly vestiges of Victorian America, such as corsets, parasols, and other accoutrements of the complex and restrictive dress of that age. These cowgirls rode their horses astride, saying that the impractical and uncomfortable sidesaddle "should be relegated to the oblivion of the hoop skirt of our grandmothers." In their view, no American woman should endure such a cumbersome relic.[42]

Like Catlin's Native Americans and some members of Cody's troupe, 101 cowgirls found much to criticize about city dwellers. These western women saw New York females as weaklings: "If some New York women were to get some of the bumps we girls get they would be broken apart. Why? Because they get up at 10 o'clock, dance the tango all night, and think they are really living." City women encumbered themselves with paraphernalia like purses; carried parasols to hide from the health-giving rays of the sun; and girded their bodies with corsets. Western women stayed slim and stood straight without them. For cowgirls, practicality determined what they wore. An active life on the Plains required big hats, high-heeled boots, a "loosely knotted neckerchief," and functional "bifurcated skirts." Real cowgirls would not ride without them. Florence LaDue reflected this philosophy when she returned a fancy dress purchased for her in New York and exchanged it for material from which she could make a comfortable western outfit.[43]

Spurning the criticism that the 101's women heaped on city-bound Americans, New Yorkers praised the beauty, prowess, and sagacity of these cowgirls while remaining silent about actions considered "unfeminine." The Millers did not take official positions on explosive issues such as woman's suffrage, but their cowgirls openly challenged Victorian stereotypes. Nearly everyone regarded them as simple, patriotic, wholesome, and robust outdoorswomen who set standards of beauty and femininity. In New York in 1914, these women were judged primarily by their talents; in later years advertising for the show would stress their physical attractiveness.

The 1914 season marked another milestone when Zack Miller took a show to London for the Anglo-American Exposition, a commemoration of one hundred years of peace between the United States and Great Britain and a celebration of "the progress which has been made by the British and American people in every branch of civilisation during the past century." Displays heralded American accomplishments in education, science, transportation, literature, and art. A friendly reviewer noted that the 101 reflected the "lighter side of the Exposition," which also included amusement park–style rides, animal acts, and large models of New York City and the Panama Canal. Lavish advertisements heralded the 101 as "America's Greatest American Show" "Depicting Frontier Life As It Really Is." These notices said Zack Miller led the "Hero Horsemen of the 101 Ranch." The show occupied the "Colossal Stadium" at Shepherd's Bush, a structure with well over ten thousand seats. The 101 offered an "Indian Reservation," where the curious could get a close look at the Cheyennes, Choctaws, Kiowas, Poncas, and Sioux. The 101 Ranch Wild West show followed the pattern of Catlin and Cody by staging a private opening for special guests and the press.[44]

Outwardly many parallels existed between the 101 show at this exposition and Cody's at the world's fairs, but Zack Miller did not follow the role established by his predecessors. For one thing, he ignored grandiose themes like material and cultural progress and connections between nations to focus upon his family's accomplishments and the 101 Ranch. He claimed that all his performers were "born and reared on the 101 Ranch," rodeos had originated there, and the 101 brand symbolized the 110,000 acre ranch, which he noted was "larger than many entire European principalities."[45]

While self-aggrandizement represented a break from George Catlin's and Buffalo Bill Cody's mostly respectful attitude toward Great Britain and its notables, the country the Millers visited had undergone significant changes. American western entertainments toured many nations now, so exhibiting in England no longer caused much of a stir. Zack Miller, like his predecessors, claimed friendship with "British Royalty," and he also said that George V commanded a performance for himself, his mother, and Empress Marie of Russia. The party enjoyed the entertainment and took several rolls of snapshots, but no royalty asked to meet Miller.[46] Perhaps a lack of personal recognition precipitated Zack's casual social style abroad.

Upon meeting the Earl of Lonsdale, Miller dispensed with formality and called him "Lonsdale" instead of "Your Lordship." According to Miller's account, the earl enjoyed this, although it disturbed others in attendance. Sometimes Miller became callous when dealing with people. Some Britons took offense at bulldogging in the show, which led to a public outcry and protests from humane societies. Zack regarded such sentiments as quaint and paid a weekly fine rather than discontinue the act, which afforded tremendous publicity.[47]

The four-act show opened to the public on 16 May 1914. Those in attendance saw an arena floor representing the plains of Oklahoma, behind which rose panels of elaborately painted mountain scenery, substantial enough to include a causeway for people on horseback. The program began with an introduction of the various groups and individuals in the show, followed by a vignette depicting settlers building a corral and cabin and then celebrating with demonstrations of cowboy and cowgirl skills. This ended abruptly, however, when Native Americans attacked, surrounded the settlers, burned the cabin, drove off the cattle, and made the settlers flee. In the second act, called "Indian Ceremonies and Prairie Pastimes," Indians pitched their tepees, lit campfires, and demonstrated their sports and ceremonies, including a war dance. When a stagecoach appeared, warriors chased it until cowboys rode to the rescue. Again the settlers built a cabin and held a rodeo. Another act portrayed pioneers on the Santa Fe Trail. The last scene featured Arizona's Grand Canyon, where Native Americans descended its walls along the Bright Angel Trail (the causeway on the pained scenery), entered the arena, ambushed settlers, and set the wagon train ablaze. After a fierce struggle, the pioneers chased away the Indians.[48]

In London, as in New York, the cowgirls enchanted attendees, causing newspapers to publish their photographs, praise their frontier skills, and call them regular employees of the 101. A female journalist noted that the cowgirls "knew quite as much about cattle and riding as did the men" and that cowboys treated cowgirls with "Courtesy without 'chivalry.'" Cowgirls camped outdoors and lamented London's big city ways. The press reported that they were all wholesome women, mostly the daughters and sisters of small ranchers in Oklahoma.[49] Cowboys and Indians also received favorable mention in the press, but cowgirls became the special favorites of English journalists.

Success in England prompted the Millers to plan a continental tour, but international events intruded. On 28 June 1914, while the 101 Wild West show entertained Londoners at Shepherd's Bush, a Serbian terrorist assassinated Archduke Francis Ferdinand of Austria, and World War I erupted. England needed horses for its military effort; consequently, on 7 August Zack Miller received an impressment order saying that the Millers would receive market value for their livestock. Looking back, Miller said that the loss of so many show animals took "fire and color" from the entertainment for many years. In addition, securing transportation back to the United States for the troupe and equipment cost the Millers about $25,000.[50] Despite the setback, they returned to the United States for more Wild West shows.

In 1915, the Millers made money, largely because they employed Jess Willard, the heavyweight boxing champion. He had won his title in a grueling twenty-six-round bout in Havana with Jack Johnson, an outspoken black champion. When Willard joined the show, he traveled with his manager, trainer, sparring partners, and sometimes his wife in a special ten-thousand-dollar railroad car. Reportedly, Willard received a thousand dollars a day, plus a percentage of the gate receipts. During the summer and fall of 1915 while the "Cowboy pugilist" appeared with the show, he earned perhaps one hundred thousand dollars.[51]

Newspapers pictured Willard in fighting stances and in cowboy outfits. Linking him to ranch life proved easy because he was a Kansan with cowboy experience who rode well and talked easily with reporters about life in the West. The Millers even claimed that Willard had worked at the 101. The boxer explained that the Wild West show allowed him to return to his "first principles." Willard initially rode in street parades, but the Millers discontinued this because many people saw Willard there but skipped the show. Willard later appeared in the grand entry, participated in acts where cowboys rode to the rescue of others, and, late in the season, he may have ridden broncos. His main feature was an aftershow at which patrons paid an additional twenty-five cents to see him box three rounds with a sparring partner and then demonstrate how he had knocked out Jack Johnson.[52] The Millers profited from the crowds that flocked to see Willard, but headlining an athlete rather than a frontier hero indicated that Wild West shows required something extraordinary to make money. For the remainder of their careers in show business, the Millers would search for stars, western or nonwestern, to attract customers.

In 1916 Americans contemplated the prospect of war in Mexico and Europe, and the 101 Ranch Wild West show followed the mood in the country by taking a decidedly militaristic turn. In March Francisco "Pancho" Villa crossed the border and raided Columbus, New Mexico. This first invasion of the United States since the War of 1812 outraged Americans, and the government responded by sending troops led by John J. "Blackjack" Pershing to pursue Villa into Mexico. Villa eluded his would-be captors, but nonetheless Mexicans resented the intrusion.

The Millers commemorated these events by reproducing the battle of Columbus with some of its actual participants. Those wanting precise information could turn to the printed programs and get the details: Villa, with nearly a thousand men, had crossed into the United States, killed seventeen of its citizens, stolen ninety-two horses from the army, looted, set fire to the hotel, and then fled across the border. Thirty-five U.S. soldiers pursued him and inflicted heavy casualties on the fleeing army.[53] Villa's audacity incensed Americans, but paled to insignificance when compared with events in Europe.

The war that began while the Millers visited England became a conflagration that demanded America's attention. President Wilson advocated neutrality, but his sympathies, like those of the American public, moved more and more toward the Allies because of German submarine warfare, the sinking of the *Lusitania,* U.S. insistence on the rights of neutral nations, and a skillful English press corps that denigrated the Central Powers. By 1916, Wilson advocated "preparedness," a policy of strengthening U.S. armed forces.

In this time when war threatened, the Millers added the "Military Pageant 'Preparedness'" to their western show. According to publicity, it offered "a rousing exhilarating display of military power in embryo" with "picturesqueness", and at the same time with a realism that quickens the blood and creates a furor of patriotic enthusiasm." Obviously, the Oklahomans hoped to generate excitement for war, to encourage men and women to join the armed forces, and to make money in the process. "Preparedness" began with the band playing a "stirring military march," after which a musician, mounted on horseback, appeared and bugled for the assembly of troops. "Uncle Sam's crack cavalry, whole batteries of rapid-fire and field guns," detachments of infantry, representatives from the "flying corps," members of the Red Cross and commissary, and "other essential units of the United States army," appeared and demonstrated military maneuvers, camp life, survival in trenches, scouting, sharpshooting, athletics, and horsemanship. No one could question the authenticity or patriotism of all this, because furloughed soldiers performed the action. Frontier border warfare and a "Troupe of Imperial Japanese," Arabs, and cossacks added to the military emphasis. The show concluded with "Equestrian Maneuvers and Flags of different nations, introducing the Rough Riders of the World in a Final Salute."[54]

All this resembled Buffalo Bill's Wild West and Congress of Rough Riders during the Spanish-American War, and for good reason: Cody toured with the Millers' show in 1916. Publicity lauded him as the one person with sufficient influence to get soldiers furloughed for the show. He participated in scenes of border and modern warfare. The old scout had hoped to buy the 101 show, but instead joined it as an employee, making $100 a day plus a portion of gate receipts when they exceeded $2,750. Despite some profitable stints that excited Cody, the season proved unspectacular.[55] In the end, the Millers paid the aged man only about one-tenth of what Jess Willard had earned the previous year.

Presenting Villa's raid and extolling "Preparedness" reflected the Millers' willingness to attune their show to conditions in the United States, but times differed from those on the eve of the Spanish-American War. Many Americans feared involvement in war in Europe, particularly one that seemed only loosely tied to American interests. Woodrow Wilson—thin, graying, and professorial—was no Rough Rider. And, despite all their bluster about Mexico and "Preparedness," the Millers were not soldiers or internationalists, but businessmen with oil, livestock, and agricultural products in a seller's market. Consequently, they sold their interest in the show to Edward Arlington (but kept exclusive rights to the name *101 Ranch*), and left entertainment for a time. Arlington tried to bring Jess Willard and Cody together in a new show, but Arlington failed because Willard rejected the offer and Cody did not survive the winter.[56]

In this prewar stint, the Millers had competed successfully with other traveling entertainments, but failed to breathe new life into Wild West shows. Although many people were familiar with the Millers, the 101 Ranch, and even its cowgirls, the show did not rivet public attention on ranchers or transform them into popular heroes. No new ideas, grand themes, or really original acts propelled the show, and it had not triumphed abroad.

While out of entertainment from 1917 to 1925, the Millers corresponded with others in the business, discussed reorganizing their show, hosted rodeos, and, in 1920, helped organize the Cherokee Strip Cow Punchers' Association, a nostalgic group that brought together old-time cowboys, met on the 101, and elected Joe Miller president of the organization for life.[57] Certainly contrariety existed when Miller decided to head a cowboy group because he believed ranchers, not their hired hands, best represented the livestock industry. However, the recognition that the position offered and his paternalistic feelings probably prompted him to help a group he considered romantic but "disappearing Americans."

In 1924 the Millers prepared to reenter the Wild West show business. They dispatched "a troupe of Indians and four cowboys" to Buenos Aires for a show and paid sixty thousand dollars to the Walter L. Main show for twenty railway cars, animals such as elephants and camels, and circus paraphernalia. However, a devastating flood postponed reorganization of the show until the winter of 1924–25. That spring the National Editorial Association met again in Oklahoma, and the Millers obliged with a Wild West exhibit at the 101. Flush from wartime prosperity, the Millers put over $300,000 into the new entertainment, which was ready for the road that same spring. An insider with the show wondered how much value the Millers received for their money.[58]

The show belonged exclusively to the Millers now, their former partner Edward Arlington having declined an offer to rejoin them. The Oklahomans believed that they could succeed without him because they genuinely "liked the game" and believed "the time was ripe for a real Wild West attraction." In addition, Cody's death in 1917 left a void they anticipated filling. Did not the West still hold "strong appeal . . . for every red-blooded American, young and old"? From a business perspective, the Millers believed that the show offered diversification for the "empire within itself." They remembered the year 1910 when the ranch lost money, but profits from the show saved the 101's operation. Opportunity for fun, travel, and excitement also influenced their decision. They had a private railroad car, "a veritable palace on wheels," and the train transported an auto for the family's use.[59]

It took between thirty and forty railroad cars to transport the big, new show and five acres of canvas to house it; a thousand humans and nearly as many animals traveled with the show; it included a sideshow, and when the people, animals, and equipment lined up for a street parade, they stretched for over a mile. However, when the Millers asked their old friend Edward Arlington about advice on scheduling, he said something that should have chilled the enthusiasm: follow the John Ringling circus by two weeks, "practically stand for stand," because the 101 would be able to pick up business from days when the circus was rained out.[60] In other words, people who missed a circus might accept the 101 as a substitute. Such advice indicated Arlington's awareness that Wild West shows were losing their appeal and that the great days of tented entertainment had passed in the United States.

Perhaps the Millers sensed that the public demanded new things in the 1920s, because they radically changed the show by adding "a new conception of art." Loosely translated, this meant that Joe added large doses of classical dance and elaborate spectacles featuring the ancient world. The showmen scoured the globe for ballerinas and other professional dancers and renamed their show "The Miller Brothers 101 Real Wild West and Great Far East."[61]

Spectacles featuring the ancient world brought a new concept of history into Wild West shows. To this point, the Plains, its peoples, and its past constituted the backward-looking aspect of the entertainment. Certainly *vaqueros,* gauchos, and cossacks had appeared in Cody's Congress of Rough Riders, but that Wild West show featured American history and specifically the winning of the West as the great achievement of the Western Hemisphere. Cody saw Europe and Asia as tired and inferior to a youthful and vigorous United States. Lillie, of course, had presented the "Far East" and its people as exotic, but he had featured incidents, not representations of actual historical events. Now the Millers supplemented their western acts with lessons on ancient history in which dancers dominated scenes, elephants and camels eclipsed horses, and few opportunities existed to compare cultures or cogitate current events and foreign policy.

Maybe inspiration for the Far Eastern portion of the show came from Pawnee Bill, a "life-long friend of the Millers," or perhaps they studied entertainment in the contemporary United States. Certainly Hollywood produced many movies featuring dance, exotic locales, and long looks at the female form. The Millers must have known that circuses added spectacles and that moviegoers thrilled to Rudolph Valentino's desert romances. Whatever the source of ideas and images, the Far Eastern segment offered a mosaic of diversion: music, dance, pageantry, tumblers, Captain Swift's zouaves, romantic antiquity, elaborate settings, "combat and contests," exotic peoples, and trained elephants. Perhaps the Millers hoped to provide something for everyone. According to one prominent western historian, the new show encompassed "stereotypes from all corners of the earth."[62]

The Far Eastern portion comprised about one-third of the total program.

Wanting the best dancers money could buy, Joe Miller traveled to New York, Zack to "Mexico City, New Orleans, and Cuba," and agents for the organization scoured Asia. Joe bragged that some of his dancers came from Ziegfeld's Follies, but that entertainment, while more refined than burlesque, got much of its appeal from "gags and gals" and hiring performers from it did little to elevate the tone of the show.[63]

For the Millers, "youth, beauty and grace were the prime requisites of those who wanted to get on the show." In an advertisement seeking one hundred dancers, the Millers specified that they prized physical attractiveness, not skill. According to their notice, women needed "some experience in dancing" to apply, but to get a job they "must be young and good looking." Programs for the show called attention to its "dazzling Oriental dance girls of youth and charm" and "beautiful horsewomen," both white and Native American. The cowgirls' contracts specified that they would wear appropriate costumes and dance in the spectacles, if instructed to do so. This was quite a change from Cody's day, when a concern for modesty caused him to prohibit female performers from wearing trousers.[64] The Millers seemed anxious to copy the sexuality in Lillie's enterprise in the hope of generated excitement and revenue.

Elaborate spectacles highlighted the Miller's Far Eastern portion. The act "Arabia," for example, featured an Egyptian noblewoman named Fatima whose caravan included dancers, slaves, camels, and elephants. Russians and Arabs performed feats of equestrianism for Fatima and her entourage; her "girls" danced for the riders; and then the Russians did the same for the women. The sun goddess spectacle from 1927, with supposed ties to mythology, depicted a beautiful sun goddess receiving homage from other male and female deities.[65]

Another spectacle, "Moscow," offered much dancing and an exciting view of Asia's peoples. Cossacks, long a staple in Wild West shows, enchanted Americans anew in the 1920s because of the Bolshevik Revolution in 1917. Historically soldiers for the czars, they fled their country when the Bolsheviks came to power. Their anticommunism, manliness, colorful costumes, musical ability, and dances appealed to Americans. In addition, many of the Millers' compatriots hoped for a softening of communism and improvement in American-Soviet relations. The Millers, however, did not use the cossacks to discuss the Bolshevik Revolution, czarist Russia, or relations between the United States and the Soviet Union. Edward Arlington congratulated them for including cossacks, saying: "everything Russian is very much in vogue right now." In an effort to capitalize on the cossacks' popularity, the Millers sent them on an off-season tour; however, some ran away, others refused to finish tours, and at times American audiences did not warm to them.[66]

The spectacle "Julius Caesar" recreated Caesar's triumphant return to Rome and included a celebratory "CIRCUS MAXIMUS," containing the 101 Ranch "ROMANETTE Ballet" that offered unusual fare for a Wild West show: an "Oriental dance" by a ballerina "on the back of an elephant," animal acts, "Roman standing chariot races, gladiators in combat and an exhibition of Roman light cavalry in lance tilts." A romantic relationship involving the lovely Minerva and a charioteer provided the dramatic underpinning for all this pageantry. The act ended with the arrival of elephants laden with wedding gifts for the happy couple. The original proposal for this act had come from a medical doctor named Harold Ingraham and included a scene in which two mummies "come to life and execute an Egyptian" during a dance. Newspaper accounts did not mention the death scene, so the Millers apparently drew the line at including murderous mummies in their Wild West show.[67]

Unlike Cody, the Millers saw no problem with making their show more circus-like. A publicity agent indicated that billing the 101 show remained flexible, and circumstances dictated whether to call it a Wild West show or a circus. At times, it was both: in 1928, publicity asserted that the show was "Combining the Greatest, Newest and Most Amazing Circus and Wild West Show of All Times." A 1925 advertisement told readers that the 101 contained "battalions of clowns" and a "complete three-ring circus" in addition to Wild West features.[68] In this time when circuses often included a western segment and the Millers' entertainment contained a circus, Wild West shows lost their identity as a distinctive form of entertainment.

Those "battalions of clowns" changed the mood of the 101's offerings. Earlier Wild West shows included comic variety acts, but they remained separate features. Now clowns, including a female impersonator, sometimes appeared with cossacks and western performers and mimicked the zouaves during their intricate military maneuvers.[69] Such added features undermined the seriousness of the acts and marked a departure from Cody's touting of educational benefits, calling his exhibition "America's National Entertainment," and even forbidding anyone to use the word *show* to describe it.

In the Millers' production western acts remained traditional, except that dance sometimes crept into them. In 1930, for example, act seventeen depicted "INDIAN WAR DANCES With the CHIEF WASHINGTON TRIO OF Bow and Arrow marksmen," which featured "the 'POCAHONTAS INDIAN BALLET.'" Another act, "PIONEER DAYS in 'HAPPY HICKORY CANYON,'" closed with "the PIONEER HAPPY HICKORY BALLET." The frontier portion, however, mostly featured what the Millers presented before World War I: introduction of the performers, rodeo, sharpshooting, roping and rope tricks, a buffalo hunt, the pony express, a stagecoach holdup, catching a horse thief and dragging him, equestrianism, and Indian dances. Near-deafening gunfire, cowboys, and Native Americans still prevailed. Western spectacles such as the Mountain Meadow Massacre or an attack on covered wagons finished shows. Such acts often ended with canvas covers on the wagons ablaze.[70]

The western portion of the show, while still popular, faced serious competition from rodeos, Indian exhibitions, and movies. For its part, rodeo had grown up in the 1920s with a World Series of Rodeo at Madison Square Garden. Its popularity increased so much that even Indians could not escape it; some entertainers wanted Indians with rodeo skills. Ironically, taking rodeos to indoor arenas in the East constituted a rediscovery of what Cody, Salsbury, and the Millers had already accomplished with their shows. Journalists wrote enthusiastically about them, calling rodeo cowboys and cowgirls the genuine articles and explaining the intricacies of bronco riding, bulldogging, and other events. To compete, the Millers filled their printed programs with information about rodeo events, claimed that the 101's performers ranked among the best contestants, called their entertainment "wilder than any Rodeo that was ever staged," and alleged that the 101 had pioneered these exhibitions of western skill. Despite such claims, the Millers knew that the best riders and ropers now chose lucrative careers in rodeo over Wild West shows.[71] During their heyday, Wild West shows provided the only option for cowboys and cowgirls who wanted to travel and perform. In the 1920s, however, rodeos attracted both top performers and enthusiastic crowds.

Likewise, Native American performers seeking audiences did not need to apply at Wild West shows because they could appear in a variety of educational and noneducational entertainments, such as agricultural fairs, expositions, pageants, and powwows, where they demonstrated traditional dress, habitations, dances, handiwork, agricultural products, and lifestyles. In addition, entertainers, like circus people, wanted Indians to add variety to their offerings.[72] Things had changed from Catlin's day, when his lecture halls were the best place to see Indians and get ethnography lessons, and the time when Cody's arena and camp provided the only opportunity to study Indians.

Like rodeos and powwows, movies depleted Wild West show audiences. The Millers soon found they could not avoid this new medium's influence. In 1911, for example, Joe Miller considered an entertainment combining movies and Wild West show acts with live performers. A 101 printed program told viewers that the mule appearing in the clown Dan Dix's act had appeared in the movie

*Through the Back Door* featuring Mary Pickford. Sometimes the 101 Ranch even provided colorful Plains characters and authentic locales for early western movies.[73]

To meet the challenge of films, the Millers sought movie celebrities as headliners for their show. First, they wooed Tom Mix, a prewar employee but now a star in silent westerns. The Millers cajoled, flattered, threatened, and warned about the unstable nature of the motion picture business to persuade Mix to join or buy the 101 show. Failing with Mix, in 1929 the Millers hired the Hollywood actor Jack Hoxie. He limited his performing to a thirty-minute aftershow for which patrons paid an additional twenty-five cents. Ticket holders saw Hoxie and his faithful dog Bunk subdue villains, his favorite leading lady Dixie Starr, Hoxie's horses Golden Stallion and Scout (also known as White Outlaw), an Indian named Chief Clearsky billed as the "'Indian Al Jolson,'" a dancer called "Half Pint" who did the Charleston, a cossack who performed a knife dance, and a knife thrower. In 1931, Zack telegraphed William S. Hart, a star of silent westerns, about joining the show. The Millers even contacted Jess Willard again and wrote Blackjack Pershing, hero of World War I and pursuer of Pancho Villa, to join them.[74]

In looking for that elusive feature to reverse their fortunes, Zack Miller resurrected old Wild West show features: a "Congress of Rough Riders of the World" in 1928 and a "Military Pageant" in 1929. In acts reminiscent of Cody's shows, English horseguards and lancers, French dragoons, German "Death Head Huzzars," Italian cavalry, Mexican *rurales,* zouaves, and American cavalry dressed in the blue uniforms of their Indian-fighting days appeared before audiences.[75] These experiments were short-lived, perhaps because disillusionment following World War I soured most Americans on military spectacles.

Often the Millers improvised. In a letter to a friend, George Miller indicated: "I have nothing new in mind but presume new ideas will hatch as we go along." Some "new ideas" had little connection to the West or the Far East. These included "THE EUROPEAN TRAMPOLINE WONDERS," an acrobat somersaulting over an auto, and "Suicide" Ted Elder, who stood with one foot on each of two racing horses as they leaped over an automobile. In 1928, teams of cowboys and cossacks played polo, and a fox hunt provided an opportunity for riders to maneuver their trained horses through an obstacle course. The following year a "Bloodless" Mexican bullfight illustrated the techniques, excitement, and pageantry of the bullring.[76]

An "evolutions show" in the 1925 sideshow included a man dressed as "The Missing Link" and another as "Big Joe the 'Gorilla.'" In a publicity venture, Joe Miller took these two characters to Dayton, Tennessee, "to appear as witnesses in the Scopes Evolution trial, should expert testimony be admitted in the case." The Millers even considered featuring a manhunt with "five or six good trail hounds," as big as possible, after a fugitive.[77]

A powerful theme might have rekindled enthusiasm for the show. The Millers found no way to exploit the lingering spirit of frontier anxiety as would Tom Mix. The ideas that the Millers had already pushed—paternalistic cattle kings as heroes and the end of big ranches—had not struck a responsive chord in the United States. The theme of progress had worked for their predecessors in Wild West shows: George Catlin harangued at his impassioned best when defending Indians and lambasting land-grabbing settlers, and Buffalo Bill Cody masterfully combined nostalgia, changing concepts of national growth, and patriotism in his appearances at world's fairs. But even the old showman Cody recognized that the Wild West show had become a tired idea after the turn of the century and that Americans found little romantic in the modern West and projects such as irrigation. Perhaps the concept of progress still held the seed of some grand new idea, but the Millers did not find it—nor does evidence indicate that they did much thinking about it.

The Millers brought automobiles into the arena, but did not link the internal combustion engine directly to western themes or ideas about progress. Automobile acts included auto polo, which featured men driving automobiles instead of riding horses, and the "Clown Police with his Bucking Ford," which highlighted Hoots Killinger most likely imitating the antics of the Keystone Cops in their articulated vehicles. Patrons opening printed programs found numerous advertisements for automobiles and automobile-related products. In 1929, George Miller, recognizing the irresistible appeal of the automobile, attempted to strike a deal with the Ford Motor Company to give away a new Ford at the show every evening. In 1930, "A Free Automobile Show, which included Chevrolet Number One" (the first Chevrolet produced) traveled with the 101 show.[78]

As in the show, automobiles began replacing horses in the lives of the performers and in the Miller family itself. Back in Oklahoma, George W. Miller's widow, Mary Anne, scurried around the far-flung ranch in a motorized vehicle. Native American performers sometimes saved their show earnings to buy autos and took them along on tours. Cowboys on the 101 became adept at handling the "tin lizzies." A reporter for the *New York Times* observed: "Down on the 101 Ranch near Bliss, Oklahoma, what a cowboy can do with a Model T or a motorcycle should please the Society of Gasoline Engineers. The ranch owners, of course, rebelled at this change: but it was either remove this story-book setting or go broke." Another reporter noted that the 101's cowboys preferred

singer Rudy Valee to western music and devoted their free time to playing golf
and bridge. Certainly mechanization changed conditions on the 101 Ranch
because the need for working cowboys decreased; in fact, by 1928 the Millers
employed more cowhands in their entertainment than in the actual operation
of the ranch. By the end of the 1920s, when the rest of the country was em-
bracing machines, the Millers still lived in two worlds—one of machines and
the other of cowboys.[79]

By this time, however, the Millers began acknowledging tiredness in the entertainment. George Miller referred to their "old stereotyped show," and Joe,
always an advocate, confided that he managed it poorly, adding, "I am going
to try the show this one more year. If it does not make good I will charge the
whole thing up to fun and amusement, put the old cars on a hill and ride out
and look [at] them occasionally and think of the fun we had spending the money
they represent." Undoubtedly, poor management contributed to their problems,
because the Millers collected hundreds of thousands of dollars each season, but
failed to make a profit. Two shows daily, usually at 2:00 and 8:00 P.M., brought
in $6,000.00 to $8,000.00 on some days. General admission prices ran $.75
for adults and $.50 for children, while reserved seats in the grandstands were
$1.50 and box seats cost $3.00. In addition, sideshows, concerts and after-show
features required separate tickets.[80]

On the debit side of the ledgers appeared transportation, publicity, food for
crews and livestock, and salaries—a combined total of $10,000.00 per week.
Salaries for employees varied, with some receiving as little as $10.00 a month
(five of it paid monthly and another five paid at the end of the season), and
top performers commanding $140.00 a month. George Miller, a level-headed
businessman, fretted constantly about expenses. Joe's generosity led him to give
away numerous passes to the show and allow many guests to eat meals with
performers. Managing the show sapped energy from its owners during seasons
that sometimes stretched to "eight long and strenuous months." During the off-
season, the Millers spent hours writing letters, attending to legal and financial
considerations, and inquiring about prospects for touring with groups of Indians or a full-fledged Wild West show in England, France, Germany, Russia,
South Africa, and South America. The Millers made no such ventures, although
they did serve as contract agents for European entertainers (mostly German)
needing Native American performers.[81]

Financially the postwar show flopped. Although ranch records indicate a loss
of $457,405.94 between 1925 and 1929, they do not reflect the entire cost of the
show. Zack blamed Joe's devotion to it for the family's eventual bankruptcy

because he neglected other duties and channeled money needed for ranching into the entertainment.[82]

The Millers cited myriad other problems for their failure: stiff competition from Ringling Brothers, Sells-Floto Circus, and other traveling shows; poor scheduling; inclement weather; tents that sometimes collapsed; railway accidents; runaways at street parades; a bronco that kicked a spectator in the head; anti-rodeo groups; lawsuits; performers who drank and became violent; broken bones and fatal accidents in the arena; and hostility from the Department of the Interior toward shows perpetuating stereotypes of Indians.[83]

In the midst of these difficult times death destroyed the family unit that George W. Miller had hoped to preserve. Two of the brothers died in automobile-related accidents during a short period: Joe in October 1927 and George in February 1929. With George's death, the show and ranch passed to Zack, who was assisted by the next generation of Millers—Joe C. Miller Jr. and George W. Miller. Zack became as enthusiastic about the entertainment as Joe had been; however, he found no more success than his brothers. During difficult times, he thought about escape and frontier times, saying that he would find it exciting to pioneer in South Africa.[84]

Zack probably planned to run the show until he could sell it. The Millers had tried to peddle their show for a number of years, particularly after Joe's death. In 1928, the American Circus Corporation offered to purchase it for $185,000 as part of a campaign to buy smaller entertainments. Letting go of the 101 Ranch Wild West show for the tendered amount represented a financial loss, but it would have rid the Millers of a huge expense. The deal failed at the closing because although the Millers agreed to allow the American Circus Corporation to use the name *101 Ranch,* they refused to relinquish the term *Miller Brothers.*[85]

The Great Depression, which dwindled show attendance, devastated the ranch. Production of livestock, farm goods, and oil continued, but prices and demand plummeted. By 1931, financial failure threatened the 101 Ranch. When forced to choose between devoting his full time to the ranch or to the entertainment, Zack chose the latter. The show went on the road in 1931 with a nearly empty cash box. Successful stands near home enabled the show to move eastward. Zack played it in direct competition with larger shows, perhaps to get the American Circus Corporation to buy it to eliminate a competitor. However, no offer came, and on the evening of 4 August 1931, creditors closed the show in Washington, D.C.[86]

Like Catlin and Cody, Zack learned about "harpies of the law" when they came to the ranch in 1932. Zack, lacking the cash to pay them, grabbed a near-by shotgun and chased them out of the house, firing a couple of shots into the floor to speed the intruders on their way. The *New York Times* concluded that Miller had "resorted to the forceful rule of the West." While the shooting provided personal satisfaction for Miller, it served no productive purpose. In March 1932, auctioneers sold the properties of the ranch. Nevertheless, during that year and the following one, Miller took small Wild West shows on the road.[87]

Many Oklahomans felt that the impossible occurred when the 101 Ranch collapsed. The 101 and its proprietors symbolized things dear to people of the state: progressive farming, large-scale ranching, fortunes in oil, and the spirit of the Old West. They had patronized the 101 Ranch Wild West show, taken pride in it as an Oklahoma institution, and claimed the Millers as leading citizens. The Millers had enjoyed their status as celebrities and they willingly assumed the many roles associated with them. In good times, they could ranch, farm, produce oil, and bankroll a Wild West show; but even the Millers could not emerge unscathed from the Great Depression.

Thus, the Millers' career in Wild West shows ended. They had assumed leadership in this traditional form of western entertainment in an attempt to preserve it and glorify themselves and the "empire within itself." In the years before World War I, they built a viable entertainment, but after that they could only transform their show into a conglomeration of dance, spectacles from ancient history, circus acts, clowns, rodeo events, western segments, sharpshooting, and western movie stars. Because their show lacked a specific focus, one-by-one the components of the earlier Wild West shows—seriousness of purpose, the West as the central attraction, and patriotism—all slipped away. But perhaps the greatest change was that the Wild West show had stopped evolving and ceased to be the "raw material of America." The Millers failed to find new themes to invigorate their show.

During their tenure in show business, the Millers found movies inescapable. They supplied livestock and authentic westerners for them and even made a few themselves. However, the Millers remained wedded to Wild West shows. In 1927, for example, Joe paid little attention to a Pathé crew working on the ranch. Moviemakers came to the 101 to film *Trail Dust,* many one-reelers, and scenes for the classic *North of 36.* A four-reeler called *On with the Show* made on the 101 even featured their Wild West show. Native Americans and others in the troupe generally enjoyed seeing themselves and familiar environs on screen. The Millers savored the notoriety that movies brought, and called attention to such stars as Will Rogers, Neal Hart, Hoot Gibson, Mabel Normand,

and Helen Gibson, all products of the ranch. But most of all, they heralded Tom Mix.[88]

This man, whom the Millers could legitimately claim as a product of their ranch and Wild West show, became the preeminent cowboy star of the 1920s. Youngsters idolized him and almost every American knew that in Tom Mix's slick productions about the West, good always triumphed over evil in ways that satisfied people of the postwar generation. Tom Mix found exactly what eluded the Millers, the medium and the message for western romanticism in the 1920s.

# "Rugged Virtue in the Saddle":
# Tom Mix from Wild West Shows to Movies
# and Back Again

he train carrying Buffalo Bill's Wild West show steamed into town, the troupe disembarked, and workers transported and set up the entertainment's tents at the Clearfield Fairgrounds in Pennsylvania. Somewhere in the throng of youngsters savoring the excitement was a ten year old named Tom Mix. When the show began, Mix sat transfixed by Cody, Annie Oakley's sharpshooting, painted Indians, colorfully costumed cowboys, and the Congress of Rough Riders. The day impressed the youngster so much that he vowed to go West someday, become a sheriff, and arrest outlaws. And Mix knew exactly in whose footsteps he wished to follow. From that time, Buffalo Bill was his hero.[1]

As soon as the show left town, Mix began duplicating Wild West show skills. He purchased an old single-shot revolver and while practicing with it, accidentally discharged the weapon, embedding a bullet deep in his leg. Undaunted, he continued shooting. Lassoing proved equally dangerous; Mix went to the local stockyards, encircled his waist with one end of a rope, tied it there, and lassoed a bull that dragged him until a worker at the stockyards noticed the desperate situation and rescued the boy.[2]

Finding horses proved easy for the aspiring showman. When Mix was born in Driftwood, Pennsylvania, in 1880, his father, Edwin E. Mix, used teams of these animals to pull downed timber from forests and haul logs to local saw-mills. These were not the wiry mustangs from the Plains that Tom admired in the Wild West show; but he practiced bareback riding, mounting, dismounting, and standing on the backs of galloping animals, thereby earning the reputation of being able to "ride anything that could walk." An athletic boy, larger and stronger than his playmates, Tom enjoyed rough-and-tumble games, possessed an iron will, and regarded education with indifference. Football and baseball interested him, and he played on the DuBois High School football team, even though he had dropped out of school after completing the fourth grade.[3]

As a youngster, Mix found that money meant power. He saw the wealthy, like his father's employer, move commoners around like pawns and take their land. Obviously, those with money lived happily while the poor suffered; so money-making, or "making a million," as he phrased it, became an important goal for the youngster.[4]

Mix first chose the military to achieve fame. Perhaps seeing Buffalo Bill's Wild West and Congress of Rough Riders made him admire both frontiersmen and soldiers. The outbreak of the Spanish-American War in 1898 prompted eighteen-year-old Mix to enlist in the army. Unlike Theodore Roosevelt, he missed Cuba and instead languished in batteries guarding American cities against possible attack by the Spanish navy. Then he missed quelling the insurrection in the Philippines. Honorably discharged in April 1901, Tom reenlisted upon learning of the Boer War in Africa, but again fighting eluded him. Exasperated, he deserted in 1902.[5]

Mix, with a bride named Grace Allin, went West seeking adventure and perhaps sanctuary from military officials. Once settled in Oklahoma, Mix moved closer and closer to performing in Wild West shows. His rugged good looks gave him his start. He lacked only about an inch of measuring six feet and weighed 175 pounds. Dark skin, wavy hair, piercing eyes, broad shoulders, and an athletic appearance caught people's attention. All this, along with charisma and an inclination for showmanship, led to a nonremunerative position as a drum major in the Oklahoma Cavalry Band, despite a lack of musical ability and no membership in the militia. Mix accompanied the group to St. Louis for the 1904 world's fair, where he met Will Rogers, who worked as a rodeo clown with the Zack Mulhall Wild West show. The following spring, a cowboy brigade formed to attend Theodore Roosevelt's second inauguration as president, and Mix journeyed to Washington, D.C., to help celebrate. There socializing abounded, and Mix renewed his acquaintance with Will Rogers and met other performers in the Mulhall show.[6]

When not traveling, Tom Mix worked as a ranch hand, tended bar, and probably helped apprehend outlaws. Zack Miller of the 101 Ranch met Mix while
he was grousing about indoor work as a bartender and offered him a job at the
ranch, probably at a salary of fifteen dollars a month. By this time, his marriage
to Grace Allin had been annulled, and he had wed Kitty Jewell Perrine, but that
union lasted less than a year.[7]

The 101 Ranch was a comfortable environment and an excellent place to learn
western mythology, roping, riding, and other Wild West show activities. In later
years, he attributed his success "to the training I received and experienced when
working under the 101 brand." He arrived with minimal cowboy skills, but they
improved enough to enable him to compete in rodeos. Enthusiasm for the sport
overshadowed his good sense in 1910, when he "borrowed" a 101 horse to enter
a local rodeo. In it, Tom broke a leg, and then the mount disappeared. The
Millers filed charges for loss of their property, but Tom somehow got out of the
mess without having to serve time in jail or pay for the animal.[8] Undaunted,
he continued to compete in rodeos.

During this time, Mix learned to look and act the part of a cowboy. A co-
worker on the 101 remembered: "He walked as he rode, with a swaggering self-
assurance. He was tall and straight and lithe and dark as an Indian. Which made
his white teeth gleam whiter from his wide smile." He delighted in riding bucking broncos in front of guests at Riverside Camp, the 101's dude ranch. With a
flair for the dramatic, he made his cowboy performances look glorious in front
of the greenhorns. Talk, or spinning yarns for the guests, comprised much of
his activities. According to Zack Miller, Tom quickly mastered the art of "ped-
dling loads to the pilgrims." He told them "windies about the ranch, its wild
and bloody history, and that sort of thing." Mix fabricated an adventure-filled
life for himself that included glorious service in the Boer War and adventures
as a Texas Ranger. Miller also declared: "Tom could color a story redder than a
Navajo blanket." And Zack added: "He told his scary tales so often that he finally
got to believing them himself. . . . Especially the one about his being half Indian."[9]

Working at the 101 taught him the skills he would use throughout his life,
but, more importantly, it gave him credibility. Before the dudes, Mix rehearsed
his acts, perfected his appearance and demeanor, and practiced his "windies."
All this prepared him for Wild West show arenas and silent western movies.

For the next several years, Mix appeared in the Miller brothers' show and other
smaller entertainments. During the early twentieth century, many such shows
existed, and securing employment in them proved easy. Here, Mix learned about

crowd-pleasing action and showmanship; but little about ideas and interpretations of the West. Like the shows themselves, which stressed entertainment and not edification, Mix's life lacked direction.

At first, Mix played a small part in the Miller brothers' entertainment, but because he would try new and difficult things, his contribution grew. He became the rustler dragged to death behind a galloping horse, and, thereafter, took many dusty trips over the ground with a rope attached to a steel eye concealed in his leather coat. Tom trumpeted what he did: "These ranch shows are just as important as cleaning up a band of rustlers. The old ways are going fast. We've got to keep on showing people what they were."[10] For several years, Mix devoted his energies to such productions.

By 1909 Mix had a third wife, Olive Stokes, a westerner who made Annie Oakley her model. This handsome young couple joined the Wilderman Wild West show, where Tom performed riding and rope tricks. When he insisted on a pay raise, his boss refused, so the Mixes headed to Seattle for the Alaska-Yukon-Pacific Exposition. Hoping to attract people gathered there, the Mixes hired sixty-five performers and founded a Wild West show of their own. In addition to standard features—a battle scene among Native Americans, an attack on a stagecoach, and bulldogging—Tom and a friend named Charlie Tipton donned armor and jousted. A local newspaper called Mix the "WORLD'S CHAMPION BULLDOGGER," and he began using the title. The show made no money and soured Olive on show ownership.[11]

Next, the Mixes joined Will A. Dickey's Circle D Wild West Show and Indian Congress, where Tom cared for the livestock. This stint proved important because the Selig Polyscope Film Company of Chicago came to film Dickey's cowboys and Indians. Although he had been hired to tend stock, the crew photographed Mix along with the cowboys.[12]

Mix's break came in 1909 when Selig filmed *Ranch Life in the Great Southwest* in Dewey, Oklahoma. This early documentary about roundups featured well-known rodeo stars in action. Here Mix served as a stock handler and safety man. Despite his lack of credentials, Tom asked the director, Francis Boggs, for a part in the film. Boggs agreed, to the consternation of the rodeo champions, and featured Tom in a bronco-busting sequence. Released in 1910, *Ranch Life* billed Mix as an "Ex-Deputy United States Marshal and Bronco Expert."[13]

Mix quickly became a regular in Selig's short productions and appeared in movies such as *On the Little Big Horn; or, Custer's Last Stand* (1909) and *The Range Rider* (1910). He also acted in movies about those wars which had inspired him about a decade earlier: *Briton and Boer* (1909 or 1910) and *Up San Juan Hill*

(1910). In 1913 he appeared in *A Prisoner of Cabanas,* another film about the Spanish-American War.[14] Given the young actor's enthusiasm for the West and warfare, such roles must have pleased him.

With some time between pictures in 1910, Mix joined Mulhall's Wild West show at the Appalachian Exposition in Roseville, Tennessee. Tom contemplated organizing another Wild West show of his own, but his wife objected, fearing financial disaster. Mix also claimed that in between movies he had gone to Mexico in 1908 with the Miller brothers' show when Bill Pickett faced the Mexican bull. Mix may also have acted as a deputy sheriff in Oklahoma during this busy period.[15]

In 1911, Selig moved to Hollywood and offered Tom a new contract. His next films were shot on location in Canon City, Colorado. Mix and others in the Selig group spent time "singing, drinking, dancing with the barflies and 'raising hell' in general." He claimed that in a rodeo in Canon City in 1911, he set the world's record for steer roping and bulldogging. In Colorado, Mix devoted some Sunday afternoons to presenting free Wild West shows for inmates at the state penitentiary. He went with Guy Weadick to Canada for a Wild West show stint and appeared in Vernon Seavers' Young Buffalo Show.[16]

In 1912, Mix's contract with Selig expired, and the next year he became Selig's business partner and moved to Hollywood. There the young actor received his own studio, camera crew, and a salary of $250 a week for acting. Soon, however, he began writing scripts and directing, and his weekly pay jumped to $1,000. In 1917, financial problems, none the fault of Mix, collapsed the company.[17]

The ease with which Mix moved among rodeos, Wild West shows, and movies revealed their interconnectedness. During this time, Tom continued to compete in rodeos, despite injuries. For their part, filmmakers visited ranches like the 101 and Wild West shows to get action shots. In this age before stunt men and sophisticated camera work, producers found Wild West show performers the best bet for daredevil feats. Show people liked these jobs, which provided off-season employment, good money for a few days' work, and publicity. Once it was filmed, producers marketed the material as a series of unrelated incidents or sequences of action held together with a simple plot.[18]

In this period when movies depended on performers in live entertainment, Tom Mix and others could move easily into movies from Wild West shows and rodeos. The Miller brothers vaunted the 101 as a proving ground for western stars and pointed proudly to their products: Tom Mix, Dan Dix, Helen Gibson, Tommy Grimes, Neal Hart, Charles "Buck" Jones, Mabel Normand, and Vester Pegg. Others who gained skills in Wild West shows and circuses and moved on to movies included Art Acord, William Boyd, Hoot Gibson, Ken Maynard, Jack Hoxie (who appeared with the Miller brothers' show in the 1920s), and Tim McCoy.[19] Like Tom Mix, who idolized Buffalo Bill, this generation of actors and actresses came from the world of entertainment, not the West.

While working with Selig, Mix, with the help of cohorts from his show days, such as Sid Jordan, transferred what he had learned from Wild West shows to movies. Mix stamped his personality on the movies, particularly those in which he both acted and directed. Unencumbered by scripts, Mix and his friends concocted an exciting situation—a runaway, for example—and began the action. Mix thrived in this environment featuring daredevil stunts, spontaneity, cowboy skills, and athletic ability. Wild West show–style action blossomed in movies without dialogue. In *The Law and the Outlaw* (1913), for example, Tom's foot caught in a stirrup, and he reproduced his Wild West show act in which a horse dragged him. Movies such as *The Telltale Knife* (1914), *The Man from the East* (1914), *The Moving Picture Cowboy* (1914), *Slim Higgins* (1915), and *Roping a Bride* (1915) featured other abilities he had mastered during his show days, including marksmanship, fancy riding, and rodeo skills.[20]

Early western movies offered an array of tough western characters, so Mix assumed a variety of roles, including cowboys, sheriffs, Indians, Mexicans, "half-breeds," gamblers, horse thieves, and outlaws. His willingness to play Indians and sundry other frontier types separated him from Cody, who eschewed actors and insisted that only authentic westerners appear in his show. Mix was different—he belonged to an age of grease paint, costuming, and role playing when filmmakers did not seek out Indians when white actors wanted the parts.[21] Often he played rough-hewn men who were so clumsy and socially inept that they failed to woo and win celluloid heroines. Also, in movies such as *When the Cook Fell Ill* (1914) and *Never Again* (1915), alcohol figured prominently in the plot. Films such as *The Life Timer* (1913), *The Way of the Red Man* (1914), *Jimmy Hayes and Muriel* (1914), *A Child of the Prairie* (1915), and *The Man from Texas* (1915) brimmed with violence and death.[22] This unpolished part of Mix's career evoked Cody's "gladiatorial combat revived" stage. After World War I, Mix would change; myriad character roles, failure with women, enthusiasm for alcohol, and violence would all vanish from his repertoire.

In these prewar years, Mix reflected the "realism" of western movies stars such as Broncho Billy Anderson, who got his start in *The Great Train Robbery,* and William S. Hart, the reigning cowboy celebrity. Mix mirrored their appearance by wearing functional clothing instead of glamorous costumes. In at least two movies, *Religion and Gun Practice* (1913) and *Slim Higgins* (1915), Mix played a

Hart-like role, the "good badman," or a character who went afoul of the law and then reformed because of a good woman's love. In keeping with "realism," Mix and others in the Selig crew often gave little thought to background scenery and shot sequences in front of the stark walls of sheds.[23]

A high level of energy, spontaneity, and a fertile imagination served Mix well during this time. He could always devise another adventure, and he could write and direct quickly, producing a film in a day or two. For writing a script, he received $25, and one-reelers brought a budget of $500, about $350 of which covered salaries and expenses. The remainder, usually about $150, represented Tom's pay for his roles as "director, actor, and general handy-man." He ended up earning pretty good money for a man who began work as a cowboy for perhaps $15 a month. Mix adapted quickly to silent movies, although he remained enthusiastic about Wild West shows and their live audiences.[24]

Wild West shows, after all, offered much that films could not: smells of smoke, dust, animals, and gunpowder; reports from rifles and pistols; shrieks from Indians and cowboys; and the sound and vibrations from horses' hooves pounding the earth. Music remained, but pianists and organists in theaters could not match the power of brass bands in Wild West shows. Nor could these early films offer proximity to frontier heroes and Plains animals.

Wild West show arenas eclipsed black-and-white photography with a kaleidoscope of colors: westerners in bright flannel shirts, Native Americans bedecked with feathers and paint, soldiers in gleaming uniforms, and Cody sporting richly embroidered buckskins. Wild West shows bombarded the senses in ways that movies could not; however, many people preferred darkened rooms where images flickered across small screens. Theatergoers could view subjects familiar to Wild West show audiences, such as galloping horses, Indian attacks, cowboys, and gunplay. Americans, in an increasingly industrial society, flocked to movies because they offered cheap and convenient entertainment featuring escapism, humor, patriotism, and reassurance that virtuous and hardworking people succeeded. Steadily, movies gained respect as more and more middle-class Americans attended them.[25]

World War I generated support for films at a time when Wild West shows lacked leadership. Cody died the year the United States entered the fight, and the Millers busied themselves with selling grain, livestock, and oil for the war effort. Western entertainment cried out for some charismatic person to represent the West. Mix, it turned out, was the right person at the right place at the right time.

Mix joined Fox Studios in 1917 and began a spectacular rise to fame. In twelve years there, about sixty Mix films appeared, and they all made money. He got his own production unit called Mixville, replete with horses, cattle, wagons, frontier-style buildings, and quarters for actors and actresses. In 1927 he made about fifteen thousand dollars a week in pictures. Not surprisingly, Mix abandoned Wild West shows, except for a short stint in 1924, when he miscalculated his movie-making schedule and signed with the Miller brothers' show. It took a breach of contract suit to get him in the arena. Tom Mix left live entertainment because he knew movies would dominate western entertainment, an insight that had escaped Cody and the Millers. For Mix, basic arithmetic told the story: thousands of people might attend Wild West shows, but movies could "reach millions."[26]

His movies did "reach millions"; consequently, Mix attained fame and participated fully in the extravagances of Hollywood during the Jazz Age. Soon after his arrival there, he divorced Olive and married Victoria Forde, an actress and a Hollywood insider. With a salary that sometimes exceeded $800,000 a year, Mix had money and spent it freely. He bought a ranch in Arizona and a six-acre Beverly Hills lot on which he built a mansion worth $350,000. He staffed it with a butler and servants and filled his seven-car garage with $75,000 to $100,000 worth of expensive imports. According to Olive Stokes Mix: "This residence was a manifestation of his extravagance, the ultimate symbol of success achieved." Hollywood's celebrities gathered there so regularly that Mix asserted: "I reckon I'm the only man in America ever to run a night-club and never have no cover charge." When yachts became popular, Mix purchased one, although he seldom used it. Everywhere and upon everything he put his T-M brand. He claimed not to have lost his virtue in the process, although he nearly worshipped money, smoked, drank liquor, and married and divorced regularly.[27]

Mix reflected the complexities of the 1920s—he personified crass materialism and enjoyed the nightlife of this golden playtime, yet he built his career around its mood of disquietude and nostalgia. The Millers failed in the 1920s, but Mix understood the decade perfectly. Entertainers could have money and live extravagantly as long as they separated their private lives from their public performances. Mix grasped other things that eluded the Millers: the majority of Americans preferred cowboys over ranchers, the West extended beyond the borders of the 101, and Americans eschewed tainting western romanticism with "high art," the Far East, or ancient history.

Mix comprehended that World War I profoundly impacted American thought and values. What began as an idealistic venture to "make the world safe for democracy" degenerated into a morass of trench warfare, mustard gas, and American blood spilled on foreign soil. The war's end brought sobering statistics: over fifty thousand Americans died in battle and nearly four times that number suffered wounds.[28] Ironically, Mix, who yearned for military combat but missed it, capitalized on his nation's revulsion for bloodshed after World War I.

Disillusionment marked the postwar period, when most Americans concluded that their sacrifices had not improved the world. In keeping with this mood, Congress rejected the peace treaty with its provision for an international peace-keeping organization called the League of Nations. Books such as Harry Elmer Barnes's *Genesis of the World War* and Sidney B. Fay's *Origins of the World War* informed readers that England and France contributed to the outbreak of the war and then misled Americans about their roles. In the 1920s, Americans re-acted with isolationism and cynicism.[29] Times had changed significantly from the 1890s, when people applauded the Spanish-American War and Cody's com-mingling of military and western themes.

Many Americans found domestic affairs equally disconcerting and worried about the Bolshevik Revolution reaching the United States, urbanization, and mechanization eroding the democracy and individualism developed on the fron-tier. The typical American now worked in a factory, lived in a congested city, and loved automobiles more than horses. With such distance from their fron-tier origins, American-style individualism and democracy might perish.[30]

Even traditional morality and beliefs about human nature changed. Women bobbed their hair, smoked cigarettes in public, and allowed their knees to peek out from under short skirts. Hollywood brazenly promoted actresses with "It," a term that everyone knew meant sex appeal. Youngsters drove automobiles and drank bootleg liquor from hip flasks. New philosophies, including existential-ism, branded traditional values as deceptions, and those who read books by Sigmund Freud learned that humans often acted irrationally. The murder of Bobby Franks electrified Americans and led to lessons in the "new psychology" at the highly publicized murder trial. The defense attorney Clarence Darrow characterized the defendants Richard A. Loeb and Nathan F. Leopold as typi-cal human beings. Darrow convinced the jury that passion could move anyone to kill, and Leopold and Loeb received life imprisonment rather than the death sentence. Other messages emanated from Freud's theories: the libido made sex-ual urges irresistible and the power of the id predestined many to neurotic and socially unacceptable behavior. Imaginative literature like that of Sherwood Anderson and Theodore Dreiser popularized Freud's ideas of neurosis and un-restrained sensuality.[31]

The carnage of World War I, disillusionment with its aftermath, Freudian psychology, and an uncertain future translated into what the historian Roderick Nash has termed "nervousness." According to Nash, "Americans from 1917–1930 constituted a *nervous* generation, groping for what certainty they could find." The frontier past looked good to Americans seeking things predictable and soothing. Some even formed the Buffalo Bill American Association to venerate that famous figure. Mix, too, capitalized on Cody's appeal by commenting that he drew his inspiration from Cody's Wild West show and had worked closely with him on several occasions.[32]

Mix could also capitalize on this nervousness by showcasing his talents. When he began at Fox, he had experience on the 101 Ranch, in rodeos, in several Wild West shows, and in short films. With this diverse background, he could pick and choose from a variety of sources and create movies that fit Americans' current tastes. Mix selected carefully and modified several Wild West show themes to fit the mood of his nation.

In the broadest sense, he softened and simplified much from Wild West shows. Specifically, he recast the image of the cowboy, minimized bloodshed, emphasized morality over historical accuracy, amplified the importance of villains, and marginalized women and Native Americans. Consequently, beginning in 1917, his movies differed from Wild West shows and his early films. The new ones became "breezy and, cheerful, 'streamlined' *entertainment* that rarely attempted a realistic re-creation of the West, offering instead action and excitement spiced with a boyish sense of fun."[33]

Mix could metamorphose himself into an idealized cowboy and make his movies into unadulterated entertainment partly because of the death of Cody and the passing of the great days of Wild West shows. With Cody gone, Mix did not compete for the public's favor with someone who possessed impeccable frontier credentials, promoted grand themes, and insisted on a degree of historicity in his productions. Philosophically, Mix differed from his predecessors in Wild West shows, who had strong convictions about the frontier. Catlin had advocated for Plains Indians; Cody had promoted "gladiatorial combat," progress, the military, and agriculture; and the Millers had emphasized ranches and ranchers. Ironically, Mix's lack of bona fide achievements and causes to champion actually benefited him because this allowed him the freedom to refashion himself into whatever he wished to become. Establishing a suitable persona came naturally; he had perfected his "windies" before the dudes at the 101 and knew which tales impressed people. Mix was a wonderfully malleable man—free from actual accomplishments and strong convictions about the Plains. For him, alleged western deeds and skillful press agents served as the "raw material of America."

Mix mythology was dazzling puffery, perfectly suited for what the journalist

Frederick Lewis Allen called the "ballyhoo years." Publicity refashioned Mix into a born-and-bred westerner: El Paso, Texas, became his birthplace, some Cherokee blood coursed through his veins, and his father had served as a captain in the Seventh U.S. Cavalry. Mix said that he grew up with cowboys and did not "even remember ever learning to ride a horse or even throw a lasso or handle a six-shooter. He just naturally did those things from the beginning."[34] As for military prowess, Tom Mix claimed to have attended Virginia Military Academy, captured machine guns during the Mexican Revolution, and served as a scout and a Rough Rider for Theodore Roosevelt in Cuba. After convalescing from wounds received there, Mix went to the Philippines to help suppress the insurrection. Moreover, he won the Boxer Rebellion and the Boer War nearly singlehandedly.

Mix said that he had worked as a cowboy in Colorado, Texas, Oklahoma, Arizona, Kansas, New Mexico, Wyoming, North Dakota, and South Dakota before distinguishing himself as a Texas Ranger, a deputy U.S. marshal, and a fearless sheriff in a dozen western towns. According to one story, while in law enforcement in Kansas Mix arrested and jailed 113 "bootleggers and gamblers" in one fell swoop. In addition, he designated himself a rodeo champion and the owner of two ranches. Breaking into Hollywood required time as a stunt man, and here too Mix proved fearless: he strangled a wolf with his bare hands, bulldogged a buffalo, rescued an actress from a bull, and dragged a hungry leopard by its tail to protect a leading lady.[35] During the twelve years at Fox Studios, Mix and press agents churned out these and other imaginary deeds for a public enamored of fantasy worlds created in Hollywood.

Mix understood that cowboys had become America's darlings by the 1920s. One historian of western films called Mix's ticket to fame "commercialization of the cowboy." Moving away from history, the casts of hundreds of Wild West shows, and the "realism" of prewar westerns, Mix and his press agents telescoped everything admirable about the West into a single glorified figure. The innocence and purity of Catlin's Native Americans, Cody's prowess, and the freedom from historicity found in the fictional hero in *The Virginian* lingered in Mix's idealized cowboys. Weaknesses vanished, including Cody's view that cowboys lacked the adaptability necessary for the modern world and the Millers' view that ranchers outshined their hired help. Mix recognized the irresistible appeal of the mythical cowboy and became, according to some, "the greatest cowboy star of all times."[36]

Mix claimed to have discovered this westerner, knocked off the rough edges, and rescued him from oblivion. Looking back at his career in 1928, he proclaimed: "I sorta made the American cowboy from an ornery sort of cuss into a pretty nice feller that everyone likes." Mix argued that outlaws, Indian fighters, pioneers, miners, and pony express riders had received too much attention. Mix worked to give the cowboy legend "its proper scope and glory." To do this he jettisoned realism. He had experienced enough life in the West to know its mundane and routine side; however, his movies depicted a place where "'Westerners spent twenty-four hours a day shooting it out with one another.'" But, Mix maintained, this is what Americans wanted, and he provided it.[37]

By the 1920s, Americans valued a good story about the West more than authenticity. Two epic movies indicated much about American taste. *The Covered Wagon* (1923) followed a caravan on the Oregon Trail and *The Iron Horse* (1924) chronicled the building of the transcontinental railroad. While the settings and props in the movies were historically correct, the plots were not. Other persons popularized the West without knowing much about it. For example, Zane Grey, a New York dentist-turned-author, penned legions of best-selling western novels. The *Saturday Evening Post* carried short romantic pieces on the West written by Mary Roberts Rinehart and others with little direct experience on the Plains.[38] Earlier Wild West showmen had built their careers around the belief that bona fide experts on the frontier should tell their own stories, but most Americans rejected that supposition in the 1920s.

Mix attuned himself to this age by listening to the public and adjusting his product accordingly. Olive Stokes Mix recalled that her husband "checked carefully on the effect of his films on the public." Tom Mix kept a file of comments and reactions to his movies. Professionals thanked him for making films that helped them relax and forget their problems.[39] Mix offered a romanticized vision of a past age and played a rugged individualist, impeccably moral and courageous, who brought villains to justice with no need for, and no interference from, big government. Those in theaters did not need to contemplate anything confusing or realistic because he proffered unadulterated escapist entertainment.

Audiences demanded predictable productions, and his movies had a standard plot, or a "nicely blended recipe," which Mix explained: "I ride into a place owning my horse, saddle, and bridle. It isn't my quarrel, but I get into trouble doing the right thing for somebody else. When it's all ironed out, I never get any money reward. I may be made foreman of the ranch and I get the girl, but there is never a fervid love scene." Olive Stokes Mix delineated the formula similarly: "They consisted of plenty of action, a simple plot, a very white hero, an impossibly incorrigible villain, a number of dangerous schemes to be foiled, and a helpless heroine to be rescued at the last moment." A reviewer of *Painted Post* (1928) commented: "the studio gave him the old rubber-stamp plot: hold-up, kidnapping, bandit chase, spectacular rescue," and other critics chided him for a lack of originality, but when Mix varied his plots or played nonwestern characters, fans protested.[40]

Mix's standardized product played well in the 1920s. When many Americans, including F. Scott Fitzgerald, worried that crassness and materialism were corrupting society, Mix played cowboys who never got a "money reward" and lived simple lives. In addition to representing the antithesis of the money-grubbers, Mix personified individualism. In this age when mainstream Americans believed that their big and bureaucratic nation stifled individual effort, Mix proved that one determined cowboy could make a difference. Unlike the Wild West shows, where groups of cowboys rode to the rescue, Mix usually acted alone. This fit an age that credited the frontier with nurturing individualism.[41]

Mix represented "rugged virtue in the saddle," fought for justice, and demonstrated that truth and justice triumphed in his mythical West. About the question of historical accuracy, he explained: "The real truth is basically there, because Good always did eventually overcome Evil in the real winning of the West." Mix believed that his movies instilled moral virtue because they remained "clean" and "wholesome," and he portrayed a character who did the "right thing because it was the right thing to do."[42]

Mix added boyish charm, prowess, a passion for justice, and a sense of humor to these screen characters. His prewar movies included humor, and at Fox, Tom's commitment to it grew. After World War I, he created an "engaging but uncomplicated" persona and avoided roles with ambiguity or psychological depth.[43] In every circumstance, he remained a thoroughly predictable cowboy.

Indians usually appeared as war-painted savages who opposed civilization, but they presented few problems for white folks in Mix's movies.[44] This marked a significant change from Buffalo Bill's Wild West show arenas where war-whooping Indians on horseback made an impact that few forgot. Mix's movies could not replicate such scenes because early westerns lacked both sound and color. In addition, with the Indian wars a part of history, they became a less potent symbol of opposition to American-style progress than during Cody's time. Perhaps, too, Mix diminished the importance of Indians because the only ones he knew were the dispossessed Poncas on the 101 Ranch.

Instead of Native Americans, Mix made slovenly cheats and bullies his favorite adversaries. The movie format allowed development of despicable villains who preyed on those weaker than themselves, performed sequences of scurrilous deeds, and humiliated their victims in frames of printed dialogue. Mix defeated the badmen with nonstop daredevil riding, desperate chases, expert shooting, fisticuffs, knife throwing, fancy roping, and fights atop speeding trains.

In addition to renegades, Mix made villains of people in positions of power. In *The Coming of the Law* (1919), Big Bill Dunlavey, a corrupt political boss, ran Dry Bottom, New Mexico. *The Wilderness Trail* (1919) featured Mix attempting to please Old Angus Fitzpatrick, a "domineering, vindictive, jealous, [and] cunning" boss. *Horseman of the Plains* (1928) pitted Tom and his horse Tony against unscrupulous creditors. In it, Mix and Tony played "mortgage lifters" who rescued hardworking people from predatory creditors.[45] Obviously, Mix contemporized the cowboy by pitting himself against modern villains.

While western badmen became stronger, female characters weakened. As Olive Stokes Mix put it, they were Tom's "reward" for being so good and so heroic. In his movies, women appeared as "spotless," helpless, and pathetic innocents whom chivalrous Mix rescued from evil villains and runaway horses. In *The Coming of the Law*, Tom knocked out Big Bill Dunlavey for insulting Nellie Hazelton, saved her from dastardly Yuma Ed, and protected her during a chase scene. Nellie won Mix's heart by nursing him back to health after he was dragged behind his horse and beaten, offering a glass of buttermilk when he came to call, and expressing gratitude for her rescue.[46]

Derring-do on Mix's part and a dependent woman always caused the two characters to fall hopelessly in love. Tom's movies often ended with an embrace and talk of marriage, but never a "fervid love scene."[47] In these ways, Mix reaffirmed that sex roles and sexual behavior remained steadfast. Unlike the Millers' Wild West show, women in Mix's movies did not talk of going off to war or dance in tutus on elephants' backs. Instead they represented virginal heroines who disproved Freud's notion that libidos ran wild and did not dress or act like flappers. Mix's films sanctioned a gender-based double standard by illustrating that women who ventured into the male world invited trouble. Had Annie Oakley and Edith Tantlinger applied for positions with Mix, he would have instructed them to leave their guns at home, learn submissiveness, get a pitcher of buttermilk, and practice feminine wiles.

In this period of despair about World War I's mayhem, Mix played cowboys who eradicated evil without spilling blood. Before World War I, William S. Hart's westerns parlayed bloodshed as a part of "realism." When aroused, Hart telegraphed his anger with piercing stares and triumphed in brawls because of his bulldog-like determination. He flailed opponents with his fists, left them in bloody heaps, and then staggered away blood-soaked and disheveled. Realism, violence, and characters who were a mixture of good and bad became Hart's stock-in-trade.[48]

In contrast, in postwar movies Mix kept his composure and seldom ruffled his clothes or bled; instead, he usually outsmarted and outmaneuvered his opponents. If pushed to physical force, Tom used his fists adroitly to knock out villains but seldom bloodied or killed them. A reviewer of *The Everlasting Whisper* (1925) commented: "He makes the villains look like mere amateurs, both with the agility of his movements and his quick thinking." In *Terror Trail* (1933), a journalist noted that the "mortality rate is unusually low." In it, Mix captured a gang of horse thieves in a "bloodless climax" by "substituting unbroken steeds for their regular mounts," then subduing them one-by-one when bucked off the horses. In movies, he threatened villains with his guns, lassoed them singly or in groups, tossed them into streams, dunked them in horse tanks, and beat them with athletic stunts like swinging across the room on chandeliers or climbing walls of nearly perpendicular box canyons.[49] If gunplay seemed imminent, Mix often demonstrated his ability with firearms to dissuaded badmen from starting trouble.[50] Avoiding gunplay fit the mood of a nation disillusioned with war, but marked a departure from the sanguinary Wild West show tradition.

The "very white hero" promoted conservative values like those found in the *McGuffey Readers* and other contemporary schoolbooks that portrayed a simple, rural, preindustrial, and pre-Freudian world where people could distinguish between right and wrong. To serve as a model for America's youngsters Mix promoted perseverance, humility, and hard work and avoided tobacco, swearing, gambling, and strong drink. When a script included such behavior he declared, "This won't do," and explained: "The role I play on screen has got to represent a man of ideals." "We've got to convince the boyhood of America that drinking and gambling are bad, that physical fitness always wins out over dissipation, that a good life brings rewards and evildoing brings punishment." Olive Stokes Mix recalled: "He wrote frequently to clergymen to verify that his pictures were not detrimental to the millions of his youthful fans." He kept a file about what people wanted in movies, savored fan mail from children, and treasured the praise of parents.[51]

Instructing young people about morality marked a departure from Wild West shows. Previous showmen touted their performances as living history lessons beneficial to everyone, including children. Catlin's shows and books had inaugurated a tradition of cultivating youngsters' interest in the West that Buffalo Bill and the Millers continued. Unlike his predecessors, Mix instead emphasized virtue over historical content. Fox Studios recommended that theater owners send letters to Boy Scouts and Girl Scouts, indicating that Mix represented the traits they taught: patriotism, courage, kindness to animals, personal health, cheerfulness, courtesy, and honor. Under Mix's tutelage, much of the intellectual content about the West dissipated, and the cowboy became a whitewashed stereotype largely aimed at youths.[52]

As for horses, George Catlin began a romantic veneration of them as symbols of freedom that was continued by Cody. Mix's movies equally celebrated horses, despite the appearance of automobiles and airplanes in his westerns. Mix mainly stayed on horseback in films one observer called "filled with anachronisms."[53]

Mix could not hide his affection for horses. Fans who turned to "The Loves of Tom Mix" in their *Photoplay* in 1929 found an article featuring the horses, not the women, in Mix's life. According to the Mix legend, "an animal was never 'dumb' to Tom. He always treated them with kindness and deep respect." Moreover, publicity stated that they sensed his affection, that he could ride any horse, and that Mix manhandled anyone who mistreated them. During his years in entertainment, Mix used three mounts—Old Blue, Tony, and Tony Jr.—and loved them dearly. According to the *New York Times,* Mix reported to the set late on Old Blue's birthday because Mix had visited the grave of his beloved companion. He made the movie *Just Tony* (1922) as a tribute to his equine friend, but one writer criticized the picture as "a lot of sentimental tosh about animals."[54]

Usually, however, reporters saw Mix and his horses as a heroic team. On screen, Tony performed wonders: if someone bound Mix's hands, Tony undid the knot; when Mix needed to be elevated, Tom encircled his waist with a rope, located a pulley or tree branch, and Tony pulled him up cliffs, to haylofts, and to robbers' hideouts; and Mix always make quick getaways because Tony waited patiently for his master to jump into the saddle. Tony also assisted Tom by kicking, biting, bumping, and otherwise jostling villains at appropriate times.[55] Tony embodied all that a machine was not: a flesh-and-blood companion who loved, anticipated needs, assisted in sundry ways, and listened sympathetically.

As a film star, Mix replicated the action he first saw as a youngster in Buffalo Bill's Wild West show: riding, lassoing, marksmanship, and anything else requiring rough-and-tumble physicality. Posters for Mix's movies promised feats of prowess, and in theaters audiences saw him jump on and off countless horses, stop runaway teams and speeding trains, demonstrate sharpshooting, fight Indians, chase villains, leap great chasms on horseback, lasso scores of badmen, and rescue stagecoaches. Mix rarely varied plots of movies; he just added more liveliness. When trains, automobiles, motorcycles, and airplanes appeared in his movies, they served mostly as novel accessories for action. He jumped from automobiles, hung from the wings of airplanes, and he and his horses leaped into the open doors of boxcars of moving trains.[56]

Reflecting the Wild West show tradition, he saw soul-stirring deeds as the lifeblood of entertainment and believed that downgrading the quality or quan-

tity of it robbed ticket holders of what they paid to see: "I try to make the pictures so that when a boy pays, say, 20 cents to see it, he will get 20 cents worth,
not 10. If I drop, you see, it would be like putting my hand in his pocket and
stealing a dime."[57]

Moreover, Mix believed that he, and he alone, should perform those feats
credited to him, because, after all, people paid to see *him*. Consequently, he did
most of his own stunts, risking his life in the process and often ending up in the
hospital. As he grew older, the studio employed some doubles, whom, along with
film crews, Mix swore to secrecy. According to a stunt man, Mix never accepted
other people substituting for him. To allow them to do their work, the studio
often lured Mix off the set with some ruse. When Mix returned, he would "raise
hell."[58] Personally performing the action recorded on film reflected a philosophy of entertainment learned in Wild West shows, where no substitutes existed. Calling oneself a champion shot or rider, only to have someone else actually
perform the shooting or riding, represented behavior unacceptable to Wild West
show performers.

Mix's devil-may-care temperament led to abrasions, bruises, and broken
bones. These, along with alleged war wounds, enhanced the Mix legend. By the
end of Mix's career, he claimed to have overcome twenty-three broken or cracked
ribs, eight different breaks in his arms, three fractures of his left leg, two clean
breaks of his legs, and several bullet wounds. When he suffered from a serious
illness, the *New York Times* reported: "An iron physique, built on the cattle plains
of the West, may save Tom Mix from death."[59] Like Catlin, Cody, and the 101's
cowgirls, Mix saw himself as a physically superior person inured to hardship
and impervious to serious injury because of a lifetime spent in nature.

During the 1920s, boxing flourished, and Mix mastered this sport too. Off-
screen, Mix sparred with the heavyweight champion Jack Dempsey himself and
used his pugilistic skill to silence bullies and to protect women, just as he did
in movies. He relied on his fists to teach respect to a surly former prize fighter
who served as a cook with his production crew. Tiring of verbal harassment from
an entertainer named "Weavin' Will" Morrissey, Mix knocked him down. When
the cowboy star recognized his daughter's suitor as the man who had mistreated the film star Clara Bow, he struck him on the jaw, kicked him in the pants,
and explained: "The sock was for Clara and the kick for me." Obviously, he
believed that aggressive virility could eradicate evil wherever it existed. This
combination of physical and moral superiority supported what Catlin, Cody,
and the Millers had said about westerners, and it appealed to Americans in the
1920s, who associated wilderness with vigor, patriotism, and character.[60]

In this age enamored of nature, western movies such as *The Covered Wagon*

(1923) and *The Iron Horse* (1924) offered theatergoers long looks at the unspoiled American landscape, and Fox Studios enhanced action in Mix's movies with breathtaking locales. Mix supported this enthusiastically and asked that his movies be filmed in national parks because glimpses of such spectacular scenery might encourage visitation to these places. *Sky High* (1922), set in the Grand Canyon, supplemented Mix-style action with the rugged grandeur of the park. Fisticuffs with a burly badman on the very brink of the canyon brought fans to the edges of their seats.[61] Like his predecessors in Wild West shows, Mix stressed the importance and magnitude of the western landscape.

Mix tried to look as stunning as the scenery, an attitude traceable to Wild West shows. Attention to the distinctive and colorful costumes of Plains peoples went back to Catlin, who recorded the details of Indians' dress in his paintings, collected their clothing and implements of war, and donned a shaman's costume to delight his customers. In the fight with Yellow Hand, Cody intentionally wore a flamboyant *vaquero* outfit, and his golden buckskins, embroidered shirts, and tight pants set a standard for western raiment. Brightly garbed cowboys, cossacks, Arabs, *vaqueros,* gauchos, and military groups from around the world transformed his arena into a pulsating sea of color, and distinctive outfits enabled those at Wild West shows to identify everyone in arenas at a glance. Surely when Mix attended Buffalo Bill's Wild West show he had noted the colorful and ornate costumes.[62]

Mix made clothing a line of demarcation between himself and villains. Badmen in his films looked shabby and usually wore dark outfits. Mix believed that his role as hero required that he always look well-groomed even if he had just subdued a band of desperados. Often Mix appeared in white costumes, including the large white hats that became his trademark, but he did not simply dress himself in white and the villains in black. Olive Stokes Mix described her husband's dress as "flamboyant, colorful outfits, business suits trimmed with leather; sports jackets that were so loud they screamed to high heaven . . . brilliant cowboy hats and gaily decorated, hand-tooled boots."[63]

Sometimes he rode on a twenty-five-hundred-dollar saddle ornamented with silver. Mix loved, collected, and wore diamonds. He often donned a horsehair belt with a diamond-encrusted buckle emblazoned with "Tom Mix, America's Champion Cowboy." The black-and-white movies did not capture the bright colors of his outfits, but contrasting tones reproduced well. His fancy clothing intrigued moviegoers in this fashion-conscious age, and reviewers of films often described what the star wore. Few cared that the costumes bore no resemblance to those of working cowboys. After all, this was show business.[64]

Like his predecessors in Wild West shows, Mix tested his appeal abroad.

Because his silent movies relied on action, drama, and simple plots rather than dialogue, European youngsters could easily understand and appreciate Mix's films. Recognizing this, Fox Studios sent him to Europe in 1925. Claiming that no famous westerner had toured London and Paris since Cody in 1905, a reporter for the *New York Times* indicated: "his arrival will create a far greater furor in London and Paris than did 'Buffalo Bill' and his hundreds of Indians and cowboys years ago." The journalist explained: "many more persons have seen Mix on the screen than had ever heard of 'Buffalo Bill's' Wild West in the olden days."[65] If the Millers read such accounts, they undoubtedly noted that reporters ignored their excursion abroad in 1914.

Mix approached the tour with an entertainer's flair. His horse Tony arrived in New York in his own private railroad car and visited the toy section of Gimbel's department store. Mix talked about Tony and his upcoming trip on WGBS, a local radio station. With an eye to publicity, Mix, in full cowboy regalia, rode Tony into the dining room of New York's fashionable Hotel Astor. He stayed astride the animal and greeted friends and chatted with Will Rogers about their experiences as young men in Zack Mulhall's Wild West show. Finally, Mix rode out of the dining room, reappeared on foot, and acted nonchalant. Then the banquet began.[66] Mix's audacity intrigued the guests and made them wonder if this man's blatant disregard for social convention would continue when he went abroad.

Mix vowed that Europe would not change him and even apologized for planning the trip, since he had not yet seen all of the United States. He refused to change his dress for Europeans. For the trip, he bought a number of white hats, a half dozen pairs of boots, a diamond-studded watch, twenty-two suits, and an ample supply of burgundy-colored formal wear. Also, he ordered leather calling cards because of the rumor that the haughty French tore up paper ones and threw them in the faces of visiting Americans. Nor would he soil his palate with exotic European food. On some leather cards appeared a picture of the typically western meal of ham and eggs with the French translation printed beneath the picture. Thus, he could order his favorite meal without learning any French.[67] In his efforts to remain unquestionably American, Mix exaggerated the Wild West show tradition of cowboys maintaining western dress, eating frontier food, and shunning European languages.

Mix, his fourth wife, Victoria, and their daughter, Thomasina, arrived in England aboard the *Aquitania* on 14 April 1925. The entertainer rode Tony down the gangplank to greet a crowd that included hundreds of cheering fans, the town council of Southampton, and the mayors of Southampton, Brighton, and Hove. He wore an elaborate cowboy outfit that included a large white hat, a short fur-collared fawn riding coat, yellow gloves, a bow tie, and spurs so long that he tripped over them. In keeping with his cowboy image, he brought several firearms. From Southampton, the Mixes and Tony proceeded by train to Waterloo Station in London, where another crowd greeted him.[68]

That night Mix spoke from the London Broadcasting Station, where he told tales about his experiences in the Spanish-American War, the Boer War, and the American frontier. He also explained that he had become an actor because a moving picture company sought a good cowboy capable of performing stunts. Mix knew he could do all the outfit asked because he "had been doing very little else but that ever since I was a kid of five on my father's ranch way back in Texas in the real pioneer days."[69]

During other talks, the American indicated his pleasure about visiting England and that this was his first trip abroad and his first vacation in ten years. He discussed the lovable English rogue Dick Turpin, a role that Mix had recently played. Because he might make a movie about Sir Walter Raleigh, he visited the Tower of London. Tom delighted English youngsters by signing autographs, talking, and lecturing them about morality and physical fitness.[70]

Like Zack Miller, Mix remained an intractable westerner when dealing with elite Britishers. On the second day in England, Mix and a swarm of publicity agents from Fox Studios visited Sir Alfred Bower, the lord mayor of London. During this hour-long visit, they discussed hunting and the mayor's days as a bicycle racer and "all-around athlete." The lord mayor and his wife offered Mix port wine, which he refused, explaining that he preferred coffee, the traditional cowboy beverage. Tom left behind one of his famous white hats and a Mexican rug. An English journalist protested the brashness of Mix and his entourage, who called Sir Alfred Bower the "mayor guy," told him how to pose with Tom, and waited until a sizable crowd gathered before leaving the mansion. The final insult was Mix's refusal to give a speech to the admirers waiting outside the building.[71]

Mix created bedlam when he rode Rotten Row, a fashionable bridle path in Hyde Park. Several hundred youngsters followed him, and police arrived to keep order. Tom delighted his admirers with trick riding. Supposedly unfamiliar with local custom, Mix proceeded down the wrong side of the path and thereby caused utter confusion and ruined the riding for others. About the experience, Mix commented: "I got more kick out of this . . . than out of my stunts for the pictures, and Rotten Row is the finest bridle path I've ever ridden on."[72]

At a formal dinner for him at the Savoy Hotel, Tom made his entrance dressed in a "puce-coloured tuxedo" and riding Tony. This act, reminiscent of the one in New York, brought cheers from the crowd. Mix rode twice around the room before Tony departed. Thomas Ormiston, president of the Cinematographic Exhibitors' Association, then proposed a toast to Mix, who responded with a short humorous speech. Mix explained that he had brought Tony, so that when he made a faux pas, he could "make a quick get-away," although that might prove difficult "with all these automobiles on the wrong side of the road." Mix added a few serious comments about keeping his movies clean and instructive because he knew that England's youngsters idolized him. He said that visiting England had been "one of the greatest wishes of his life" because his current wife was English. A short film documenting a typical day's work on Mix's ranch ended the evening.[73]

With the trip to Great Britain, Mix followed the Wild West show pattern of going abroad and remaining a patriotic westerner. His cockiness resembled that of Zack Miller, but differed from Catlin's "green horn from the backwoods" demeanor and Cody's efforts to make Europeans "esteem us better." Mix called the trip a "holiday" and "just a look-around visit," a predictable attitude during a time people in the United States saw Europe as a "playground" and resented that these nations had called for assistance during World War I and then refused to pay their war debts.[74]

Mix had no investment in the trip to recoup, so he did not need to give shows or please audiences. And unlike Catlin, who carted six tons of artifacts and paintings to Europe, and Cody and the Millers, who transported hundreds of people and animals, Mix brought virtually no accoutrements, demonstrated few western skills, and did not camp outdoors to establish his western persona. Mix's "show," in the form of silent movies, had preceded him to Europe, and while there he simply confirmed the rigid cowboy stereotype established in his films. With Mix, the cowboy was *the* representative of the West, and that image alone ensured the success of the trip. Mix gave a new twist to Cody's argument about cowboys' unadaptability by turning inflexibility into a virtue and charming the English with it. Mix brought the cowboy stereotype to England and made no concessions. His lack of concern about the British-American relationship indicated the broader feeling that the United States—like the image of the cowboy—no longer needed to establish its credentials abroad.

Some Britons saw Mix's trip for what it was: a short visit subsidized by his studio and orchestrated by an entourage of publicity agents to get maximum exposure for the money spent. An English reporter protested this in an article entitled "This Mix Business: What London Wants Is a Society for Putting Americans in Their Place." The English periodical *Punch* lampooned Mix, as it had the others in Wild West shows, by observing that this American lacked polish.[75] As a casual visitor, Mix largely ignored diplomacy, made insipid remarks, and seemed interested in only those people and places that related to his movie career.

After England, Mix went to Paris. When Tony left, "hundreds of boys . . . tumbled over each other in their efforts to catch a glimpse of the horse" in a cargo ship purportedly carrying him. However, Tony was probably not aboard because he arrived in France by airplane. About fifty thousand fans greeted Mix and Tony in Paris. This crowd snarled traffic and prevented many Parisians from going home. Because of the congestion and confusion, the station master forbade Mix to ride Tony. Putting his family in the horse van along with Tony, Mix rode atop it to the hotel amid cheers from admirers and "hoots, cat-calls, and whistling—the French equivalent of hissing" from some inconvenienced by the American. The next day, Mix began a round of widely publicized horseback rides, autograph signings, and a visit to a Boy Scout conclave. After France, Mix proceeded to Belgium, Holland, and Germany. Throughout his travels, he presented white Stetson hats, forty-seven in all, to those he wished to impress.[76]

On 21 July 1925, Mix returned to North America and stopped in Toronto, Boston, Washington, D.C., Buffalo, Detroit, St. Louis, and Denver before returning to Hollywood. During these travels, he visited Boy Scouts and stopped regularly at hospitals for children and disabled veterans. Everywhere Americans cheered him. Mix basked in this attention and declared that being home felt good because "the pomp and vanity of feudal Europe was tiring."[77] After the tour, Tom returned to Fox Studios.

By the late 1920s, Mix had enjoyed a meteoric rise to stardom, made a fortune, and completed a successful tour abroad. In the process of accomplishing those things, he had carefully sifted the Wild West show tradition, kept some of its components, and jettisoned others. Specifically, he had polished and streamlined the cowboy image, increased the emphasis on morality, tailored his films for a more youthful audience, and altered the images of badmen, women, and Indians. Mix had also embraced and expanded other old Wild West show themes. He had exalted horses and the past and emphasized physical prowess, nonstop action, and the uplifting qualities of nature. Tom took elaborate costuming to a degree beyond that previously seen in Wild West shows, and he visited Europe and claimed to be America's representative westerner. Ironically, his formula for success carried the seeds of destruction, because once Mix had established these parameters, he stuck stubbornly with what he knew and the world of entertainment bypassed him.

Mix's success spawned imitators. Wanting a safe investment, Hollywood often turned to B grade westerns—low budget products brimming with Mix-style action and sometimes featuring established stars such as Buck Jones, Hoot

Gibson, Ken Maynard, and Tim McCoy. New names also appeared: Gary Cooper, George O'Brien, John Wayne, and singers like Gene Autry and Roy Rogers. Each star claimed a part of Mix's appeal; for example, Buck Jones excelled in riding, glamorous Fred Thompson duplicated Mix's stunts and preached morality to children, Hoot Gibson mastered comedy, John Wayne personified physical prowess, and Gene Autry and Roy Rogers copied Mix's ostentatious dress.[78]

Western movie themes began to change, which undermined Mix's popularity. The greater introspection, frustration, and despair fostered by the depression led to a return of realism and violence in movies. Mix watched disgustedly and lashed out at Johnny Mack Brown for playing Billy the Kid. Tom Mix did not appreciate anyone glamorizing outlaws, particularly "sissies" like modern-day hoodlums. Mix argued "that the gangster gunman of to-day is a clumsy amateur and coward and that one old-time gun thrower could account for a room full of racketeers."[79] However, in this topsy-turvy age when cherished American values failed, the movie-going public often preferred outlaws to Mix's ideas about honesty, altruism, and good overcoming evil.

Not just Mix suffered; the whole western movie industry faced hard times. In March 1929, the Hollywood commentator Cal York penned the following for *Photoplay:*

The western films that were a wow
Are only so much footage now,
And all those steeds we thought so nice
Are hauling wagons labelled "Ice."

The next issue of *Photoplay* carried a more thoughtful, but equally devastating, article. In it, the editor James R. Quirk declared that Charles Lindbergh's recent transatlantic flight "put the cowboy into discard as a type of national hero. The Western novel and motion picture heroes have slunk away into the brush, never to return." He wrote that Mix and his cohorts "must swap horses for aeroplanes or go to the old actors' home." Since Lindbergh's achievement, boys hesitated to plunk down dimes to see cowboys because they preferred entertainment reflecting current and exciting events. Quirk overstated his case, but statistics indicated a decline in the genre: in 1928, 141 westerns appeared, followed by a drop to 92 in 1929, and another fall to 79 in 1930.[80]

Something new—sound in westerns—further muddled Mix's future. In 1928, the year his contract with Fox expired, the studio released *In Old Arizona* starring Warner Baxter as the Cisco Kid and Edmund Lowe as the Texas Ranger pursuing him. In addition to action, theatergoers heard the sounds of the

West—hoofbeats, gunshots, and even the sizzle of bacon in a frying pan.[81] Adding sound restored an ingredient jettisoned in the transition from Wild West shows to silent movies. Now actors and actresses could converse and develop character that way instead of relying on visual cues such as standardized dress, stereotypes, and nonstop action. George Catlin, the lecturer, would have welcomed the return of dialogue. However, this made Mix squirm because what he had learned in Wild West shows and transferred to movies fell out of fashion in talkies.

Unhappy with a changing world, Mix lashed out at Hollywood. He blamed his failing marriage on all those "parasites" who came to his house to drink, eat, smoke, swim, and play bridge and tennis and then left behind "cigarette stubs, empty bottles and empty lives." Even making movies lost its appeal. Now, instead of getting on with shooting films, studios mired themselves "with a lot of supervisors and yes-men and assistant yes-men and more red tape than an Indian agent."[82]

During 1928, Mix went on a "vaudeville tour" that took him back before live audiences. He discussed escape to Argentina, where he planned to ride the pampas, befriend those "real colorful hombres" called gauchos, and live a style of life reminiscent of that in the Old West. There, with his own movie company, he could make traditional, action-packed silents. His plans for money-making also included starting a diversified "company" for buying real estate and building a "light and power" system.[83]

In chatting about Argentina, Mix followed a pattern established by Catlin, Cody, and Zack Miller. When each man's particular view of the West lost appeal, he broadened his view of the world. Catlin proposed a "museum of mankind" and fled to South America after the loss of his collection; Cody and Salsbury made their show international with a Congress of Rough Riders; and Miller dreamed of South Africa. Even in his talk about real estate, Mix followed the lead of Catlin and Cody, who hoped to make windfall profits in that business. But, like his predecessors, he lacked business ability and would not leave show business. Mix returned to the United States, having made no movies and no money.

Mix signed a contract with the Film Booking Office (FBO) under the direction of Joseph P. Kennedy and produced action-filled silents: *Son of the Golden West* (1928), *King Cowboy* (1928), *Outlawed* (1929), *The Drifter* (1929), and *The Big Diamond Robbery* (1929). None was a hit, and commentators panned some. *Photoplay* carried these comments: "King Cowboy—FBO—Please, Mr. Mix, don't do anything like this again" and "Outlawed—FBO—Not so hot, Mr. Mix, not so hot!" FBO reorganized into RKO, which specialized in sound and worsened matters for Mix, who had trouble delivering convincing dialogue. A review of *The Drifter* reported "Tom Mix is bowing out" of movies and that "vaudeville is calling him." In a disparaging remark about Wild West shows, this writer added: "He'll probably break little glass balls with a rifle."[84] Sure enough, Mix returned to Wild West shows.

In 1929, 1930, and 1931, Mix appeared with an abbreviated Wild West show in the Sells-Floto Circus, that entertainment where Buffalo Bill spent some of his last years. Fan magazines reported the position paid ten thousand dollars per week for a thirty-five-week season in 1930, excellent wages (if accurate) for a down-on-his-luck celebrity during the depression. Mix led the opening procession, did trick riding, and then returned after the circus portion with forty or fifty westerners to present Wild West show acts.[85]

Mix explained his return by claiming such shows remained his "first love." There was some truth to that statement because even at the height of his movie career, Mix had sometimes given free "Wild West Exhibitions" featuring rodeo skills and sharpshooting for his fans. Furthermore, live entertainment brought direct and ego-building contact with adoring fans, including children who spent Saturdays watching his silents at matinees. He claimed happiness for the "first time since I left the range" and called circus personnel "*real* folks" who worked hard and cared for one another. While such things indicated a continuing interest in live performances, Mix had resisted returning to them. The Miller brothers, for example, had tried everything—flattery, threats, and cajolery—to sell him their Wild West show or feature him in it, but Mix had refused to return.[86]

Clearly, Mix had reacted to the changes wrought by sound in movies by fleeing to Argentina, continuing to work in silent westerns, and returning to a Wild West show. In 1932 and 1933, he tried "talkie" westerns for Universal Sound Pictures with dashing titles such as *The Rider of Death Valley, Texas Bad Man, Destry Rides Again, My Pal, The King, The Fourth Horseman, Hidden Gold, Flaming Guns, Hollywood on Parade, Terror Trail,* and *Rustler's Roundup.* He learned his lines, but failed to master sound. He talked of retirement from pictures, traveling in a show, and another trip to Europe. In 1933, he inaugurated a radio program for Ralston Purina Company in which he combined two Mix standbys—adventure and instructing young people about morality—with pitches for Ralston's cereals. The radio show proved popular and continued to 1950, about ten years after he died.[87]

In 1934 Mix joined the Sam B. Dill Circus as a performer, bought it the next year for four hundred thousand dollars, and promptly changed the name to the Tom Mix Circus and Wild West. Running the show during the Great Depression proved difficult, however. To finance it—and combat communism and criminals' influence on America's youngsters—Mix made a fifteen-part cinema serial called *The Miracle Rider* in which he played a Texas Ranger in the modern West. The serial included just about everything: morality lessons, superstitious Native Americans, automobiles, bomb-like bullets made of a metal called X-94 being secretly mined on an Indian reservation, bad guys hiding in underground strongholds and sending secret telegraph and radio messages, remote-controlled glider airplanes, runaway trucks, and Mix and Tony Jr., a stallion who replaced the original Tony, saving the day with western heroics. Although disjointed, it made almost a million dollars for the Mascot film company.[88] With *The Miracle Rider,* Mix updated the western theme with gadgets, the modern West, and even a new enemy—madmen intent on world domination. However, *The Miracle Rider* did not revitalize his career.

In addition to his myriad professional difficulties, Mix faced personal problems in the late 1920s. The stock market crash cost him around a million dollars as well as his Beverly Hills mansion and Arizona ranch. Adding to his woes, a grand jury indicted him for failure to pay taxes. He began drinking heavily, lost his normally optimistic outlook, nearly died from a ruptured appendix, and suffered several injuries. He also spent a lot of time in court fighting the back taxes charge, battling with Zack Miller about a breach of contract suit concerning Mix's refusal to appear in the 101 show, enduring another divorce, fighting for custody of a daughter, and trying to prevent the marriage of another one. Beset from every side, Mix went abroad, leaving a grown daughter named Ruth to run the show. Although she worked hard, the Tom Mix Circus failed during his absence.[89]

Mix's second tour of England stretched from the fall of 1938 to the spring of 1939. His arrival produced enthusiastic crowds of twenty thousand fans in many cities. Mix brought with him three American rodeo stars named Jack Knapp, Joe Bowers, and Bud Carlell, as well as Tony Jr. Tom's modest Wild West show resembled Catlin's offerings as much as Cody's and the Millers' large shows. The entertainments, given twice nightly, began with Tom making a dramatic entrance on the "Wonder Horse" Tony Jr., after which the horse retired from the arena. Then came standard Wild West show acts, such as "characteristic ranch sports, shooting, rope-spinning, and whip wizardry."[90]

To demonstrate marksmanship, Mix contorted his body and fired from nearly every conceivable position, as had Johnnie Baker in Cody's show. Mix demonstrated the quick draw with revolvers, twirled them, and perforated spinning targets. For a grand finale he shot at the cutting edge of a butcher's cleaver, apparently splitting the bullet and sending pieces of lead to break objects placed on either side of the cleaver. The show also included variety acts, presented by

English performers, that changed from city to city and included trapeze artists, dancers, comedy musicians, comics of other kinds, roller-skating cossacks,
and performing pigeons.[91]

Despite everything, some saw the old entertainer as "still more of a hero than
the cinema world imagines," "a statuesquely romance figure in bright cowboy
trappings," and "a commanding and colorful figure." Wherever he went, adults
and children clustered about him and asked for autographs. Tom still told captivating stories about his heroism in the military and the West, working with
Buffalo Bill Cody, whom he might play in an upcoming movie, and how one
of Mix's uncles killed Billy the Kid. Mix explained that he did much of his own
silver work, a skill learned from Navajos, and that he had been a fire chief and
a colonel in the "United States Air Force." To link himself with the British Isles,
Mix told about his grandfather, a Scottish minister who went to Texas and spread
the word of God among cowboys by following them into saloons, cornering
them there, and reforming them.[92]

Despite favorable press and self-aggrandizement, everyone—including Mix
himself—recognized the end of his great days as a western star. On one occasion, he told a reporter that he did not enjoy appearing in a "circus," but he
would stay because he was not a quitter. All in all, he said, he would have been
happiest if he had stayed in the West and "stuck to cow-punching." Journalists
characterized Mix as a reminder of a former time, a man "reared in the true
Western tradition when the West really was 'tough.'" Mix agreed that the frontier had changed, roads joined most of the country, and the few remaining
outlaws hovered near the Mexican border. Mix talked freely about being fifty-
eight years of age, and reporters regularly called him a star of a previous age.
Remembering watching Mix's silent movies as youngsters, journalists lamented the passing of a genre in which "men had to be quick on the draw and able
to ride hell for leather if they wished to live"; movies in which "womanhood
was revered and protected"; and a mythical West where good always triumphed.[93] Like Buffalo Bill, Mix in his last years symbolized a bygone era.

At every opportunity, Mix praised old-style western films for their values and
traditions and lambasted contemporary ones. According to Mix, Hollywood's
present products lacked authenticity because "the men who make them have
never seen cowboys; they see a Madison Square Garden rodeo, a dude ranch,
and one Indian, and think they know all about the West. Then they take a croon-
er, put him on a horse, and call him a 'cowboy.'" "Crooners," or singing cowboys, aggravated Mix, who railed that in all his western experiences, he had never
seen a cowboy riding a horse and playing a guitar at the same time. Perhaps they
"crooned" because they could not ride, rope, or shoot. Tom could not under-

stand why studios would spend two hundred thousand dollars for these impostors to make a single movie.[94]

Mix probably could not recognize that he had inspired much of what these scorned singers and their films offered: standardized plots, morality lessons replacing history, minimal violence, women and Native Americans playing marginal roles, and pretty cowboy dress.[95] Like his predecessors in Wild West shows, Mix learned that new generations of western entertainers took what worked from one period, updated and popularized it, and left the veterans in the business confused, nostalgic, and sometimes bitter. Crooners pilfered from Mix in the same thankless way that he had taken elements from Wild West shows, suited them to the 1920s, and transferred them to silent movies.

During this final trip abroad, Mix avoided gauche publicity stunts and became more humble, friendly, and philosophical. Perhaps, he said, his two daughters in Wild West shows handled horses better than he did. He listed "loyalty, friendship, and appreciation" as the three most important words in the English language. Some interviews took unexpected turns when Mix discussed human nature, political economy, international affairs, reverence for God, and enthusiasm for Abraham Lincoln. He explained that he admired delicate prairie wildflowers, and to protect them, he had spent a lifetime directing his mounts around these plants.[96]

He praised the English people for their "selflessness," their "extreme courtesy," the "unhurried way in which they go about their business," "their friendly competition," and their strong sense of family. About the tense international situation, Mix said that he had contacted his old FBO director, Joseph P. Kennedy, now ambassador to England, asking what he might do for the English in the event of war. Should hostilities begin, he promised to join the English "in some useful capacity."[97] Like Cody and the Millers, he expressed a willingness to fight.

Mix returned from Europe before hostilities began, made appearances in the United States, and talked of reentering entertainment. Perhaps a tour in South America, where his movies remained popular, would convince everyone that he still had many fans. Surely there were producers in Hollywood who still recognized his appeal. With that in mind, Mix visited Twentieth Century-Fox, an enterprise that owed much to the popularity of his westerns. Out of respect for him, John Ford, busy filming *The Grapes of Wrath,* found the time to take Mix to lunch. Those at the studio that day remember a defeated Mix attired in a white cowboy outfit looking like a relic from the past.[98] Mix learned, as the other showmen had before him, that western entertainment discarded its principles without remorse.

While contemplating the future, Mix traveled about the nation, stopping to visit with fans and friends. After an appearance in Phoenix, Mix sped across the desert in his Cord roadster. He drove too fast for conditions, left the road to avoid hitting a crew of highway workers, overturned his car, and died near Florence, Arizona, on 12 October 1940. A suitcase flew forward during the crash, cleanly breaking his neck, but leaving his body unmarked. Even in death Mix looked good, dressed in his typical flamboyant style. In the pockets of this man intent on "making a million" were six thousand dollars in cash and fifteen hundred dollars in traveler's checks. Tom Mix was buried in an ornate silver casket engraved with the initials T.M. Fans everywhere, including a club in Lisbon, Portugal, mourned his passing.[99]

The manner of Mix's death reflected much about the man. Dashing recklessly befitted this western hero, who always escaped desperate situations with courage, quick thinking, and athleticism. An elaborate cowboy costume was his trademark and reflected a Wild West show tradition of attention to the distinctive and colorful clothing styles of westerners. No blood marked his regalia, an appropriate occurrence for this man who converted the blood-and-thunder of Wild West shows into nearly bloodless movies. Mix died in a remote desert setting because he lived there. Arizona suited him, he had explained, because it still offered areas untouched by civilization.

Despite such pronouncements, Mix was a man filled with contradiction, not just someone trying to avoid progress. Certainly, Mix "made his million" in the 1920s playing a cowboy who venerated the preindustrial West, but he also drove a Cord roadster, an American automobile long on gadgetry and luxury, which featured forward-looking innovations such as front-wheel drive and electrically controlled gear selection.[100] This contrariety—cowboy and automobile aficionado—symbolized Mix. He had attuned himself perfectly to 1920s, a nervous age that looked forward and accepted progress, but also looked backward in time and revered the past as simple and wholesome. The 1920s had been Mix's decade, and he did not fare well after that; however, technology intrigued him and he seemed always to find the money to buy those things he wanted.

Assessing this man was not easy for people of his own age. After all, how seriously should others regard a fellow who wore outlandish outfits, rode horses into formal banquet halls, failed to make the transition from silent westerns to talkies, and then criticized everything he saw on screen after that? Perhaps the best contemporary evaluation came late in his career when a journalist linked Mix's Wild West show and film careers by calling him the "greatest of all screen heroes of the 'Wild West school.'"[101] The connection between movies and the "'Wild West school'" represented Mix's place in the history of entertainment.

He learned his craft in Wild West shows, left them for movies, and then returned to live entertainment. An astute showman, he recognized the decline of tented entertainment, knew that movies and skillful press agents represented the future in western entertainment, and sensed that the mythical cowboy figure encapsulated the frontier experience for most Americans. By extracting the cowboy from Wild West shows and making him into "rugged virtue in the saddle," Mix became the preeminent western star of the 1920s, "made a million" for himself, and established a kind of cowboy movie hero who endured until the middle of the twentieth century.

# CONCLUSION

Just over one hundred years elapsed between George Catlin's first public exhibitions and Tom Mix's death in the Arizona desert. While time and geography separated them, Wild West shows linked these men, as well as Buffalo Bill Cody and the Miller brothers. Certainly, a number of similar entertainments existed, but these four showmen best represented the Wild West show tradition. In addition to creating the most popular exhibitions, they, more than any others, brought the adventure-filled "Wild West" into American culture. These individuals and their shows illustrate much about popular entertainment, the parent culture, and images and ideas about the uniqueness of the West.

As entertainers, they promoted themselves and their views of the West by tantalizing people with the proposition that they had missed something special because a particular phase of Plains history was nearing its end or had already passed. To satisfy the public's curiosity, the showmen vowed to use authentic props and real westerners—even if they did not always follow through—to reproduce for audiences the most significant sights, sounds, and experiences of the Plains. However, the showmen knew their programs must have broad appeal; consequently, audiences generally saw scenes featuring heroic figures performing adventurous deeds in wilderness settings. In this regard, Catlin glorified Plains Indians and eulogized them as "vanishing Americans," Cody celebrated the Anglo-Saxon settlement of the frontier, the Millers tried to rally enthusiasm for cattle kings, and Mix adulated the romanticized cowboy.

In the evolution of western entertainment, Wild West shows linked Indian captivity narratives, which dated back to colonial times, and a particular type of cowboy movie that lasted into the 1950s. About 1800, George Catlin reacted with fear when he saw his first Indian because of his familiarity with accounts of the Wyoming Valley Massacre but changed his perception of Indians when he came to know On-o-gong-way. Thereafter, he devoted himself to encouraging Americans to see Native Americans as flesh-and-blood humans. In the late nineteenth and early twentieth centuries, Buffalo Bill Cody gave Wild West shows their most recognized form by glorifying Manifest Destiny and expansion abroad. However, as the twentieth century progressed, Wild West shows became a tired idea, and the Millers bankrupted themselves trying to rejuvenate the genre in an era when rodeos, Indian powwows, and movies (particularly those of Tom Mix) adapted those features from Wild West shows with the most appeal.

Wild West shows were vigorous and intense live entertainment. Hearts beat a little faster when Catlin related the mysteries of the O-kee-pa, donned his medicine man outfit, and brought "real" Indians before city-bound Americans and Europeans. Cody's show bombarded audiences with vivid posters, music from the brass band, the thunder of firearms, smells of gunpowder and animals, pulsating hooves on arena floors, the careening Deadwood stage, and the dramatic duel to death with Yellow Hand. Mix made audiences cheer when he used action reminiscent of the shows to triumph over villainy. Overall, the shows offered a forceful kind of entertainment uncommon in today's world.

These showmen measured success by ticket sales and applause, so they kept their presentations experimental, always seeking that perfect but elusive combination of peoples, ideas, and images of the West. Even successful programs required modification to entice people to purchase tickets a second or third time. Additionally, what pleased one generation might bore the next. Consequently, in its hundred-year history, Wild West shows entertained and edified patrons with a variety of things: paintings, museum-style displays, speeches, play-acting, vignettes of domestic scenes and warfare, grand spectacles, rodeo acts, dance, Plains animals, and movies. They also offered an array of characters, such as Plains Indians, scouts, cowboys, cowgirls and other western women, ranchers, exotic peoples, and representatives of the great armies of the world. As entertainment, then, Wild West shows evolved in form and personnel to meet the needs of successive generations of Americans.

In addition to their place in the history of public performance, Wild West shows revealed significant aspects of the parent culture. They were particularly important reflectors of American values because they were self-consciously

American institutions devoted to defining their nation's values and history through the lens of the frontier experience.

As interpreters of the West and the nation, the shows explored issues such as expansion, progress, and violence. When Catlin lambasted his society for its misguided Indian policy and its westward push that displaced more Native Americans, most in Jacksonian America rejected him as a hopeless, out-of-touch romantic. Buffalo Bill Cody, on the other hand, celebrated Manifest Destiny before American audiences from 1883 to 1887, linked the ideas of frontier expansion and progress for international audiences in the years 1887–93, and subsequently promoted growth tied to imperialism and militarism. The Millers publicized themselves as progressive ranchers and championed the 101 as the crowning achievement in civilizing the Plains. Sensitive to the mood of the 1920s, Tom Mix reflected the nation's nervousness about internationalism and untrammeled progress and cut his movies loose from these themes. He chose to entertain his fans with nonstop action and morality lessons. By doing this, he abandoned key ingredients of Wild West shows.

These entertainers usually tied progress to struggles and bloodshed. After all, the American public wanted to associate heroism, adventure, and hard-fought battles with extending civilization to the Plains. Catlin first cast Native Americans as honorable people and victims of aggressive and misguided U.S. policies, but he quickly learned that battle cries, talk of scalping, and accounts of warfare brought the most paying customers into his lecture halls. For Buffalo Bill Cody, westward expansion meant conflict, and he heralded the "the rifle as an aid to civilization" and "Resplendent Realism of Glorious War." The Miller brothers saw the history of the Plains as a blood-drenched saga and bristled with bellicose talk when war with Mexico threatened. During their heyday, then, Wild West shows parlayed a nationalistic message that sanctioned America's efforts to grow, on this continent and elsewhere, and to kill those who stood in the way. Consequently, scores of Native Americans, Spaniards, Boxers, and Mexicans fell before Americans in Wild West show arenas. Only after World War I did the emphasis on violence abate when Mix tailored his movies to a nation tired of killing and disillusioned with their experiment to "make the world safe for democracy." By minimizing bloodshed, Mix eliminated another staple of Wild West shows.

In addition to validating growth, progress, and the use of force, the showmen delineated aspects of America's national character by contrasting their nation with Europe and other parts of the world. Catlin ventured abroad feeling "trembling excitements and fears" during a time when Americans fretted about their cultural inferiority and sought approval from Europeans. However, his letters home and the comments by Native Americans recorded in *Notes of Eight Years' Travels and Residence in Europe* reflected the typical American observation that Europeans suffered from overcivilization. In lectures, he presented Native Americans as nature's nobles, an accolade that Cody and others in Wild West shows ascribed to themselves and others in their troupes. Cody represented an assertive nation and went abroad in 1887 determined to make Europeans "esteem us better." During the 1890s, he and his show reflected a country determined to win respect with hardihood and militarism. In an international age, he added a Congress of Rough Riders and provided foreigners in the arena for audiences to compare with his westerners.

On the eve of World War I, when the Millers went to London, and in the 1920s, when Tom Mix traveled abroad, these showmen treated Europeans with a callousness befitting a homeland confident of its superiority. So throughout their history, Wild West shows revealed Americans' propensity to see themselves as innocent nature's people and to judge their own virtue and progress by measuring themselves against Europeans.

In addition to illustrating aspects of national character, these entertainers endeavored to demonstrate the uniqueness of the West. After all, they were in the "Wild West" business, and they needed to separate themselves and their region from the rest of their nation to attract paying customers. Consequently, no hint of the ordinary tainted the inhabitants, circumstances, or the places of their Wild West. In this regard, Catlin's Native Americans differed from money-grubbing and land-grabbing Jacksonian Americans and Cody's scouts contrasted dramatically with clerks and factory workers.

The world presented in Wild West show arenas proved so intoxicating that Americans would allow nothing mundane to creep into this mythical place. When the showmen ventured into ordinary occupations—like Catlin and Cody as real estate developers and the Millers touting themselves as successful businessmen—they failed to excite their audiences. Tom Mix understood this infatuation and propelled himself into the limelight with the proposition that his Wild West differed from mainstream America in the 1920s and offered silent films filled with horses, athleticism, simple plots featuring good triumphing over evil, and plenty of action. While Mix retained much that had made his predecessors successful in entertainment, he moved the Wild West show tradition away from commitments to history, live performers, authentic props, and westerners portraying themselves.

A continuing search for a properly heroic figure or figures to personify the Wild West marked the history of these exhibitions. White Americans and western Europeans found Catlin's Indians interesting, but so exotic and culturally separate that they could not accept a *beau savage* as the lone representative of the Plains. Cody brought a variety of peoples into his arenas, but attention focused on the cowboy as the representative westerner. Such high regard for the cowhand must have aggravated the Miller brothers, who founded a show to promote ranchers, not cowboys, as the central figures of Plains history. Ironically, Tom Mix, one of their own hired hands, lionized the mythical cowboy and customized that figure into a "very white hero" who remained ensconced in movies into the 1950s.

In addition to the cowboy, images of painted Indians on horseback, blazing revolvers, stagecoach robberies, buffalo hunts, chases, and other Wild West show features permeated American culture. One need go no farther than television or magazines to realize that advertisers still use the lure of exploration and adventure in the West to sell four-wheel drive vehicles, the glamor of the mythical West to sell jeans, and scenes of rugged westerners relishing alcohol and tobacco products to entice other Americans to use them.

The issue of *U.S. News and World Report* that appeared on 21 May 1990 reveals that Americans still cogitate ideas and images of the West. The cover of this periodical carries a photograph of Buffalo Bill, Pawnee Bill, and Buffalo Jones, and the table of contents says about the accompanying article: "How the West Was Really Won. Historians are shattering the old myths." The text explains that the "old myths" include westerners as the embodiment of self-sufficient individualism and innocent children of nature; white males as heroes and agents of change; Indians as noble savages, ignoble savages, and vanishing Americans; and the West as a refuge from civilization's problems. However, according to the article, much that was unsavory flourished in the West—greed, monopoly, poverty, dispossession, and racial discrimination—but western mythology rejected such realities.

The section of the article entitled "How the myth was spun" explains that Wild West shows and Tom Mix's movies helped gloss over the negative aspects of the westward movement and contributed to the creation of the glorious mythology that infixed a positive view of the frontier in the psyches of Americans.[1] Certainly, as the authors of the *U.S. News and World Report* article suggest, Wild West shows were important spinners of glorious myths about the West. However, in fairness to the showmen, they did explore various interpretations of the West and acknowledged the diversity of its inhabitants.

Wild West shows represented a hundred-year experiment with western themes. Instead of promoting white Anglo-Saxon males as heroes, George Catlin vilified them, praised Indians, lamented the slaughter of buffalo, and angrily denounced the ruination of wilderness. While Cody peppered his exhibitions with strong doses of Anglo-Saxonism, he also recognized ethnic diversity in the West by including Hispanics, blacks, and some whose ancestry was part Indian in his early contingents of cowboys. He defended Native Americans' right to defend their homeland, battled those bureaucrats who enforced bad Indian policy, hired Mexicans as performers, brought women before audiences, and made his camp a demonstration of harmonious international living. By investing in mining and irrigation, he personified the proposition that America's ideas about business extended to the frontier. The Millers challenged prevailing ideas about the Plains by offering a patrician view of the West and endeavoring to make agribusiness acceptable to Americans. Tom Mix played a variety of western characters early in his movie career and occasionally tried nonwestern themes later, but his fans always insisted that he return to his familiar cowboy role.

Although each of these entertainers promoted a particular perspective about the Plains and its people, none could force his views on a powerless and unresponsive public. Because the shows were both businesses needing paying customers and popular entertainments wherein Americans saw a reflection of themselves and their nation, audiences determined much of the content. The shows remained experimental by providing an array of people, images, and ideas, and the showmen shaped and reshaped the "raw material of America" as they watched the reactions. That the white cowboy emerged as the most memorable icon of the West indicates much about national character and the public's power to determine the direction of "America's National Entertainment." Mix's cowboy—not Catlin's Indian, Cody's scout, or the Millers' rancher—outlasted his competitors, but even this "very white hero" became outdated after the 1950s. The history of Wild West shows is especially important because these entertainments were incubators and crucibles of ideas about the West for a hundred years.

Contemporary society offers no single live entertainment that duplicates Wild West shows. However, the issues that they raised remain: Are westerners different from other Americans and if so, what explains their uniqueness? To what extent should people in the United States tolerate (or perhaps promote) violence as a solution to problems in society? Is progress good when it consumes wilderness, erodes tradition, diminishes the quality of life, and dispossesses poor people and minority groups? Is militarism compatible with our society, and should we send our armed forces to other nations to enforce America's view of how the world should be? Can we as a people balance white males' accomplishments on the frontier with issues of race and gender? Tourists still wonder how they should behave abroad and how much reverence they should have for European antiquity. Wild West showmen contemplated these and other fundamental issues—the "raw material of America"—for a hundred years and offered western views of them to audiences at home and abroad. In this way, Wild West shows provide an important window for examining the history of popular entertainment, America's national character, and the evolution of images and ideas about the West.

# NOTES

## Abbreviations

AHC    American Heritage Center, Owen Wister Western Writer's Reading Room, University of Wyoming, Laramie

AOS    Annie Oakley Scrapbook, William F. Cody Collection, Manuscript Collection 6, Buffalo Bill Historical Center, McCracken Research Library, Cody, Wyo.

BBHC    William F. Cody Collection, Manuscript Collection 6, Buffalo Bill Historical Center, McCracken Research Library, Cody, Wyo.

*BBWW*    *Buffalo Bill's Wild West*

CFP    Catlin Family Papers, Archives of American Art, Smithsonian Institution, Washington, D.C.

CPS    Col. W. F. Cody's Private Scrapbook, vol. 12 of the Nate Salsbury Scrapbooks, William F. Cody Collection, Western History Department, Denver Public Library

DPL    William F. Cody Collection, Western History Department, Denver Public Library

GC    General Correspondence

GCP    George Catlin Papers

GLC    Maj. Gordon W. Lillie Collection, Western History Collections, Bizell Memorial Library, University of Oklahoma

GTBP    George T. Beck Papers, William F. Cody Collection, American Heritage Center, Owen Wister Western Writer's Reading Room, University of Wyoming, Laramie

JBS    Johnny Baker Scrapbook, William F. Cody Collection, Western History Department, Denver Public Library

LC        Motion Pictures and Television Reading Room, Motion Picture, Broadcast-
          ing, and Recorded Sound Division, Library of Congress, Washington, D.C.
LFFS      L. F. Foster Scrapbook, National Anthropological Archives, Smithsonian In-
          stitution, Washington, D.C.
MB        Miller Brothers 101 Ranch Collection, Western History Collections, Bizell
          Memorial Library, University of Oklahoma
NCFA      National Collection of Fine Arts and the National Portrait Gallery Library,
          Washington, D.C.
SI        Smithsonian Institution, Washington, D.C.
NSS       Nate Salsbury Scrapbooks, William F. Cody Collection, Western History
          Department, Denver Public Library
UO        Western History Collections, Bizell Memorial Library, University of Okla-
          homa
WFCC      William F. Cody Collection

## Introduction

1. John M. Burke, "Buffalo Bill's Wild West and Congress of Rough Riders of the
World," *First Appearance,* DPL; *Philadelphia Sunday Dispatch,* 6 June 1885, vol. 1, NSS.
2. For other shows, see *Boston Morning Post,* 12 Sept. 1838 and 24 Sept. 1838; *New York
Morning Herald,* 7 June 1839; Russell, *Wild West,* 121–27; Buscombe, *BFI Companion,*
32; *Official Souvenir Program,* author's collection; Moses, *Wild West Shows,* 274–76.
3. For theatrical histories, see Deahl, "History," and Blackstone, *Buckskins, Bullets,
and Business.* For the musical history, see Masterson, "Sounds of the Frontier." Masterson also helped with recording *The Wild West: Music from the Epic Mini Series.* The music
on the compact disc is important as are the explanatory notes with it. See also White,
"Frederick Jackson Turner."

## Chapter 1: "The Raw Material of America"

1. Catlin, *Life amongst the Indians,* 15–25. I have retained Catlin's system of recording
Native American names in a phonetic, hyphenated style followed by a translation in
parentheses. For most individuals he discussed, no modern spellings exist. Additionally, I find Catlin's intentions admirable. He wanted to record names as the Indians themselves pronounced them. I have not verified the accuracy of Catlin's translations.
2. Ibid.
3. Ibid., 25–26.
4. Ibid., 26–28; Catlin, *Last Rambles amongst the Indians,* 2.
5. Catlin, *Life amongst the Indians,* 24–28.
6. Ibid., 12–14, 29–34. See also "Putnam Catlin," unidentified book, 280, Family
Histories and Genealogies, CFP.

7. Catlin, *Life amongst the Indians*, 29–39.

8. Catlin, *Letters and Notes*, 1:3; Hone, *Diary*, 1:434.

9. Catlin, *Letters and Notes*, 2:225.

10. "Introduction," *BBWW* (1907 program), DPL; *Bristol Press* (England), 16 July 1903, and *Leicester News* (England), 18 Sept. 1903, both in vol. 11, NSS. For different views on the origins of the Wild West show phenomenon, see Russell, *Lives and Legends*, 287; McCracken, *George Catlin*, 184; and Goetzman, *Exploration and Empire*, 190.

11. Catlin, *Letters and Notes*, 1:5.

12. For a different view, see Dippie, *Catlin*, 14–22.

13. "Family Histories and Genealogies," CFP; Putnam to George, 4 Aug. 1817, 21 Jan. 1818, and 15 Feb. 1830, all in Roehm, *Letters*, 3–13, 15, 19–20, 44–46; Catlin, *Letters and Notes*, 1:2; Truettner, *Natural Man*, 11–15; Catlin, "North American Indian Sketchbook," Original Indian Drawings, Indian Gallery, GCP, 1840–60, SI. For Catlin's desire to record the Native American way of life, Truettner cites Donaldson, *George Catlin Indian Gallery*, 715.

14. Catlin to General Peter B. Porter, Secretary of War, 22 Feb. 1829, Buffalo and Erie County Historical Society, Buffalo, N.Y.

15. W. F. Cody to General Nelson A. Miles, 15 June 1882, GC, BBHC (in the register of letters the date is listed as 1880).

16. Catlin, *Letters and Notes*, 1:3; *New York Commercial Advertiser*, 24 July 1832.

17. *New York Commercial Advertiser*, 21 June 1834; Satz, *American Indian Policy*, 11–12. Catlin doubted that Indians would be allowed to keep the land the government had promised them; see Catlin, *Letters and Notes*, 2:118.

18. Ewers, *George Catlin*, 502; McCracken, *Catlin and the Old Frontier*, 26–27; Viola, *Indian Legacy*, 13–14.

19. The two most reliable sources for Catlin's western travels are Truettner, *Natural Man*, 15–36, and Dippie, *Catlin*, 21–46. Putnam to George, 21 Jan. 1831 and 23 June 1831, George to Francis, 10 June 1836, and Polly to Francis, 21 Aug. 1838, all in Roehm, *Letters*, 50, 53–54, 90–91, 136.

20. *New York Commercial Advertiser*, 13 Nov. 1832; *Morning Courier and New-York Enquirer*, 3 Oct. 1837; Catlin, *Letters and Notes*, 1:106. For information on Catlin's artistic techniques, see Truettner, *Natural Man*, chap. 5; Catlin, "Original Sketch and Notebook," Notebooks, etc., GCP, 1821–90, SI; and Catlin, "North American Indian Sketchbook," Original Indian Drawings, Indian Gallery, GCP, 1840–60, SI.

21. See *Boston Morning Post*, 27 Aug. 1838, 19 Sept. 1838, and see 26 Sept. 1838 for an example of a travel account; *New York Commercial Advertiser*, 13 July 1836, 15 July 1836, and 18 July 1836.

22. Ekirch, *Idea of Progress*, 38–71; Wecter, *Hero in America*, 200–221; Pessen, *Jacksonian America*, chaps. 2–6; Ward, *Andrew Jackson*, 207–13.

23. On 1 July 1833 the *Cincinnati Daily Gazette* reprinted Catlin's letter to the *New York Commercial Advertiser*, which had been printed on 21 June 1833, and commented

that it had reprinted others; *American and Commercial Daily Advertiser* (Baltimore), 4 July 1838; *Boston Commercial Gazette*, 16 Aug. 1838; *New York Commercial Advertiser*, 20 Oct. 1832, 20 Feb. 1833, 20 June 1834, 20 Oct. 1834.

24. *New York Commercial Advertiser*, 24 July 1832, 13 Nov. 1832, 22 Aug. 1834, 26 Dec. 1835; Catlin, *Letters and Notes*, 2:132.

25. For "vagueness" and the West, see Boorstin, *The Americans*, 223–41; *New York Commercial Advertiser*, 21 June 1834; Catlin, *Letters and Notes*, 1:62–66; Ewers, *George Catlin*, 502; Crane, "Noble Savage," 45–46; Orians, "Cult," 3–15; White, "Frederick Jackson Turner," 17.

26. *Pittsburgh Gazette*, 12 Apr. 1833.

27. *Cincinnati Daily Gazette*, ads, 18 May 1833, 11 Oct. 1833, 28 Oct. 1833, and 15 Nov. 1833; *New Orleans Bee*, 24 Mar. 1835 and 3 Apr. 1835; *New Orleans Observer*, 11 Apr. 1835; "Letter from Mr. Catlin," 554–61; *Pittsburgh Gazette*, 12 Apr. 1833 and 23 Apr. 1833; Hall, "Mr. Catlin's Exhibition," 535; *New Orleans Courier*, 2 Apr. 1835.

28. Larkin, *Reshaping*, 204–5, 209–10, 211–13, 218–19, 224–31; Dulles, *History of Recreation*, 100–121, 131–35; *Daily Albany Argus*, 17 June 1837 and 26 May 1837; *Cincinnati Daily Gazette*, 12 Nov. 1833 and 24 Dec. 1833; Bode, *American Lyceum*, 32–33.

29. Boorstin, *The Americans*, 307–24; Elson, *Guardians of Tradition*, 8–9; Atherton, *Main Street*, 203–4; "Hubbard Winslow's Fourth of July Oration," *Boston Morning Post*, 12 Sept. 1838; *Boston Daily Evening Transcript*, 11 Sept. 1838; Bode, *American Lyceum*, 3–24, 27, 30, 47–49, 186–88, 228–34; Dulles, *History of Recreation*, 91–95.

30. Bode, *American Lyceum*, 30, 47, 60, 62, 63, 65, 70–72, 82, 84, 91, 145–46, 190, 205–7, 213–14, 216–17, 221–28; *Essex Register* (Salem), 29 Oct. 1838 and 5 Nov. 1838; *United States Gazette* (Philadelphia), 5 Sept. 1838; Catlin, *Catalog* (1837); reprint of article from *United States Gazette* (Philadelphia), n.d., in Catlin, *Descriptive Catalog* (1848).

31. McCracken, *George Catlin*, 179; Haberly, *Pursuit*, 94; Putnam to George and Clara, 26 Dec. 1835, and George to Francis, 10 June 1836, both in Roehm, *Letters*, 82–84, 90–91, and see editor's comment on 90; "Letter from Mr. Catlin," 554–55. The business and financial information comes from Certificates, etc., roll 2136, GCP, 1821–90, SI. See receipts for 6 July 1836, 1 Aug. 1836, and 3 Jan. 1837.

32. George to Henry and Francis, 1 Aug. 1836, and Putnam to Francis, 11 Sept. 1836, 12 Oct. 1836, and 25 Nov. 1836, all in Roehm, *Letters*, 92–93, 94–95, 96–98; Catlin, *Letters and Notes*, 2:160–78; Catlin, "Mineral Chart and Lithograph," GCP, SI; *New York Commercial Advertiser*, 19 Sept. 1837, 25 Sept. 1837, and 30 Sept. 1837.

33. Putnam to Francis, 11 Apr. 1837 and 17 June 1837, and George Catlin to Francis, 28 Dec. 1836, all in Roehm, *Letters*, 107–8, 110, 102–3; *Oneida Whig* (Utica), 7 Mar. 1837; *Daily Albany Argus*, 15 May 1837 and 17 June 1837; *New York Commercial Advertiser*, 13 July 1837; *Troy Daily Whig*, 6 July 1837, 8 July 1837, 11 July 1837, 13 July 1837, 15 July 1837, and 24 July 1837.

34. *New York Commercial Advertiser*, 21 June 1834; Crane, "Noble Savage," 76–114.

35. *Morning Courier and New-York Enquirer*, 5 Dec. 1837; James Hall to Catlin, 12 Feb.

1836, Correspondence, GCP, 1821–90, SI; Viola, *Indian Legacy,* 80; *New York Commercial Advertiser,* 25 Oct. 1837; Hone, *Diary,* 1:385–86; *New York Evening Post,* 4 Oct. 1837. For comments on Bird's book, see Williams, preface, v–vi; Keiser, *Indian in American Literature,* 95, 144.

36. Putnam to Francis, 16 Oct. 1837 and 8 Sept. 1838, Clara to Abigail, 29 Sept. 1838, and Putnam to James, 4 Jan. 1839, all in Roehm, *Letters,* 121–22, 137, 139, 142; *New York Commercial Advertiser,* 17 Sept. 1839; George to Burr, n.d. (probably 2 or 3 Sept. 1838), Correspondence, GCP, 1821–90, SI; Catlin, *Notes of Eight Years' Travels,* 1:4; *Boston Daily Evening Transcript,* 22 Nov. 1838; *Boston Morning Post,* 17 Aug. 1838 and 15 Nov. 1838; freight receipts dated 2 July 1836, 9 May 1837, 21 Sept. 1837, 20 July 1838, 28 July 1838, and 28 Oct. 183? (last number illegible), hotel receipts dated Aug. 1833, 22 July 1837, 9 Oct. 1837, and 3 Apr. 1838, and labor and materials bill dated 28 Apr. 1838, all in Certificates, etc., roll 2136, GCP, 1821–90, SI. For advertisements indicating tickets were available from local businesses, see *New York Evening Post,* 26 Sept. 1837, and *New York Commercial Advertiser,* 27 Sept. 1837.

37. Printing receipt dated 25 May 1838, Certificates, etc., roll 2136, GCP, 1821–90, SI; George to Burr, 18 Aug. 1839, Correspondence, GCP, NCFA; *New York Evening Post,* 1 Nov. 1837; Hone, *Diary,* 1:290–91.

38. Robertson, *History,* 224–25; Larkin, *Reshaping,* 139; *Philadelphia Daily Focus,* 30 June 1838; Putnam to Francis, 16 Oct. 1837, in Roehm, *Letters,* 121–22; *New Orleans Courier,* 2 Apr. 1835; *New York Commercial Advertiser,* 25 Oct. 1837; *New York Morning Herald,* 26 Oct. 1837; *Essex Register* (Salem), 5 Nov. 1838; *Washington Daily National Intelligencer,* 16 Apr. 1838.

39. *American and Commercial Daily Advertiser* (Baltimore), 4 July 1838 and 16 July 1838; *Baltimore Sun,* 4 July 1838; rent receipts dated 1 Aug. 1836 and 3 Nov. 1837, Certificates, etc., roll 2136, GCP, 1821–90, SI; *Washington Daily National Intelligencer,* 9 Apr. 1838; Larkin, *Reshaping,* 135–37, 141–42; *Washington Globe,* 23 May 1838; Putnam to Francis, 8 Sept. 1838, in Roehm, *Letters,* 137.

40. *Daily Albany Argus,* 15 May 1837; *New York Evening Post,* 25 Sept. 1837; *Washington Globe,* 10 May 1838; *Boston Morning Post,* 18 Aug. 1838; *New York Commercial Advertiser,* 25 Oct. 1837; *United States Gazette* (Philadelphia), 5 Sept. 1838; *Morning Courier and New-York Enquirer,* 2 Oct. 1837 and 5 Dec. 1837; *Washington Daily National Intelligencer,* 9 Apr. 1838 and 9 May 1838; *Essex Register* (Salem), 5 Nov. 1838; *Boston Daily Evening Transcript,* 10 Sept. 1838 and 10 Nov. 1838; quotes about shaman outfit in Catlin, *Letters and Notes,* 1:40.

41. *Boston Daily Evening Transcript,* 7 Nov. 1838; *Pittsburgh Gazette,* 23 Apr. 1833, 3 May 1833, and 7 May 1833; *Cincinnati Daily Gazette,* 1 July 1833; *New York Morning Herald,* 26 Oct. 1837; *Boston Daily Evening Transcript,* 22 Nov. 1838; *New York Evening Post,* 21 Oct. 1837; *New York Commercial Advertiser,* 20 Nov. 1839; Putnam to Francis, 4 May 1838, in Roehm, *Letters,* 130.

42. *Pittsburgh Gazette,* 23 Apr. 1833; *Morning Courier and New-York Enquirer,* 2 Oct.

1837, 3 Oct. 1837, and 5 Dec. 1837; *New Orleans Courier,* 2 Apr. 1835; *United States Gazette* (Philadelphia), 5 Sept. 1838; *Essex Register* (Salem), 29 Oct. 1838 and 5 Nov. 1838; Buckingham, *America,* 1:95.

43. For information about Catlin's appearance, see Dippie, *Catlin,* 3; bill for satin vest and doeskin trousers, Certificates, etc., roll 2137, GCP, 1821–90, SI; Haberly, *Pursuit,* 82; "Francis Catlin's Diary of His Trip to Belgium," in Roehm, *Letters,* 363. *London Globe and Traveller,* 15 Feb. 1840; "Catlin's Indian Gallery," *John Bull* (London), 16 Feb. 1840, 80; Catlin, *Catalog* (1837), 11.

44. *Morning Courier and New-York Enquirer,* 5 Dec. 1837; *Pittsburgh Gazette,* 23 Apr. 1833.

45. Ewers, *George Catlin,* 502; Truettner, *Natural Man,* 36.

46. *Pittsburgh Gazette,* 23 Apr. 1833; *Essex Register* (Salem), 5 Nov. 1838. Catlin's *Catalog* (1837) indicated tribal affiliation, name, and biographical information about individuals. *United States Gazette* (Philadelphia), 5 Sept. 1838.

47. *Pittsburgh Gazette,* 12 Apr. 1833 and 23 Apr. 1833; *Cincinnati Daily Gazette,* 18 May 1833; Satz, *American Indian Policy,* 112–14.

48. *Pittsburgh Gazette,* 23 Apr. 1833; Hall, "Mr. Catlin's Exhibition," 535; *United States Gazette* (Philadelphia), 5 Sept. 1838.

49. *New York Commercial Advertiser,* 30 Sept. 1837; Catlin, *Letters and Notes,* 1:55–57.

50. Catlin, "North American Indian Sketchbook," Original Indian Drawings, Indian Gallery, GCP, 1840–60, SI; Truettner, *Natural Man,* 69; Catlin, *Letters and Notes,* 1:60–62, 85, 94–95, 2:25–28, 83, 223–25, 238–46.

51. *Pittsburgh Gazette,* 23 Apr. 1833; reprint of *Philadelphia Evening Post,* n.d., in Catlin, *Descriptive Catalog* (1848); *New York Morning Herald,* 11 Oct. 1837; *American and Commercial Daily Advertiser* (Baltimore), 20 July 1838; *Baltimore Sun,* 19 July 1838. On 21 June 1834 and 20 October 1834 the *New York Commercial Advertiser* printed comments by Catlin in which he criticized the government for not protecting Native Americans from settlers, "traders and trappers" in particular. In an article in the 22 June 1836 issue of the *New York Commercial Advertiser,* Catlin was quoted as saying that he feared for his life should he return to the frontier because of his deteriorating relationship with the American Fur Company. On 8 March 1838, the *New York Commercial Advertiser* discussed the introduction of smallpox to the Mandans and reported that an American Fur Company ship carried a passenger who introduced the disease. Catlin's name is not mentioned in the article, but he most likely was the source of the information. Catlin's *Letters and Notes,* 2:249–56, contains a ringing indictment of the fur trade, missionaries, and the American government. Dippie characterizes the relationship between Catlin and the American Fur Company as contentious (*Catlin and His Contemporaries,* 61). For Catlin's prediction of a Sioux war, see *Boston Morning Post,* 15 Nov. 1838. Truettner, *Natural Man,* 69–78, 79–80; Berkhoffer, *White Man's Indian,* 88; Slotkin, *Regeneration,* 294; Orians, "Cult," 2–15.

52. *Pittsburgh Gazette,* 23 Apr. 1833; Crane, "Noble Savage," 29, 46; Mathews, "Cat-

lin Collection," 597–98; Catlin discussed Mandan origins in *New York Commercial Advertiser*, 20 Feb. 1833.

53. *Pittsburgh Gazette*, 23 Apr. 1833; *New York Commercial Advertiser*, 10 Jan. 1833; Catlin, *O-kee-pa; Boston Morning Post*, 17 Nov. 1838; *New York Evening Post*, 30 Dec. 1837; for the particulars of the decimation of the Mandans by smallpox, see *New York Commercial Advertiser*, 8 Mar. 1838; Putnam to Francis, 18 Mar. 1838, in Roehm, *Letters*, 127; *Washington Daily National Intelligencer*, 9 May 1838.

54. Ewers, *George Catlin*, 500; reprint of article from *Philadelphia Enquirer*, n.d., in Catlin, *Catalog* (1848); *New York Commercial Advertiser*, 20 Oct. 1832 and 13 Nov. 1832; *New York Morning Herald*, 11 Oct. 1837; *Washington Globe*, 26 Apr. 1838; *Baltimore Sun*, 4 July 1838; *United States Gazette* (Philadelphia), 5 Sept. 1838.

55. *New York Evening Post*, 25 Sept. 1837; *Boston Daily Evening Transcript*, 10 Nov. 1838; *Boston Morning Post*, 28 Aug. 1838; *Washington Daily National Intelligencer*, 9 May 1838 and 15 May 1838; *Washington Globe*, 10 May 1838; Buckingham, *America*, 1:104; *United States Gazette* (Philadelphia), 5 Sept. 1838.

56. *Boston Daily Evening Transcript*, 10 Nov. 1838; Catlin, *Catalog* (1837), 13, 35; *Morning Courier and New-York Enquirer*, 11 June 1839; *New York Sun*, 10 July 1838 and 12 June 1839; Catlin, *Letters and Notes*, 1:31, and note on 153–54; Combe, *Notes*, 1:70.

57. *New York Commercial Advertiser*, 25 Oct. 1837 and 26 Oct. 1837; *Morning Courier and New-York Enquirer*, 24 Oct. 1837; *New York Morning Herald*, 26 Oct. 1837; Callender, "Sauk," 652. In a note in *Letters and Notes*, 1:221–22, Catlin estimated 1,200–1,400 attended, and in *Letters and Notes*, 2:212, he set the figure at 1,500.

58. *New York Commercial Advertiser*, 26 Oct. 1837; *New York Morning Herald*, 26 Oct. 1837; Catlin, *Letters and Notes*, 2:212–13n.

59. *New York Commercial Advertiser*, 26 Oct. 1837; Catlin, *Letters and Notes*, 1:221–22n.

60. *New York Commercial Advertiser*, 26 Oct. 1837; *New York Morning Herald*, 26 Oct. 1837; Catlin, *Letters and Notes*, 1:32–34.

61. *New York Morning Herald*, 26 Oct. 1837; *New York Commercial Advertiser*, 26 Oct. 1837.

62. *New York Commercial Advertiser*, 26 Oct. 1837.

63. *New York Evening Post*, 21 Oct. 1837, 31 Oct. 1837, and 1 Nov. 1837; *New York Commercial Advertiser*, 26 Oct. 1837 and 1 Nov. 1837.

64. *New York Commercial Advertiser*, 31 Oct. 1837 and 1 Nov. 1837; *New York Morning Herald*, 3 Nov. 1837; *New York Evening Post*, 27 Oct. 1837; *Morning Courier and New-York Enquirer*, 25 Oct. 1837 and 1 Nov. 1837.

65. *New York Morning Herald*, 28 Nov. 1837; *New York Commercial Advertiser*, 26 Nov. 1837 and 27 Nov. 1837; Catlin, *Catalog* (1837), 3, 22.

66. *New York Morning Herald*, 1 Nov. 1837; *New York Commercial Advertiser*, 5 Feb. 1838, 20 Feb. 1838, 19 Mar. 1838, and 4 Jan. 1840; *Morning Courier and New-York Enquirer*, 1 Nov. 1837; Satz, *American Indian Policy*, 102–3; *Washington Daily National Intelligencer*, 18 May 1838; *Washington Globe*, 26 Apr. 1828.

67. *New York Commercial Advertiser,* 27 Mar. 1838, 28 Mar. 1838, 29 Mar. 1838, 5 Feb. 1838, and 6 Feb. 1838; *Washington Daily National Intelligencer,* 18 Apr. 1838; Putnam to Francis, 18 Mar. 1838, in Roehm, *Letters,* 127.

68. *Essex Register* (Salem), 5 Nov. 1838.

69. *Morning Courier and New-York Enquirer,* 1 Nov. 1837; *Charleston Courier,* n.d., reprinted in *Morning Courier and New-York Enquirer,* 26 Jan. 1838; Ross qtd. in *Washington Daily National Intelligencer,* 18 May 1838.

70. *Morning Courier and New-York Enquirer,* 5 Dec. 1837; *New York Commercial Advertiser,* 1 Dec. 1837, 28 Nov. 1838, and 17 Sept. 1838; George to Burr, n.d. (probably 2 or 3 Sept. 1838), Correspondence, GCP, 1821–90, SI; *New York Morning Herald,* 5 Dec. 1837.

71. *New York Commercial Advertiser,* 1 Dec. 1837; Catlin, *Catalog* (1837), 1–36; Combe, *Notes,* 1:70; Catlin, *Letters and Notes,* 1:43–44; *Morning Courier and New-York Enquirer,* 29 Nov. 1837 and 30 Dec. 1837; *Boston Daily Evening Transcript,* 17 Sept. 1838 and 3 Oct. 1838; *Boston Morning Post,* 12 Oct. 1838; *American and Commercial Daily Advertiser* (Baltimore), 17 July 1838.

72. *Washington Daily National Intelligencer,* 16 Apr. 1838 and 18 May 1838; *Boston Morning Post,* 17 Oct. 1838; *Troy Daily Whig,* 11 July 1837; *New-York Evening Star* qtd. in *Boston Commercial Gazette,* 16 May 1838; Catlin, *Catalog* (1848), 68–83; Catlin, *Notes of Eight Years' Travels,* 1:app. A.

73. Combe, *Notes,* 1:70; *Boston Morning Post,* 17 Oct. 1838; George to Burr, 29 Dec. 1838, Correspondence, GCP, 1821–90, SI; Putnam to Francis, 15 Apr. 1839, in Roehm, *Letters,* 144; *New York Commercial Advertiser,* 22 Feb. 1838; *Boston Daily Evening Transcript,* 17 Sept. 1838 and 25 Oct. 1838.

74. *Boston Morning Post,* 12 Oct. 1838.

75. Putnam to Francis, 4 May 1838, 12 July 1838, 23 Sept. 1838, and 4 Jan. 1839, all in Roehm, *Letters,* 130, 133, 137, 142; George to Burr, n.d. (probably 2 or 3 Sept. 1838), Correspondence, GCP, 1821–90, SI; *Troy Daily Whig,* 11 July 1837; *Washington Daily National Intelligencer,* 16 Apr. 1838; *New York Evening Post,* 8 Aug. 1839; *Boston Morning Post,* 10 Sept. 1838.

76. *Pennsylvanian* (Philadelphia), 28 Mar. 1839 and 22 May 1839; *North American* (Philadelphia), 29 Mar. 1839 and 10 May 1839; *New York Commercial Advertiser,* 17 Sept. 1839; Putnam to Francis, 4 Jan. 1839, in Roehm, *Letters,* 142; Putnam to George, 19 Jan. 1839, Correspondence, GCP, NCFA.

77. Thomas Sully to Catlin, 16 July 1837, Correspondence, GCP, 1821–90, SI; *New York Evening Post,* 12 Dec. 1837; *Morning Courier and New-York Enquirer,* 1 Jan. 1838; *Baltimore Sun,* 13 July 1838, 17 July 1838, and 21 July 1838.

78. *Morning Courier and New-York Enquirer,* 1 Jan. 1838; Putnam to Francis, 15 Apr. 1839, in Roehm, *Letters,* 144; "Catlin's Indian Gallery," 164; *United States Gazette* (Philadelphia), n.d., reprinted in *New York Courier,* 21 Nov. 1838; *American and Commercial Daily Advertiser* (Baltimore), 9 Aug. 1838; Catlin, letter to the editor, *New York Commercial Advertiser,* 26 Nov. 1839 and 30 Oct. 1838.

79. Catlin, letter to the editor, *New York Commercial Advertiser,* 26 Nov. 1839.

80. *New York Commercial Advertiser,* 25 Nov. 1839; *New York Journal of Commerce,* 28

Nov. 1839; Henry Clay to the Earl of Selkirk (Thomas Douglas), 7 July 1838, Benjamin Silliman, General Letter of Introduction, 14 Oct. 1839, and Thomas Sully to J. Wright, 12 June 1837, all in Correspondence, GCP, 1821–90, SI; *Boston Commercial Gazette,* 16 Aug. 1838; Catlin, *Notes of Eight Years' Travels,* 1:1–2, 50; Hone, *Diary,* 1:434.

## Chapter 2: "Trembling Excitements and Fears"

1. Catlin, *Notes of Eight Years' Travels,* 1:34–35; *London Morning Post,* 25 Jan. 1840; *London Spectator,* 25 Jan. 1840; *Athenaeum* (London), 29 June 1839 and 1 Feb. 1840.

2. *London Morning Chronicle,* 30 Jan. 1840; Catlin, *Notes of Eight Years' Travels,* 1:37.

3. Dippie, *Catlin,* 69, 447; Catlin, *Notes of Eight Years' Travels,* 1:34–37; *London Globe and Traveller,* 19 Feb. 1840; *New York Commercial Advertiser,* 4 Sept. 1838.

4. Catlin, *Notes of Eight Years' Travels,* 1:34, 36–37; John Murray to George Catlin, n.d., Correspondence, GCP, NCFA; for examples of Catlin's social success, see Catlin, *Notes of Eight Years' Travels,* 1:40–43, 2:67–68.

5. George to Parents, 17 Feb. 1840, in Roehm, *Letters,* 156–58.

6. Catlin, *Descriptive Catalogue* (1840), 3.

7. *London Court Journal,* 1 Feb. 1840; "Catlin's Indian Gallery," *John Bull* (London), 16 Feb. 1840. At least one reviewer did not accept the role; see *Athenaeum* (London), 27 May 1848, 3 June 1848, and quote from 2 Oct. 1841.

8. For American attitudes toward Europe, see Rahv, *Discovery,* xi–xiii; Strout, *American Image,* 18–19, 62–63, 68–70; Boorstin, *America,* 11–16, 121–22; Mowat, *Americans,* 103–22; Dulles, *Americans Abroad,* 1–2, 24–25, 30–31, 41–43, 66–68, 86–87, 93–95; George to Putnam, 3 Mar. 1842, in Roehm, *Letters,* 237.

9. *London Morning Post,* 25 Jan. 1840; *London Saturday Journal,* 15 Feb. 1840. For advertising and financial receipts, see reproduction of handbill in Haberly, *Pursuit,* 119; Briggs, *Social History,* illustration on 233; unidentified and undated worksheet showing $9,433 paid for advertising, "Receipt Book" with "List of News Papers in London 184?" (probably 1841), orders for printed materials, 14 June 1841, 19 Aug. 1841, and 3 Sept. 1841, receipt for painting the front of Egyptian Hall, n.d., and bills dated 14 Jan. 1840 and 22 Jan. 1840, all in Certificates, etc., roll 2136, GCP, 1821–90, SI; receipt for posting bills, 23 May 1843?, Certificates, etc., roll 2137, GCP, 1821–90, SI; for Britain purchasing collection, see George to Parents, 29 June 1840, in Roehm, *Letters,* 173; "Article III," 421–22.

10. Undated and unidentified financial worksheet, Certificates, etc., roll 2136, GCP, 1821–90, SI. According to this document, the lectures attracted 5,075 patrons and generated £338 2s 0d and the gallery attracted 27,425 and generated £1642 17s 6d; *London Morning Post,* 4 Feb. 1840; *London Times,* 3 Feb. 1840; Catlin, *Descriptive Catalog* (1840), 3, 7–9, 11–12, 14–30, 42, 45.

11. *London Morning Post,* 8 Feb. 1840 and 14 Feb. 1840; *London Times,* 8 Feb. 1840; *London Globe and Traveller,* 5 Feb. 1840; *London Saturday Journal,* 15 Feb. 1840; "Catlin's Indian Gallery," *John Bull* (London), 16 Feb. 1840.

12. *London Morning Post,* 14 Mar. 1840 and 4 Feb. 1840; *London Globe and Traveller,* 15 Feb. 1840 and 27 Feb. 1840; "Mr. Catlin's Lectures and Exhibitions," unidentified clipping from England, n.d., Clippings, Indian Gallery, GCP, 1840–60, SI.

13. Ainsworth, "Editor's Preface," vi; Billington, *Land of Savagery,* 18–25, 30–32; for attitudes about Cooper's works, see a review of *The Pathfinder* in *London Globe and Traveller,* 9 Mar. 1840; *Athenaeum* (London), 1 Feb. 1840; "Article III," 403–4; *Court Journal,* 1 Feb. 1840, cited in Foreman, *Indians Abroad,* 161–62; for Catlin's helpfulness to Indians abroad, see Archibald Douglass to Catlin, n.d., Correspondence, GCP, NCFA.

14. Catlin, *Notes of Eight Years' Travels,* 1:47–49.

15. "Article III," 421; George to Putnam, 31 Aug. 1840, Catlin Papers, Missouri Historical Society, St. Louis, cited in Dippie, *Catlin,* 98, 459; Clara to Putnam and Polly, 28 Feb. 1841, in Roehm, *Letters of George Catlin,* 208–9.

16. Burr to Francis, 7 Feb. 1841, in Roehm, *Letters of George Catlin,* 207; "Article III," 421.

17. Catlin, *Notes of Eight Years' Travels,* 1:50–60; Catlin to Thomas Phillipps, 24 Dec. 1841, Correspondence, GCP, 1840–60, SI. By 1868, perhaps sixty thousand of his books had sold; see Donaldson, *George Catlin Gallery,* 525–26. "Article VI," 415–30; "Reviews," *Athenaeum* (London), 2 Oct. 1841, 19 Feb. 1842; "Catlin's North American Indians," 44–52; "Vindication of the United States," 202–11.

18. "Mr. Catlin's Lectures and Exhibitions," unidentified clipping, n.d., Clippings, Indian Gallery, GCP, 1840–60, SI; "Catlin's Indian Gallery," *John Bull* (London), 16 Feb. 1840, 80; *London Morning Post,* 14 Mar. 1840.

19. Catlin, *Notes of Eight Years' Travels,* 1:69–77.

20. Ibid., 1:77–78.

21. Ibid., 1:87–90; Burr to Francis, 7 Feb. 1841, in Roehm, *Letters,* 206–7.

22. George to Putnam, 30 Sept. 1840, Clara to Putnam and Polly, 29 Oct. 1840, and Burr to Francis, 7 Feb. 1841, all in Roehm, *Letters,* 193–94, 196, 207; *London Morning Post,* 8 Feb. 1840; Catlin, *Notes of Eight Years' Travels,* 1:94–95; Nye, *Unembarrassed Muse,* 184–85; "Tableaux Vivants of the Red Indians," Handbills, Indian Gallery, GCP, 1840–60, SI.

23. *London Times,* 19 Apr. 1841; *Northern Times* (Sunderland), 24 Mar. 1843, Clippings, GCP, NCFA; "Tableaux Vivants of the Red Indians" and "Manners and Customs of the North American Indians," both in Handbills, Indian Gallery, GCP, 1840–60, SI; Catlin, *Notes of Eight Years' Travels,* 1:94–97.

24. George to Putnam, 19 June 1841 and 3 Apr. 1842, both in Roehm, *Letters,* 212–13, 245; James Sheridan Knowles to Catlin, 11 Feb. 1843 or 11 July 1843 (microfilm unclear), Correspondence, GCP, 1821–90, SI; Benjamin Silliman to Catlin, 9 May 1842, and George to Clara, n.d., both in Correspondence, GCP, NCFA; *Northern Times* (Sunderland), 24 Mar. 1843, Clippings, GCP, NCFA; *Manchester Guardian,* 25 Oct. 1843 and 8 Nov. 1843; Catlin, *Notes of Eight Years' Travels,* 1:99–100.

25. Catlin, *Notes of Eight Years' Travels,* 1:101–3; Stuart, *Short History,* 6–9, 21–30; Foreman, *Indians Abroad,* 171–72; *London Times,* 5 Apr. 1844.

26. Catlin, *Notes of Eight Years' Travels*, 1:99–100, 103.

27. Ibid., 1:107–9, note on 154; *Manchester Guardian*, 11 Nov. 1843.

28. Catlin, *Notes of Eight Years' Travels*, 1:vi, 103–6, 152–59, see also the contradictory statement on 2:302–4.

29. Stuart, *Short History*, 6, 9–11.

30. *Manchester Guardian*, 11 and 18 Nov. 1843; "Ojibbeway Indians," unidentified clipping, in Handbills, Indian Gallery, GCP, 1840–60, SI; *London Morning Chronicle*, 4 Mar. 1844; *London Era*, 21 Jan. 1844; *London Times*, 29 Dec. 1843.

31. Catlin, *Notes of Eight Years' Travels*, 1:124–27, 151; *London Times*, 5 Dec. 1843; *London Era*, 17 Dec. 1843; *London Spectator*, 2 Mar. 1844.

32. Stuart, *Short History*, 11–13; Catlin, *Notes of Eight Years' Travels*, 1:128–41, 146; "Visit of Ojibbeway"; *London Times*, 22 Dec. 1843. Sources differ on which Ojibway delivered the speech to the queen; see "Ojibbeway Indians," unidentified clipping, Handbills, Indian Gallery, GCP, 1840–60, SI; *Descriptive Catalog* (1840), n.p.

33. Catlin, *Notes of Eight Years' Travels*, 1:124–27, 143; Haberly, *Pursuit*, 139. Catlin said that the partnership produced a one-thousand-dollar profit for him in a month; Haberly estimated profits of four hundred dollars a day split between the two men. Haberly's figures are probably more accurate. *London Spectator*, 30 Dec. 1843; *London Era*, 31 Dec. 1843.

34. *London Times*, 29 Dec. 1843; *London Spectator*, 30 Dec. 1843; *London Era*, 31 Dec. 1843; *Manchester Guardian*, 18 Nov. 1843.

35. *London Era*, 31 Dec. 1843; *Manchester Guardian*, 15 Nov. 1843 and 25 Nov. 1843; *London Spectator*, 30 Dec. 1843; Catlin, *Notes of Eight Years' Travels*, 1:114–19, 147–48.

36. Dickens, *American Notes*, 196; Dickens, "Noble Savage," 468.

37. Mumby, *Phillipps Study*, 54; *London Spectator*, 2 Mar. 1844; Catlin, *Notes of Eight Years' Travels*, 1:152–59.

38. Catlin, *Notes of Eight Years' Travels*, 1:144, 155–57.

39. "Ojibbeway Indians," 14.

40. *London Times*, 1 Apr. 1844, 2 Apr. 1844, 3 Apr. 1844, and 13 Apr. 1844; Catlin, *Notes of Eight Years' Travels*, 1:185–86.

41. *London Times*, 2 Apr. 1844, 10 Apr. 1844, 11 Apr. 1844, 12 Apr. 1844, 13 Apr. 1844, 14 Apr. 1844, and 15 Apr. 1844; "'Strong Wind,'" 173; "Important," 179; Catlin, *Notes of Eight Years' Travels*, 1:186–88; *Detroit Advertiser* article reprinted in *London Times*, 15 Jan. 1845. On 5 October 1844 the *London Times* carried the news that a newspaper called the *Patriot* reported that the couple had separated; the father of the bride denied the report; see *London Times*, 7 October 1844. He said that the newlyweds had landed in New York on 31 August and were on their way to upper Canada.

42. *London Morning Chronicle*, 21 Mar. 1844. After leaving Catlin's employment, Joc-o-sot (sometimes Joc-o-set) remained in England for a time, and then died on the return trip to America. See Foreman, *Indians Abroad*, 195.

43. *London Era*, 31 Mar. 1844 and 14 Apr. 1844; *London Morning Herald*, 6 June 1844.

44. *London Times*, 24 July 1844; *Liberty (Mo.) Weekly Tribune*, 22 Apr. 1859 and 4 June 1859; Taylor, *Views A-Foot*, 18–19.

45. *London Times,* 24 July 1844; Denslow, *Out of the Past,* 3–35; Catlin, *Unparalleled Exhibition,* 2–4; Catlin, *Notes of Eight Years' Travels,* 2:1–2. George H. C. Melody to the Honorable Secretary of War, Sept. 1843, and Melody to V. Ellis, Editor "Old School Democrat," 20 June 1843, Letters Received by the Office of Indian Affairs, National Archives, Washington, D.C.

46. Catlin, *Unparalleled Exhibition,* 1, 5–7, 9–13; Catlin, *Notes of Eight Years' Travels,* 2:2–14.

47. Catlin, *Notes of Eight Years' Travels,* 1:107–8, 148–49, 2:53–54; "Movements of the Ojibbeways," 79; *London Spectator,* 2 Mar. 1844; *London Times,* 22 Dec. 1843 and 6 Feb. 1844.

48. Catlin, *Notes of Eight Years' Travels,* 2:7–8, 11–12, 29, 42–43, 48–52, 63–64, 80–85; Foreman, *Indians Abroad,* 185; *London Morning Herald,* 8 Aug. 1844; *London Times,* 5 Aug. 1844; *London Era,* 11 Aug. 1844; Catlin, *Unparalleled Exhibition,* 13–14.

49. *London Era,* 11 Aug. 1844.

50. *London Morning Herald,* 21 Aug. 1844; Catlin, *Unparalleled Exhibition,* 16, 18–28.

51. Catlin, *Unparalleled Exhibition,* 24–25; *London Morning Herald,* 26 Aug. 1844; Catlin, *Notes of Eight Years' Travels,* 2:33–34.

52. *London Era,* 21 Jan. 1844.

53. "Real Scalps," 3.

54. Catlin, *Notes of Eight Years' Travels,* 2:118; "The Encampment," Handbills, Indian Gallery, GCP, 1840–60, SI; *London Morning Herald,* 28 Aug. 1844.

55. *London Morning Herald,* 22 Aug. 1844; *London Era,* 25 Aug. 1844; *London Times,* 27 Aug. 1844 and 18 Sept. 1844; "The Encampment" and "Vauxhall Gardens," both in Handbills, Indian Gallery, GCP, 1840–60, SI; Catlin, *Notes of Eight Years' Travels,* 2:78–79.

56. Catlin, *Notes of Eight Years' Travels,* 2:119, 124; *London Era,* 11 Aug. 1844 and 25 Aug. 1844.

57. George to Clara, 5 Jan. 1844, and James Sheridan Knowles to Catlin, 11 Feb. 1843, both in Correspondence, GCP, 1821–90, SI; Catlin, *Notes of Eight Years' Travels,* 2:130, 134, 140–41, 144–47, 151, 157, 159–62, 169, 171–74, 177–80, 184, 186, 197–99; for Catlin's remarks about subduing horses by breathing into their nostrils, see "Indian Mode," 200.

58. George to Clara, n.d., letterhead reads: "J. Dewar, Perth, Scotland," and n.d., written from Edinburgh, both in Correspondence, GCP, 1821–90, SI; George to Clara, n.d., Correspondence, GCP, NCFA.

59. Catlin, *North American Indian Portfolio,* 4.

60. Ibid., 5–6, 7–12, 13.

61. Ibid., 7.

62. Thomas Phillipps to Catlin, 12 July 1851, Correspondence, GCP, 1840–60, SI; Billington, *Land of Savagery,* 24–25, 30–32; Crane, "Noble Savage," 4–9; Beetem, "George Catlin," 129–44; Catlin, *Notes of Eight Years' Travels,* 2:318, 1:196.

63. Catlin, *Notes of Eight Years' Travels,* 2:194–204, 209, 211–16, 227–31, 247; *Galignani's Messenger* (Paris), 17 Apr. 1845, 6 June 1845, 19 June 1845, and 24 June 1845; Fore-

man, *Indians Abroad,* 189–91; "Agence Spéciale de Publicite," 15 June 1845 (this bill is from an advertising clearinghouse sent to Catlin), Certificates, etc., roll 2137, GCP, 1821–90, SI; Catlin, *Catalogue Raisonné; Le Constitutionnel* (Paris), 22 June 1845; Beetem, "George Catlin," 130; *Le Charivari* (Paris), 22 July 1845.

64. *Galignani's Messenger* (Paris), 6 June 1845 and 5 July 1845; Catlin, *Notes of Eight Years' Travels,* 2:210, 244–45; G. d'Eichtheil, Secretary of Société Ethnologique, to Catlin, 27 June 1846, Correspondence, GCP, 1821–90, SI; Beetem, "George Catlin," 129–44.

65. Catlin, *Notes of Eight Years' Travels,* 2:219–20.

66. Ibid., 2:272–74; *Galignani's Messenger* (Paris), 14 June 1845, 24 June 1845, 26 June 1845, and 5 July 1845; "American Indians in Europe," 2; "Paid Out for the Exhibition," expense ledger for 2–14 June 1845, Certificates, etc., roll 2137, GCP, 1821–90, SI; Foreman, *Indians Abroad,* 193.

67. *Galignani's Messenger* (Paris), 30 July 1845, qtd. in Haberly, *Pursuit,* 167–68. For the closeness of George and Clara Catlin, see George to Clara, 5 Jan. 1844; n.d., written from Newcastle-on-Tyne; and n.d., written from Glasgow, all in Correspondence, GCP, 1821–90, SI. Eliza Dart to Mrs. Mary Hartshorn, 30 Jan. 1847 and 9 Dec. 1849, Letters, CFP; Catlin to Thomas Phillipps, 4 Oct. 1847, Correspondence, GCP, 1840–60, SI.

68. *Galignani's Messenger* (Paris), 29 Mar. 1845, 28 July 1845, 4 Aug. 1845, and 19 Aug. 1845; Dippie, *Catlin,* 108–9; "Dance of the Wabunnoog," Handbills, Indian Gallery, GCP, 1840–60, SI.

69. *Galignani's Messenger* (Paris), 29 Mar. 1845.

70. Catlin, *Notes of Eight Years' Travels,* 2:278–79, 280; *Galignani's Messenger* (Paris), 20 Aug. 1845 and 15 Oct. 1845; Beetem, "George Catlin," 132; *La Presse* (Paris), 8 Oct. 1845.

71. Catlin, *Notes of Eight Years' Travels,* 2:285–89; *Galignani's Messenger* (Paris), 20 Oct. 1845 and 28 Nov. 1845; Catlin to Thomas Phillipps, 19 Feb. 1841, Correspondence, GCP, 1840–60, SI; Catlin, "Memorial of George Catlin," 3.

72. Catlin, *Notes of Eight Years' Travels,* 2:295–97, 302; Foreman, *Indians Abroad,* 195; "Indians Exhibited," 2; Truettner, *Natural Man,* 49; Dippie, *Catlin,* 109; Donaldson, *George Catlin Indian Gallery,* 695. Truettner and Dippie correct Catlin's numbers. Catlin said seven Indians contracted smallpox; the correct number is eight. Two Indians died in Belgium and one died after returning to London. Donaldson estimated Catlin's losses at $1,700.

73. Catlin, *Notes of Eight Years' Travels,* 2:302; "Indians Exhibited," 2.

74. *London Times,* 2 June 1848; Catlin to Thomas Phillipps, 8 May 1849, 5 July 1850, 14 Dec. 1850, and 1 Oct. 1860, all in Correspondence, GCP, 1840–60, SI; George to Francis, 7 June 1868, and George to Librarian of the "Historical Society of N. York," 10 Oct. 1870, both in Roehm, *Letters,* 345, 405.

75. Catlin, *Descriptive Catalog* (1848); handwritten draft of Catlin, *Notes of Eight Years' Travels,* NCFA. This document shows that Catlin wrote the book hurriedly and made few revisions. For favorable reviews, see "Savage Views," 406–10, and "Catlin's Notes

in Europe," *London Spectator,* 27 May 1848, 515–16. For an unfavorable review, see "Reviews—Catlin's Notes of Eight Years' Travels and Residence with His North American Indian Collection, with Anecdotes of Incidents of the Travels and Adventures of Three Different Parties of American Indians Whom He Introduced to the Courts of England, France, and Belgium. 2 vols. With Numerous Illustrations," *London Athenaeum,* 27 May 1848, 529–31, 3 June 1848, 552–53.

76. "Memorial of American Artists in Paris," 4–5; "Memorial of American Citizens in London," 5–6; Catlin to Daniel Webster, 4 Apr. 1852, in Roehm, *Letters,* 442.

77. Dippie, *Catlin,* 36–37; George to Francis, 18 May 1844, in Roehm, *Letters,* 103–5, 289. For conditions that encouraged immigration, see Livesay, *Andrew Carnegie,* 3–13; Catlin, *Notes for the Emigrant,* 9–10, 15.

78. Catlin, *Notes for the Emigrant,* 3, 6, 8, 11–14.

79. Handbill for Valley of the Mississippi Lecture, 9 Apr. 1850, Printed Material, etc., GCP, 1821–90, SI; Catlin to Thomas Phillipps, n.d., 14 Dec. 1850, and 12 Jan. 1851, all in Correspondence, GCP, 1840–60, SI.

80. Catlin, *Proposed Creation of Museum of Mankind,* GCP, 1840–60, SI; Catlin, *Notes of Eight Years' Travels,* 1:61–64.

81. Catlin to Thomas Phillipps, 12 Jan. 1851, Correspondence, GCP, 1840–60, SI; *New York Times,* 10 June 1851; "Mr. Catlin's Indian Family," 254–55.

82. Roehm, *Letters,* 317–18; Dippie, *Catlin,* 143–55.

83. Catlin, *Last Rambles,* 51; Catlin to Thomas Phillipps, 23 Jan. 1853, Correspondence, GCP, 1840–60, SI.

84. Truettner, *Natural Man,* 53; Catlin to William Blackmore, 16 Apr. 1871, Correspondence, GCP, 1840–60, SI; George to Francis, 7 June 1868, in Roehm, *Letters,* 346.

85. Catlin, *Last Rambles,* 52; Catlin to Thomas Phillipps, 27 Nov. 1854, 3 Nov. 1857, 31 Dec. 1857, and 1 Oct. 1860, all in Correspondence, GCP, 1840–60, SI; George to "My Dear Sweet, little Louise," 22 Apr. 1860, Correspondence, GCP, 1821–90, SI; Catlin, *Life amongst the Indians,* vii, 307; Catlin to William Blackmore, 16 Apr. 1871, Correspondence, GCP, 1821–90, SI; Catlin, "Synopsis," Printed Material, etc., GCP, 1821–90, SI.

86. "Francis Catlin's Diary of His Trip to Belgium," in Roehm, *Letters,* 354–71, quote on 360; Catlin, *Life amongst the Indians,* 4.

87. Catlin, *Last Rambles,* 347–48.

88. Catlin to Thomas Phillipps, 1 Oct. 1860, Correspondence, GCP, 1840–60, SI; "Francis Catlin Diary," George to Burr, 9 Sept. 1868, George to Francis, 9 Sept. 1868, 18 Sept. 1868, 4 Jan. 1869, 9 Jan. 1869, 13 Jan. 1869, 26 Jan. 1869, 17 Feb. 1869, 17 Mar. 1869, 11 June 1869, 26 Oct. 1869, 17 Dec. 1869, 5 Feb. 1870, 26 Feb. 1870, 3 Mar. 1870, and appendix X, all in Roehm, *Letters,* 348–53, 358–60, 376–400, 445–48.

89. George to Francis, 29 Aug. 1870, in Roehm, *Letters,* 401–2, 411; M. Dulieu to Catlin, 16 July 1870, Correspondence, GCP, NCFA; Catlin, *North and South American Indians; Jersey City (N.J.) Journal,* 24 Dec. 1872, *New York Herald,* 24 Dec. 1872, *New York Times,* 24 Dec. 1872, and *Jersey City (N.J.) Times,* 24 Dec. 1872, all in Obituary Notes, GCP, NCFA; Joseph Henry, SI, to D. S. Gregory, Jersey City, N.J., 29 Oct. 1872, Cor-

respondence, GCP, 1821–90, SI; "George Catlin," 16; Henry, "Report of the Secretary," 13–54.

90. Catlin, *Last Rambles*, 146.

## Chapter 3: "The Gladiatorial Contest Revived"

1. Cody, *Life*, 20–25.

2. Ibid., 26–27.

3. Ibid., 28–29.

4. Merk, *Manifest Destiny*, 24–27, 187, 264–65. For different views on Manifest Destiny and mission, see Burns, *American Idea*, 187–90, and Weinberg, *Manifest Destiny*, 1, 116, 208–12. For views of patriotism and war in schoolbooks, see Elson, *Guardians*, 145, 325–31.

5. Cody, *Life*, 39, 48–49, 55–85, 127–29, 131–33.

6. Ibid., v–viii, 48, 66, 85, 89–90, 105–7, 111–18, 134–280, 312, 319, 360–61. For different opinions about Cody's veracity, see Walsh, *Making of Buffalo Bill*, v, 21, 203–4; Russell, *Lives and Legends*, 6; and Blake, *Blake's Western Stories*.

7. *Hartford Courant*, n.d., qtd. in Walsh, *Making of Buffalo Bill*, 228; Cody, *Life*, 282; Fees, "Flamboyant Fraternity," 1–8.

8. Fees, "Flamboyant Fraternity," 2; Cody, *Life*, 173–74, 269, 295–305.

9. Cody, *Life*, v, 263–64; Russell, *Lives and Legends*, 386–415; Henry Nash Smith, *Virgin Land*, 113–25; "Chronology," 14; Curti, "Dime Novels," 172–88; Johannsen, *House*; Ingraham, *Adventures*, 91–105; McIntyre, foreword, xxiii–xxv; *BBWW* (1885 program), BBHC. Buffalo Bill rated a biography in the series Histories of Poor Boys Who Have Become Rich; these were included with packages of Duke Cigarettes. See *Life of Buffalo Bill*, DPL.

10. Cody, *Life*, 310–11, 312, 313–19, 320–28, 364–65; Cody to John Wallace Crawford, 22 Apr. 1879, 30 Sept. 1879, 5 Oct. 1879, and 4 July 1882, all in box 1, DPL; *New York Times*, 31 Mar. 1873, qtd. in Walsh, *Making of Buffalo Bill*, 181; *New York Dramatic Mirror*, 23 Aug. 1884, cited in Deahl, "History," 25; "Bowery Theatre," DPL.

11. Rahill, *Melodrama*, 226, 234–36; Dulles, *History*, 213–14; Russell, *Lives and Legends*, 202–3.

12. Cody, *Life*, 320–28; Walsh, *Making of Buffalo Bill*, 180–81; Cody, *Buffalo Bill's Own Story*, 265–66.

13. Cody to John Wallace Crawford, 22 Apr. 1879, box 1, DPL; Cody, *Life*, 307–10.

14. Cody, *Life*, 277–78; Cody to Sam (probably "Buckskin" Sam Hall), 2 Sept. 1879, GC, BBHC.

15. Walsh, *Making of Buffalo Bill*, 202; Cody, *Life*, 340.

16. Cody, *Life*, 344; King, *Campaigning*, iii.

17. Cody, *Life*, 342–47, 360, quote on 355–56; King, *Campaigning*, 42; Russell, *Lives and Legends*, 254; Cody to Louisa Cody, 18 July 1876, and Ed Goodman to Father, 29 May 1886, both in GC, BBHC; Walsh, *Making of Buffalo Bill*, 197, 254; Fellows and

Freeman, *This Way,* 139, 193. The scalp is now a part of the collections at the Buffalo Bill Historical Center in Cody, Wyoming.

18. King, *Campaigning,* 42.

19. For an analysis of Cody's career on stage, see Nieuwnhuyse, "Six Guns."

20. Salsbury, "Origin," 205–8. For background information on Nate Salsbury, see "Mr. Nate Salsbury, Director," *BBWW* (1885 program), BBHC; Cody to Sam (probably "Buckskin" Sam Hall), 5 July 1879, GC, BBHC. The most complete account of Buffalo Bill serving as grand marshal appears in Yost, *Buffalo Bill,* 116–22.

21. *Wild West* (1883 exhibition program), BBHC; Deahl, "History," 16–17; Russell, *Lives and Legends,* 289, 293–94; Salsbury, "Origin," 207; Fellows and Freeman, *This Way,* 66–67. *Wild West* (1883 Chicago Driving Park program), DPL.

22. *Wild West* (1883 Chicago Driving Park program), DPL; *Hartford Courant,* n.d., in Fellows and Freeman, *This Way,* 64–65, quote on 69; Cody to "Sister," 8 Feb. [1883], and Cody to "Sister and Brother," 24 Sept. 1883, both in GC, BBHC; Deahl, "History," 18; Salsbury, "Origin," 207–9.

23. Wrobel, *End of American Exceptionalism,* viii, 13–25; Slotkin, *Gunfighter Nation,* 81; Moses, *Wild West Shows,* 12.

24. Nye, *Unembarrassed Muse,* 190; Dulles, *History,* 282–86; Schlesinger, *Rise,* xiv; *Philadelphia Sunday Dispatch,* 6 June 1885, vol. 1, NSS; Fellows and Freeman, *This Way,* 83.

25. Frank Norris, *Blix, Moran of the Lady Letty* (1899), qtd. in Henry Nash Smith, "The West," 280–82; *Philadelphia Sunday Dispatch,* 6 June 1885, vol. 1, NSS.

26. *Hamilton (Ont.) Daily Spectator and Tribune,* 27 Aug. 1885, *Pittsburgh Commercial Gazette,* 22 Sept. 1885, *New York World,* 16 July 1886, and *New York Telegram,* 30 June 1886, all in vol. 1, NSS.

27. *New York Sun,* 27 June 1886, *Kingston (Ont.) Daily News,* 20 Aug. 1885, *St. Louis Sunday Sayings,* 9 May 1886, *Philadelphia Record,* 9 June 1886, *Philadelphia Times,* 7 June 1886, and *Ottawa Free Press,* 17 Aug. 1885, all in vol. 1, NSS; "A Historical Coach of the Deadwood Line," *BBWW* (1885 program), BBHC.

28. *New York World,* 16 July 1886, vol. 1, NSS; Burke, *"Buffalo Bill,"* 238–39.

29. *Montreal Daily Witness,* 12 Aug. 1885, vol. 1, NSS; Pancoast, *Trail Blazers,* 32; Rennert, *One Hundred Posters,* 3–5.

30. Pancoast, *Trail Blazers,* 31–32, 181–83; Rennert, *One Hundred Posters,* 3–5 (for representative poster images of Buffalo Bill, see 17, 24, 25, 32, 49, 60, 61, 63, 71, 77, 87, 108, 112); *Swansea Leader* (Wales), 23 June 1903, vol. 1, NSS; Fellows and Freeman, *This Way,* 33.

31. Pancoast, *Trail Blazers,* 33; *New York Times,* 26 June 1886; Fellows and Freeman, *This Way,* 17–19, 22–23, 83, 138; Walsh, *Making of Buffalo Bill,* 97, 183–84.

32. *Boston Herald,* 31 July 1885, *Montreal Daily Witness,* 14 Aug. 1885, and *Detroit Post,* 5 Sept. 1885, all in vol. 1, NSS; Walsh, *Making of Buffalo Bill,* 259–60.

33. Ed Goodman to Father, 29 May 1886, GC, BBHC; *Burlington (Vt.) Free Press and Times,* 6 Aug. 1885, *New York Sun,* 27 June 1886, and *New York Morning Journal,* 26 June 1886, all in vol. 1, NSS.

34. *Daily British Whig* (Kingston, Ont.), 20 Aug. 1885, *Hamilton (Ont.) Daily Spectator and Tribune,* 27 Aug. 1885, *New York Sun,* 27 June 1886, and *New York Star,* 27 June 1886, all in vol. 1, NSS; *New York Times,* 27 June 1886; Fellows and Freeman, *This Way,* 69–70; Pancoast, *Trail Blazers,* 32; *Times* (no city), n.d., and *Taggert's Time* (no city), n.d., both in AOS.

35. Dulles, *History,* 212; *Montreal Gazette,* 15 Aug. 1885, *St. Louis Sunday Sayings,* 4 Oct. 1885, *Philadelphia Daily News,* 8 June 1886, and *New York Dispatch,* 27 June 1886, all in vol. 1, NSS; *New York Times,* 26 June 1886.

36. Atherton, *Main Street,* 134; Fellows and Freeman, *This Way,* 106–19; *St. Louis Sunday Sayings,* 4 Oct. 1885, vol. 1, NSS; Dubofsky, *Industrialism,* 18–19; *1897 Sears Roebuck Catalog.*

37. *Dispatch* (no city), n.d., *Evening Star* (no city), 15 May 1895, unidentified clipping (probably 1895), and *Albany Express,* 21 May 1895, all in AOS; *London (Ont.) Advertiser,* 2 Sept. 1885, *London (Ont.) Free Press,* 2 Sept. 1885, and *Brick Pomeroy's Democrat* (New York), 10 July 1886, all in vol. 1, NSS; Fellows and Freeman, *This Way,* 65; *New York Times,* 31 Oct. 1886, and *Manchester Guardian,* 29 Apr. 1887, both in JBS.

38. *Hamilton (Ont.) Daily Spectator and Tribune,* 27 Aug. 1885, vol. 1, NSS; *Evening Star* (no city), 15 May 1895, and *Daily Telegraph* (no city), n.d., both in AOS; "Buffalo Bill's 'Wild West,'" 150; for the length of the show, see *Hamilton (Ont.) Daily Spectator and Tribune,* 27 Aug. 1885, and *Indianapolis Sentinel,* 30 Sept. 1885, both in vol. 1, NSS. The length of the monologue was determined by reading it aloud. Ed Goodman to "Dear Mother," 4 July 1886, GC, BBHC.

39. "Buffalo Bill's 'Wild West,'" 150–51; *Brick Pomeroy's Democrat* (New York), 10 July 1886, vol. 1, NSS; *Washington Times,* n.d., and *Evening Democrat* (Aterbury or Waterbury), n.d., both in AOS.

40. "Buffalo Bill's 'Wild West,'" 151; *Brick Pomeroy's Democrat* (New York), 10 July 1886, vol. 1, NSS; Webb, "Buffalo Bill," 14–15, BBHC.

41. *Hamilton (Ont.) Daily Spectator and Tribune,* 27 Aug. 1885, vol. 1, NSS.

42. Ibid.; *New York Evening Telegram,* 26 June 1886, vol. 1, NSS. For descriptions of the sights, sounds, and moods of the Wild West show, see unidentified clipping (probably 1895), *Evening Democrat* (Aterbury or Waterbury), n.d., AOS; *New York Sun,* 27 June 1886 and 11 July 1886, *Brick Pomeroy's Democrat* (New York), 10 July 1886, and *Montreal Daily Post,* 11 Aug. 1885, all in vol. 1, NSS. For the music of the shows, see Masterson, "Sounds," vi.

43. *Wild West* (1883 Chicago Driving Park program), DPL; *BBWW* (1884 program), DPL; *Burlington (Vt.) Free Press and Times,* 6 Aug. 1885, vol. 1, NSS; *New York Times,* 29 June 1886.

44. *Boston Daily Globe,* 28 July 1885, and *Burlington (Vt.) Free Press and Times,* 6 Aug. 1885, both in vol. 1, NSS; *Wild West* (1883 Chicago Driving Park program), DPL; *BBWW* (1884 program), DPL; "Buffalo Bill's 'Wild West,'" 151–52.

45. For sources on the image of early cowboys, see Frantz and Choate, *American Cowboy,* chaps. 1 and 9, and French, "Cowboy," 219–34. Atherton, *Main Street,* 65;

Chester A. Arthur's remark in Henry Nash Smith, *Virgin Land,* 122–23; "Murderous Cowboys," *New York Times,* 16 Feb. 1886.

46. Cody to Sam (probably "Buckskin" Sam Hall), 23 May 1879 and 5 July 1879, GC, BBHC; Cody, *Life,* 276–77, 363; Katzive, introduction, 57.

47. *Montreal Daily Witness,* 12 Aug. 1885, and *Montreal Gazette,* 15 Aug. 1885, both in vol. 1, NSS.

48. *Wild West* (1883 exhibition program), BBHC.

49. *New York Telegram,* 30 June 1886, and *Philadelphia Item,* 7 June 1886, both in vol. 1, NSS; *Wild West* (1883 exhibition program), BBHC; "'Buck' Taylor, King of the Cowboys," *BBWW* (1885 program), BBHC; Henry Nash Smith, *Virgin Land,* 123–24.

50. Rennert, *One Hundred Posters,* 6, 20–23; *Boston Saturday Evening Express,* 25 July 1885, *Burlington (Vt.) Free Press and Times,* 6 Aug. 1885, and *Philadelphia Daily News,* 9 June 1886, all in vol. 1, NSS; *Wild West* (1883 exhibition program), BBHC; *Wild West* (1883 Chicago Driving Park program), DPL; "Buffalo Bill's 'Wild West,'" 153, 156.

51. Rennert, *One Hundred Posters,* 6, 19; *New York Times,* 29 June 1886; Ed Goodman to Father, 29 May 1886, GC, BBHC; *Philadelphia Evening Call,* 11 June 1886, *Boston Evening Transcript,* 28 July 1885, *Philadelphia Item,* 7 June 1886, *New York Times,* 26 June 1886, *New York World,* 16 July 1886, and *Boston Daily Globe,* 28 July 1885, all in vol. 1, NSS.

52. *BBWW* (1884 courier), DPL (the library lists this as an 1885 courier, but Bogardus was not with the show in that year); *BBWW* (1887 program), DPL; *BBWW* (1885 program), BBHC.

53. "The Rifle as an Aid to Civilization," *BBWW* (1885 program), BBHC.

54. Rennert, *One Hundred Posters,* 6, 10–11, 18–19, 22–29, 32, 37, 39, 40–41, 50, 52–58, 67; Atherton, *Cattle Kings,* 242–43, 275.

55. "Buffalo Bill's 'Wild West,'" 152–53; *Wild West* (1883 Chicago Driving Park program), DPL; *BBWW* (1884 program), DPL; *Albany Express,* 21 May 1895, AOS; *BBWW* (1885 program), BBHC; *New York Dramatic Mirror,* 14 June 1884, and *New Orleans Daily Picayune,* 9 Mar. 1885, cited in Deahl, "History," 21, 30; Fellows and Freeman, *This Way,* 73–75; Russell, *Lives and Legends,* 319.

56. "A Practical 'All-Round Shot,'" *BBWW* (1885 program), BBHC; "Buffalo Bill's 'Wild West,'" 154; *New York Times,* 26 July 1886; *Boston Post,* 28 July 1885, and *Boston Daily Globe,* 28 July 1885, both in vol. 1, NSS.

57. *BBWW* (1886 program), DPL; *New York Times,* 7 Apr. 1901; "Buffalo Bill's 'Wild West,'" 153; Fellows and Freeman, *This Way,* 73; Riley, *Life,* 36; Rennert, *One Hundred Posters,* 80, 83, 105.

58. "Shoots like a Man," 148–49.

59. Riley, *Life,* 27, 30–31; Cody, *Life.*

60. *Philadelphia Item,* 7 June 1886, and *Philadelphia Daily News,* 9 June 1886, both in vol. 1, NSS; *BBWW* (1885 program), BBHC; *New York Times,* 29 June 1886; Walsh, *Making of Buffalo Bill,* 249; Riley, *Life,* 34; Wood-Clark, *Beautiful,* 10; Tompkins, *West,* 37–45.

61. *Wild West* (1883 Chicago Driving Park program), DPL; "The Hunt of the Bison" and "The Buffalo" in *BBWW* (1885 program), BBHC; *Philadelphia Daily News,* 9 June 1886, *Boston Saturday Evening Express,* 25 July 1885, and *Toronto Globe,* 24 Aug. 1885, all in vol. 1, NSS; *New York Times,* 26 June 1886.

62. *New York Times,* 26 June 1886; *Boston Evening Transcript,* 28 July 1885, vol. 1, NSS; Ekirch, *Man and Nature,* 47, 81; Roderick Nash, *Wilderness,* 24, 25–30, 40–42; for the disappearance of big game animals, see *New York Times,* 8 Aug. 1886, 23 Oct. 1886, 30 Apr. 1888, 21 May 1888, and 11 June 1888.

63. Walsh, *Making of Buffalo Bill,* 257–58; *BBWW* (1885 program), BBHC; *Dayton Daily Herald,* 20 May 1886, cited in Deahl, "History," 47–48; "Buffalo Bill's 'Wild West,'" 156; *Philadelphia Item,* 13 June 1886, vol. 1, NSS; Dulles, *History,* 182–85, 198–99, 201.

64. Arpad and Lincoln, *Buffalo Bill's Wild West,* 36; *Toronto Globe,* 24 Aug. 1885, and *Montreal Gazette,* 11 Aug. 1885, both in vol. 1, NSS; *New York World,* 31 July 1886, cited in Deahl, "History," 56; *BBWW* (1885 program), BBHC; *New York Times,* 25 Nov. 1886; Merk, *Manifest Destiny,* 33–34, 86–106, 157–79, 210; Cody, *Life,* 119–24, 148, 158–60, 194, 209, 227–28.

65. *BBWW* (1885 program), BBHC; White, "Frederick Jackson Turner," 52, 54.

66. Moses, *Wild West Shows,* 23–25, 116.

67. Slotkin, *Regeneration,* 17; *BBWW* (1907 or 1908 program), DPL; *BBWW* (1898 courier), 5, 11–12, 27, DPL; *Toronto Globe,* 24 Aug. 1885, vol. 1, NSS; unidentified clipping, 1879, box 1, 1879–80 Stage Notices Scrapbook, BBHC.

68. Moses, *Wild West Shows,* 19–20.

69. Rennert, *One Hundred Posters,* 10, 11, 56, 58, 68; Ralph, "Behind the 'Wild West' Scenes," 775.

70. *New York Telegram,* 30 June 1886, vol. 1, NSS.

71. "Buffalo Bill's 'Wild West,'" 152; *Toronto Globe,* 24 Aug. 1885, vol. 1, NSS.

72. "Buffalo Bill's 'Wild West,'" 155; "A Historical Coach of the Deadwood Line," *BBWW* (1885 program), BBHC; *Grand Rapids Morning Telegram,* 12 Sept. 1885, vol. 1, NSS; Chidsey, *John the Great,* 100.

73. *New York Daily Graphic,* 29 June 1886, *Toronto Globe,* 24 Aug. 1885, and *Hamilton (Ont.) Daily Spectator and Tribune,* 27 Aug. 1885, all in vol. 1, NSS; Chidsey, *John the Great,* 102; Pancoast, *Trail Blazers,* 32.

74. *Boston Saturday Evening Express,* 25 July 1885, and *Philadelphia Times,* 8 June 1886, both in vol. 1, NSS; Ed Goodman to "Dear Ma," 8 May 1886, GC, BBHC; Pancoast, *Trail Blazers,* 32; Tuska, "American Western Cinema," 41.

75. *Wild West* (1883 Chicago Driving Park program), DPL; *Omaha Daily Herald,* 18 May 1883, cited in Deahl, "History," 11.

76. "Buffalo Bill's 'Wild West,'" 156; *Philadelphia Times,* 8 June 1886, *Hamilton (Ont.) Daily Spectator and Tribune,* 27 Aug. 1885, *Ohio State Journal* (Columbus), 29 Sept. 1885, *Boston Daily Globe,* 28 July 1885, *New York Evening Telegram,* 26 June 1886, and *Toronto Globe,* 24 Aug. 1885, all in vol. 1, NSS; *New York Times,* 26 June 1886 and 29 June 1886.

77. White, "Frederick Jackson Turner," 21.

78. Masterson, "Sounds," 252–83; Deahl, "History," 35–36, and reprint of *Chicago Tribune*, 18 May 1885, on 42; *Toronto Globe*, 24 Aug. 1885, *Hamilton (Ont.) Daily Spectator and Tribune*, 27 Aug. 1885, and *Boston Post*, 28 July 1885, all in vol. 1, NSS; *BBWW* (1885 program), BBHC.

79. Fellows and Freeman, *This Way*, 132; Moses, *Wild West Shows*, 41, 44, 46.

80. Moses, *Wild West Shows*, 25–27, 30; Yost, *Buffalo Bill*, 151; Utley, *Lance*, 260–67; *Columbus Daily Times*, 29 Sept. 1885, and *Ohio State Journal* (Columbus), 29 Sept. 1885, both in vol. 1, NSS.

81. "History of Sitting Bull," *BBWW* (1885 program), BBHC; *Detroit Evening Journal*, 5 Sept. 1885, *Boston Post*, 28 July 1885, *Burlington (Vt.) Free Press and Times*, 6 Aug. 1885, *Toronto Globe*, 24 Aug. 1885, *Columbus Daily Dispatch*, 29 Sept. 1885, and *Detroit Post*, 5 Sept. 1885, all in vol. 1, NSS; Walsh, *Making of Buffalo Bill*, 255–56. The contract between Sitting Bull and John Burke is reproduced in Havighurst, *Annie Oakley*, 49.

82. Anderson, *Sitting Bull*, 143; Walsh, *Making of Buffalo Bill*, 255; *Columbus Daily Times*, 29 Sept. 1885, *Montreal Daily Witness*, 12 Aug. 1885, and *Boston Daily Globe*, 28 July 1885, all in vol. 1, NSS.

83. *Toronto Globe*, 24 Aug. 1885, *Detroit Evening Journal*, 5 Sept. 1885, *Grand Rapids Evening Leader*, 13 Sept. 1885, *Ohio State Journal* (Columbus), 27 Sept. 1885, and *St. Louis Sunday Sayings*, 4 Oct. 1885, all in vol. 1, NSS.

84. *St. Louis Sunday Sayings*, 4 Oct. 1885, vol. 1, NSS; Vestal, *Sitting Bull*, 251; Russell, *Lives and Legends*, 317; Moses, *Wild West Shows*, 31.

85. "Buffalo Bill's 'Wild West,'" 156; *New York Morning Journal*, 26 June 1886 and 18 July 1886, *Philadelphia Times*, 7 June 1886, *New York Telegram*, 30 June 1886, *Montreal Gazette*, 15 Aug. 1885, *New York Daily Tribune*, 1 Aug. 1886, and *New York Star*, 30 July 1886 and 6 Aug. 1886, all in vol. 1, NSS.

86. *New York Star*, 1 Aug. 1886, *Richmond County Advance*, 31 July 1886, *New York Daily Tribune*, 15 Aug. 1886, and *New York Daily News*, 18 Aug. 1889, all in vol. 1, NSS; *New York Times*, 19 Aug. 1886.

87. *New York Morning Journal*, 26 June 1886, and *Ohio State Journal* (Columbus), 27 Sept. 1885, both in vol. 1, NSS.

88. *New Orleans Daily Picayune*, 2 Feb. 1885, qtd. in Deahl, "History," 29; Ward, *Andrew Jackson*, 3–29.

89. Mackaye, *Epoch*; *New York Times*, 14 Nov. 1886, 25 Nov. 1886, and 28 Nov. 1886; Walsh, *Making of Buffalo Bill*, 262.

90. "Programme: A History of American Civilization," in *BBWW* (1886 program), DPL; *New York Times*, 31 Oct. 1886, 14 Nov. 1886, 25 Nov. 1886, and 30 Nov. 1886.

91. *New York Times*, 25 Nov. 1886; "Programme: A History of American Civilization," in *BBWW* (1886 program), DPL.

92. *New York Times*, 25 Nov. 1886.

93. "Programme: A History of American Civilization," in *BBWW* (1886 program), DPL; *New York Times*, 31 Oct. 1886, 25 Nov. 1886, and 30 Nov. 1886.

94. "Programme: A History of American Civilization," in *BBWW* (1886 program), DPL; *New York Times*, 31 Oct. 1886, 25 Nov. 1886, 28 Nov. 1886, 4 Jan. 1886, 23 Jan. 1886, and 6 Feb. 1887; Ed Goodman to "Ma, Pa, sisters and brothers," 20 Nov. 1886, GC, BBHC; Deahl, "History," 60. For thoughts on why the cowboy rather than the miner became the folk hero of the frontier, see Duane A. Smith, *Rocky Mountain Mining Camps*, 79–80, 255–56.

95. *New York Times*, 25 Nov. 1886 and 28 Nov. 1886.

96. Moses, *Wild West Shows*, 23; *New York Times*, 12 Sept. 1886; Walsh, *Making of Buffalo Bill*, 254; Fellows and Freeman, *This Way*, 74; *The Spirit of the Times* (New York), 7 Aug. 1886, *Montreal Herald*, 15 Aug. 1885, *Indianapolis Sentinel*, 30 Sept. 1885, and *St. Louis Sunday Sayings*, 4 Oct. 1885, all in vol. 1, NSS; Cody to John Wallace Crawford, Staten Island, 21 July 1886, box 1, DPL.

97. *New York World*, 31 July 1886, vol. 1, NSS; Walsh, *Making of Buffalo Bill*, 261; Fellows and Freeman, *This Way*, 70.

98. *Montreal Herald*, 14 Aug. 1885, *Columbus Daily Times*, 29 Sept. 1885, and *Wolverhampton Express-Star* (England), 18 June 1903, all in vol. 11, NSS; Ed Goodman to "My dear Mother," 22 Nov. 1886, GC, BBHC; Leavitt, *Fifty Years*, 141–42; Johannsen, *House*, 1:38–39; *New York Dramatic Mirror*, 12 Mar. 1887, cited in Deahl, "History," 61.

99. *New York Times*, 31 Mar. 1887; *Columbus Daily Times*, 29 Sept. 1885, vol. 1, NSS.

100. Twain's letter reprinted in *Washington Chronicle*, 30 May 1886, vol. 1, NSS; *New York Times*, 31 Mar. 1887.

## Chapter 4: "To Esteem Us Better"

1. Cody, *Story of the Wild West*, 711–13.

2. Ibid., 713; Ed Goodman to "My dear Ma and Pa," 22 Apr. 1887, and W. F. Cody to "My Dear General," 15 June 1882 (the register lists the date as 1880), both in GC, BBHC; Wilson, "Exporting America," 11. Richard Wilson kindly provided me with a written copy of his paper.

3. Cody, *Story of the Wild West*, 710, 717–18; *Illustrated London News*, 16 Apr. 1887; *Fame and Fortune* (no city), 21 Apr. 1887, *London Observer*, 24 Apr. 1887, and *London Era*, 23 Apr. 1887, all in JBS.

4. Curti, "America," 246–77; Ed Goodman to "My dear Ma and Pa," 22 Apr. 1887, and *Sporting Life*, 10 May 1887, both in AOS; *St. James's Gazette* (London), 10 May 1887, and *London Observer*, 8 May 1887, both in JBS; *American Exhibition*, DPL; *London Times*, 1 Nov. 1887.

5. *American Exhibition*, DPL; *St. James's Gazette* (London), 10 May 1887, JBS; *London Times*, 1 Nov. 1887.

6. Cody, *Story of the Wild West*, 730.

7. *London Times,* 10 June 1851.

8. Cody, *Story of the Wild West,* 730; Hand, *I Was after Money,* 15–16; *London Daily News,* 16 Apr. 1887, and *Manchester Guardian,* 29 Apr. 1887, both in JBS; *London Penny Illustrated Paper,* 7 May 1887; Willson, *History,* 648–77; Bailey, *Diplomatic History,* 421–38.

9. Ed Goodman to "My dear Ma and Pa," 22 Apr. 1887, GC, BBHC; *Sheffield Daily Telegraph,* 22 Apr. 1887, *Manchester Telegraph,* 28 Apr. 1887, and *Pall Mall Gazette* (London), 10 May 1887, all in JBS; Walsh, *Making of Buffalo Bill,* 270; Wilder, *People,* 115–16.

10. Burke, *"Buffalo Bill,"* 210–14; *New York Times,* 29 Apr. 1887; *Illustrated Bits* (no city), 12 Mar. 1887, and *Daily Telegraph* (no city), 29 Apr. 1887, both in JBS.

11. Walsh, *Making of Buffalo Bill,* 266; "Buffalo Bill's Wild West," in *American Exhibition,* DPL; *St. James's Gazette* (London), 10 May 1887, *London Metropolitan,* 30 Apr. 1887, *Court and Society* (no city), 23 Mar. 1887, *London Morning Post,* 12 Apr. 1887, and *London Era,* 23 Apr. 1887, all in JBS.

12. *Court and Society,* 23 Mar. 1887, *Fame and Fortune* (London), 12 May 1887, and *Sporting Life,* 10 May 1887, all in JBS; John M. Burke, "Salutatory," and "The Cowboys," and general accounts of the program, in *BBWW* (1887 program), DPL.

13. Derry, "Corsets and Broncs," 2–4. Derry observes that the passenger list for the *State of Nebraska* names sixteen women in the Wild West show troupe (including Oakley and Smith), but notes that it is impossible to tell "precisely how many were among the cast as opposed to family members or aides." My figure of a dozen is an estimate. Wilson, "Exporting America," 12–13; *London Era,* 23 Apr. 1887, *Fame and Fortune* (London), 12 May 1887, and *St. James's Gazette* (London), 10 May 1887, all in JBS; *BBWW* (1887 program), DPL; "With the Indians," 269; "Robert at the American Exhibition," 10.

14. *Sporting Life,* 10 May 1887, *Pall Mall Gazette* (London), 10 May 1887, and *Daily Telegraph* (no city), 10 May 1887, all in JBS; "Robert at the American Exhibition," 10; "With the Indians," 269.

15. Walsh, *Making of Buffalo Bill,* 266–68, 169; Cody, *Story of the Wild West,* 730–31, 735, 737; *Illustrated London News,* 21 May 1887; *London Times,* 22 May 1887.

16. Rennert, *One Hundred Posters,* 7, 34–35; Walsh, *Making of Buffalo Bill,* 267; Cody, *Story of the Wild West,* 734, 735–37; *Illustrated London News,* 21 May 1887; *Kate Field's Washington,* 19 July 1893, vol. 3, NSS.

17. Cody, *Story of the Wild West,* 742–43; *Galignani's Messenger* (Paris), 17 Mar. 1890, Scrapbook for Italy, BBHC.

18. *London Times,* 21 May 1888; *World* (no city), 11 May 1887, and *Pall Mall Gazette* (London), 3 June 1887, both in AOS.

19. Cody, *Story of the Wild West,* 331–34.

20. Walsh, *Making of Buffalo Bill,* 270–72; *London Times,* 1 Nov. 1887; *Courier of London,* 9 May 1887, JBS; Riley, *Life,* 37–42; *Truth* (no city), 23 May 1887, AOS.

21. Burke, *Prairie to Palace,* 133; *London Penny Illustrated Paper,* 14 May 1887; *London Metropolitan,* 30 Apr. 1887, JBS.

22. *London Times,* 29 Apr. 1887; *Illustrated London News,* 16 Apr. 1887.

23. Cody, *Story of the Wild West*, 719, 707; *Illustrated London News*, 16 Apr. 1887.

24. Willson, *History*, 648–77; Rosa and May, *Buffalo Bill*, 118–19; Wilson, "Exporting America," 7–8.

25. Fees, "Flamboyant Fraternity," 6; *Courier of London*, 9 May 1887, JBS.

26. *London Times*, 1 Nov. 1887; Cody, *Story of the Wild West*, 719, 747, 748–50; Leavitt, *Fifty Years*, 143; *Topical Times* (no city), 22 Oct. 1887, AOS; Walsh, *Making of Buffalo Bill*, 270; Ed Goodwin to Parents, 4 Nov. 1887, GC, BBHC; for Cody acting like a "proud and profane son," see Moses, *Wild West Shows*, 59.

27. Cody, *Story of the Wild West*, 750–55; *Inaugural Invitation Exhibition*, DPL.

28. *Inaugural Invitation Exhibition*, DPL; Ed Goodwin to Parents, 4 Mar. 1888 and 11 Mar. 1888, GC, BBHC; Cody, *Story of the Wild West*, 756–57, 761–62, 764.

29. *London Times*, 21 May 1888; Cody, *Story of the Wild West*, 716–17, 724–30, 756–57, 766.

30. *London Times*, 31 May 1888 and 12 Aug. 1888; *Washington Post*, 24 Sept. 1888, cited in Deahl, "History," 77, 75, and text, 74, 81; Rennert, *One Hundred Posters*, 7, 34–35.

31. *London Times*, 8 May 1889, 9 Oct. 1889, and 28 Apr. 1889; *Le Voltaire* (France), 15 Oct. 1889, Scrapbook for France, 1889, BBHC.

32. *BBWW* (1893 program), 58, DPL; *Truth* (no city), 23 May 1889, AOS; *La France Militaire*, 25 Aug. 1889, and *La Liberté* (France), 17 Oct. 1889, Scrapbook for France, BBHC.

33. Elson, *Guardians*, 128–43; Strout, *American Image*, 16, 19; Bloom-Wilson, "Exporting America," 1; Billington, *Land of Savagery*, 34–35, 219–40; *Independence Luxembourgeoise*, 21 Aug. 1889, and clipping identified as "New-York Paper," both in Scrapbook for France, BBHC.

34. *La Charge*, 11 Aug. 1889, *American Musician*, 17 Aug. 1889, and *New York Tribune*, 31 Aug. 1889, all in Scrapbook for France, BBHC; *New York Times*, 23 June 1889.

35. *New York Times*, 18 May 1890 and 23 June 1889.

36. Unidentified newspaper advertisement in French, *La France Militaire*, 25 Aug. 1889, *Petit Courrier Angers*, 12 Oct. 1889, *Le Parisien*, 22 Aug. 1889, *Courrier du Nord-Est*, 12 Sept. 1889, *San Francisco Chronicle*, n.d., and *Le Gil-Blas*, 8 Aug. 1889, all in Scrapbook for France, BBHC; Romein, *Watershed*, 209; Billington, *Land of Savagery*, 49; "With the Indians," 269; Bloom-Wilson, "Exporting America," 10; Burke, *"Buffalo Bill,"* 234; wages computed from "Yearly Income" table in Balfour, *Kaiser*, 441.

37. *BBWW* (1889 French program), Campbell Collection, UO; clipping identified as "New-York Paper," *New York Tribune*, 31 Aug. 1889, unidentified clipping about the Boston Rifle Team, *La France Militaire*, 25 Aug. 1889, and *Republique Illustrée*, 10 Aug. 1889, all in Scrapbook for France, BBHC.

38. *New York Tribune*, 31 Aug. 1889, *La France Militaire*, 25 Aug. 1889, and *New York Herald*, 28 Apr. 1889, all in Scrapbook for France, BBHC; "Gabriel Dumont," *BBWW* (1889 French program), 44, Campbell Collection, UO; *New York Times*, 28 Apr. 1889. Gabriel Dumas (sometimes Dumont) was advertised as an attraction, but probably did not actually reach France.

39. Bloom-Wilson, "Exporting America," 7–8; unidentified clipping about the Bos-

ton Rifle Team, *Le Parisien,* 22 Aug. 1889, *Galignani's Messenger* (Paris), 28 Aug. 1889, *Telegraphe,* 8 Oct. 1898, *La Charge,* 11 Aug. 1889, and *San Francisco Chronicle,* n.d., all in Scrapbook for France, BBHC; *New York Times,* 28 Aug. 1889 and 24 Nov. 1889; Walsh, *Making of Buffalo Bill,* 267; Hassrick, "The Artists," 25.

40. *La Louveraineté,* 6 Aug. 1889, in Scrapbook for France, BBHC.

41. *Republique Illustrée,* 10 Aug. 1889, *New York Herald,* 28 Apr. 1889, *New York Sun,* 28 Apr. 1889, *Galignani's Messenger* (Paris), 23 Oct. 1889, and *La Louveraineté,* 6 Aug. 1889, all in Scrapbook for France, BBHC; *New York Times,* 23 June 1889 and 28 Apr. 1889; "protection of virtue" quote identified as Scrapbook for France, BBHC, in Bloom-Wilson, "Exporting America," 11.

42. *Ville de Paris,* 7 Aug. 1889, cited in Bloom-Wilson, "Exporting America," 8; *La Louveraineté,* 6 Aug. 1889, in Scrapbook for France, BBHC.

43. *Truth* (no city), 23 May 1887, AOS; *New York Times,* 23 June 1889.

44. *Republique Illustrée,* 10 Aug. 1889, *New York Herald,* 28 Apr. 1889, *Rosier de Marie,* 17 Aug. 1889, *Moniteur de L'Armée,* 6 Sept. 1889, *La France Militaire,* 25 Aug. 1889, *Petit Courrier Angers,* 12 Oct. 1889, and *Le Petit Parisien,* 22 Aug. 1889, all in Scrapbook for France, BBHC; Billington, *Land of Savagery,* 29, 46; Hassrick, "The Artists," 25.

45. *New York Herald,* 10 Aug. 1889, *L'Observateur Français,* 7 Oct. 1889, and *L'Autorite,* 1 Oct. 1889, all in Scrapbook for France, BBHC.

46. *Galignani's Messenger* (Paris), 23 Oct. 1889, in Scrapbook for France, BBHC.

47. Paret, *Makers,* 260; David L. Chapman, *Sandow,* 2–4; Bloom-Wilson, "Exporting America," 12; unidentified clipping about the Boston Rifle Team, *L'Union Nationale,* 7 Sept. 1889, and *La Louveraineté,* 6 Aug. 1889, all in Scrapbook for France, BBHC.

48. *Le Gil Blas,* 22 Aug. 1889, in Scrapbook for France, BBHC; *New York Times,* 23 June 1889.

49. *Republique Française* (Paris), 14 Oct. 1889, and *London Star,* 5 Mar. 1890, both in Scrapbook for France, BBHC. The lamp's cost in current dollars would be about $27,400.

50. *Galignani's Messenger* (Paris), 23 Oct. 1889, in Scrapbook for France, BBHC; "Route, 1889–1891," WFCC, AHC; Strout, *American Image,* 28; Elson, *Guardians,* 147, 150–56; Burke, *"Buffalo Bill,"* 238; *New York Times,* 22 Dec. 1889 and 18 May 1890; *Galignani's Messenger* (Paris), 4 Mar. 1890, Scrapbook for Italy, BBHC; *BBWW* (1893 program), 58–59, DPL; Walsh, *Making of Buffalo Bill,* 277–78.

51. Walsh, *Making of Buffalo Bill,* 278; *New York Times,* 18 May 1890; *Diario de Barcelona,* 22 Dec. 1889, and *New York Clipper,* 18 Jan. 1890, both in AOS; *Berliner Tageblatt* (Berlin), 26 July 1890 and 27 July 1890, Scrapbook for Germany, BBHC; Moses, *Wild West Shows,* 87.

52. "Route, 1889–1891," WFCC, AHC; Strout, *American Image,* 110, 134–37; Dulles, *Americans Abroad,* 80–82; Higham, *Strangers,* 24, 65–66, 74.

53. Seton-Watson, *Italy; New York Herald* (Paris ed.), 16 Mar. 1890, *Garro di Tespi* (Rome), 16 Feb. 1890, *La Riforma* (Rome), 20 Feb. 1890, and *Il Corrierre Italiano* (Florence), 14 Mar. 1890 and 18 Mar. 1890, all in Scrapbook for Italy, BBHC.

54. *La Tribuna* (Rome), 20 Feb. 1890 and 21 Feb. 1890, *Galignani's Messenger* (Paris), 17 Mar. 1890 and 27 Mar. 1890, *Il Secolo Illustrado* (Milan), 9 Mar. 1890, *La Riforma* (Rome), 20 Feb. 1890, *Il Messaggero* (Rome), 20 Feb. 1890 and 7 Mar. 1890, *L'Opinione* (Rome), 21 Feb. 1890, *La Voce della Verita* (Rome), 21 Feb. 1890, *L'Opinione Nazionale* (Florence), 14 Mar. 1890, *Roman Herald,* 1 Mar. 1890, *Capitan Fracassa* (Rome), 21 Feb. 1890, *Il Diritto* (Rome), 27 Feb. 1890, *Il Corriere Italiano* (Florence), 14 Mar. 1890, *La Nazione* (Florence), 13 Mar. 1890, and *Gazzetta Dell' Emilia* (Bologna), 30 Mar. 1890, all in Scrapbook for Italy, BBHC; *New York Times,* 18 May 1890.

55. *Il Messaggero* (Rome), 7 Mar. 1890, *La Nazione* (Florence), 16 Mar. 1890, clipping identified as "New-York paper," *La Riforma* (Rome), 20 Feb. 1890, *Galignani's Messenger* (Paris), 27 Mar. 1890, and *Il Vero Monello* (Florence), 9 Mar. 1890, all in Scrapbook for Italy, BBHC; *Denver Republican,* 7 Apr. 1890, CPS.

56. *La Tribuna* (Rome), 20 Feb. 1890, *La Riforma* (Rome), 20 Feb. 1890, *New York Herald* (Paris ed.), 11 Mar. 1890, and *Galignani's Messenger* (Paris), Mar. 1890, all in Scrapbook for Italy, BBHC.

57. *Roman Herald,* 1 Mar. 1890, *New York World,* 5 Mar. 1890, *Galignani's Messenger* (Paris), 4 Mar. 1890, *Rome-Carro di Terpi,* 22 Feb. 1890 and 23 Feb. 1890, *New York Herald,* 5 Mar. 1890, *La Tribuna* (Rome), 25 Feb. 1890, *New York Herald* (Paris ed.), n.d., and *Sportsman's Journal,* 15 Mar. 1890, all in Scrapbook for Italy, BBHC. For the gondola tour, see Walsh, *Making of Buffalo Bill,* photo following page 278. Wilson, "Visual Images," 9; Burke, *"Buffalo Bill,"* 260–62; *BBWW* (1893 program), 33–35, 62–63, DPL; *New York Times,* 18 May 1890.

58. *Roman Herald,* 1 Mar. 1890, *New York Herald* (Paris ed.), 3 Mar. 1890, 4 Mar. 1890, and 5 Mar. 1890, *Pall Mall Gazette* (London), Mar. 1890, *Galignani's Messenger* (Paris), 4 Mar. 1890, *Sportsman's Journal,* 15 Mar. 1890, and *La American Register* (Paris), 15 Mar. 1890, all in Scrapbook for Italy, BBHC.

59. *Il Messaggero* (Rome), 26 Feb. 1890, *Roman Herald,* 1 Mar. 1890, *La Voce della Verita* (Rome), 28 Feb. 1890, and *La American Register* (Paris), 15 Mar. 1890, all in Scrapbook for Italy, BBHC; Rosa and May, *Buffalo Bill,* 217; Yost, *Buffalo Bill,* 10.

60. *L'Opinione* (Rome), 21 Feb. 1890, *La Nazione* (Florence), 16 Mar. 1890, and *Galignani's Messenger* (Paris), 17 Mar. 1890 and 27 Mar. 1890, all in Scrapbook for Italy, BBHC.

61. Walsh, *Making of Buffalo Bill,* 278; *Galignani's Messenger* (Paris), 4 Mar. 1890, in Scrapbook for Italy, BBHC; *New York Times,* 18 May 1890.

62. Walsh, *Making of Buffalo Bill,* 278; *Galignani's Messenger* (Paris), 4 Mar. 1890, in Scrapbook for Italy, BBHC; *New York Times,* 18 May 1890. Cody's remark may refer to Spanish currency, because at the time he was discussing the poor in both Italy and Spain.

63. *La Tribuna* (Rome), 20 Feb. 1890, *Corriere della Sera* (Milan), 2 Apr. 1890 and 3 Apr. 1890, and *La Riforma* (Rome), 20 Feb. 1890, all in Scrapbook for Italy, BBHC; *Arena* (Verona), 14 Apr. 1890, CPS; *New York Times,* 18 May 1890.

64. *New York Herald* (Paris ed.), 16 Mar. 1890, and *Galignani's Messenger* (Paris), 17 Mar. 1890, both in Scrapbook for Italy, BBHC.

65. Item identified as "Clipping from U.S.A.," *New York Clipper,* 1 Mar. 1890, and *Galignani's Messenger* (Paris), 17 Mar. 1890, all in Scrapbook for Italy, BBHC.

66. *Capitan Fracassa* (Rome), 21 Feb. 1890, *La Tribuna* (Rome), 21 Feb. 1890, article identified as "Don Chisciotte della Mancia" (Rome), 21 Feb. 1890, *La Voce della Verita* (Rome), 21 Feb. 1890, *La American Register* (Paris), 15 Mar. 1890, *Galignani's Messenger* (Paris), 17 Mar. 1890, *La Nazione* (Florence), 7 Mar. 1890, and *Il Vero Monello* (Florence), 16 Mar. 1890, all in Scrapbook for Italy, BBHC.

67. *Arena* (Verona), 14 Apr. 1890, CPS.

68. *L'Italia* (Milan), 4 Apr. 1890 and 5 Apr. 1890, CPS.

69. *Truth* (no city), 27 Mar. 1890, article in English marked "Unknown," *Capitan Fracasse* (Rome), 1 Mar. 1890, *Il Secolo* (Milan), 5 Mar. 1890 and 6 Mar. 1890, *Il Messaggero* (Rome), 7 Mar. 1890, *New York Herald* (Paris ed.), 5 Mar. 1890, 6 Mar. 1890, and 11 Mar. 1890, and *Galignani's Messenger* (Paris), 17 Mar. 1890, all in Scrapbook for Italy, BBHC.

70. *Truth* (no city), 27 Mar. 1890, article in English marked "Unknown," *New York Herald,* 5 Mar. 1890, *La Lotta* (Florence), 12 Mar. 1890, *La Capitale* (Rome), 5 Mar. 1890 and 6 Mar. 1890, and *Galignani's Messenger* (Paris), 17 Mar. 1890, all in Scrapbook for Italy, BBHC. *New York Times,* 18 May 1890; *New York Sun,* 31 Mar. 1890, CPS.

71. *Truth* (no city), 27 Mar. 1890, *La Lotta* (Florence), 12 Mar. 1890, *New York World,* 10 Mar. 1890, and article in English marked "Unknown," all in Scrapbook for Italy, BBHC; *BBWW* (1893 program), 29–30, DPL.

72. *Il Messaggero* (Rome), 8 Mar. 1890, in Scrapbook for Italy, BBHC; *Abbonamonto Postale* (Milan), 6 Apr. 1890, CPS.

73. "Route, 1889–1891," WFCC, AHC; *Strassburger Stadtnachrichten* (Strasbourg), 24 Oct. 1890, and *Wiener Tagesblatt* (Vienna), 29 May 1890, both in Scrapbook for Germany, BBHC. The route book also contains the gross receipts for all cities visited from 1889 to 1891.

74. *Tagesblatt und Anzeiger* (Leipzig), 26 June 1890, Scrapbook for Germany, BBHC; Higham, *Strangers,* 9–11, 15, 25; Strout, *American Image,* 141; Elson, *Guardians,* 143–46; Hughes, *Consciousness and Society,* 43.

75. *Morgenblatt* (Dresden), 31 May 1890, and *Volks Zeitung* (Vienna), 8 May 1890, both in CPS; Billington, *Land of Savagery,* 30, 34–35, 45–57; Hughes, *Consciousness and Society,* 34–35, 43; Stackelberg, *Idealism Debased,* 19, 25–26, 37, 85, 144.

76. *Volks Zeitung* (Vienna), 8 May 1890, *Muenchener Neuste Nachrichten* (Munich), 19 Apr. 1890, *Morgenblatt* (Dresden), 31 May 1890, and *Neues Tagesblatt* (Dresden), 28 May 1890, all in CPS; *Dresdener Journal* (Dresden), 7 June 1890, Scrapbook for Germany, BBHC.

77. *Nachrichten* (Dresden), 1 June 1890, and *Journal* (Dresden), 31 May 1890, both in CPS; *Leipziger Tagesblatt und Anzeiger* (Leipzig), 17 June 1890, and *Hamburger Nachrichten* (Hamburg), 25 Aug. 1890, both in Scrapbook for Germany, BBHC; Paret, *Makers,* 254–58; Walsh, *Making of Buffalo Bill,* 293–94.

78. *Nekarbote* (Cannstatt), 15 Oct. 1890, *Württembergische Landeszeitung* (Stuttgart), 16 Oct. 1890, *Berliner Tagesblatt* (Berlin), 23 July 1890, *Kleine Presse* (Frankfurt), 7 Oct.

1890 and 9 Oct. 1890, *Anzeiger* (Dresden), 31 May 1890, *Tagesblatt* (Dresden), 11 June 1890, *Hamburger Nachrichten* (Hamburg), 25 Aug. 1890 and 5 Sept. 1890, unidentified clipping (probably from Berlin), 23 July 1890, and *Staatsbürger Zeitung* (Berlin), 1 Aug. 1890, all in Scrapbook for Germany, BBHC; *Journal* (Dresden), 3 June 1890, *Stadt Anzeiger* (Brauschürg), 17 July 1890, *Galignani's Messenger* (Paris), 29 Apr. 1890, *Neue Freie Presse* (Vienna), 8 May 1890, *Nachrichten* (Dresden), 2 June 1890, *Muenchener Tagesblatt* (Munich), 21 Apr. 1890, *Muenchener Neuste Nachrichten* (Munich), 21 Apr. 1890, and *Nachrichten* (Munich), 30 Apr. 1890, all in CPS; wages computed from "Yearly Income" table in Balfour, *Kaiser,* 441.

79. *Deutsche Volkszeitung* (Hanover), 5 July 1890, *Germania* (Berlin), 25 July 1890, unidentified clipping (probably from Dresden), n.d., *Berliner Zeitung Presse* (Berlin), 24 July 1890, and *Wiener Tagesblatt* (Vienna), 29 May 1890, all in Scrapbook for Germany, BBHC; *Neue Freie Presse* (Vienna), 8 May 1890, CPS.

80. *Tagesblatt und Anzeiger* (Leipzig), 26 June 1890, *Neuste Nachrichten* (Hanover), 2 July 1890, and *Tagesblatt und Anzeiger* (Leipzig), 26 June 1890, all in Scrapbook for Germany, BBHC; *Muenchener Neuste Nachrichten* (Munich), 19 Apr. 1890, and *Neues Tagesblatt* (Dresden), 28 May 1890, both in CPS.

81. *Dresdener Journal* (Dresden), 7 June 1890, and unidentified clipping (probably from Berlin), 23 July 1890, both in Scrapbook for Germany, BBHC; *Neues Tagesblatt* (Dresden), 28 May 1890, CPS.

82. *Continental* (Dresden), 31 May 1890, CPS; unidentified clipping (probably from Dresden), n.d., *Anzeiger* (Dresden), 8 June 1890, *Stadt Anzeiger* (Brauschürg), 17 July 1890, and unidentified clipping (probably from Berlin), 23 July 1890, all in Scrapbook for Germany, BBHC.

83. *General Anzeiger* (Leipzig), 22 June 1890, *Illustrierte Zeitung* (Leipzig), 12 July 1890, *Tagesblatt* (Branschweig), 17 July 1890, *Das Kleine Journal* (Berlin), 23 July 1890, *Berliner Börsen Courier* (Berlin), 23 July 1890, *Staatsbürger Zeitung* (Berlin), 26 July 1890, *Dresdener Journal* (Dresden), 7 June 1890, and *Berliner Zeitung Presse* (Berlin), 24 July 1890, all in Scrapbook for Germany, BBHC; *Muenchener Tagesblatt* (Munich), 21 Apr. 1890, *Neues Tagesblatt* (Dresden), 28 May 1890, and *Wiener Tagesblatt* (Vienna), 11 May 1890, all in CPS.

84. *Berliner Tagesblatt* (Berlin), 27 July 1890, Scrapbook for Germany, BBHC; *Nachrichten* (Munich), 3 May 1890, CPS.

85. *Tagesblatt* (Munich), 29 Apr. 1890, *Fremdenblatt* (Munich), 30 Apr. 1890, and *Nachrichten* (Munich), 5 May 1890, all in CPS. *Frankfurter Zeitung* (Frankfurt), 30 Sept. 1890, and *Nachrichten* (Frankfurt), 9 Oct. 1890, both in Scrapbook for Germany, BBHC; Moses, *Wild West Shows,* 95.

86. *Landeszeitung* (Branschweig), 19 July 1890, *Unterhaltungsblatt* (Branschweig), 19 July 1890, and *Staatsbürger Zeitung* (Berlin), 26 July 1890, all in Scrapbook for Germany, BBHC; Walsh, *Making of Buffalo Bill,* 280; Moses, *Wild West Shows,* 94–98.

87. Prucha, "Thomas Jefferson Morgan," 193–203; Morgan, "Wild West Shows," 309–12; Moses, *Wild West Shows,* 93, 98.

88. "Improved by Travel" (reprint of telegram from Jno. Robinson, missionary, Pine Ridge Agency), 30 July 1888, "The Sioux and Wild West Shows" (contains reprint of *New York Sun* editorial, n.d.), "Explicit Denial of the Various Charges Made against 'Buffalo Bill,'" (reprint of article from *Herald's* European edition, 24 July 1890), and "Buffalo Bill's Indians Examined Officially" (reprint from *Lincoln Journal,* 3 Dec. [1890]), all in *BBWW* (1893 program), 33, 35–36, 49–50, DPL; Cody to Mike (M. R. Russell), 27 Dec. 1899, BBHC; Moses, *Wild West Shows,* 64, 101, 103–4.

89. *Anzeiger und Tagesblatt* (Freiberg), 1 June 1890, Scrapbook for Germany, BBHC; Mooney, *Ghost-Dance Religion,* v–viii; Utley, *Last Days,* 69, 98.

90. General Nelson A. Miles to Col. Cody, 24 Nov. 1890, BBHC; Utley, *Last Days,* 124; Walsh, *Making of Buffalo Bill,* 287; *BBWW* (1893 program), 50–53, 61–62, DPL.

91. Utley, *Last Days,* 5, 146–66, 200–230; Vestal, *Sitting Bull,* 300–301.

92. For different views of the Sitting Bull incident, see Russell, *Lives and Legends,* 354–69, and Wilson, "Exporting America," 13. "'Buffalo Bill' Victorious" (editorial from *New York Sun,* 10 Mar. [1891]), *BBWW* (1893 program), 34, 61–62, DPL; *New York Times,* 7 Mar. 1892 and 19 Mar. 1892; Walsh, *Making of Buffalo Bill,* 291–92; Moses, *Wild West Shows,* 109–11.

93. Salsbury, "Origin," 205–6; Walsh, *Making of Buffalo Bill,* 293; Deahl, "History," 89–90.

94. "Route, 1889–1891," WFCC, AHC; Deahl, "History," 90.

95. *New York Times,* 26 June 1892; Walsh, *Making of Buffalo Bill,* 295, 297; Remington, "Buffalo Bill," 847.

96. Burg, *Chicago's White City,* xiii, 336; Garland, *Son of the Middle Border,* 458; Muccigrosso, *Celebrating,* 80.

97. Burg, *Chicago's White City,* 112–13, 195–97.

98. Ibid., 216, 218–19, 221–24; Muccigrosso, *Celebrating,* 165–67. The "sliding scale" quote comes from Rydell, *All the World's a Fair,* 65; Rydell is quoting Denton J. Snider, *World's Fair Studies* (Chicago: Sigma, 1895), 237.

99. *Kate Field's Washington,* 19 July 1893, vol. 3, NSS; *Chicago Sunday Democrat,* 2 July 1893, *Chicago Daily News,* 27 May 1893, *Chicago Post,* 6 Aug. 1893, *Chicago Globe,* 18 June 1893, *Chicago Herald,* 1 Nov. 1893 and 5 Nov. 1893, and *Chicago Mail,* 21 Oct. 1893, all in vol. 2, NSS; Fellows and Freeman, *This Way,* 74.

100. *Chicago Times,* 28 July 1893 and 30 July 1893, *Times* (no city), 23 Apr. 1893, *Chicago Dispatch,* 5 Aug. 1893, *New York Rider and Driver,* n.d., *Chicago News,* 12 May 1893, *Chicago Post,* 17 Aug. 1893, and *Daily Globe* (no city), Apr. 29, 1893, all in vol. 2, NSS; *Kansas City Star,* 15 Mar. 1893, vol. 3, NSS; "Ghost-Dancers in the West," *BBWW* (1983 program), 38, DPL; Leavitt, *Fifty Years,* 141; *Chicago Times,* 27 Apr. 1893, AOS; *New York Times,* 19 Mar. 1892; Walsh, *Making of Buffalo Bill,* 299. Debate abounds over who brought the original Sitting Bull cabin to the fair and where it was located. "Actual relics" of Wounded Knee appeared at several sites. See Walsh, *Making of Buffalo Bill,* 299; Moses, *Wild West Shows,* 139; Utley, *Lance,* 312; and Rydell, *All the World's a Fair,* 95.

101. *BBWW* (1893 program), 2, 4, 51, 54–55, DPL; *Dispatch* (no city), 4 Apr. 1893, vol. 2, NSS; *New York Times,* 17 Feb. 1893.

102. *Kate Field's Washington,* 19 July 1893, vol. 3, NSS; *Chicago Dispatch,* 4 Apr. 1893, vol. 2, NSS; *BBWW* (1893 program), 51, DPL; Rennert, *One Hundred Posters,* 15, 106.

103. *Chicago Inter Ocean,* 8 May 1893, *Chicago Herald,* 15 May 1893, and *Chicago Daily News,* 24 June 1893, all in vol. 2, NSS.

104. Burg, *Chicago's White City,* 257–58; Wrobel, *End of American Exceptionalism,* 36.

105. For the suggestion that Buffalo Bill and Frederick Jackson Turner delivered the same message, see Wish, *American Historian,* 188, and Nachbar, introduction, 7. *Chicago Inter Ocean,* 11 June 1893, and *Chicago Dispatch,* 5 Aug. 1893, both in vol. 22, NSS; banner in *BBWW* (1893 courier), DPL.

106. Cody, *Story of the Wild West,* v–vi; Burke, *"Buffalo Bill,"* 250–51; *BBWW* (1893 program), 61, DPL.

107. *Chicago Inter Ocean,* 11 June 1893, and *Chicago Evening Journal,* 2 Sept. 1893, both in vol. 2, NSS; *BBWW* (1888 program), 7, DPL; *BBWW* (1893 courier), DPL; *BBWW* (1893 program), 62–64, DPL; Cody, *Story of the Wild West,* 17, 756–57; Burke, *"Buffalo Bill,"* 260–61.

108. *London Era,* 23 Apr. 1887, JBS; *Chicago Globe,* 28 June 1893, vol. 2, NSS; *BBWW* (1893 program), 4, 5, 25, 35, 45–47, DPL; Roderick Nash, *Wilderness,* 141–60; Burke, *"Buffalo Bill,"* 17–18, 49–50, 159–60; Cody, *Story of the Wild West,* 308–9.

109. *BBWW* (1893 program), 11, DPL; *Chicago News,* 5 May 1893, vol. 2, NSS; Burke, *"Buffalo Bill,"* 12, 17.

110. *Chicago Herald,* 8 July 1893, vol. 2, NSS.

## Chapter 5: "Resplendent Realism of Glorious War"

1. *Marshalltown (Iowa) Times-Republican,* 22 Sept. 1899, vol. 8, NSS; "Resplendent Realism of Glorious War," in *BBWW* (1899 program), DPL.

2. *New York Sunday Telegraph,* 26 Mar. 1899, and *Wilkes-Barre (Pa.) Record,* 20 May 1899, both in vol. 8, NSS; *BBWW* (1899 program), 33–34, 36, DPL.

3. *Baltimore Sun,* 18 Apr. 1899, *New York Sunday Telegraph,* 26 Mar. 1899, and *New York Times,* 30 Mar. 1899, all in vol. 8, NSS.

4. *BBWW* (1899 program), 32; *Syracuse Post-Standard,* 17 July 1899, vol. 8, NSS; *Lancaster Examiner and Express,* 23 June 1898, *Wheeling Intelligencer,* 5 July 1898, and *New York Daily News,* 3 Apr. 1898, all in vol. 7, NSS; *Providence Journal,* 1 June 1897, vol. 6, NSS.

5. *New York Evening Telegram,* 24 Apr. 1900, vol. 9, NSS; *New York Sunday Telegraph,* 26 Mar. 1899, *Boston Journal,* 15 June 1899, *New York Times,* 26 Mar. 1899 and 30 Mar. 1899, *Syracuse Post-Standard,* 17 July 1899, and *New York Commercial Advertiser,* 23 Mar. 1899, all in vol. 8, NSS; *Route-Book,* 42, DPL. Sell and Weybright reproduced this route book, see 238.

6. *New York Morning Telegraph,* 7 Apr. 1899, and *Chicago Record,* 24 Aug. 1899, both in vol. 8, NSS.

7. Wisan, "The Cuban Crisis," 43–54; *New York Press,* 22 July 1894, vol. 4, NSS; *Philadelphia Evening Herald,* 4 May 1898, vol. 7, NSS; Jacobs, *Rise of the American Film,* 11, 14.

8. *Albany Argus,* 15 June 1898, *New York World,* 30 Mar. 1898, *Brooklyn Citizen,* 27 Apr. 1898, and *Philadelphia Call,* 2 May 1898, all in vol. 7, NSS; *BBWW* (1898 program), v, DPL; Rennert, *One Hundred Posters,* 90–91.

9. Cody to George T. Beck, 4 June 1898, GTBP; Cody to Kerngood, 3 Aug. 1898, GC, BBHC; *Buffalo Bill Bids You Good Bye,* BBHC; *Kansas City Star,* 22 Sept. 1898, *Minneapolis Tribune,* 8 Aug. 1898, and *Brooklyn Daily Times,* 27 Apr. 1898, all in vol. 7, NSS.

10. "Buffalo Bill and the Bullfighters," *BBWW* (1899 program), 27–28, DPL.

11. *New York Journal,* 10 May 1894, vol. 4, NSS; *Steubenville Gazette,* 18 July 1896, vol. 5, NSS; *Brooklyn Daily Eagle,* 11 Apr. 1897 and 13 Apr. 1897, vol. 6, NSS; *Wilkes-Barre Record,* 20 May 1899, and *Louisville Evening Post,* 3 May 1899, both in vol. 8, NSS; *Baltimore Sun,* 23 Apr. 1901, vol. 10, NSS; *BBWW* (1898 courier), 7, DPL.

12. *New York Times,* 2 May 1894 and 6 May 1894; *The Argus,* n.d., AOS; *Utica Observer,* 13 June 1901, vol. 10, NSS.

13. *New York Mail and Express,* 28 Apr. 1897, and *New York Daily Tribune,* 3 May 1897, both in vol. 6, NSS.

14. *BBWW* (1899 program), 63, DPL; *Syracuse Post-Standard,* 17 July 1899, *Syracuse Journal,* 17 July 1899, *New York Evening Telegram,* 28 Mar. 1898 and 30 Mar. 1898, all in vol. 8, NSS; *World,* 27 May 1894, vol. 4, NSS; *Albany Evening Journal,* 14 June 1898, vol. 7, NSS; *BBWW* (1897 program), 3, DPL; *Buffalo Bill Bids You Good Bye,* BBHC.

15. *BBWW* (1894 program), 2–3, DPL; *Rough Rider,* 3, DPL; *New York World,* 13 May 1894, and *New York Recorder,* 6 Apr. 1894, both in vol. 4, NSS; for poster art, see Rennert, *One Hundred Posters,* 8, 11, 13, 41, 43, 69, 83, 86.

16. *New York Recorder,* 13 May 1894, vol. 4, NSS; *First Appearance,* DPL; *Brooklyn Eagle,* 16 June 1894, and *Harper's Young People,* 26 June 1894, both in vol. 4, NSS; *Bay City Times-Press,* 31 July 1896, vol. 5, NSS. The term *nationalist nineties* is from Higham, *Strangers,* 68–105.

17. *BBWW* (1907 courier), 9, DPL; *Lansing State Republican,* 8 July 1901, vol. 10, NSS; *Holyoke Daily Transcript,* 29 June 1899, vol. 8, NSS; *Morning Journal* (no city), 20 May 1894, vol. 4, NSS; Wrobel, *End of American Exceptionalism,* 54, 88.

18. *BBWW* (1901 program), 60–61, DPL; *New York Telegraph,* 3 Apr. 1901, vol. 10, NSS; *Route-Book,* 21–23, DPL; *New York Sun,* 13 May 1894, vol. 4, NSS; *Marshalltown (Iowa) Times-Republican,* 22 Sept. 1899, vol. 8, NSS; *New York Times,* 6 May 1894 and 10 May 1894.

19. *First Appearance,* DPL.

20. Etulain, "Origins," 58; Wrobel, *End of American Exceptionalism,* 53–68.

21. Wrobel, *End of American Exceptionalism,* 53–68; *Trenton Evening News,* 16 May 1898, vol. 7, NSS.

22. Wrobel, *End of American Exceptionalism,* chaps. 3–5.

23. *Grand Island (Neb.) Daily Independent,* 2 Sept. 1898, vol. 7, NSS.

24. *Cincinnati Enquirer,* 5 May 1901, vol. 10, NSS. The term *New Manifest Destiny* is from DeSantis, *Shaping of Modern America,* 121.

25. *Topeka State Journal,* 19 Sept. 1898, vol. 7, NSS.

26. *Marietta (Ohio) Daily Register,* 19 July 1900, vol. 9, NSS; *Topeka State Journal,* 19 Sept. 1898, vol. 7, NSS; *Louisville Evening Post,* 3 May 1899, vol. 8, NSS; Cody to Beck, 17 Aug. 1896, GTBP; Cody to A. A. Anderson, 26 Mar. 1903, GC, BBHC. For the politics of expansionism, see Merk, *Manifest Destiny,* 241, and Wrobel, *End of American Exceptionalism,* 64.

27. *Philadelphia Evening Bulletin,* 3 May 1898, vol. 7, NSS; *Dayton Daily News,* 10 May 1899, vol. 8, NSS; *New York Mail and Express,* 24 Apr. 1900, and *New York Commercial Advertiser,* 28 Apr. 1900, vol. 9, NSS.

28. Burke, *"Buffalo Bill,"* vii.

29. Ibid., 85–98. *Chicago Inter Ocean,* 7 Sept. 1897, vol. 6, NSS; *New York Mail and Express,* 9 Apr. 1898, vol. 7, NSS; *Lima (Ohio) Times-Democrat,* 3 Aug. 1899, and *Muncie Times,* 4 Aug. 1899, both in vol. 8, NSS. For discussions of the mythology about Little Bighorn, see Slotkin, *Fatal Environment,* 3–12, and White, "Frederick Jackson Turner," 27, 29, 32, 34–43, 45.

30. Rennert, *One Hundred Posters,* 9, 15, 64, 104–5.

31. Pringle, *Roosevelt,* 129, 257; *Chicago Record,* 22 Aug. 1899, vol. 8, NSS; *New York Herald,* 24 Apr. 1900, vol. 9, NSS.

32. Wrobel, *End of American Exceptionalism,* 66; White, "Frederick Jackson Turner," 50.

33. Pringle, *Theodore Roosevelt,* 130; *BBWW* (1899 program), 32–33, 36, DPL; *New York Press,* 15 Apr. 1899, vol. 8, NSS.

34. *Keokuk (Iowa) Evening Press,* 19 Aug. 1898, vol. 7, NSS; *Philadelphia Evening Bulletin,* 29 May 1899, vol. 8, NSS.

35. *Evening Press,* 19 Aug. 1898, vol. 7, NSS; *Philadelphia Press,* 16 May 1900, and *Hartford Daily Courant,* 26 June 1900, both in vol. 9, NSS; *New York Evening Sun,* 30 Mar. 1899, *St. Cloud Journal-Press,* 11 Sept. 1899, and *Rochester Post Express,* 21 July 1899, all in vol. 8, NSS.

36. Cherny, *Righteous Cause,* 80–81; Higham, *Strangers,* 106–30; Curti, *Roots,* 212–17.

37. *BBWW* (1899 program), DPL; *Dayton Daily News,* 10 May 1899, vol. 8, NSS.

38. *New York Press,* 3 Apr. 1901, vol. 10, NSS.

39. Elson, *Guardians,* 161–65; Higham, *Strangers,* 18, 25, 31, 167, 170.

40. *New York Journal,* 3 Apr. 1901, and *New York Telegraph,* 3 Apr. 1901, both in vol. 10, NSS; *BBWW* (1901 program), DPL.

41. *New York Press,* 4 Apr. 1901, *New York Telegraph,* 3 Apr. 1901, and *New York Evening Sun,* 3 Apr. 1901, all in vol. 10, NSS.

42. *St. Paul Globe,* 10 Aug. 1898, vol. 7, NSS; *New York Press,* 3 Apr. 1901 and 5 Apr. 1901, and *New York Daily Tribune,* 3 Apr. 1901, all in vol. 10, NSS; Pringle, *Roosevelt,* 206; for imperialists and anti-imperialists, see Merk, *Manifest Destiny,* 228–60.

43. "The Wave of Progress at the Foothills of the Rockies," *Historical Sketches and Programme* (1903), DPL; *BBWW* (1907 or 1908 program), DPL.

44. Rennert, *One Hundred Posters,* 9 and foldout between pages 56 and 57. Henry Nash Smith (*Virgin Land,* 9) cites the line of poetry as from "Verses on the Prospect of Planting Arts and Learning in America," *The Works of George Berkeley, D.D.,* ed. Alexander C. Fraser, 4 vols. (1901), 4:364. Merk (*Manifest Destiny* 256–57) says Americans resisted linking Manifest Destiny and imperialism. Perhaps that sentiment moved the entertainers to take such extraordinary measures to link the two concepts.

45. Wrobel, *End of American Exceptionalism,* 43–44; *Plymouth Mercury* (England), 30 July 1903, vol. 10, NSS; *Cleveland Press,* 20 July 1896, vol. 5, NSS; "Buffalo Bill, His Time, and His Town," Lucille Nichols Patrick Papers, AHC. For typical letters, see Cody to Frank, 21 Dec. 1895, Cody to Mike (M. R. Russell), 27 Dec. 1899, and 14 Mar. 1901, and Cody to Sister Julia, 12 Mar. 1903, all in GC, BBHC.

46. Cody to Beck, 2 July 1895, 17 June 1897, GTBP; *Ideal Western Lands,* 1–8, WFCC, AHC.

47. *BBWW* (1897 program), 14, DPL; *Harrisburg (Pa.) Daily Telegraph,* 6 Aug. 1897, vol. 6, NSS; *Toledo Times,* 1 July 1901, and *Sioux City Daily Tribune,* 5 Aug. 1901, both in vol. 10, NSS; William F. Cody, "The Big Horn Basin: An American Eden," *Success* (June 1900): 212, vol. 9, NSS; *Ideal Western Lands,* 11, WFCC, AHC.

48. *Worchester Daily Telegram,* 3 June 1900, vol. 9, NSS; see also Henry Nash Smith, *Virgin Land,* and Wrobel, *End of American Exceptionalism.* The themes of the myth of the garden and the Wild West run throughout these books. For a different view, see Fees, "In Defense," 141–49.

49. Cody to Beck, 29 Mar. 1895, 5 May 1895, 7 May 1895, 9 May 1895, 27 July 1895, 15 Sept. 1895, 16 Sept. 1895, 25 Sept. 1895, 29 Sept. 1895, 31 Oct. 1895, 26 Mar. 1896, 3 Apr. 1896, 9 Apr. 1896, 28 Apr. 1896, 13 May 1896, 17 May 1896, 25 May 1896, 5 July 1896, 14 July 1896, 17 Aug. 1896, 31 Aug. 1896, 18 Sept. 1896, 7 Oct. 1896, 20 July 1898, and 10 Mar. 1899, all in GTBP.

50. Cody to Beck, 14 June 1895, 6 Sept. 1899, and 2 Aug. 1902, all in GTBP; "Body of Cody to Lie in State in Denver Capitol" (no city), n.d., box 1, Memorial Museum Clippings, Chicago Paper, AHC; "Buffalo Bill, His Time, and His Town," Lucille Nichols Patrick Papers, AHC; *Baltimore News,* 23 Apr. 1901, vol. 10, NSS; Cody to C. L. Hinckle, 15 Apr. 1901, 27 Apr. 1901, and 17 May 1901, GC, BBHC; design of the military college on letterhead of Cody to Mike (M. R. Russell), 3 Feb. 1902, GC, BBHC; *BBWW* (1909 courier), BBHC.

51. *Buffalo Bill's TE Ranch,* 2, DPL (see also the letterhead on Cody to Laraue, 7 Dec. 1916, BBHC); *BBWW* (1909 courier), 29, BBHC; Cody to C. L. Hinckle, 17 May 1901, 4 June 1901, and 2 July 1904, Cody to E. E. Arbuckle, 16 June 1916, Cody to Elwell, 31 Aug. 1908, and Cody to Sister Julia, 19 Mar. 1903, 19 July 1903, and 12 Apr. 1903, all in GC, BBHC; *Kokomo (Ind.) Daily Dispatch,* 2 July 1894, vol. 5, NSS; Cody to Bell, 13 Mar. 1909, box 1, DPL; *BBWW* (1901 program), DPL. For more on Cody's divorce, see letters, clippings, and documents in the Hon. Richard H. Scott Collection, AHC.

52. There is a voluminous body of literature on the uncertainty of Americans in the 1890s. The following offer representative interpretations: Commager, *American Mind,* 41–54; Hofstadter, *Age of Reform,* 23–59; Hofstadter, "Manifest Destiny," 173–200; Hays, *Response to Industrialism,* 4–23, 188–93; Wiebe, *Search for Order,* 11–43; Marx, *Machine in the Garden,* 340–65; Roderick Nash, *Wilderness,* 144–45; Schlesinger, *Rise,* xiv; and Wrobel, *End of American Exceptionalism,* 13–26, 27–41. Masterson, "Sounds," 63–64. Masterson cites Remington's remarks as being quoted in *Buffalo Bill's Wild West and Congress of Rough Riders of the World* (1895 program), 48–49, DPL.

53. *Trinidad (Colo.) Chronicle-News,* 10 Sept. 1898, vol. 7, NSS; *Rochester Herald,* 8 July 1900, vol. 9, NSS.

54. *BBWW* (1898 courier), 30, DPL; *Columbus (Ind.) Daily Morning Times,* 16 Apr. 1896, vol. 5, NSS; *St. Paul Globe,* 10 Aug. 1898, vol. 7, NSS.

55. *Manchester Evening News,* 14 Apr. 1903, *Liverpool Journal of Commerce,* 5 May 1903, *Oxford Times,* 27 June 1903, *Birmingham Gazette,* 2 June 1903, and *Portsmouth News,* 10 Aug. 1903, all in vol. 10, NSS.

56. J.M.B., "A Terse Compilation of Frontier History," unidentified Buffalo Bill and Pawnee Bill program, Jacob M. Schwoob Collection, AHC; *New York Sun,* 26 May 1894 and 27 May 1894, and *Brooklyn Eagle,* 16 June 1894, all in vol. 4, NSS; *Hamilton Daily Democrat,* 6 May 1896, vol. 5, NSS.

57. "Introduction," *BBWW* (1907 or 1908 program), DPL; *BBWW* (1907 courier), 12, DPL; *BBWW* (1898 courier), 11–12, DPL; *Manchester Evening Chronicle,* 27 Apr. 1903, vol. 10, NSS; *BBWW* (1909 program), BBHC.

58. *Bristol Press* (England), 16 July 1903, and *Leicester News* (England), 18 Sept. 1903, both in vol. 10, NSS; *BBWW* (1907 program), DPL; *BBWW* (1898 courier), 5, 27, DPL; *Newcastle-on-Tyme Evening Chronicle,* 9 July 1904.

59. *BBWW* (1894 program), 3, DPL; *New York Mail and Express,* 9 Apr. 1898, vol. 7, NSS.

60. *BBWW* (1899 program), 27, DPL; *New York Sun,* 3 Apr. 1898, vol. 7, NSS.

61. *New York Morning Journal,* 12 June 1894, and *New York Recorder,* 22 May 1894, both in vol. 4, NSS; for a discussion of the "cult of motherhood," see Green, *Light of the Home,* 29–58; *Historical Sketches and Programme* (1902), 24, GLC.

62. Rennert, *One Hundred Posters,* 7, 9, 10, 15, 28, foldouts A and B between pages 56 and 57, 58, 62, 85, 100–101.

63. *Transcript* (no city), 14 July 1894, *Burlington Free Press and Times,* 20 July 1895, and *Press* (no city), 20 Apr. 1895, all in AOS; *New York Commercial Advertiser,* 9 June 1894, vol. 4, NSS; *Terre Haute Gazette,* 25 June 1896, vol. 5, NSS; *New York Daily News,* 31 Mar. 1898, vol. 7, NSS; *Philadelphia Evening Bulletin,* 15 May 1900, vol. 9, NSS; *Route-Book,* 8, DPL; *Official Souvenir,* 20, 22, BBHC.

64. *BBWW* (1898 courier), 4, DPL; *Historical Sketches and Programme* (1902), DPL; *BBWW* (1900 program) 4, DPL; *BBWW* (1907 program), DPL; *Boston Post,* 13 June 1899, vol. 8, NSS; *New York World,* 30 Mar. 1898, and *Denver Times,* 7 Sept. 1898, both in vol. 7, NSS; *Historical Sketches and Programme* (1903), DPL; *BBWW* (1898 program), DPL.

65. *Portsmouth Times,* 13 July 1895, *Philadelphia Inquirer,* n.d., *New York Recorder,* n.d., *South Wales Argus,* 16 Jan. 1895, and *Record* (no city), n.d., all in AOS; for Annie Oakley's departure, see Kasper, *Annie Oakley,* 162–69, and Riley, *Life,* 60–61.

66. *Liverpool Post,* 5 May 1903, vol. 10, NSS; *Historical Sketches and Programme* (1903), DPL; *BBWW* (1907 courier), 25, DPL; *L'Independent* (Pau), 27 Sept. 1905; *La Republique* (Brive), 27 Sept. 1905; Rennert, *One Hundred Posters,* 12.

67. *New York Advertiser,* 19 Apr. 1894, and *New York Journal,* 8 June 1894, both in vol. 4, NSS; *Aurora (Ill.) News,* 20 Aug. 1896, vol. 5, NSS.

68. Cody to Beck, 26 Mar. 1895, WFCC, AHC; *Kokomo (Ind.) Daily Dispatch,* 2 July 1896, vol. 5, NSS; *Cortland Evening Standard,* 15 June 1901, vol. 10, NSS; Cody to William A. Bell, 12 Oct. 1902, 5 Jan. 1903, and 28 Mar. 1903, all in box 1, DPL; Griffin, *Four Years,* 16; Fellows and Freeman, *This Way,* 78–79.

69. *Route-Book,* 68, DPL.

70. *Bloomington (Ind.) Bulletin,* 29 May 1896, and *Columbus (Ind.) Evening Republican,* 12 May 1896, both in vol. 5, NSS; *Kansas City Star,* 22 Sept. 1898, and *Omaha Sunday World-Herald,* 28 Aug. 1898, both in vol. 7, NSS; Cody to E. W. Lenders, 10 Sept. 1908, Lenders Papers, AAA, SI.

71. *Parkersburg (W.Va.) Daily Sentinel,* 29 Apr. 1896, *Winona Republican,* 8 Sept. 1896 and 9 Sept. 1896, and *Dixon Sun,* 22 Aug. 1896, all in vol. 5, NSS; *Route-Book,* 25, 33, 38, DPL; *St. Albans (Vt.) Evening Messenger,* 7 June 1897, vol. 6, NSS; *Muncie Times,* 4 Aug. 1899, vol. 8, NSS; *Trinidad (Colo.) Chronicle-News,* 10 Sept. 1898, vol. 7, NSS; for daily schedule and street parades, see *Route-Book,* 20, 23–43, DPL; Cody to Beck, 10 Sept. 1895, and 11 May 1896, GTBP; for travel by rail, see Milt Hinkle, "The Way a Wild West Show Operated," *Frontier Times* (Feb.–Mar. 1909): 22–23, and n.p., William F. Cody file, Jacob M. Schwoob Collection, AHC.

72. *Champaign (Ill.) Daily News,* 1 June 1896, *Chicago Journal,* 2 June 1896, and *Burlington (Iowa) Gazette,* 19 June 1896, all in vol. 5, NSS; *Racine Daily Times,* 7 Aug. 1900, vol. 9, NSS; *Reading Telegram,* 5 June 1901, vol. 10, NSS; Webb, "Buffalo Bill," 16, BBHC; Fellows and Freeman, *This Way to the Big Show,* 84; Hamid, *Circus,* 63–64.

73. *Detroit Evening News,* 12 Aug. 1899, and *Philadelphia Evening Bulletin,* 29 May 1899, both in vol. 8, NSS; *New York Evening Sun,* 3 Apr. 1901, vol. 10, NSS.

74. Wetmore, *Last,* xiii–xiv, 2–3, 65, 99–100, 225–26; *Bradford Argus* (England), 5 Oct. 1903, vol. 10, NSS.

75. *BBWW* (1899 program), 26, DPL.

76. See Wister, *The Virginian,* 360, where the Virginian asks people not to mistake him for a Wild West show cowboy.

77. Ibid., 8, 37, 105, 228, 341–44, 363–64.

78. Rosa and May, *Buffalo Bill,* 161, 166; Wrobel, *End of American Exceptionalism,* 71; *Harrisburg Daily Telegraph,* 6 Aug. 1897, vol. 6, NSS; *Williamsport (Pa.) Gazette and Bulletin,* 18 May 1899, vol. 8, NSS.

79. Blackstone, *Buckskins, Bullets, and Business,* 28; *Welshman* (Carmarthen), 6 May

1904; *Williamsport (Pa.) Gazette and Bulletin,* 18 May 1899, vol. 8, NSS; *Burton Mail* (England), 23 Oct. 1903, vol. 10, NSS; "Buffalo Bill's Wild West—Season 1906," DPL; Cody to Mike (M. R. Russell), 29 Aug. 1904, Cody to Sister Julia, 29 Dec. 1903, 6 Oct. 1903, and 14 June 1905, and Cody to Hinckle, 7 May 1904, all in GC, BBHC; "Buffalo Bill's Wild West, Seasons 1893 to 1905," postcard with route in Leaflets folder, box 5, WFCC, AHC.

80. *Swansea Leader* (Wales), 23 June 1903, *Manchester Guardian,* 14 Apr. 1903, *Birmingham Express,* 9 June 1903, *Liverpool Express,* 22 May 1903, *London Star,* 4 Apr. 1903, and *London Answers,* 9 May 1903, all in vol. 10, NSS; *Historical Sketches and Programme* (1903 program), DPL; Rennert, *One Hundred Posters,* 7, 30; Fellows and Freeman, *This Way,* 143, 148, 152–53; for bill printing and posting, see "Tickets and Paper Report, England, 1903–1904," box 2, WFCC, AHC, as well as "Summary Billposting—1903," "Billposting Summary, 1904," and "Printing Bills, 1904," all in France folder, box 1, WFCC, AHC.

81. *Birkenhead News,* 23 May 1903, *Norwich Mercury,* 22 Aug. 1903, *Manchester Weekly Times,* 10 Apr. 1903, *Liverpool Courier,* 5 May 1903, *Swansea Leader* (Wales), 14 July 1903, *Bristol Times-Mirror,* 21 July 1903 and 22 July 1903, and *Liverpool Journal of Commerce,* 5 May 1903, all in vol. 10, NSS; *Historical Sketches and Programme* (1903 program), DPL; *Staffordshire Sentinel,* 21 Apr. 1904. The 1904 program is detailed in *Welshman* (Carmarthen), 6 May 1904, and *Llandudno Advertiser,* 6 May 1904.

82. *Llandudno Advertiser,* 6 May 1904; *Glasgow Evening Citizen,* 1 Aug. 1904; *Sunderland Daily Echo,* 16 July 1904.

83. *Welshman* (Carmarthen), 6 May 1904; *Llandudno Visitor's Herald,* 30 Apr. 1904.

84. Griffin, *Four Years,* 55, 62–67, 69–73; *New York Herald* (European ed.), 3 Apr. 1905, RSC; *Semaine de Bayonne,* 20 Sept. 1905; *Courrier de Bayone,* 4 Oct. 1905; *La Depeche* (Toulouse), 8 Oct. 1905, 13 Oct. 1905, 14 Oct. 1905, and 16 Oct. 1905; *Memorial des Pyrenees* (Pau), 4 Oct. 1905 and 5 Oct. 1905; *L'Eclaireur* (Nice), 10 Mar. 1906; *L'Eclair* (Montpellier), 25 Oct. 1905; Wetmore, *Le Dernier,* box 1, WFCC, AHC; for figures on advertising, see "Press Reports, France, 1905," "Paper and Ticket Reports, France, 1905," and "Excursion Flyers, France, 1905," all in box 2, WFCC, AHC.

85. Griffin, *Four Years,* 57–61.

86. For material on the program in France, see *BBWW* (1905 program), 2–3, BBHC. Millis, *Martial Spirit,* 136; Bailey, *Diplomatic History,* 466; Hughes, *Consciousness and Society,* 344; *La Depeche* (Toulouse), 8 Oct. 1905; *Semaine de Bayonne,* 20 Sept. 1905, 27 Sept. 1905, and 30 Sept. 1905; *Journal Avenir* (Bayonne), 23 Sept. 1905, 25 Sept. 1905, and 26 Sept. 1905; Griffin, *Four Years,* 55.

87. "Buffalo Bill's Wild West—Season 1906," DPL; *BBWW* (1907 courier), 18–21, DPL; Griffin, *Four Years,* 76.

88. *BBWW* (1907 courier), 20–21, DPL; "Buffalo Bill's Wild West—Season 1906," DPL; Cody to James A. Bailey, 25 Mar. 1906, GC, BBHC.

89. Griffin, *Four Years,* 85; Cody to Elwell, 28 May 1906 and 16 July 1906, GC, BBHC; Deahl, "History," 147–48.

90. Cody to Mr. McCaddon, 25 May 1907, and Cody to Elwell, 1 June 1908, both in GC, BBHC; *BBWW* (1907 program), DPL; *BBWW* (1907 courier), photographs on 3 and 9, DPL.

91. *BBWW* (1907 program), DPL.

92. Ibid.; *BBWW* (1907 courier), 14, 16–17, DPL.

93. Webb, "Buffalo Bill," 4, BBHC; "Football Playing Horses," *BBWW* (1909 program), BBHC; *BBWW* (1907 program), DPL; *BBWW* (1907 courier), 10–11, DPL.

94. *BBWW* (1907 courier), 11, DPL; Rennert, *One Hundred Posters,* 12, 74.

95. *BBWW* (1907 courier), DPL; Jacobs, *Rise of the American Film,* 11–21.

96. Judson, "The Movies," 68–72; Cody to Clarence Buell and wife, undated (library dates it 1908; the letterhead, not the text, is significant), Cody to Elwell, 13 Dec. [1914], and Cody to Jake Schwoob, 23 Dec. 1914, all in GC, BBHC; Moses, *Wild West Shows,* 223–24; Muller, *My Life,* 273–81, 290–91; "Buffalo Bill—in Action," 33–40, and Lee, untitled typewritten ms., 1–2, 5–26, both in William F. Cody file, LC.

97. Russell, *Lives and Legends,* 447–49.

98. Shirley, *Pawnee Bill,* 13, 19, 115–47; Lynn, *Blazing Horizon,* 113–14; Sullivan, "Major Lillie's Own Story," box 9, GLC; *Season 1900,* 31, 33, 35, 37, BBHC; for other Wild West shows, see Russell, *Wild West,* 121–27.

99. *Season 1900,* 35, BBHC; Rennert, *One Hundred Posters,* 99.

100. Lynn, *Blazing Horizon,* 177–78; Shirley, *Pawnee Bill,* 141–44; *New York Times,* 5 Apr. 1894, and *New York Dramatic Mirror,* 25 Aug. 1894, both in vol. 4, NSS; Freeman and Fellows, *This Way,* 56, 62–64.

101. Winch, *Thrilling Lives,* 101–38, 147–55, 165–73, 187–93, 207–15; *BBWW* (1909 program), BBHC.

102. Sullivan, "Major Lillie's Own Story," 8–9, box 9, GLC; Cody to Beck, 27 May 1909, GC, BBHC; "In Union There Is Strength," *Buffalo Bill Bids You Good Bye,* BBHC.

103. *BBWW* (1909 program), BBHC; *Pioneer Scouts,* BBHC; Webb, "Buffalo Bill," 4, BBHC.

104. *Pioneer Scouts,* BBHC; Webb, "Buffalo Bill," 4, BBHC.

105. *BBWW* (1909 courier), BBHC; *BBWW* (1909 program), BBHC.

106. *BBWW* (1909 courier), 28, BBHC; Rennert, *One Hundred Posters,* 12, 79.

107. *Buffalo Bill Bids You Good Bye,* cover and 12, BBHC; Cody to Elwell, 22 June 1908, GC, BBHC; Winch, *Thrilling Lives,* 217–18.

108. Hamid, *Circus,* 62–64, 68; Webb, "Buffalo Bill," 11–12, BBHC; Russell, *Lives and Legends,* 451; Rennert, *One Hundred Posters,* 16, 111; *Birmingham Express,* 9 June 1903, vol. 10, NSS.

109. Rosa and May, *Buffalo Bill,* 198–200, 202–3. For copies of the documents, see box 18, GLC. For Pawnee Bill's account, see "When the Noose was Tightened," *Daily Oklahoman* (Oklahoma City), 15 July 1934, and "Pawnee Bill Talks about the Show's Fall," *Daily Oklahoman* (Oklahoma City), 22 July 1934.

110. Joe Miller to Wm. E. Hawks, 25 Aug. 1913, and Joe Miller to Wm. A. Bell, 25 Aug. 1913, GC, box 102, MB.

111. *Story Book and Program,* BBHC; Cody to Sister Julia, 22 Oct. 1915, and Cody to Buck (probably E. E. Arbuckle), 27 July 1915, both in GC, BBHC.

112. *Miller and Arlington* (1916 program), BBHC; see also Cody to Elwell, 11 June 1916, GC, BBHC for a letterhead that shows the content and look of "preparedness."

113. Fellows and Freeman, *This Way,* 160–61; unidentified obituary, box 1, WFCC, AHC. The Cody Collection at the Denver Public Library and the Cody file in the Jacob M. Schwoob Collection at the American Heritage Center also contain clippings about Cody's death. Final quote from Pancoast, *Trail Blazers,* 34.

## Chapter 6: "An Empire within Itself"

1. Collings and England, *101 Ranch,* 27–28, 45–46; Gipson, *Fabulous Empire,* 181–84; *Miller Bros. and Arlington* (1915 program), Show Scripts, MB.

2. Gipson, *Fabulous Empire,* 183–86.

3. Gerald Nash, *American West,* 26–27; Schlebecker, "A Day at the 101 Ranch," 6–7; Collings and England, *101 Ranch,* 69–121; Gipson, *Fabulous Empire,* 185–87; *Daily Oklahoman* (Oklahoma City), 6 Feb. 1927; *Official Review,* Show Scripts, MB; for film documenting the 101, see listing by reel, Oklahoma (state) file, LC.

4. Collings and England, *101 Ranch,* xxix; *Official Review,* Show Scripts, MB; *Miller Bros. and Arlington* (1915 program), Show Scripts, MB; *Miller Brothers* (1927 program), Show Scripts, MB.

5. Collings and England, *101 Ranch,* xxix, 53, 129–36, 159, 164; *Daily Oklahoman* (Oklahoma City), 6 Feb. 1927; *Official Review,* Show Scripts, MB; *Miller Bros. and Arlington* (1915 program), Show Scripts, MB.

6. *Daily Oklahoman* (Oklahoma City), 6 Feb. 1927; *Miller Bros. and Arlington* (1915 program), Show Scripts, MB; *Official Review,* Show Scripts, MB; Atherton, *Cattle Kings,* 36, 73–77; Gipson, *Fabulous Empire,* 208.

7. *Daily Oklahoman* (Oklahoma City), 6 Feb. 1927; Collings and England, *101 Ranch,* 142, 145, 136–38; Gipson, *Fabulous Empire,* 226.

8. *Official Review,* Show Scripts, MB; *New York City Commercial,* 25 Apr. 1914, Outsize Scrapbook for 1914, MB; *Ponca City (Okla.) Courier,* 12 June 1905; Collings and England, *101 Ranch,* 142–44; Gipson, *Fabulous Empire,* 227–31; the thirty thousand figure is from Roth, "101 Ranch," 419; the hundred thousand estimate is from *Ponca City (Okla.) Courier,* 12 June 1905, and *Official Review,* Show Scripts, MB.

9. *Official Review,* Show Scripts, MB; *New York City Commercial,* 25 Apr. 1914, Outsize Scrapbook for 1914, MB; *Ponca City (Okla.) Courier,* 12 June 1905; Collings and England, *101 Ranch,* 142–44; Gipson, *Fabulous Empire,* 232–34.

10. Hanes, *Bill Pickett,* viii, 20, 25–26, 46–47.

11. Debo, *Geronimo,* 400–427; Moses, *Wild West Shows,* 177–78; Gibson, *Fabulous Empire,* 228–30.

12. Collings and England, *101 Ranch,* 146–48, 161; Gipson, *Fabulous Empire,* 243–53; Hanes, *Bill Picket,* 63, 65–67.

13. Collings and England, *101 Ranch*, 161; Hanes, *Bill Pickett*, 63, 65–70; Moses, *Wild West Shows*, 179; "A Centenary of Peace and Progress," *American Register and Colonial World* (London), 31 May 1914; *Miller Bros. and Arlington* (1911 or 1914 program), BBHC (the copyright date on the cover of this program is 1911, but the material suggests it is actually from 1914).

14. *Ponca City (Okla.) Courier*, 2 Apr. 1908.

15. *Miller Brothers* (1927 program), Show Scripts, MB.

16. *Boston Transcript*, 15 Apr. 1909, *Boston Herald*, 15 June 1909, and *White Plains (N.Y.) Reporter*, 17 July 1909, all in Scrapbooks, MB; *New York Evening Mail*, 18 Apr. 1914, Outsize Scrapbook for 1914, MB; *Official Review*, Show Scripts, MB; *Miller Brothers* (1927 program), Show Scripts, MB; unsigned carbon copy of letter (probably from Joe Miller) to Princess Wenona, 3 Jan. 1911, and unsigned carbon copy (probably from Joe Miller) to Sammy Garrett, 2 Jan. 1911, GC, box 100, MB.

17. Moses, *Wild West Shows*, 168–69.

18. Wrobel, *End of American Exceptionalism*, 91–93; Atherton, *Cattle Kings*, 241–42.

19. Croly, *Promise;* Weyl, *New Democracy;* Wrobel, *End of American Exceptionalism*, 79–82; for more on the frontier as "unlimited opportunity," see Slotkin, *Regeneration*, 5.

20. *Miller Bros. and Arlington* (1915 program), Show Scripts, MB; *Miller Brothers* (1927 program), Show Scripts, MB; *Official Review*, Show Scripts, MB; *Indianapolis News*, 13 Sept. 1915, Scrapbooks, MB; *Daily Oklahoman* (Oklahoma City), 6 Feb. 1927; Gipson, *Fabulous Empire*, 411.

21. Joe to Billie Burke, 7 Sept. 1913, and Joe to Lute P. Stover, n.d., both in GC, box 102, MB; Frank Butler to Zack Miller, 20 July 1909, and *Holyoke Telegram*, 11 Aug. 1915, both in Scrapbooks, MB; *Grand Rapids Michigan Herald*, 19 Apr. 1914, *Schenectady Star*, 30 Apr. 1914, *New York City Variety*, 17 Apr. 1914, *North American* (Philadelphia), 6 May 1914, *Philadelphia Star*, 7 May 1914, and *Richmond (N.Y.) News*, 2 May 1914, all in Outsize Scrapbook for 1914, MB; *Official Review*, Show Scripts, MB; Collings and England, *101 Ranch*, 186–87; Buffalo Bill to Stacy, 29 Apr. 1908, GC, BBHC; Gipson, *Fabulous Empire*, 255, 259; Rennert, *One Hundred Posters*, 16, 107.

22. *Boston Herald*, 15 June 1909, *Boston Post*, 18 June 1909, and *Meriden (Conn.) Morning Record*, 12 July 1909, all in Scrapbooks, MB; *Official Review*, Show Scripts, MB; *Ponca City (Okla.) Courier*, 2 Apr. 1908; *Miller Bros. and Arlington* (1911 or 1914 program), BBHC; Collings and England, *101 Ranch*, 175–78. The stage was not authentic; see Joe Miller, Jr. to R. M. Harvey, 8 Jan. 1929, GC, box 82, MB; and Roth, "101 Ranch," 423n.

23. Unsigned carbon (probably from Joe Miller) to High Chief, May 1911, GC, box 100, MB; unsigned carbon initialed EMB to Amos Hawk, 19 Mar. 1926, GC, box 81, MB; *Meriden (Conn.) Morning Record*, 12 July 1909, Scrapbooks, MB; *Official Review*, Show Scripts, MB; *Miller Bros. and Arlington* (1915 program), Show Scripts, MB; *Ponca City (Okla.) Courier*, 2 Apr. 1908; Collings and England, *101 Ranch*, 169, 174–78.

24. *Ponca City (Okla.) Courier*, 2 Oct. 1913 and 2 Apr. 1908; *Boston Transcript*, 15 July

1901, Scrapbooks, MB; *Miller Bros. and Arlington* (1915 program), Show Scripts, MB; *New York City Mail,* 20 Apr. 1914 and 24 Apr. 1914, Outsize Scrapbook for 1914, MB.

25. *Utica (N.Y.) Press,* 7 May 1914, and *New York Evening Sun,* 18 Apr. 1914, both in Outsize Scrapbook for 1914, MB; *Official Review,* Show Scripts, MB; *Miller Bros. and Arlington* (1915 program), Show Scripts, MB; clipping (probably from *Boston Herald* about 15 June 1909), Scrapbooks, MB; Joe to Frank Paul, 3 Jan. 1910, GC, box 100, MB; Collings and England, *101 Ranch,* 76, 165.

26. Unless otherwise noted, material on Mexico is from Meyer and Sherman, *Course of Mexican History,* chaps. 27–28, 30, and Cumberland, *Mexico,* chaps. 8–9. Unless otherwise noted, the account of the 101 show in Mexico is from Hanes, *Bill Pickett,* chap. 5, and Gipson, *Fabulous Empire,* 259–76. *Daily Oklahoman* (Oklahoma City), 24 Mar. 1929; *New York Evening Journal,* 9 Nov. 1926, Printed Material, MB.

27. Rennert, *One Hundred Posters,* 16, 107; *Miller Bros. and Arlington* (1910 courier), BBHC.

28. Joe to Park A. Findley, 31 July 1913, GC, box 102, MB; Zack to G. Gregory Gorman, 3 Mar. 1929, GC, box 80, MB; *New York Evening Sun,* 18 Apr. 1914, *New York World,* 20 Apr. 1914, and *New York Telegraph,* 20 Apr. 1914, all in Outsize Scrapbook for 1914, MB; *Miller Brothers* (1927 program), Show Scripts, MB; *Daily Oklahoman* (Oklahoma City), 24 Mar. 1929.

29. *New York Telegraph,* 20 Apr. 1914, *New York Tribune,* 20 Apr. 1914, *New York Times,* 26 Apr. 1914, and *New York World,* 3 May 1914, all in Outsize Scrapbook for 1914, MB.

30. *New York World,* 22 Apr. 1914, *New York Mail,* 21 Apr. 1914, and *New York Tribune,* 27 Apr. 1914, all in Outsize Scrapbook for 1914, MB.

31. *New York Evening Sun,* 25 Apr. 1925, Outsize Scrapbook for 1914, MB.

32. *New York Telegram,* 3 May 1914 and 19 Apr. 1914, Outsize Scrapbook for 1914, MB.

33. *New York Press,* 22 Apr. 1914, Outsize Scrapbook for 1914, MB.

34. *New York Sun,* 21 Apr. 1914, and *Utica (N.Y.) Press,* 7 May 1914, both in Outsize Scrapbook for 1914, MB; *Miller Bros. and Arlington* (1915 program), Show Scripts, MB; Rennert, *One Hundred Posters,* 15, 98; clipping from *New Castle News* (probably England), 22 June 1915, Ethyl Parry Bradford folder, BBHC.

35. *New York Variety,* 17 Apr. 1914, *New York Globe,* 18 Apr. 1914, *New York Telegraph,* 19 Apr. 1914 and 20 Apr. 1914, *New York Press,* 22 Apr. 1914 and 26 Apr. 1914, *New York Mail,* 20 Apr. 1914, *New York Sun,* 21 Apr. 1914, and *New York Post,* 25 Apr. 1914, all in Outsize Scrapbook for 1914, MB; *Official Review,* Show Scripts, MB.

36. *New York Press,* 22 Apr. 1914, *New York Commercial,* 25 Apr. 1914, *New York Journal of Commerce,* 25 Apr. 1914, and *New York Telegraph,* 20 Apr. 1914, all in Outsize Scrapbook for 1914, MB; *Miller Bros. and Arlington* (1915 program), Show Scripts, MB; *Miller Bros. and Arlington* (1910 courier), MB; *Miller and Arlington* (1916 program), BBHC; Rennert, *One Hundred Posters,* 107.

37. *Milwaukee Free Press,* 29 July 1913, Ethyl Parry Bradford folder, BBHC; *New York Mail,* 1 May 1914, Outsize Scrapbook for 1914, MB; *Official Review,* Show Scripts, MB;

see also Collings and England, *101 Ranch*, 165–66, for an account apparently copied from the *Official Review.*

38. *Miller Bros. and Arlington* (1915 program), Show Scripts, MB; *Philadelphia Press,* n.d., Outsize Scrapbook for 1914, MB.

39. *Miller Bros. and Arlington* (1915 program), Show Scripts, MB; *Philadelphia Press,* n.d., and *New York Press,* 22 Apr. 1914, Outsize Scrapbook for 1914, MB.

40. Rennert, *One Hundred Posters,* quotes on 16, image on 107; Rosa and May, *Buffalo Bill,* 92.

41. *New York Tribune,* 3 May 1914, *New York Evening Sun,* 29 Apr. 1914, *New York Evening Mail,* 18 Apr. 1914, *New York Tribune,* 19 Apr. 1914, and *Philadelphia Press,* n.d., all in Outsize Scrapbook for 1914, MB; *Official Review,* Show Scripts, MB; promotional stickers for Miller Brothers 101 Ranch Real Wild West show, San Francisco Exposition, 1915, folder 1–2, BBHC. These stickers have been reproduced in Wood-Clark, *Beautiful,* 2.

42. *Miller Bros. and Arlington* (1915 program), Show Scripts, MB; *Philadelphia Press,* n.d., Outsize Scrapbook for 1914, MB.

43. *New York Evening Sun,* 29 Apr. 1914, *Philadelphia Inquirer,* 3 May 1914, and *New York Telegram,* 29 Apr. 1914, all in Outsize Scrapbook for 1914, MB; Collings and England, *101 Ranch,* 166.

44. *Newark Evening Star,* 2 May 1914, Outsize Scrapbook for 1914, MB; *London Globe,* 11 May 1914 and 16 May 1914; *American Register and Colonial World* (London), 31 May 1914; *Norfolk Chronicle* (London), 17 July 1914; *London Daily Sketch,* 23 May 1914, 1 June 1914, 1 July 1914, and 8 July 1914; *London Standard,* 18 May 1914; *London Stage,* 21 May 1914.

45. *Norfolk Chronicle* (London), 17 July 1914; *American Register and Colonial World* (London), 31 May 1914; *London Morning Advertiser,* 25 May 1914; *Official Review,* Show Scripts, MB.

46. Moses, *Wild West Shows,* 169; Gipson, *Fabulous Empire,* 338–41; Collings and England, *101 Ranch,* 181–82. Collings cites *London Daily Chronicle,* 26 June 1914, as her source for the royal visit.

47. Gipson, *Fabulous Empire,* 337–39.

48. *London Globe,* 11 May 1914 and 13 May 1914; *American Register and Colonial World* (London), 31 May 1914.

49. *London Morning Advertiser,* 25 May 1914; *London Graphic,* 23 May 1914; *American Register and Colonial World* (London), 31 May 1914; Reeves, "Skirt Round-Up," 634; Collings and England, *101 Ranch,* 179–80. Collings attributes her material on cowgirls to *London Daily Mirror,* 27 May 1914, and *London Daily Citizen,* 11 July 1914.

50. Collings and England, *101 Ranch,* 182 (this includes a copy of the impressment order); Moses, *Wild West Shows,* 186–88; Hanes, *Bill Pickett,* 134; Gipson, *Fabulous Empire,* 355. The 101 Ranch show advertised extensively in the *London Standard.* Advertisements stopped on 27 August 1914.

51. *Poughkeepsie (N.Y.) Evening Enterprise,* 31 July 1915, *Ansonia Evening Sentinel,* 3 Aug.

1915, *Reading Eagle,* 25 Aug. 1915, *Tulsa Daily World,* 5 Oct. 1915, *Easton Daily Free Press,* 16 Aug. 1915, and *Springfield Daily Republican,* 11 Aug. 1915, all in Scrapbooks, MB.

52. *Houston Daily Post,* 24 Oct. 1915; *Poughkeepsie (N.Y.) Enterprise,* 4 Aug. 1915, *Springfield Daily Republican,* 11 Aug. 1915, unidentified clipping entitled "Ranch People in Parade Here," n.d., *Newark Evening News,* 20 Aug. 1915, *San Antonio Express,* 1915, and *Allentown Morning Call,* 18 Aug. 1915, all in Scrapbooks, MB.

53. *Miller and Arlington* (1916 program), BBHC; *Buffalo Bill (Himself)* (1916 program), BBHC.

54. *Miller and Arlington* (1916 program), BBHC; *Buffalo Bill (Himself)* (1916 program), BBHC.

55. *Miller and Arlington* (1916 program), BBHC; Moses, *Wild West Shows,* 248–49; Yost, *Buffalo Bill,* 397–99. Yost cites Stella Adelyne Foote, *Letters from Buffalo Bill* (Billings, Mont.: privately published, 1954), 77–78, for the season's business affairs; Russell, *Lives and Legends,* 461; and Walsh, *Making of Buffalo Bill,* 356.

56. Hanes, *Bill Pickett,* 139–40; *Miller Bros.* (1929 program), 9, Show Scripts, MB; *Miller Bros.* (1930 program), 5, Show Scripts, MB; unidentified clipping, vol. I, LFFS.

57. Collings and England, *101 Ranch,* 145–46, 155–57; *New York Times,* 13 Sept. 1925; Joe to R. S. Bixby, 5 Jan. 1922, Joe to Billie Burke, 17 Aug. 1923, and Billie Burke to Joe, 11 Aug. 1923, all in GC, box 73, MB.

58. Foreman, *Indians Abroad,* 209; Miller Brothers 101 Ranch to Mrs. Bell Mahan, 11 June 1924, GC, box 86, MB; Joe to Harry McDonald, 28 July 1924, GC, box 85, MB; Joe to J. D. Newmann, 19 Sept. 1924, Edward P. Newmann to Miller Bros. Ranch, 30 Sept. 1924, and Joe to Robert Nicholson Seed Company, 23 Jan. 1924, all in GC, box 88, MB; W. F. Christian, "A Foreword," *Miller Brothers Official Season's Route,* 2, Show Scripts, MB; item marked "101 Ranch Wild West Show," n.d., Misc. unnumbered box, MB; George L. Miller to Helen Gibson Smith, 6 Aug. 1923, GC, box 73, MB; George to Mrs. Joe C. Miller, 22 Dec. 1928, GC, box 87, MB; *Pendleton East Oregonian,* 26 Jan. 1932, Outsize Scrapbook for Pawnee Bill, Lillie Collection, UO; Collings and England, *101 Ranch,* 155, 183–86, 216–17.

59. George to General Don Joaquin Amaro, 7 Feb. 1928, GC, box 73, MB; C. W. Finney to Joe, 29 July 1927, GC, box 79, MB; *Miller Brothers Official Season's Route,* Show Scripts, MB; *Daily Oklahoman* (Oklahoma City), 24 Mar. 1929; Collings and England, *101 Ranch,* 183.

60. *Miller Brothers Official Season's Route,* Show Scripts, MB; Edward Arlington to C. W. Finney, 2 Mar. 1927, GC, box 73, MB; *Henryetta (Okla.) Daily Free Lance,* 13 Oct. 1926; *New York Times,* 22 July 1928 and 23 July 1928; *Daily Oklahoman* (Oklahoma City), 24 Mar. 1929 and 20 Oct. 1929; Collings and England, *101 Ranch,* 183; Moses, *Wild West Shows,* 252.

61. Collings and England, *101 Ranch,* 185. The title is from the cover of *Official Program* (1926), Printed Material, MB.

62. Collings and England, *101 Ranch,* 227; Jacobs, *Rise of the American Film,* 338–43, 358–59, 395–415; *Miller Brothers* (1927 program), Show Scripts, MB; *Miller Bros.* (1929

program), 7, 11, 13, 15–17, 19, 25, 31, Show Scripts, MB; *Miller Bros.* (1930 program), 7, 11, 13, Show Scripts, MB; *Miller Brothers 1929 Route Book,* 3, Show Scripts, MB; *Official Program* (1926), Printed Material, MB; *Program* (undated), Printed Material, MB; *New York Times,* 23 July 1925; *Daily Oklahoman* (Oklahoma City), 18 Apr. 1925; Nye, *Unembarrassed Muse,* 190; Atherton, *Cattle Kings,* 77.

63. Collings and England, *101 Ranch,* 184–85; Nye, *Unembarrassed Muse,* 177.

64. Collings and England, *101 Ranch,* 184; *Daily Oklahoman* (Oklahoma City), 11 Mar. 1930; *Program* (undated), Printed Material, MB; Wild West and Great Far East Show Co., Inc. employment contract with Jewell Austin, 29 Mar. 1928, and employment contract with Vera Hodge, 15 Feb. 1928, both in GC, box 82, MB; Derry, "Corsets and Broncs," 7.

65. Collings and England, *101 Ranch,* 184–85; *Miller Brothers* (1927 program), Show Scripts, MB.

66. *Official Program* (1926), Printed Material, MB; Edward Arlington to Joe, 7 Apr. 1926, and George to Prince Andronikoff, 8 Oct. 1928, both in GC, box 73, MB; W. F. Christian to Charles L. Sasse, 8 Nov. 1926, GC, box 92, MB; Joe to Art Eldridge, 22 Nov. 1926, GC, box 78, MB; C. W. Finney to Joe, 28 Dec. 1926, and George to Mohamed Ethawary, 31 Dec. 1927, both in GC, box 79, MB; Joe to Stefan Bondareff, 23 Mar. 1927, GC, box 74, MB; George to Apanassi Boulanoff and John Minacft (c/o San Antonio Jail, San Antonio, Texas), 12 Mar. 1928, GC, box 75, MB; Diggins, *Proud Decades,* 56; for a representative article reflecting the interest in and attitudes about cossacks, see Hindus, "Russia's Flaming Cossack," 14.

67. *Miller Bros.* (1930 program), 11, Show Scripts, MB; *Miller Brothers* (1929 program), 16–17, Show Scripts, MB; Harold Carlton Ingraham to Joe, 23 Oct. 1926, GC, box 83, MB; *New York Times,* 23 July 1928.

68. R. M. Harvey to Joseph Jr., 16 Feb. 1929, GC, box 82, MB; *New York Times,* 22 July 1928; *Daily Oklahoman* (Oklahoma City), 18 Apr. 1925.

69. *Program* (undated), Printed Material, MB; *Miller Bros.* (1930 program), 11, 13, Show Scripts, MB.

70. *Miller Bros.* (1930 program), 29, Show Scripts, MB; *Miller Brothers* (1927 program), Show Scripts, MB; R. M. Harvey to Zack, 23 Feb. (1929 or 1930), GC, box 82, MB; *Official Program* (1926), Printed Material, MB; Zack to Peters Cartridge Company, 23 Feb. 1929, George W. to Peters Cartridge Company, 12 Mar. 1929, and George to Bill Penny, 14 Feb. 1928, all in GC, box 90, MB; Zack to "Texas" Bud Snell, 26 Jan. 1929, GC, box 93, MB; Zack to George Skyeagle, 23 Jan. 1929, GC, box 93a, MB; unsigned carbon from "Treasurer of the Miller Brothers' 101 Ranch Show" to Ray O. Lyon, 24 Mar. 1930, and Western Show Company, Inc. employment contract with Helen Lowe, 23 Jan. 1929, both in GC, box 85, MB.

71. *New York Times,* 24 Oct. 1926, 26 Oct. 1927, 24 Oct. 1928, 12 Oct. 1929, 1 Nov. 1930, and 12 Oct. 1931; Moses, *Wild West Shows,* 255; Westermeier, *Man, Beast, Dust,* 292–93; Becker, "Rodeo," 195–200; Arthur Chapman, "Rodeo Dollars," 28–30; Dye, "They Ride 'Em," 34–33; Earle, "Ride 'Im, Cowboy," 906–11; *Miller Brothers* (1927 program),

Show Scripts, MB; *Miller Bros.* (1929 program), 9, 13, 15, Show Scripts, MB; George to American Royal Building, 20 Feb. 1929, GC, box 91, MB; The 101 Ranch Show Co. to Jimmie McBride, 5 Mar. 1927, GC, box 87, MB; *Daily Oklahoman* (Oklahoma City), 6 Feb. 1927.

72. Moses, *Wild West Shows,* 150, 195–222, 252–72.

73. Unsigned carbon copy of letter (probably from Joe Miller) to O. Marrimar, 3 Jan. 1911, GC, box 100, MB; *Program* (undated), Printed Material, MB; Balshofer and Miller, *One Reel,* 76–80; for an example of offering the 101 ranch and crew for work in movies, see Joe to Kinemacolor Co. of America, 4 Oct. 1913, GC, box 102, MB.

74. Joe to Tom Mix, 29 Aug. 1927, George W. to Tom Mix, 19 Nov. 1929, GC, box 87, MB; unsigned carbon (probably from George Miller) to Tom Mix, 23 Nov. 1927, George to Tom Mix, 2 Feb. 1928, George to Jack Hill, 24 Feb. 1928, and carbon copy of telegram from Zack to William S. Hart, 31 May 1931, all in GC, box 82, MB; J. D. Newmann to Zack, 1 Feb. 1930, GC, box 89, MB; "In re: Western Show Corp. vs Tom Mix Memorandum," n.d., Misc. unnumbered box, MB; *Miller Bros.* (1929 program), 23, Show Scripts, MB; *Miller Bros.* (1930 program), 15, Show Scripts, MB; Joe to Ray O. Archer, 16 May 1923 (telegram), 26 May 1923, 28 May 1923, and 28 June 1923, all in GC, box 73, MB; Joe to R. M. Rickerstaff, 15 Sept. 1924, GC, box 88, MB; *Daily Oklahoman* (Oklahoma City), 15 Oct. 1929.

75. *New York Times,* 22 July 1928; *Official Program* (1926), Printed Material, MB; *Miller Bros.* (1929 program), 27, 29, Show Scripts, MB; George to Albert Hodgini, 24 Feb. 1928, GC, box 82, MB.

76. George to George L. Myers, 23 Sept. 1928, GC, box 87, MB; *Miller Bros.* (1930 program), 13, 15, Show Scripts, MB; *Miller Brothers 1929 Route Book,* 7, Show Scripts, MB; *Miller Bros.* (1929 program), 24, Show Scripts, MB; T. O. Manning to R. O. Scatterday, 16 Mar. 1929, GC, box 93, MB; George to Don Henderson, 23 Mar. 1928, GC, box 82, MB; Zack to John F. McGrail, 9 Feb. 1929, GC, box 88, MB; Zack to Eduardo de Leon, 9 Feb. 1929, GC, box 78, MB; *New York Times,* 23 July 1928; *Daily Oklahoman* (Oklahoma City), 15 Apr. 1928.

77. *Miller Brothers Official Season's Route,* Show Scripts, MB; George to Albert Hodgini, 24 Feb. 1928, GC, box 77, MB.

78. *London Morning Advertiser,* 14 May 1914; *Miller Brothers Official Season's Route,* Show Scripts, MB; *Miller Bros.* (1930 program), 27, Show Scripts, MB; George to R. M. Harvey, 28 Jan. 1929, GC, box 82, MB; for examples of advertisements for autos, parts, and accessories, see *Miller Brothers* (1927 program), Show Scripts, MB, and *Miller Bros.* (1930 program), Show Scripts, MB.

79. *Miller Brothers* (1927 program), Show Scripts, MB; *Miller Brothers 1929 Route Book,* 24, Show Scripts, MB; Moses, *Wild West Shows,* 265; *New York Times,* 22 July 1928, 2 Nov. 1930, magazine section, 16 Sept. 1931 and 6 Sept. 1931; *Daily Oklahoman* (Oklahoma City), 22 Apr. 1928.

80. Unsigned carbon copy (probably from George Miller) to Tom Mix, 23 Nov. 1927, GC, box 82, MB; Joe to Art Eldridge, 24 Nov. 1926, GC, box 78, MB; Joe to Edward

Arlington, 23 May 1924, GC, box 73, MB; W. F. Christian to Charles L. Sasse, 8 Nov. 1926, GC, box 92, MB; C. W. Finney to Joe, 29 July 1927, GC, box 79, MB; *Miller Bros.* (1929 program), 23, Show Scripts, MB; *New York Times,* 23 July 1928; Gipson, *Fabulous Empire,* 362–65.

81. "Approximate Salary List and Expenses, Season 1926" sent by C. W. Finney to George, n.d., and letter, 29 July 1927, George to Mr. C. W. Finney, 13 Aug. 1936, and George to F. J. Frink, 31 July 1926, all in GC, box 79, MB; Joe to Edward Arlington, 23 May 1925, Wild West and Great Far East Show Co., Inc. employment contract with Jewel Austin, 29 Mar. 1928, and Joe to E. F. Burnett, 27 Oct. 1925, all in GC, box 73, MB; Zack to Eduardo de Leon, 9 Feb. 1929, and Joe to Art Eldridge, 22 Nov. 1926, both in GC, box 78, MB; Western Show Co. Inc., employment contract with Helen Lowe, 23 Jan. 1930, GC, box 85, MB; carbon copy initialed EMB to Amos Hawk, 19 Mar. 1926, GC, box 81, MB; *Miller Brothers Official Season's Route,* Show Scripts, MB; *Miller Brothers* (1927 program), Show Scripts, MB; Zack to Boswell Brothers Circus and Menagerie (Johannesburg), 3 Mar. 1925, GC, box 75, MB; Joe to G. L. Cherpin (Paris), 10 Jan. 1927, GC, box 76, MB; Joe to Paul Schultze (Berlin), 19 Apr. 1926, and Paul Schultze to Joe, 19 Feb. 1927, both in GC, box 92, MB; Gipson, *Fabulous Empire,* 200; *Daily Oklahoman* (Oklahoma City), 24 Mar. 1929; Moses, *Wild West Shows,* 265.

82. "Receipts and Disbursement," Misc. unnumbered box, MB; Gipson, *Fabulous Empire,* 368.

83. *Miller Brothers 1929 Route Book,* 9, 10, 23, 25, Show Scripts, MB; *Miller Brothers Official Season's Route,* Show Scripts, MB; Joe to Edward Arlington, 23 May and 9 June 1925, Edward Arlington to C. W. Finney, 2 Mar. 1927, and telegram from W. E. Button (Sheriff of Jefferson County, Watertown, N.Y.) to Manager 101 Ranch, 18 July 1925, all in GC, box 73, MB; Charles M. Willoughby to W. F. Christian, 7 Dec. 1925, GC, box 81, MB; Joe to Ernie Black, 29 Sept. 1927, GC, box 74, MB; Sam R. Sumner and city attorney of Wenatchee, Wash. to 101 Ranch Wild West Show, 18 Aug. 1926, and unsigned carbon to R. L. Spalsbury, 5 Nov. 1927, both in GC, box 92, MB; George to C. W. Finney, 10 Oct. 1928, GC, box 80, MB; Joe to Billie Perry, 1 Aug. 1925 (this letter says three cowgirls were kicked out of the show), and Charles H. Burke to George, 4 Feb. 1928, both in GC, box 90, MB; Gipson, *Fabulous Empire,* 364, 369–71; *Hattiesburg American,* 29 Oct. 1929; *Daily Oklahoman* (Oklahoma City), 27 May 1927; *New York Times,* 26 July 1928, 28 July 1928, and 2 Aug. 1929; for an anti-rodeo article, see *New York Times,* 12 July 1925.

84. *New York Times,* 3 Feb. 1929; Moses, *Wild West Shows,* 265; *Miller Bros.* (1929 program), 5, 22, Show Scripts, MB; *Miller Bros.* (1930 program), 21, Show Scripts, MB; Frank Gavin to Editor, Billboard Publishing Company, 21 Jan. 1928, GC, box 75, MB.

85. Unsigned carbon (probably from George Miller) to Tom Mix, 23 Nov. 1927, unsigned letter from 101 Ranch to Tom Mix, 19 Nov. 1929, and George to Sarah R. Henry, 16 Dec. 1928, all in GC, box 82, MB; Zack to Tex Sherman, 10 Dec. 1930, GC, box 93, MB; George to Mrs. J. C. Miller, 22 Dec. 1928, GC, box 87, MB; George to Walter

L. Wilson, 21 Dec. 1928, GC, box 75, MB. *Daily Oklahoman* (Oklahoma City), 18 Dec. 1928.

86. Gipson, *Fabulous Empire,* 374–78; Collings and England, *101 Ranch,* 192; Johnson, "Passing," 33–34; *New York Times,* 16 Aug. 1931, 17 Aug. 1931, and 19 Aug. 1931.

87. *New York Times,* 25 Mar. 1932; Zack to Henry S. Johnson, 18 July 1933, Misc. unnumbered box, MB; Collings and England, *101 Ranch,* 198–211.

88. Moses, *Wild West Shows,* 227; Balshofer and Miller, *One Reel a Week,* 76, 79–80; Joe to Elmer Pearson, 25 Aug. 1925 and 30 Aug. 1927, GC, box 90, MB; *Miller Brothers Official Season's Route,* Show Scripts, MB; *Miller Brothers* (1927 program), Show Scripts, MB; *New York City Press,* 19 Apr. 1924, Outsize Scrapbook for 1914, MB; *Daily Oklahoman* (Oklahoma City), 6 Feb. 1927 and 1 Oct. 1923; E. W. Lenders to J. G. Braecklein, 2 June 1924 and 21 July 1924, Lenders Papers, AAA, SI; Collings and England, *101 Ranch,* 199, 167.

## Chapter 7: "Rugged Virtue in the Saddle"

1. Paul E. Mix, *Life and Legend,* 15, 20; Olive Stokes Mix, *Fabulous Tom Mix,* 48–49; Nicholas, *Tom Mix,* 3–4; *London Daily Express,* 15 Apr. 1925; *San Francisco Examiner,* 27 Nov. 1931, LFFS. The Olive Stokes Mix account places the incident in El Paso, Texas, an obvious attempt to uphold the myth that Tom Mix was born a westerner. Tom Mix could not have attended Buffalo Bill's Wild West show when he claimed; Cody's show was in Europe in 1890.

2. Paul E. Mix, *Life and Legend,* 20, 22, 27.

3. Ibid., 15–18, 21, 25, 27, 172.

4. Ibid., 24–25. "Making a Million" was the title of a six-part series by Mix about his efforts to become wealthy; see Tom Mix, "Making a Million."

5. Paul E. Mix, *Tom Mix,* 29–42, 173–74; Brownlow, *War,* 302–4.

6. Paul E. Mix, *Tom Mix,* 43–45; Nicholas, *Tom Mix,* 4.

7. Paul E. Mix, *Tom Mix,* 45–47, 53, 174; Gipson, *Fabulous Empire,* 233–34. The dates of the meeting between the Millers and Mix and employment at the ranch vary in different accounts. According to the *Daily Oklahoman* (Oklahoma City, 6 Feb. 1927), Mix's salary on the 101 was twenty dollars a month. See also Norris, *Tom Mix Book,* 13.

8. Collings and England, *101 Ranch,* 218; Brownlow, *War,* 304–5.

9. Cruikshank, "Tom Takes the Rainbow Trail," 49; *New York Times,* 25 Jan. 1933; Paul E. Mix, *Tom Mix,* 46–47; Collings and England, *101 Ranch,* 166; Gipson, *Fabulous Empire,* 233–34; Theodore Strauss, "The Return of a Two-Gun Hero," *New York Times,* 8 Sept. 1940.

10. Paul E. Mix, *Tom Mix,* 47–48, 50, 65; Olive Stokes Mix, *Fabulous Tom Mix,* 49.

11. Olive Stokes Mix, *Fabulous Tom Mix,* 42–44, 48–52, 54–63, 93.

12. Ibid., 63–67; Paul E. Mix, *Tom Mix,* 52, 74.

13. Paul E. Mix, *Tom Mix,* 74–78. According to Nicholas, the movie featured Tom Mix rescuing a herd of cattle from rustlers (*Tom Mix,* 13).

14. Buscombe, *BFI Companion,* 370; Kaminsky, "Tom Mix," 687. The release date given in different sources for *Briton and Boer* varies.

15. Paul E. Mix, *Tom Mix,* 51–52, 78; Olive Stokes Mix, *Fabulous Tom Mix,* 68–72, 74–75, 79–80, 87–88; Brownlow, *War,* 305; Norris, *Tom Mix Book,* 13; for an account of Mix's experiences with the Mulhall show, see *New York Times,* 12 Apr. 1925.

16. Paul E. Mix, *Tom Mix,* 80–81; Lincks, "Tom Mixes In," 110. According to Theodore Strauss, Mix won the title "World's Cowboy Championship" at the Cheyenne rodeo in 1907 ("The Return of a Two-Gun Hero," *New York Times,* 8 Sept. 1940). According to the *New York Times,* Mix "won the National roping and riding contest for cowboys at Prescott, Ariz., in 1909, and one at Canyon City, Colo., in 1911" (13 Oct. 1940).

17. Olive Stokes Mix, *Fabulous Tom Mix,* 88, 92–95, 97, 103, 128; Paul E. Mix, *Tom Mix,* 78–82, 84, 88–92; Tom Mix, "Making a Million" (June 1928), 70–71, 112.

18. Brownlow, *War,* 307, 253–62; Olive Stokes Mix, *Fabulous Tom Mix,* 116–17; Esselman, "Camelot," 15; for correspondence connecting the 101 Ranch, its Wild West show, and movies, see P. S. Greeney to Joe Miller, 26 Dec. 1910, and unsigned carbon copy of a letter (probably from Joe Miller) to C. Harriman, 3 Jan. 1911, GC, box 100, MB; Joe Miller to Kinemacolor Co. of America, 4 Oct. 1913, GC, box 102, MB; and *Daily Oklahoman* (Oklahoma City), 6 Feb. 1927.

19. Collings and England, *101 Ranch,* 166–67; *Daily Oklahoman* (Oklahoma City), 1 Oct. 1923, 24 Mar. 1929, 15 Oct. 1929, and 20 Oct. 1929; Buscombe, *BFI Companion,* 32.

20. Hyams, *Life and Times,* 32; Olive Stokes Mix, *Fabulous Tom Mix,* 30, 110–13, 116–17; Paul E. Mix, *Tom Mix,* 98–99; Tom Mix, "Making a Million" (Jan. 1928), 111–12; publicity item for *The Law and the Outlaw,* copyright description registered with the Copyright Office, 7 June 1913, LU 815 and 816, LC. Sometimes the dates and prefixes stamped on the publicity items submitted to the Copyright Office differ from those given in *Motion Pictures, 1912–1939: Catalog of Copyright Entries, Cumulative Series.* I have used the dates and prefixes used in the catalog. *The Telltale Knife,* 15 Oct. 1914, LP 3552; *The Man from the East,* 28 Nov. 1914, LP 3852; *The Moving Picture Cowboy,* 14 Sept. 1914, LP 3395; *Slim Higgins,* 11 Feb. 1915, LP 4442; and *Roping a Bride,* 26 Jan. 1915, LP 4312, all copyright descriptions in LC.

21. *When the Cook Fell Ill,* 9 July 1914, LP 3009; *Why the Sheriff Is a Bachelor,* 10 Oct. 1914, LP 3505; *An Apache's Gratitude,* 1 Aug. 1913, LU 1058; *The Mexican,* 24 Sept. 1914, LP 3445; *The Marshall's Capture,* 28 June 1913, LU 886; *The Sheriff of Yavapai County,* 21 Mar. 1913, LU 499; *A Muddle in Horse Thieves,* 29 Oct. 1913, LU 1481; and *The Taming of Texas Pete,* 24 July 1913, LU 981, all copyright descriptions in LC; Moses, *Wild West Shows,* 272.

22. *The Telltale Knife,* 15 Oct. 1914, LP 3009; *Roping a Bride,* 26 Jan. 1915, LP 4312; *When the Cook Fell Ill,* 9 July 1914, LP 3052; *Never Again,* 28 Aug. 1915, LP 6249; *The Life Timer,* 27 Mar. 1913, LU 512; *The Way of the Red Man,* 16 Sept. 1914, LP 3393; *Jimmy Hayes and Muriel,* 30 Sept. 1914, LP 3465; *A Child of the Prairie,* 24 Feb. 1915, LP 4527; and *The Man from Texas,* 24 Feb. 1915, LP 4529, all copyright descriptions in LC.

23. Buscombe, *BFI Companion,* 370; *Religion and Gun Practice,* 29 May 1913, LU 793, and *Slim Higgins,* 11 Feb. 1915, LP 4442, both copyright descriptions in LC; Brownlow, *War,* 307; for Hart and the "good badman" role, see Hyams, *Life and Times,* 25, 28.

24. Olive Stokes Mix, *Fabulous Tom Mix,* 70–71, 76, 93–94, 99–100, 128; *New York Times,* 13 Oct. 1940; *London Evening News,* 3 Sept. 1938.

25. Moses, *Wild West Shows,* 224; Jacobs, *Rise of the American Film,* 136–56.

26. Joe Miller to Tom Mix, 20 July 1927, GC, box 87, MB; Paul E. Mix, *Tom Mix,* 105–7; Nicholas, *Tom Mix,* 22; Olive Stokes Mix, *Fabulous Tom Mix,* 99.

27. Nicholas, *Tom Mix,* 16, 19–20, 28. Many articles included information about Mix's salary; see, in particular, *New York Times,* 29 Mar. 1925. "As We Go to Press," *Photoplay* 36 (June 1929), 10; *San Francisco Examiner,* 27 Nov. 1931, LFFS; Paul E. Mix valued the mansion at $250,000 (*Tom Mix,* 101–3) and explains why stars married so often (91); *New York Times,* 27 May 1928; Olive Stokes Mix, *Fabulous Tom Mix,* 138–40; Fenin and Everson, *The Western,* 119; Chrisman, "Tom Mix," 49; for his smoking and drinking, see Cruikshank, "Tom Takes the Rainbow Trail," 112, 120, and Brownlow, *War,* 307, 324; for Mix's views on the instability of marriage for movie stars, see Tom Mix, "Making a Million" (Jan. 1928), 38.

28. Coffman, *War,* 363; Hawley, *Great War.*

29. Roderick Nash, *Nervous Generation,* 33–45.

30. Ibid., 43, 55–67, 77–90; Boorstin, *America,* 24–25.

31. Nash, *Nervous Generation,* 45–55, 115–25; Allen, *Only Yesterday,* 73–101.

32. Nash, *Nervous Generation,* 2; Wrobel, *End of American Exceptionalism,* 102–3, 107; *New York Times,* 5 Apr. 1925; *London Daily Express,* 15 Apr. 1925; *Brighton and Hove Herald,* 3 Dec. 1938; Brownlow, *War,* 301, 309.

33. Fenin and Everson, *The Western,* 116.

34. Allen, *Only Yesterday,* 155–87; Sells-Floto Circus program, 1931, quoted in Paul E. Mix, *Tom Mix,* 164; *San Francisco Examiner,* 27 Nov. 1931, LFFS.

35. Material on the Mix legend is voluminous. For standard sources, see Tom Mix, "Making a Million"; Fenin and Everson, *The Western,* 109–12; Paul E. Mix, *Tom Mix,* 53–54, 59–64, 163–71; Lincks, "Tom Mixes In," 110; Brownlow, *War,* 300–302; and Buscombe, *BFI Companion,* 31. The Mix legend permeates Olive Stokes Mix's *Fabulous Tom Mix.*

36. Wrobel, *End of American Exceptionalism,* 104–6; White, "Frederick Jackson Turner," 45–46; Buscombe, *BFI Companion,* 32, 370. Frantz and Choate assert that the cowboy was the composite of all frontiersmen (*American Cowboy,* 70–71, 139).

37. Chruikshank, "Tom Takes the Rainbow Trail," 120; Brownlow, *War,* 301; Olive Stokes Mix, *Fabulous Tom Mix,* 89–90, 99–100.

38. Fenin and Everson, *The Western,* 131–43; Jacobs, *Rise of the American Film,* 295–96; Hyams, *Life and Times of the Western Movie,* 33–34; Nye, *Unembarrassed Muse,* 293–97; for an example of romantic western literature, see Rinehart, "Summer Comes," 3–4, 66, 71–72.

39. Olive Stokes Mix, *Fabulous Tom Mix,* 141; *New York Times,* 5 Apr. 1925; *London Evening News,* 3 Sept. 1938.

40. Olive Stokes Mix, *Fabulous Tom Mix*, 100, 141; Fenin and Everson, *The Western*, 117; "The Shadow Stage," *Photoplay* 34 (July 1928), 56, and (Sept. 1928), 111; "Brief Reviews of Current Pictures," *Photoplay* 33 (Dec. 1927), 8, and 35 (Jan. 1929), 111; for review of a Mix movie combining western and Arabian themes, see the review of *King Cowboy* in "The Shadow Stage," *Photoplay* 35 (Jan. 1929), 92.

41. Wrobel, *End of American Exceptionalism*, 99–100.

42. *New York Times*, 21 Feb. 1932; Olive Stokes Mix, *Fabulous Tom Mix*, 70; Tom Mix, "Making a Million" (June 1928), 113; for the influence of melodrama on early westerns, see Rahill, *World of Melodrama*, 297, 302–4.

43. Paul E. Mix, *Tom Mix*, 87–89; Fenin and Everson, *The Western*, 114; Mordaunt Hall, "The Screen," *New York Times*, 21 Jan. 1925 and 28 Jan. 1926; Buscombe, *BFI Companion*, 31.

44. For Indians in Mix movies, see reviews of *Deadwood Coach* and *The Rainbow Trail* in Mordaunt Hall, "The Screen," *New York Times*, 21 Jan. 1925 and 3 June 1925.

45. Paul E. Mix, *Tom Mix*, 118–20, 122; review of *Horseman of the Plains* in "Brief Reviews of Current Pictures," *Photoplay* 34 (June 1928), 17, and "Shadow Stage," *Photoplay* 34 (June 1928), 82.

46. Olive Stokes Mix, *Fabulous Tom Mix*, 70; *New York Times*, 12 Oct. 1925; Paul E. Mix, *Tom Mix*, 118–20.

47. Buscombe, *BFI Companion*, 370.

48. Hart, *My Life*, 166–225, 274–300, 324–25; Jacobs, *Rise of the American Film*, 144–45; Hyams, *Life and Times*, 25, 28, 30, 32; Fenin and Everson, *The Western*, 75–107.

49. Buscombe, *BFI Companion*, 31; Chrisman, "Tom Mix," 98; *New York Times*, 12 Oct. 1925 and 11 Feb. 1933; for plot outlines of typical movies, see Paul E. Mix, *Tom Mix*, 118–24.

50. Olive Stokes Mix, *Fabulous Tom Mix*, 33–34; Lincks, "Tom Mixes In," 110.

51. For values in the *McGuffey Readers*, see Atherton, *Main Street*, 65–88; for Mix's advice to children, see Montanye, "The Ridin' Romeo," 113; Olive Stokes Mix, *Fabulous Tom Mix*, 94, 134–35, 141–42; *New York Times*, 21 Feb. 1925 and 5 Apr. 1925; *London Daily Express*, 15 Apr. 1925; Chrisman, "Tom Mix," 98.

52. Olive Stokes Mix, *Fabulous Tom Mix*, 134–35; Paul E. Mix, *Tom Mix*, 124–125; for the cowboy as hero, see Davis, "Ten Gallon Hero," 111–25.

53. Review of *Deadwood Coach* in Mordaunt Hall, "The Screen," *New York Times*, 21 Jan. 1925; Olive Stokes Mix, *Fabulous Tom Mix*, 142.

54. Tom Mix, "The Loves of Tom Mix," 30–31, 124–27; Olive Stokes Mix, *Fabulous Tom Mix*, 44–45; *London Star*, 13 Apr. 1925; *New York Times*, 12 July 1925 and 23 Apr. 1928; Fenin and Everson, *The Western*, 117–18; Review of *Just Tony* in Mordaunt Hall, "The Screen," *New York Times*, 7 Aug. 1922.

55. *London Graphic*, 11 Apr. 1925; *New York Times*, 7 Aug. 1922, 31 Mar. 1925, 3 June 1925, 2 Aug. 1925, 18 Aug. 1925, 28 Jan. 1926, and 28 Apr. 1926.

56. Paul E. Mix, *Tom Mix*, 115, posters on 126–33; *New York Times*, 21 Jan. 1925, 15 Apr. 1925, 3 June 1925, 18 Aug. 1925, and 2 Dec. 1925, 28 Jan. 1926, 15 Mar. 1926, and 28

Apr. 1926; Buscombe, *BFI Companion,* 31; Paul E. Mix, *Tom Mix,* 120–21; review of *The Drifter* in "The Shadow Stage," *Photoplay* 35 (Mar. 1929), 49. For Mix posters featuring this kind of action, see Nicholas, *Tom Mix,* 32, 33, 35, 37. The reference to a motorcycle is from *A Muddle in Horsethieves,* 29 Oct. 1913, LU 1481, copyright description in LC.

57. *New York Times,* 27 May 1928.

58. Lincks, "Tom Mixes In," 67; *Sheffield Telegraph,* 6 Oct. 1938; Olive Stokes Mix, *Fabulous Tom Mix,* 51–52, 71–72; Fenin and Everson, *The Western,* 118–19; *New York Times,* 25 Jan. 1933; Brownlow, *War,* 307, attributes the stunt double information and Mix's reaction to a letter to him from Harrey Parry.

59. Tom Mix, "Making a Million" (June 1928), 114; Olive Stokes Mix, *Fabulous Tom Mix,* 30; *Sheffield Telegraph,* 6 Oct. 1938; *New York Times,* 26 Nov. 1931.

60. *New York Times,* 5 Apr. 1925; Paul E. Mix, *Tom Mix,* 100; Olive Stokes Mix, *Fabulous Tom Mix,* 121–23; Cal York, "Gossip of All the Studios," *Photoplay,* Nov. 1928, 50–51; Chrisman, "Tom Mix," 90; Roderick Nash, *Wilderness,* 188–91; Roderick Nash, *Nervous Generation,* 77–90.

61. Fenin and Everson, *The Western,* 116, 118–19, 132, 135; Wrobel, *End of American Exceptionalism,* 106; *New York Times,* 25 Jan. 1933; Olive Stokes Mix, *Fabulous Tom Mix,* 88; Paul E. Mix, *Tom Mix,* 123; Buscombe, *BFI Companion,* 31.

62. For sources linking Mix's costumes to those in Wild West shows, see Hyams, *Life and Times,* 32, and Brownlow, *War,* 309.

63. Olive Stokes Mix, *Fabulous Tom Mix,* 139–40.

64. Tom Mix, "Making a Million" (May 1925), 110; Olive Stokes Mix, *Fabulous Tom Mix,* 38, 139–40; Reid, "Diamond Tom Mix," 101; *San Francisco Examiner,* 27 Nov. 1931, LFFS; *London Daily Mirror,* 16 Apr. 1925; Fenin and Everson, *The Western,* 119–20; Buscombe, *BFI Companion,* 31. Articles and many movie reviews include descriptions of Mix's attire; see, in particular, *New York Times,* 21 Jan. 1925, 15 Apr. 1925, 3 June 1925, 18 Aug. 1925, 2 Dec. 1925, 28 Jan. 1926, and 28 Apr. 1926. According to Nicholas (*Tom Mix,* 41) and Fenin and Everson (*The Western,* 181–90), Mix set the pattern for western costume into the 1950s.

65. *New York Times,* 29 Mar. 1925.

66. *New York Times,* 31 Mar. 1925, 4 Apr. 1925, and 12 Apr. 1925.

67. *New York Times,* 2 Apr. 1925 and 5 Apr. 1925. Details about preparations for the trip, and the number of hats, varied. A later article (*New York Times,* 9 May 1925), said Mix distributed forty-seven white hats while in Europe.

68. *London Daily Mirror,* 14 Apr. 1925, 15 Apr. 1925, and 16 Apr. 1925; *London Morning Post,* 15 Apr. 1925 and 16 Apr. 1925; *London Star,* 14 Apr. 1925; *London Daily Telegraph,* 15 Apr. 1925; *London Daily Express,* 15 Apr. 1925; *London Daily Graphic,* 15 Apr. 1925.

69. *London Morning Advertiser,* 15 Apr. 1925; *London Daily Herald,* 14 Apr. 1925; *London Daily Graphic,* 15 Apr. 1925.

70. *London Morning Advertiser,* 15 Apr. 1925; *London Daily Mirror,* 14 Apr. 1925 and 16 Apr. 1925; *London Daily Express,* 15 Apr. 1925; *London Morning Post,* 15 Apr. 1925;

*London Daily Herald,* 16 Apr. 1925 and 17 Apr. 1925. For Mix as Dick Turpin, see reviews of *Dick Turpin* in Mordaunt Hall, "The Screen," *London Times,* 26 Jan. 1925, and Dean, "Do You Know," 102.

71. *London Daily Telegraph,* 16 Apr. 1925; *London Morning Post,* 16 Apr. 1925; *London Times,* 16 Apr. 1925; *London Daily Graphic,* 16 Apr. 1925; *London Daily Mirror,* 16 Apr. 1925.

72. *London Star,* 16 Apr. 1925; *London Morning Post,* 17 Apr. 1925; *London Daily Mirror,* 17 Apr. 1925.

73. *London Morning Post,* 16 Apr. 1925; *London Daily Telegraph,* 16 Apr. 1925; *London Daily Graphic,* 16 Apr. 1925; *London Daily Express,* 15 Apr. 1925; *London Daily Herald,* 16 Apr. 1925.

74. *London Morning Advertiser,* 15 Apr. 1925; *London Daily Express,* 15 Apr. 1925; Dulles, *Americans Abroad,* 153–56; Boorstin, *America,* 20–24; Strout, *American Image,* 177–78.

75. *London Daily Graphic,* 16 Apr. 1925; "'Max' and 'Mix,'" 422; see also *London Morning Post,* 18 Apr. 1925.

76. *London Daily Chronicle,* 17 Apr. 1925; *London Star,* 17 Apr. 1925; *London Daily Graphic,* 15 Apr. 1925 (for Mix considering sending Tony to Paris by "aeroplane"); *London Daily Express,* 20 Apr. 1925; *Le Gaulois* (Paris), 19 Apr. 1925; *London Morning Post,* 15 Apr. 1925; Norris, *Tom Mix Book,* 37; *London Times,* 9 May 1925.

77. Paul E. Mix, *Tom Mix,* 109; *London Times,* 9 May 1925.

78. Buscombe, *BFI Companion,* 30–32; Fenin and Everson, *The Western,* 146–60; Hyams, *Life and Times of the Western Movie,* 32; Hardy, *Encyclopedia,* 18.

79. Jacobs, *Rise of the American Film,* 506–7, 509–13; Bushby, "New Two-Gun Man," 50, 121; *London Evening News,* 3 Sept. 1938; Chrisman, "Tom Mix," 90.

80. Cal York, "Gossip of All the Studios," *Photoplay,* Mar. 1929, 96; James R. Quirk, "Close-Ups and Long-Shots," *Photoplay,* Apr. 1929, 27; Buscombe, *BFI Companion,* 426.

81. Hardy, *Encyclopedia,* 18.

82. James R. Quirk, "Close-Ups and Long-Shots," *Photoplay,* Nov. 1928, 30; Cruikshank, "Tom Takes the Rainbow Trail," 119.

83. Caption under photo of Mix, *Photoplay* 34 (July 1928), 24; George Miller to Jack Hill c/o Tom Mix, 24 Feb. 1928, GC, box 82, MB; Cruikshank, "Tom Takes the Rainbow Trail," 119; "As We Go to Press," *Photoplay* 33 (Mar. 1928), 6.

84. Buscombe, *BFI Companion,* 371. Paul E. Mix lists an additional film, *The Dude Ranch,* and asserts that all the films were released in 1929 (*Tom Mix,* 190). "Brief Reviews of Current Pictures," *Photoplay* 35 (Apr. 1929), 146; "The Shadow Stage," *Photoplay* 35 (Mar. 1929), 49.

85. Cal York, "News! Views! Gossip! of Stars and Studios," *Photoplay,* Apr. 1930, 78; *New York Times,* 21 Feb. 1932; Paul E. Mix, *Tom Mix,* 112, 134–35; Olive Stokes Mix, *Fabulous Tom Mix,* 143–45; Chrisman, "Tom Mix," 48–49. Reports of his salary varies. Paul E. Mix and Olive Stokes Mix put the salary at $20,000. In a 1 February 1930 letter to Zack Miller, J. C. Newman claimed it was $7,000 (GC, box 89, MB). For specific acts in Mix's "Wild West Exhibition," see Nicholas, *Tom Mix,* 63–64, 66.

86. Paul E. Mix, *Tom Mix,* 135–38; Olive Stokes Mix, *Fabulous Tom Mix,* 143–46; Chrisman, "Tom Mix," 90–98; *Glenwood Post* (Glenwood Springs, Colo.), 13 July 1926, 15 July 1926, 22 July 1926; Joe Miller to Tom Mix, 29 Aug. 1927, GC, box 87, MB; Charles Wirth, Circus Editor of *The Billboard* to Joe Miller, 8 Sept. 1927, GC, box 74, MB; George Miller to Tom Mix, 23 Nov. 1927, and George Miller to Jack Hill c/o Tom Mix, 24 Feb. 1928, both in GC, box 82, MB; Zack Miller to John McGrail, 9 Feb. 1929, GC, box 88, MB; unsigned letter from one of the Millers (perhaps young George W.) to Tom Mix, 19 Nov. 1929, GC, box 87, MB; "In Re: Western Show Corp. vs Tom Mix Memorandum," n.d., Misc. unnumbered box, MB.

87. Chrisman, "Tom Mix," 43, 49, 98; Paul E. Mix, *Tom Mix,* 190–93; Kaminsky, "Tom Mix," 688; *New York Times,* 19 Dec. 1932 and 14 July 1933; for the quality of Mix's speaking voice, see *New York Times,* 20 May 1928 and 8 Sept. 1940. I listened to him speak in *The Miracle Rider* and confirmed that he often did not speak well or clearly.

88. Paul E. Mix, *Tom Mix,* 142, 145, 147, 149, 178–82; Olive Stokes Mix, *Fabulous Tom Mix,* 147–49, 157–71; Buscombe, *BFI Companion,* 239; Tuska, "American Western Cinema," 35; Fenin and Everson, *The Western,* 121; *The Miracle Rider.*

89. Paul E. Mix, *Tom Mix,* 111–12, 138–50, 178, 182; Olive Stokes Mix, *Fabulous Tom Mix,* 158, 172–73; James R. Quirk, "Close-Ups and Long-Shots," *Photoplay,* Nov. 1928, 30; "As We Go to Press," *Photoplay* 36 (July 1929), 6; *New York Times,* 9 May 1929, 12 May 1929, 10 Sept. 1929, 7 Nov. 1930, 9 Jan. 1931, 25 Jan. 1931, 20 Sept. 1931, 25 Nov. 1931, 26 Nov. 1931, 27 Nov. 1931, 28 Nov. 1931, 29 Nov. 1931, 1 July 1932, 19 Dec. 1932, 17 Jan. 1933, 25 Jan. 1933, 5 Oct. 1935, and 20 May 1936; for Mix's view of marital difficulties, see Tom Mix, "Wanted," 38–39, 125–27; for the Millers' lawsuit, see "In Re: Western Show Corp. vs Tom Mix Memorandum," n.d., Misc. unnumbered box, MB; H. L. Wentz to Zack Miller, 24 Jan. 1935, Show Scripts, MB. This last document shows the Millers were to collect ninety-five hundred dollars as a settlement.

90. *Edinburgh Evening Dispatch,* 31 Oct. 1938; *Leeds Mercury,* 17 Oct. 1938; *Birmingham Gazette,* 20 Sept. 1938; *Birmingham Mail,* 19 Sept. 1938 and 20 Sept. 1938; *Portsmouth Evening News,* 14 Feb. 1939; *Edinburgh Evening News,* 1 Nov. 1938.

91. *Birmingham Gazette,* 20 Sept. 1938; *Birmingham Mail,* 20 Sept. 1938; *Nottingham Guardian,* 3 Oct. 1938; *Edinburgh Evening News,* 1 Nov. 1938; *Portsmouth Evening News,* 14 Feb. 1939.

92. *Birmingham Gazette,* 20 Sept. 1938; *Nottingham Guardian,* 3 Oct. 1938; *Brentford and Chiswick Times,* 3 Mar. 1939; *Birmingham Mail,* 20 Sept. 1938; *Edinburgh Evening News,* 31 Oct. 1938; *Edinburgh Evening Dispatch,* 31 Oct. 1938; *Brighton and Hove Herald,* 3 Dec. 1938; *Leeds Mercury,* 17 Oct. 1938; *Hull and Yorkshire Times,* 19 Nov. 1938.

93. *London Evening News,* 3 Sept. 1938; *Nottingham Guardian,* 3 Oct. 1938; *Liverpool Weekly Post,* 10 Sept. 1938; *Hull Daily Mail,* 22 Nov. 1938; *Sheffield Telegraph,* 6 Oct. 1938; *Wolverhampton Express and Star* (England), 21 Jan. 1939.

94. *Nottingham Evening News,* 4 Oct. 1938; *Liverpool Weekly Post,* 10 Sept. 1938; *London Evening News,* 3 Sept. 1938; *Sheffield Telegraph and Star,* 11 Oct. 1938; *Brighton and Hove Herald,* 3 Dec. 1938; *Wolverhampton Express and Star* (England), 21 Jan. 1939.

95. Buscombe, *BFI Companion*, 370.

96. *Nottingham Evening News*, 4 Oct. 1938.

97. Ibid.

98. Olive Stokes Mix, *Fabulous Tom Mix*, 172–75; Brownlow, *War*, 309, 312.

99. *New York Times*, 13 Oct. 1940 and 14 Oct. 1940; Brownlow, *War*, 312; Paul E. Mix, *Tom Mix*, 151. R. E. Nelson bought the wreck on 3 October 1942 for one hundred dollars. The restored auto is on exhibit at the Imperial Palace, Las Vegas, complete with Mix's gun holster and oversized gas pedal. See Paddock and Pearson, *Imperial Palace Auto Collection*, 68.

100. Brazendale and Aceti, *Classic Cars*, 320–23.

101. *Sheffield Telegraph and Star*, 11 Oct. 1938.

## Conclusion

1. Horn and Burke, "How the West Was Really Won," 56–65. For different views among western historians on how to deal with the "Wild West" component of the discipline, see Dippie, "American Wests," 4, 11, 14, 15, 17, 18; White, "Frederick Jackson Turner," 54; and Slotkin, *Gunfighter Nation*, 66–69.

# BIBLIOGRAPHY

Newspapers

*American and Commercial Daily Advertiser* (Baltimore). 1838.
*American Register and Colonial World* (London). 1914.
*Athenaeum* (London). 1839–42, 1848.
*Baltimore Sun.* 1838.
*Birmingham Gazette.* 1938.
*Birmingham Mail.* 1938.
*Boston Commercial Gazette.* 1838.
*Boston Daily Evening Transcript.* 1838.
*Boston Morning Post.* 1838.
*Brentford and Chiswick Times.* 1939.
*Brighton and Hove Herald.* 1938.
*Le Charivari* (Paris). 1845.
*Cincinnati Daily Gazette.* 1833.
*Le Constitutionnel* (Paris). 1845.
*Courrier de Bayonne.* 1905.
*Daily Albany Argus.* 1837.
*Daily Oklahoman* (Oklahoma City). 1923, 1925, 1927, 1928–30, 1934.
*La Depeche* (Toulouse). 1905.
*L'Eclair* (Montpellier). 1905.
*L'Eclaireur* (Nice). 1906.
*Edinburgh Evening Dispatch.* 1938.
*Edinburgh Evening News.* 1938.
*Essex Register* (Salem). 1838.
*Galignani's Messenger* (Paris). 1845.

*Le Gaulois* (Paris). 1925.

*Glasgow Evening Citizen.* 1904.

*Glenwood Post* (Glenwood Springs, Colo.). 1926.

*Hattiesburg (Miss.) American.* 1929.

*Henryetta (Okla.) Daily Free Lance.* 1926.

*Hull Daily Mail.* 1938.

*Hull and Yorkshire Times.* 1938.

*Illustrated London News.* 1887.

*L'Independent* (Pau). 1905.

*John Bull* (London). 1840, 1843.

*Journal Avenir* (Bayonne). 1905.

*Leeds Mercury.* 1938.

*Liberty (Mo.) Weekly Tribune.* 1859.

*Liverpool Weekly Post.* 1938.

*Llandudno Advertiser.* 1904.

*Llandudno Visitor's Herald.* 1904.

*London Court Journal.* 1840.

*London Daily Chronicle.* 1925.

*London Daily Express.* 1925.

*London Daily Graphic.* 1925.

*London Daily Herald.* 1925.

*London Daily Mirror.* 1925.

*London Daily Sketch.* 1914.

*London Daily Telegraph.* 1925.

*London Era.* 1843–44.

*London Evening News.* 1938.

*London Globe.* 1914.

*London Globe and Traveller.* 1840.

*London Graphic.* 1914, 1925.

*London Morning Advertiser.* 1914, 1925.

*London Morning Chronicle.* 1840, 1844.

*London Morning Herald.* 1844.

*London Morning Post.* 1840, 1925.

*London Saturday Journal.* 1840.

*London Spectator.* 1840, 1843–44.

*London Stage.* 1914.

*London Standard.* 1914.

*London Star.* 1925.

*London Times.* 1887–89, 1840–41, 1843–45, 1848, 1851, 1925.

*Manchester Guardian.* 1843.

*Memorial des Pyrenees* (Pau). 1905.

*Morning Courier and New-York Enquirer.* 1832, 1837–39.

*Newcastle-on-Tyme Evening Chronicle.* 1904.
*New Orleans Bee.* 1835.
*New Orleans Courier.* 1835.
*New Orleans Observer.* 1835.
*New York Commercial Advertiser.* 1832–40.
*New York Courier.* 1838.
*New York Evening Post.* 1837, 1839.
*New York Journal of Commerce.* 1839.
*New York Morning Herald.* 1837, 1839.
*New York Sun.* 1838–39.
*New York Times.* 1851, 1886–90, 1892–94, 1901, 1922, 1925–33, 1935–36, 1940.
*Norfolk Chronicle* (London). 1914.
*Nottingham Evening News.* 1938.
*Nottingham Guardian.* 1938.
*Oneida Whig* (Utica). 1837.
*Pennsylvanian* (Philadelphia). 1839.
*Penny Illustrated Paper* (London). 1887.
*Philadelphia Daily Focus.* 1838.
*Philadelphia North American.* 1839.
*Pittsburgh Gazette.* 1833.
*Ponca City (Okla.) Courier.* 1905, 1908, 1913.
*Pourtsmouth Evening News.* 1939.
*La Presse* (Paris). 1845.
*La Republique* (Brive). 1905.
*Semaine de Bayonne.* 1905.
*Sheffield Telegraph.* 1938.
*Staffordshire Sentinel.* 1904.
*Sunderland Daily Echo.* 1904.
*Troy Daily Whig.* 1837.
*United States Gazette* (Philadelphia). 1838.
*Washington Daily National Intelligencer.* 1838.
*Washington Globe.* 1838.
*Welshman* (Carmarthen). 1904.
*Wolverhampton Express and Star.* 1939.

## Archival Sources

American Heritage Center. Owen Wister Western Writer's Reading Room. University
    of Wyoming, Laramie.
    William F. Cody Collection.
        George T. Beck Papers.
        Correspondence.

France folder.

*Ideal Western Lands Selected by the Famous "Buffalo Bill."* N.p., n.d. Box 5. Leaflets folder.

"Route of Buffalo Bill's Wild West—1889–1891." Box 1.

Lucille Nichols Patrick Papers.

"Buffalo Bill, His Time, and His Town: From the Old Cody *Enterprise* Issues—under Editor J.H. Peake." Typewritten Ms. Cody History, 1901 File.

Memorial Museum Clippings. Chicago Paper.

Jacob M. Schwoob Collection.

Milt Hinkle. "The Way a Wild West Show Operated." *Frontier Times* (Feb.–Mar. 1909): 22–23, and n.p. William F. Cody File

Unidentified Buffalo Bill and Pawnee Bill Program. N.p., n.d.

The Hon. Richard H. Scott Collection.

Author's collection. Grand Junction, Colo.

*Official Souvenir Program: Buffalo Bill's Wild West and Congress of Rough Riders of the World.* N.p.: Nebraska Game and Parks Commission, Buffalo Bill's Wild West Inc., 1971. Program of reenactment given in North Platte, Neb. Monte Montana, producer.

Buffalo Bill Historical Center. McCracken Research Library. Cody, Wyo.

William F. Cody Collection. Manuscript Collection 6.

Ethyl Parry Bradford folder.

*Buffalo Bill Bids You Good Bye: Magazine and Official Review.* New York: I. M. Southern and Co., n.d. Program, 1910.

*Buffalo Bill (Himself) and 101 Ranch Wild West Combined with the Military Pageant "Preparedness": Magazine and Daily Review.* Philadelphia: Harrison Press, n.d. Program, 1916.

*Buffalo Bill's Wild West.* Hartford, Conn.: Calhoun Printing, 1885. Program, 1885.

*Buffalo Bill's Wild West.* Paris: n.p., n.d. Program in French, 1905 or 1906.

*Buffalo Bill's Wild West Combined with Pawnee Bill's Great Far East.* Buffalo: Courier Company, 1909. Courier, 1909.

*Buffalo Bill's Wild West Combined with Pawnee Bill's Great Far East: Magazine of Daily Wonders and Daily Review.* 1st ed. Buffalo: Courier Company, 1909. Program, 1909.

1879–80 Stage Notices Scrapbook.

General Correspondence.

*Miller and Arlington Wild West Show Co. Presents Buffalo Bill (Himself) and the 101 Ranch and Military Pageant "Preparedness."* N.p., n.d. Program, 1916.

*Miller Bros. and Arlington 101 Ranch Real Wild West.* N.p., n.d. Courier, 1910.

*Miller Bros. and Arlington 101 Ranch Real Wild West.* N.p, 1911. Program, 1911 or 1914; dated 1911 but contents suggest this is a 1914 program.

Annie Oakley Scrapbook.

*Official Souvenir: Buffalo Bill's Wild West and Congress of Rough Riders of the*

*World.* Ed. M. B. Bailey. Compiled and published by Chas. R. Hutchinson. Route book, 1896.

*The Pioneer Scouts: A Book of Border Life: Magazine of Wonders and Daily Review.* Buffalo: Courier Company, 1911. Program, 1911.

Scrapbook for France, 1889. Box 4.

Scrapbook for Germany, 1890. Box 5.

Scrapbook for Italy, 1890. Box 6.

*Season 1900: Official Route Book of the Pawnee Bill Wild West Show.* Chicago: F. T. Peterson Co., n.d.

*Story Book and Program: Sells-Floto Circus: Home of 1001 Wonders.* N.p., n.d. Program, 1914.

Harry Webb. "Buffalo Bill: Saint or Devil." Typewritten Ms.

*The Wild West: Buffalo Bill and Dr. Carver: Rocky Mountain and Prairie Exhibition.* Hartford, Conn.: Calhoun Printing and Engraving Co., 1883. Program, 1883.

Denver Public Library. Western History Department.

William F. Cody Collection.

*The American Exhibition, London, 1887.* N.p., n.d. Box 2.

Johnny Baker Scrapbook for 1887.

"Bowery Theatre." New York: S. V. St. Clair, 1877. Box 2. Program for 8 September 1877.

*Buffalo Bill's (Col. W. F. Cody) Wild West and Congress of Rough Riders of the World: Historical Sketches and Programme.* New York: Fless and Ridge Printing Co., 1894. Box 2. Program, 1894.

*Buffalo Bill's (Col. W. F. Cody) Wild West and Congress of Rough Riders of the World: Historical Sketches & Programme.* New York: Fless and Ridge Printing Co., n.d. Box 2. Program, 1897.

*Buffalo Bill's (Col. W. F. Cody) Wild West and Congress of Rough Riders of the World: Historical Sketches and Programme.* New York: Fless and Ridge Printing Co., 1899. Box 2. Program, 1899.

*Buffalo Bill's TE Ranch, Ishawooa, Wyoming: Home Ranch of Col. W. F. Cody, Season of 1916, Opened to Tourists for the First Time.* Denver: Press of Western Newspaper Union, n.d. Box 1.

*Buffalo Bill's Wild West.* N.p., n.d. Box 2. Courier, 1884; the library lists this as an 1885 courier.

*Buffalo Bill's Wild West.* N.p., n.d. Box 2. Program, 1884.

*Buffalo Bill's Wild West.* Hartford, Conn.: Calhoun Printing Co., 1886. Box 2. Program, 1886.

*Buffalo Bill's Wild West.* Hartford, Conn.: Calhoun Printing Co., 1887. Box 2. Program, 1887.

*Buffalo Bill's Wild West.* Hartford, Conn.: Calhoun Printing Co., 1888. Box 2. Program, 1888.

*Buffalo Bill's Wild West.* Buffalo: Courier Company, 1907. Box 2. Courier, 1907.

*Buffalo Bill's Wild West and Congress of Rough Riders of the World.* Chicago: Blakely Printing Company, n.d. Box 2. Courier, 1893.

*Buffalo Bill's Wild West and Congress of Rough Riders of the World.* N.p.: Courier Co., n.d. Box 2. Courier, 1898.

*Buffalo Bill's Wild West and Congress of Rough Riders of the World: Historical Sketches and Programme.* Chicago: Blakely Printing Company, 1893. Box 2. Program, 1893.

*Buffalo Bill's Wild West and Congress of Rough Riders of the World: Historical Sketches and Programme.* Buffalo: J. and H. Mayer and Courier Company, 1900. Box 2. Program, 1900.

*Buffalo Bill's Wild West and Congress of Rough Riders of the World: Historical Sketches and Programme.* Buffalo: J. and H. Mayer and Courier Company, Buffalo, 1901. Box 2. Program, 1901.

*Buffalo Bill's Wild West and Congress of Rough Riders of the World: Official Programme.* New York: Fless and Ridge Printing Company, 1898. Box 2. Program, 1898.

*Buffalo Bill's Wild West: Historical Sketches and Daily Review.* New York: Courier Co., 1907. Box 2. Program, 1907.

*Buffalo Bill's Wild West: Historical Sketches and Daily Review.* Cincinnati and New York: Strobridge Litho. Co. and Courier Company Printers, 1907. Box 2. Program, 1907 or 1908.

"Buffalo Bill's Wild West—Season 1906." Box 2.

Col. W. F. Cody's Private Scrapbook. Vol. 12 of the Nate Salsbury Scrapbooks.

*First Appearance of Buffalo Bill's New and Enlarged Wild West and Congress of Rough Riders.* N.p., n.d. Box 2. Courier, 1895.

*Historical Sketches and Programme.* Buffalo: J. and H. Mayer and Courier Co., 1902. Box 2. Program, 1902.

*Historical Sketches and Programme.* London: Partington Advertising Company, 1902. Box 2. Program, 1903.

*Inaugural Invitation Exhibition of Buffalo Bill's (Hon. W. F. Cody) Wild West.* Manchester: Guardian Printing Work, 1887. Box 2. Manchester program, 1887.

*Life of Buffalo Bill.* New York: Knapp and Company, n.d. In series Histories of Poor Boys Who Have Become Rich packed in Duke Cigarettes. Box 1.

*The Rough Rider.* Buffalo: Cody and Salsbury, 1899. Oversized File. Courier, 1899.

*Route-Book: Buffalo Bill's Wild West, 1899, Containing Also the Official Routes, Seasons of 1895, 1896, 1897, 1898.* Compiled by George H. Gooch. Buffalo: Mathews-Northrup Co., n.d. Box 2.

Nate Salsbury Scrapbooks. 11 vols.

*The Wild West.* N.p., n.d. Box 2. Program, 1883.

*The Wild West: Hon. W. F. Cody and Dr. W. F. Carver's Rocky Mountain and Prairie Exhibition.* Chicago: P. L. Hanscom and Co., 1883. Box 2. Program for Chicago Driving Park, October 1883.

Library of Congress. Washington, D.C.

Motion Picture, Broadcasting, and Recorded Sound Division. Motion Pictures and Television Reading Room.

William F. Cody file.

Buffalo Bill—in Action: Col. William F. Cody Himself Stars at Meeting of Westerners—in Motion Pictures of the Old Silent Days, Assembled from Many Sources with Comments and Explanations by Don Russell." *Westerners Brand Book* 19, no. 5 (July 1962): 33–40.

Bob Lee. Untitled typewritten ms.

Copyright descriptions registered with the Copyright Office.

"Oklahoma (state)" file.

National Archives. Washington, D.C.

Letters Received by the Office of Indian Affairs, 1824–80. Miscellaneous, 1842–43.

Microfilm Copy, M234. Roll 442. Correspondence M1800 (1843).

National Collection of Fine Arts and the National Portrait Gallery Library. Washington, D.C.

George Catlin Papers.

George Catlin. Handwritten draft of *Catlin's Notes of Eight Years' Travels and Residence in Europe, with His North American Indian Collection.*

Clippings.

Correspondence.

Obituary Notes.

Smithsonian Institution. Washington, D.C.

Archives of American Art.

George Catlin Papers, 1821–90. Rolls 2136–37.

George Catlin. "Mineral Chart and Lithograph." Roll 2137.

Certificates, Account Book, Receipts, and Miscellaneous Financial Material. Rolls 2136–37.

Correspondence. Roll 2136.

Notebooks, Manuscripts, Writings, and Notes. Roll 2136

———. "Original Sketch and Notebook."

Printed Material—Petitions, Memorials, Proposals, Pamphlets, etc. Roll 2137.

George Catlin. "Synopsis of the Travels of George Catlin in Gathering His Sketches for His Indian Collection."

George Catlin Papers, 1840–60. Roll 3277. Original documents housed in the Gilcrease Museum, Tulsa, Okla.

Correspondence.

Indian Gallery.

Clippings.

Handbills.

Original Indian Drawings.

George Catlin. "North American Indian Sketchbook." Unpublished
sketchbook.

George Catlin. *Proposed Creation of Museum of Mankind.* London: W. J.
Golbourn, 1851.

Catlin Family Papers.

Family Histories and Genealogies. Roll 3023.

Letters. Roll 3024.

Emil Williams Lenders Papers. Roll 3278. Original documents housed in the
Gilcrease Museum, Tulsa, Okla.

National Anthropological Archives.

L. F. Foster Scrapbook.

University of Oklahoma. Bizell Memorial Library. Western History Collections.

Walter S. Campbell Collection.

*Buffalo Bill's Wild West.* Paris: Imprimerie Parrot, 1889. Box 72. French Program, 1889.

Maj. Gordon W. Lillie Collection.

*Historical Sketches and Programme: Buffalo Bill's Wild West and Congress of
Rough Riders of the World: Official Programme.* Buffalo: Courier Company
and J. and H. Mayer, 1902. Box 20. Program, 1902.

Legal Documents. Box 18.

Outsize Scrapbook for Pawnee Bill.

L. M. Sullivan. "Major Gordon W. Lillie's (Pawnee Bill) Own Story." Box 9.
Typewritten ms.

Miller Brothers 101 Ranch Collection.

General Correspondence. Boxes 73–83, 85–90, 91–93, 93a, 98, 100, 102.

Misc. Unnumbered box.

Outsize Scrapbook for 1914. New York Engagement.

Printed Material, Blank Forms, Misc. Box 99a.

*Official Program Miller Bros. 101 Ranch Real Wild West: Season 1926.* N.p.,
n.d. Program, 1926.

*Program: 101 Ranch Real Wild West and Great Far East.* N.p., n.d.

Scrapbooks. Box 97.

Show Scripts, Correspondence, Programs, Brochures, Probate Will of George L.

*Miller Bros. and Arlington 101 Ranch Real Wild West: Magazine and Daily
Review.* Buffalo: Courier Company, n.d. Program, 1915.

*Miller Bros. 101 Ranch Wild West Show: Daily Review.* N.p., n.d. Program,
1929.

*Miller Bros. 101 Ranch Wild West Show: Daily Review.* N.p., n.d. Program,
1930.

*Miller Brothers 101 Ranch Real Wild West and Great Far East: Magazine and Daily Review.* N.p., n.d. Program, 1927.

*Miller Brothers 101 Ranch Wild West Show: 1929 Route Book.* N.p., n.d.

*The Miller Brothers 101 Real Wild West and Great Far East: Official Season's Route, Season 1925.* Comp. Jerome T. Harriman. N.p., n.d.

*Official Review and History of the Great Wild West: Miller Bros. 101 Ranch Wild West.* New York: I. M. Southern and Co., n.d. Courier, 1909.

## Books, Articles, Chapters, Dissertations, and Papers

Ainsworth, W. Harrison. "Editor's Preface." *Nick of the Woods; or, The Jibbenainosay: A Tale of Kentucky* by Robert Montgomery Bird. 3 vols. London: Richard Bentley, 1837. v–viii.

Allen, Frederick Lewis. *Only Yesterday: An Informal History of the 1920s.* New York: Harper and Row, 1931. Reprint, New York: Harper and Row, 1964.

"American Indians in Europe—the Burial of O-ki-oui-mi, Wife of the Little Wolf at Paris." *Niles' National Register* 68 (2 Aug. 1845): 2.

Anderson, Gary C. *Sitting Bull and the Paradox of Lakota Nationhood.* New York: HarperCollins, 1996.

Arpad, Joseph J., and Kenneth R. Lincoln. *Buffalo Bill's Wild West.* Palmer Lake, Colo.: Filter Press, 1971.

"Article III." *Quarterly Review* 65 (Mar. 1840): 384–422.

"Article VI—*Letters and Notes on the Manners, Customs, and Condition of the North American Indians.* With Four Hundred Illustrations, engraved from his Original Paintings. By George Catlin. 2 vols. 8 vo. Second Edition. London: 1841." *Edinburgh Review* 74 (Jan. 1842): 415–30.

Atherton, Lewis. *The Cattle Kings.* Lincoln: University of Nebraska Press, 1972.

———. *Main Street on the Middle Border.* Bloomington: Indiana University Press, 1984.

Bailey, Thomas A. *A Diplomatic History of the American People.* 6th ed. New York: Appleton-Century-Crofts, 1958.

Balfour, Michael. *The Kaiser and His Times.* New York: W. W. Norton, 1972.

Balshofer, Fred J., and Arthur C. Miller. *One Reel a Week.* Berkeley: University of California Press, 1967.

Becker, Bob. "The Rodeo: Cowboys and Girls from Western Plains Who Risk Lives in Thrilling Feats Are Amateurs, Competing Only for Prizes." *Popular Mechanics,* Aug. 1926, 195–200.

Beetem, Robert N. "George Catlin in France: His Relationship to Delacroix and Baudelaire." *Art Quarterly* 24 (Summer 1961): 129–44.

Berkhoffer, Robert F., Jr. *The White Man's Indian: Images of the American Indian from Columbus to the Present.* New York: Random House, 1979.

Billington, Ray Allen. *Land of Savagery, Land of Promise: The European Imagery of the American Frontier in the Nineteenth Century.* New York: W. W. Norton, 1981.

Bird, Robert Montgomery. *Nick of the Woods; or, The Jibbenainosay: A Tale of Kentucky.* Ed. Cecil B. Williams. New York: American Book Company, 1939.

Blackstone, Sarah J. *Buckskins, Bullets, and Business: A History of Buffalo Bill's Wild West.* Westport, Conn.: Greenwood Press, 1986.

Blake, Herbert Cody. *Blake's Western Stories: History and Busted Romances of the Old Frontier.* Brooklyn, N.Y.: Herbert Cody Blake, 1929.

Bloom-Wilson, Harriet. "Exporting America to Europe: Verbal Images of Buffalo Bill's Wild West." Paper presented at the American Studies Association International Convention, New York, 22 Nov. 1987.

Bode, Carl. *The American Lyceum: Town Meeting of the Mind.* New York: Oxford University Press, 1956.

Boorstin, Daniel J. *America and the Image of Europe: Reflections on American Thought.* New York: Meridian Books, 1960.

———. *The Americans: The National Experience.* New York: Random House, 1965.

Brazendale, Kevin, and Enrica Aceti, eds. *Classic Cars: Fifty Years of the World's Finest Automotive Design.* New York: Exeter Books, 1981.

Briggs, Asa. *A Social History of England.* New York: Viking Press, 1984.

Brownlow, Kevin. *The War, the West, and the Wilderness.* New York: Alfred A. Knopf, 1979.

Buckingham, James Silk. *America: Historical, Statistical, and Descriptive.* 3 vols. London: Fisher, Son, and Co., 1841.

"Buffalo Bill's 'Wild West.'" Monologue from show. In *A Treasury of American Folklore: The Stories, Legends, Tall Tales, Traditions, Ballads, and Songs of the American People,* ed. B. A. Bodkin. New York: Bonanza Books, 1983. 150–56.

Burg, David F. *Chicago's White City of 1893.* Lexington: University Press of Kentucky, 1976.

Burke, John M. *"Buffalo Bill" from Prairie to Palace: An Authentic History of the Wild West.* New York: Rand McNally, 1893.

Burns, Edward McNall. *The American Idea of Mission: Concepts of National Purpose and Destiny.* New Brunswick, N.J.: Rutgers University Press, 1957.

Buscombe, Edward, ed. *The BFI Companion to the Western.* New York: Atheneum, 1988.

Bushby, Marquis. "The New Two-Gun Man." *Photoplay,* Apr. 1930, 50, 121.

Callender, Charles. "Sauk." In *Northwest, 1978.* Ed. Bruce G. Trigger. Vol. 15 of *Handbook of North American Indians.* Washington, D.C.: Smithsonian Institution, 1978. 648–55.

Catlin, George. *Catalog of Catlin's Indian Gallery of Portraits, Landscapes, Manners and Customs, Costumes &c., Collected during Seven Years' Travels amongst Thirty Eight Different Tribes, Speaking Different Languages.* New York: Piercy and Reed, 1837.

————. *Catalogue Raisonné de la Galerie Indienne de Mr. Catlin*. Paris: Inprimerie de Wittersheim, 1845.

————. *Catlin's North American Indian Portfolio: Hunting Scenes and Amusements of the Rocky Mountains and Prairies of America*. London: George Catlin, 1844.

————. *Catlin's Notes for the Emigrant to America*. London: George Catlin, 1848.

————. *Catlin's Notes of Eight Years' Travels and Residence in Europe, with His North American Indian Collection*. 2 vols. London: George Catlin, 1848.

————. *A Descriptive Catalog of Catlin's Indian Collection, Containing Portraits, Landscapes, Costumes &c., and Representations of the Manners and Customs of the North American Indians; Collected and Painted by Mr. Catlin, during Eight Years' Travels amongst Forty Eight Tribes, Mostly Speaking Different Languages; Also Opinions of the Press in England, France, and the United States*. London: George Catlin, 1848.

————. *A Descriptive Catalogue of Catlin's Indian Gallery: Containing Portraits, Landscapes, Costumes, &c. and Representation of the Manners and Customs of the North American Indians; Collected and Painted Entirely by Mr. Catlin, during Seven Years Travel amongst Forty-Eight Tribes, Mostly Speaking Different Languages; Exhibiting at the Egyptian Hall, Picadilly, London, From 10 a.m. until 6 p.m., and from 7 till 10 p.m. Admittance 1.S.* London: C. and J. Adlard, Bartholomew Close, [1840].

————. *Last Rambles amongst the Indians of the Rocky Mountains and the Andes*. New York: D. Appleton, 1867.

————. *Letters and Notes on the Manners, Customs, and Conditions of North American Indians: Written during Eight Years' Travel amongst the Wildest Tribes of Indians in North America*. 2 vols. London: George Catlin, 1844. Reprint, New York: Dover, 1973.

————. *Life amongst the Indians: A Book for Youth*. London: Sampson Low, Son, and Co., 1861.

————. "Memorial of George Catlin, Praying Congress to Purchase His Collection of Indian Portraits and Curiosities." In *Memorial of R. R. Gurley, Praying the Purchase of Catlin's Collection of Paintings and Curiosities, Illustrative of the Manners and Customs of the North American Indians*. 10 July 1848. 30th Cong., 1st Sess. Vol. I, Senate Misc. Doc. 152. 3–4.

————. *North and South American Indians: Catalogue Descriptive and Instructive of Catlin's Indian Cartoons*. New York: Baker and Goodwin, 1871.

————. *O-kee-pa: A Religious Ceremony and Other Customs of the Mandans*. Ed. John C. Ewers. Centennial ed. London: Trübner and Company, 1867; Philadelphia: Lippincott, 1867. Reprint, New Haven: Yale University Press, 1967.

————. *Unparalleled Exhibition: The Fourteen Ioway Indians and Their Interpreter, Just Arrived from the Upper Missouri, near the Rocky Mountains, North America*. London: W. S. Johnson, Nassau Steam Press, 1844.

"Catlin's Indian Gallery." *Niles' National Register* 55 (10 Nov. 1838): 164.

"Catlin's North American Indians." *Democratic Review* 11 (July 1842): 44–52.

Chapman, Arthur. "Rodeo Dollars." *World's Work* 60, no. 7 (July 1931): 28–30.

Chapman, David L. *Sandow the Magnificent: Eugen Sandow and the Beginnings of Bodybuilding.* Urbana: University of Illinois Press, 1994.

Cherny, Robert W. *A Righteous Cause: The Life of William Jennings Bryan.* Boston: Little, Brown, 1985.

Chidsey, Donald Barr. *John the Great: The Times and Life of a Remarkable American, John L. Sullivan.* New York: Doubleday, Doran, 1942.

Chrisman, J. Eugene. "Tom Mix Won His Fight for Life—Now He's Rarin' to Go." *Motion Picture Magazine,* Mar. 1932, 48–49, 90, 98.

"Chronology of Events." In *Buffalo Bill and the Wild West* by David Katzive et al. New York: Brooklyn Museum, 1981. 14–15.

Cody, William F. *Buffalo Bill's Own Story of His Life and Deeds.* Chicago: n.p., 1917.

———. *The Life of Hon. William F. Cody, Known as Buffalo Bill, the Famous Hunter, Scout, and Guide: An Autobiography.* Hartford, Conn.: Frank E. Bliss, 1879. Reprint, Lincoln: University of Nebraska Press, 1978.

———. *Story of the Wild West and Camp-fire Chats, by Buffalo Bill, (Hon. W. F. Cody). A Full and Complete History of the Renowned Pioneer Quartette, Boone, Crockett, Carson, and Buffalo Bill . . . Including a Description of Buffalo Bill's Conquests in England with His Wild West Exhibition, Where Royalty from All the European Nations Paid Him a Generous Homage and Made His Wonderful Show the Greatest Success of Modern Times.* Philadelphia: Historical Publishing, 1888.

Coffman, Edward M. *The War to End All Wars: The American Military Experience in World War I.* New York: Oxford University Press, 1968.

Collings, Ellsworth, and Alma Miller England. *The 101 Ranch.* Norman: University of Oklahoma Press, 1937. Reprint, Norman: University of Oklahoma Press, 1971.

Combe, George. *Notes on the United States of North America during a Phrenological Visit in 1838–39–40.* 2 vols. Philadelphia: Carey and Hart, 1841.

Commager, Henry Steele. *The American Mind: An Interpretation of American Thought and Character since the 1880's.* New Haven: Yale University Press, 1967.

Crane, Fred Arthur. "The Noble Savage in America, 1815–1860: Concepts of the Indian, with Special Reference to the Writers of the Northeast." Ph.D. diss., Yale University, 1952.

Croly, Herbert. *The Promise of American Life.* New York: Macmillan, 1909.

Cruikshank, Herbert. "Tom Takes the Rainbow Trail." *Motion Picture Magazine,* July 1928, 49, 112, 119–20.

Cumberland, Charles C. *Mexico: The Struggle for Modernity.* New York: Oxford University Press, 1968.

Curti, Merle. "America at the World's Fairs, 1851–1893." In *Probing Our Past,* ed. Merle Curti. New York: Harper and Brothers, 1955. 246–77.

———. "Dime Novels and the American Tradition." In *Probing Our Past,* ed. Merle Curti. New York: Harper and Brothers, 1955. 172–88.

———, ed. *Probing Our Past.* New York: Harper and Brothers, 1955.

———. *The Roots of American Loyalty.* New York: Atheneum, 1968.

Davis, David B. "Ten Gallon Hero." *American Quarterly* 6, no. 2 (Summer 1954): 111–25.

Deahl, William. "A History of Buffalo Bill's Wild West Show, 1883–1913." Ph.D. diss., Southern Illinois University, 1974.

Dean, Jesse. "Do You Know Who Dick Turpin Was?" *Motion Picture Magazine,* Apr. 1925, 102–3.

Debo, Angie. *Geronimo: The Man, His Time, His Place.* Norman: University of Oklahoma Press, 1982.

Denslow, Ray Vaughn. *Out of the Past: The Story of George Henry Curzon Melody.* N.p., 1942.

Derry, Kathryn. "Corsets and Broncs: The Wild West Show Cowgirl, 1890–1920." *Colorado Heritage* (Summer 1992): 2–4.

DeSantis, Vicent P. *The Shaping of Modern America: 1877–1920.* 2d ed. Arlington Heights, Ill.: Forum Press, 1989.

Dickens, Charles. *American Notes and Pictures from Italy.* New York: Harper and Brothers, 1842. Reprint, New York: Oxford University Press, 1987.

———. "The Noble Savage." *The Uncommercial Traveller and Reprinted Pieces Etc.* New York: Oxford University Press, 1958. Reprint, New York: Oxford University Press, 1987. 467–73.

Diggins, John Patrick. *The Proud Decades: America in War and Peace, 1941–1960.* New York: W. W. Norton, 1988.

Dippie, Brian W. "American Wests: Historiographical Perspectives." *American Studies International* 27 (Oct. 1989): 3–25.

———. *Catlin and His Contemporaries: The Politics of Patronage.* Lincoln: University of Nebraska Press, 1990.

Donaldson, Thomas. *The George Catlin Indian Gallery in the U.S. National Museum (Smithsonian Institution) with Memoir and Statistics.* Part 5 of *Report of the United States National Museum under the Direction of the Smithsonian Institution, to July, 1885.* Washington, D.C.: GPO, 1886.

Dubofsky, Melvin. *Industrialism and the American Worker, 1865–1920.* 3d ed. Wheeling, Ill.: Harlan Davidson, 1996.

Dulles, Foster Rhea. *Americans Abroad: Two Centuries of European Travel.* Ann Arbor: University of Michigan Press, 1964.

———. *A History of Recreation: America Learns to Play.* 2d ed. New York: Appleton-Century-Crofts, 1965.

Dye, Homer, Jr. "They Ride 'Em at the 4W." *Sunset Magazine,* Nov. 1927, 32–33.

Earle, G. W. "Ride 'Im, Cowboy!" *Popular Mechanics,* June 1930, 906–11.

*1897 Sears Roebuck Catalog.* Ed. Fred L. Israel. New York: Chelsea House, 1968.

Ekirch, Arthur A., Jr. *The Idea of Progress in America, 1815–1860.* New York: Columbia University Press, 1944.

———. *Man and Nature in America.* New York: Columbia University Press, 1963.

Elson, Ruth Miller. *Guardians of Tradition: American Schoolbooks of the Nineteenth Century.* Lincoln: University of Nebraska Press, 1964.

Esselman, Kathryn C. "From Camelot to Monument Valley: Dramatic Origins of the Western Film." In *Focus on the Western,* ed. Jack Nachbar. Englewood Cliffs, N.J.: Prentice Hall, 1974. 9–18.

Etulain, Richard W. "Origins of the Western." In *Critical Essays on the Western American Novel,* ed. William T. Pilkington. Boston: G. K. Hall, 1980. 56–60.

Ewers, John C. *George Catlin: Painter of Indians of the West.* Reprinted from *Annual Report of the Smithsonian Institution for 1955.* Washington, D.C.: GPO, 1955.

Fees, Paul. "In Defense of Buffalo Bill: A Look at Cody in and of His Times." In *Myth of the West* by Chris Bruce et al. Seattle: Henry Art Gallery, University of Washington; New York: Rizzoli, 1990. 141–49.

———. "The Flamboyant Fraternity." *Gilcrease Magazine of American History and Art* 6, no. 1 (Jan. 1984): 1–8.

Fellows, Dexter W., and Andrew A. Freeman. *This Way to the Big Show: The Life of Dexter Fellows.* New York: Viking Press, 1936.

Fenin, George N., and William K. Everson. *The Western: From Silence to Cinerama.* New York: Bonanza Books, 1962.

Foreman, Carolyn Thomas. *Indians Abroad, 1493–1938.* Norman: University of Oklahoma Press, 1943.

Frantz, Joe B., and Julian E. Choate, Jr. *The American Cowboy: The Myth and the Reality.* Norman: University of Oklahoma Press, 1955.

French, Warren. "The Cowboy in the Dime Novel." *Studies in English* 30 (1951): 219–34.

Garland, Hamlin. *A Son of the Middle Border.* New York: Macmillan, 1917.

"George Catlin." *American Bibliopolist: A Monthly Literary Register and Repository of Notes and Queries* 5 (Jan. 1873): 16.

Gipson, Fred. *Fabulous Empire: Colonel Zack Miller's Story.* Boston: Houghton, Mifflin, 1946.

Goetzmann, William H. *Exploration and Empire: The Explorer and Scientist in the Winning of the American West.* New York: Alfred A. Knopf, 1966.

Green, Harvey. *The Light of the Home: An Intimate View of the Lives of Women in Victorian America.* New York: Random House, 1983.

Griffin, Charles Eldridge. *Four Years in Europe with Buffalo Bill.* Albia, Iowa: Stage Publishing, 1908.

Haberly, Lloyd. *Pursuit of the Horizon: A Life of George Catlin, Painter and Recorder of the American Indian.* New York: Macmillan, 1948.

[Hall, James.] "Mr. Catlin's Exhibition of Indian Portraits." *Western Monthly Magazine* 2, no. 9 (Nov. 1833): 535–38.

Hamid, George A., as told to his son George A. Hamid, Jr. *Circus.* New York: Sterling, 1950.

Hand, Charles. *I Was after Money.* London: Partridge Publications, 1949.

Hanes, Col. Bailey C. *Bill Pickett, Bulldogger: The Biography of a Black Cowboy.* Norman: University of Oklahoma Press, 1977.

Hardy, Phil. *The Encyclopedia of Western Movies.* Minneapolis, Minn.: Woodbury Press, 1984.

Hart, William S. *My Life East and West.* Boston: Houghton Mifflin, 1929. Reprint, New York: Benjamin Blom, 1968.

Hassrick, Peter H. "The Artists." In *Buffalo Bill and the Wild West* by David Katzive et al. New York: Brooklyn Museum, 1981. 16–26.

Havighurst, Walter. *Annie Oakley of the Wild West.* New York: Macmillan, 1954.

Hawley, Ellis W. *The Great War and the Search for a Modern Order: A History of the American People and Their Institutions, 1917–1933.* 2d ed. New York: St. Martin's Press, 1992.

Hays, Samuel P. *The Response to Industrialism: 1885–1914.* Chicago: University of Chicago Press, 1957.

Henry, Joseph. "Report of the Secretary for the Year 1872." In *Annual Report of the Board of Regents of the Smithsonian Institution Showing the Operations, Expenditures, and Condition of the Institution for the Year 1872.* 42d Cong., 3d Sess., Misc. Doc. 107. Washington, D.C.: GPO, 1873. 13–54.

Higham, John. *Strangers in the Land: Patterns of American Nativism, 1860–1925.* New York: Atheneum, 1965.

Hindus, Maurice. "Russia's Flaming Cossack Is Doomed." *New York Times Magazine,* 20 Sept. 1925, 14.

Hofstadter, Richard. *The Age of Reform: From Bryan to F.D.R.* New York: Random House, 1955.

———. "Manifest Destiny and the Philippines." In *America in Crisis: Fourteen Crucial Episodes in American History.* Ed. Daniel Aaron. New York: Alfred A. Knopf, 1952. 173–200.

Hone, Philip. *The Diary of Philip Hone, 1828–1851.* Ed. Allan Nevins. 2 vols. New York: Dodd, Mead, 1927.

Horn, Miriam, and Sarah Burke. "How the West Was Really Won." *U.S. News and World Report,* 21 May 1990, 56–65.

Hughes, H. Stuart. *Consciousness and Society: The Reorientation of European Social Thought, 1890–1930.* Rev. ed. New York: Random House, 1977.

Hyams, Jay. *The Life and Times of the Western Movie.* New York: Gallery Books, 1983.

"Important—to the Ladies." *Punch* 6 (1844): 179.

"Indian Mode of Training Horses." *Chamber's Edinburgh Journal* 9 (9 July 1842): 200.

"Indians Exhibited in Europe." *Niles' National Register* 70 (7 Mar. 1846): 2.

Ingraham, Prentiss. *Adventures of Buffalo Bill from Boyhood to Manhood: Deeds of Daring and Romantic Incidents in the Life of Wm. F. Cody, the Monarch of Bordermen.*

New York: Beadle and Adams, 1881. Reprinted in *Eight Dime Novels*. Ed. E. F.
Bleiler. New York: Dover, 1974. 91–105.

Jacobs, Lewis. *The Rise of the American Film: A Critical History with an Essay, Experimental Cinema in America, 1921–1947*. New York: Teachers College Press, Columbia University, 1971.

Johannsen, Albert. *The House of Beadle and Adams and Its Dime and Nickel Novels: The Story of a Vanished Literature*. 2 vols. Norman: University of Oklahoma Press, 1950.

Johnson, Winifred. "Passing of the 'Wild West': A Chapter in the History of American Entertainment." *Southwest Review* 21, no. 1 (Oct. 1935): 33–51.

Judson, William. "The Movies." In *Buffalo Bill and the Wild West* by David Katzive et al. New York: Brooklyn Museum, 1981. 68–83.

Kaminsky, Stuart M. "Tom Mix." In *Actors and Actresses*. Vol. 3 of *International Dictionary of Film and Filmmakers*, ed. Nicholas Thomas. Detroit: St. James Press, 1992. 687–89.

Kasper, Shirl. *Annie Oakley*. Norman: University of Oklahoma Press, 1992.

Katzive, David. Introduction to "The Cowboys" by Howard R. Lamar. In *Buffalo Bill and the Wild West* by David Katzive et al. New York: Brooklyn Museum, 1981. 57.

Keiser, Albert. *The Indian in American Literature*. New York: Oxford University Press, 1933.

King, Charles. *Campaigning with Crook and Stories of Army Life*. Milwaukee: Charles King, 1880. Reprint, Ann Arbor: University Microfilms, 1966.

Larkin, Jack. *The Reshaping of Everyday Life, 1790–1840*. New York: Harper and Row, 1989.

Leavitt, Michael Bennett. *Fifty Years in Theatrical Management*. New York: Broadway Publishing, 1912.

"Letter from Mr. Catlin, Describing Scenes of the Far West." *American Turf Register and Sporting Magazine*, Aug. 1836, 554–61.

Lincks, Peggy. "Tom Mixes In." *Motion Picture Magazine*, Feb. 1919, 66–67, 110.

Livesay, Harold C. *Andrew Carnegie and the Rise of Big Business*. Boston: Little, Brown, 1975.

Lynn, Ernest. *The Blazing Horizon: The True Story of Pawnee Bill and the Oklahoma Boomers*. Chicago: Whitehouse, 1927.

Mackaye, Percy. *Epoch: The Life of Steele Mackaye, Genius of the Theatre in Relation to His Times and Contemporaries*. 2 vols. New York: Boni and Liveright, 1927.

Marx, Leo. *The Machine in the Garden: Technology and the Pastoral Ideal in America*. New York: Oxford University Press, 1967.

Masterson, Michael L. "Sounds of the Frontier: Music in Buffalo Bill's Wild West." Ph.D. diss., University of New Mexico, 1990.

Mathews, Washington. "The Catlin Collection of Indian Paintings." In *Report of the National Museum for 1890*. Washington, D.C.: GPO, 1890. 593–610.

"'Max' and 'Mix.'" *Punch* 168 (1925): 422.

McCracken, Harold. *George Catlin and the Old Frontier.* New York: Bonanza Books, 1959.

McIntyre, John T. "Foreword." In *The House of Beadle and Adams and Its Dime and Nickel Novels: The Story of a Vanished Literature* by Albert Johannsen. 2 vols. Norman: University of Oklahoma Press, 1950. xxiii–xxv.

"Memorial of American Artists in Paris." In *Memorial of R. R. Gurley, Praying the Purchase of Catlin's Collection of Paintings and Curiosities, Illustrative of the Manners and Customs of the North American Indians.* 10 July 1848. 30th Cong., 1st Sess., vol. 1, Senate Misc. Doc. 152. 4–5.

"Memorial of American Citizens Resident in London." In *Memorial of R. R. Gurley, Praying the Purchase of Catlin's Collection of Paintings and Curiosities, Illustrative of the Manners and Customs of the North American Indians.* 10 July 1848. 30th Cong., 1st Sess., vol. 1, Senate Misc. Doc. 152. 5–6.

Merk, Frederick. *Manifest Destiny and Mission in American History: A Reinterpretation.* New York: Random House, 1963.

Meyer, Michael C., and William L. Sherman. *The Course of Mexican History.* 3d ed. New York: Oxford University Press, 1987.

Millis, Walter. *The Martial Spirit.* Chicago: Ivan R. Dee, 1989.

*The Miracle Rider.* Dir. Armand Schaeffer and B. Reeves Eason. 15 episodes, 5 hours. 1935. Burbank Videos, 1991. Videocassette.

Mix, Olive Stokes. *The Fabulous Tom Mix.* Englewood Cliffs, N.J.: Prentice Hall, 1957.

Mix, Paul E. *The Life and Legend of Tom Mix.* Cranbury, N.J.: A. S. Barnes and Company, 1972.

Mix, Tom. "The Loves of Tom Mix." *Photoplay,* Mar. 1929, 30–31, 124–27.

———. "Making a Million." *Photoplay,* Jan. 1928, 38–39, 110–12; Feb. 1928, 64–65, 82, 115–19; Mar. 1928, 64–65, 86, 101–4; Apr. 1928, 68–69, 117–23; May 1928, 70–71, 82, 110–12; June 1928, 70–71, 82, 112–14.

———. "Wanted, Dead or Alive—Edmund Hoyle." *Photoplay,* Dec. 1927, 38–39, 125–27.

Montanye, Lillian. "The Ridin' Romeo." *Motion Picture Magazine,* Oct. 1921, 57, 112–13.

Mooney, James. *The Ghost-Dance Religion and the Sioux Outbreak of 1890.* Chicago: University of Chicago Press, 1965.

Morgan, Thomas Jefferson. "Wild West Shows and Similar Exhibitions." In *Americanizing the American Indians: Writings by the "Friends of the Indians," 1800–1900,* ed. Francis Paul Prucha. Lincoln: University of Nebraska Press, 1978. 309–12.

Moses, L. G. *Wild West Shows and the Images of American Indians, 1883–1933.* Albuquerque: University of Mexico Press, 1996.

*Motion Pictures, 1912–1939: Catalog of Copyright Entries, Cumulative Series.* Washington, D.C.: Copyright Office, Library of Congress, 1951.

"Movements of the Ojibbewas." *Punch* 6 (1844): 79.

Mowat, R. B. *Americans in England.* Boston, Mass.: Houghton Mifflin, 1935.

"Mr. Catlin's Indian Family and Its Manufactures: A Museum of Man in the Exhibition." *Illustrated London News,* 23 Aug. 1851, 254–55.

Muccigrosso, Robert. *Celebrating the New World: Chicago's Columbian Exposition of 1893.* Chicago: Ivan R. Dee, 1993.

Muller, Dan. *My Life with Buffalo Bill.* Chicago: Reilly and Lee, 1948.

Mumby, Alan N. L. *Phillipps Study no. 4.* Cambridge: Cambridge University Press, 1956.

Nachbar, Jack. Introduction. In *Focus on the Western,* ed. Jack Nachbar. Englewood Cliffs, N.J.: Prentice Hall, 1974. 1–8.

Nash, Gerald D. *The American West in the Twentieth Century: A Short History of an Urban Oasis.* Englewood Cliffs, N.J.: Prentice Hall, 1973.

Nash, Roderick. *The Nervous Generation: American Thought, 1917–1930.* Chicago: Rand McNally, 1971.

———. *Wilderness and the American Mind.* Rev. ed. New Haven, Conn.: Yale University Press, 1976.

Nicholas, John H. *Tom Mix: Riding Up to Glory.* Kansas City: Lowell Press, 1980.

Nieuwnhuyse, Craig Francis. "Six Guns on the Stage: Buffalo Bill Cody's First Celebration of the Conquest of the American Frontier." Ph.D. diss., University of California, Berkeley, 1981.

Norris, M. G. "Bud." *The Tom Mix Book.* Waynesville, N.C.: World of Yesterday, 1989.

Nye, Russel B. *The Unembarrassed Muse: The Popular Arts in America.* New York: Dial Press, 1970.

"The Ojibbeway Indians." *Punch* 6 (1844): 14.

Orians, G. Harrison. "The Cult of the Vanishing American: A Century View, 1834–1934." *Bulletin of the University of Toledo* 13, no. 3 (Nov. 1935): 3–15.

Paddock and Pearson, ed. *Imperial Palace Auto Collection.* Hong Kong: Motorbooks International, n.d.

Pancoast, Chalmers Lowell. *Trail Blazers of Advertising: Stories of the Romance and Adventures of the Old-Time Advertising Game.* New York: Frederick H. Hitchcock, Grafton Press, 1926.

Paret, Peter, ed. *Makers of Modern Strategy from Machiavelli to the Nuclear Age.* Princeton, N.J.: Princeton University Press, 1986.

Pessen, Edward. *Jacksonian America: Society, Personality, and Politics.* Homewood, Ill.: Dorsey Press, 1969.

Pringle, Henry F. *Theodore Roosevelt.* New York: Harcourt, Brace and World, 1956.

Prucha, Francis Paul. "Thomas Jefferson Morgan, 1889–1893." In *The Commissioners of Indian Affairs, 1821–1977,* ed. Robert M. Kvasnicka and Heerman J. Viola. Lincoln: University of Nebraska Press, 1979. 193–203.

Rahill, Frank. *The World of Melodrama*. University Park: Pennsylvania State University Press, 1967.

Rahv, Philip, ed. *Discovery of Europe: The Story of American Experience in the Old World.* Boston: Houghton Mifflin, 1947.

Ralph, Julian. "Behind the 'Wild West' Scenes." *Harper's Weekly,* 18 Aug. 1894, 775–76.

"Real Scalps! Great Attraction." *Punch* 7 (1844): 3.

Reeves, Anna Ballard. "The Skirt Round-Up." *Illustrated Sporting and Dramatic News,* 6 June 1914, 634.

Reid, Janet. "Diamond Tom Mix." *Motion Picture Magazine,* Nov. 1926, 21, 101.

Remington, Frederic. "Buffalo Bill in London." *Harper's Weekly,* 3 Sept. 1892, 847.

Rennert, Jack. *One Hundred Posters of Buffalo Bill's Wild West.* New York: Darien House, 1976.

Riley, Glenda. *The Life and Legacy of Annie Oakley.* Norman: University of Oklahoma Press, 1994.

Rinehart, Mary Roberts. "Summer Comes to the Ranch." *Saturday Evening Post,* 4 July 1925, 3–4, 66, 71–72.

"Robert at the American Exhibition." *Punch* 93 (1887): 10.

Robertson, Ross M. *History of the American Economy.* New York: Harcourt, Brace, 1973.

Roehm, Marjorie Catlin, ed. *The Letters of George Catlin and His Family: A Chronicle of the American West.* Berkeley: University of California Press, 1966.

Romein, Jan. *The Watershed of Two Eras: Europe in 1900.* Trans. Arnold Pomerans. Middletown, Conn.: Wesleyan University Press, 1978.

Rosa, Joseph G., and Robin May. *Buffalo Bill and His Wild West: A Pictorial Biography.* Lawrence: University Press of Kansas, 1989.

Roth, Barbara Williams. "The 101 Ranch Wild West Show, 1904–1932." *Chronicles of Oklahoma* 63 (Winter 1965–66): 416–31.

Russell, Don B. *The Lives and Legends of Buffalo Bill.* Norman: University of Oklahoma Press, 1960.

———. *The Wild West.* Fort Worth: Ammon Carter Museum of Western Art, 1970.

Rydell, Robert W. *All the World's a Fair: Visions of Empire at American International Expositions, 1876–1916.* Chicago: University of Chicago Press, 1984.

Salsbury, Nate. "The Origin of the Wild West Show." *Colorado Magazine,* July 1955, 205–8.

Satz, Ronald N. *American Indian Policy in the Jacksonian Era.* Lincoln: University of Nebraska Press, 1976.

"Savage Views of Civilization." *Chamber's Edinburgh Journal* 9 (24 June 1848): 406–10.

Schlebecker, John T. "A Day at the 101 Ranch." *Lloyds of America: An International Magazine of Life and Literature* 2 (July 1925): 6–7.

Schlesinger, Arthur M. *The Rise of the City, 1878–1898.* New York: Macmillan, 1933.

Sell, Henry Blackman, and Victor Weybright. *Buffalo Bill and the Wild West.* New York: New American Library, 1959.

Seton-Watson, Christopher. *Italy from Liberalism to Fascism, 1870–1925.* London: Methuen, 1967.

Shirley, Glenn. *Pawnee Bill: A Biography of Major Gordon W. Lillie.* Albuquerque: University of New Mexico Press, 1958.

"Shoots like a Man." In *National Police Gazzete,* ed. Gene Smith and Jayne Barry Smith. New York: Simon and Schuster, 1972. 148–49.

Slotkin, Richard. *The Fatal Environment: The Myth of the Frontier in the Age of Industrialization, 1800–1890.* New York: HarperCollins, 1994.

———. *Gunfighter Nation: The Myth of the Frontier in Twentieth-Century America.* New York: HarperCollins, 1993.

———. *Regeneration through Violence: The Mythology of the American Frontier, 1600–1860.* Middletown, Conn.: Wesleyan University Press, 1974.

Smith, Duane A. *Rocky Mountain Mining Camps: The Urban Frontier.* Lincoln: University of Nebraska Press, 1967.

Smith, Henry Nash. *Virgin Land: The American West as Symbol and Myth.* New York: Random House, 1950.

———. "The West as an Image of the American Past." *University of Kansas City Review* 18 (Autumn 1951): 280–82.

Stackelberg, Roderick. *Idealism Debased: From Völkish Ideology to National Socialism.* Kent, Ohio: Kent State University Press, 1981.

"The 'Strong Wind' in St. Martin's Church." *Punch* 6 (1844): 173.

Strout, Cushing. *The American Image of the Old World.* New York: Harper and Row, 1963.

[Stuart, C.] *A Short History and Description of the Ojibbeway Indians Now on a Visit to England.* London: Vizetelly Brothers and Co., 1844.

Taylor, Bayard. *Views A-Foot; or, Europe Seen with Knapsack and Staff.* New York: Columbian Publicity Co., 1891.

Tompkins, Jane. *West of Everything: The Inner Life of Westerns.* New York: Oxford University Press, 1993.

Truettner, William H. *The Natural Man Observed: A Study of Catlin's Indian Gallery.* Washington, D.C.: Smithsonian Institution Press, 1979.

Tuska, Jon. "The American Western Cinema: 1903–Present." In *Focus on the Western,* ed. Jack Nachbar. Englewood Cliffs, N.J.: Prentice Hall, 1974. 25–43.

Utley, Robert M. *The Lance and the Shield: The Life and Times of Sitting Bull.* New York: Henry Holt, 1993.

———. *The Last Days of the Sioux Nation.* New Haven, Conn.: Yale University Press, 1963.

Vestal, Stanley. *Sitting Bull: Champion of the Sioux, a Biography.* Norman: University of Oklahoma Press, 1957.

"Vindication of the United States." *Southern Literary Messenger* 11 (Apr. 1845): 202–11.

Viola, Herman J. *The Indian Legacy of Charles Bird King*. Washington, D.C.: Smithsonian Institution Press; New York: Doubleday, 1976.

"Visit of Ojibbeway to Queen." *John Bull* (London): 23 Dec. 1843.

Walsh, Richard J., in collaboration with Milton S. Salsbury. *The Making of Buffalo Bill: A Study in Heroics*. Indianapolis: Bobbs-Merrill, 1928.

Ward, John William. *Andrew Jackson: Symbol for an Age*. New York: Oxford University Press, 1962.

Wecter, Dixon. *The Hero in America: A Chronicle of Hero-Worship*. Ann Arbor: University of Michigan Press, 1963.

Weinberg, Albert K. *Manifest Destiny: A Study of Nationalist Expansionism in American History*. Chicago: Quadrangle Paperbacks, 1963.

Westermeier, Clifford P. *Man, Beast, Dust: The Story of Rodeo*. Denver: World Press, 1947.

Wetmore, Helen Cody. *Le Dernier des grands eclaireurs histoire de vie du Col. W. F. Cody*. Trans. René d'Hubert. Paris: Partington Advertising Company, 1905.

———. *Last of the Great Scouts: The Life Story of Colonel William F. Cody*. Chicago: Duluth Press, 1899. Reprint, Lincoln: University of Nebraska Press, 1966.

Weyl, Walter. *The New Democracy: An Essay on Certain Political and Economic Tendencies in the United States*. New York: Macmillan, 1912.

White, Richard. "Frederick Jackson Turner and Buffalo Bill." In *The Frontier in American Culture,* ed. James R. Grossman. Berkeley: University of California Press, 1994. 7–65.

Wiebe, Robert H. *The Search for Order: 1877–1920*. New York: Hill and Wang, 1967.

Wilder, Marshall P. *The People I've Smiled With: Recollections of a Merry Little Life*. New York: Cassel and Co., 1899.

*The Wild West: Music from the Epic Mini Series*. Aspen Recording Society. Telepictures Productions, 1993. Produced by John McEuen. Compact Disc, Digital Audio 73333 35828–2.

Williams, Cecil B. Introduction. *Nick of the Woods; or, The Jibbenainosay: A Tale of Kentucky* by Robert Montgomery Bird. New York: American Book Company, 1939. ix–lxiii.

———. Preface. *Nick of the Woods; or, The Jibbenainosay: A Tale of Kentucky* by Robert Montgomery Bird. New York: American Book Company, 1939. v–vi.

Willson, David Harris. *A History of England*. 2d. ed. Hinsdale, Ill.: Dryden Press, 1972.

Wilson, Richard B. "Exporting America to Europe: Visual Images of Buffalo Bill's Wild West." Paper presented at the American Studies Association International Convention, New York, 22 Nov. 1987.

Winch, Frank. *Thrilling Lives of Buffalo Bill and Pawnee Bill*. New York: S. L. Parsons, 1911.

Wisan, Joseph E. "The Cuban Crisis as Reflected in the New York Press." In *American Imperialism in 1898,* ed. Theodore P. Greene. Lexington, Mass.: D. C. Heath, 1955. 43–54.

Wish, Harvey. *The American Historian: A Social-Intellectual History of the Writing of the American Past.* New York: Oxford University Press, 1960.

Wister, Owen. *The Virginian: A Horseman of the Plains.* New York: Macmillan, 1902. Reprint, New York: Simon and Schuster, 1969.

"With the Indians on Derby Day." *Punch* 92 (1887): 269.

Wood-Clark, Sarah. *Beautiful Daring Western Girls: Women of the Wild West Shows.* Cody, Wyo.: Buffalo Bill Historical Center, 1991.

Wrobel, David M. *The End of American Exceptionalism: Frontier Anxiety from the Old West to the New Deal.* Lawrence: University Press of Kansas, 1993.

Yost, Nellie Snyder. *Buffalo Bill: His Family, Friends, Fame, Failures, and Fortunes.* Chicago: Swallow Press, 1979.

# INDEX

Paul Reddin is a professor of history at Mesa State College, Grand Junction, Colorado.

Typeset in 10.5/13 Adobe Garamond
with Old Towne No. 536 display
Book design by Dennis Roberts
Composed by Celia Shapland
for the University of Illinois Press
Manufactured by Cushing-Malloy, Inc.